THE BATHROOM MAN

I'll be right off the phone, have a seat in the living room," Carol suggested to the Bathroom Man as she began to wind up her call with her daughter. Only half paying attention to her new house guest, who had come to the house a week earlier and used the bathroom, Carol pointed off to her right.

The Bathroom Man took a slow step in that direction, but he didn't move far. He could see Duce's dark shadow lurking just outside the oval window in the door, and he wanted to stay where Duce would be able to see what was going to happen next.

After assuring her daughter that things were fine, Carol said good-bye and placed the portable phone down on the antique bench just inside the front door.

Carol was convinced that the Bathroom Man had stopped in to speak to her husband when he got home, so it was just a matter of finding the unexpected guest a comfortable place to sit down and wait for the rabbi's arrival.

Still standing in the entrance hall, Carol motioned for the Bathroom Man to come along with her. "Why don't you follow me into the sun parlor?" Carol suggested as she walked past him toward the living room.

Behind her the Bathroom Man was pulling a short length of lead pipe out of his clothing . . . .

BROKEN VOWS

ERIC FRANCIS

St. Martin's Paperbacks

BROKEN VOWS

Cover photograph of Fred Neulander courtesy AP/Wide World. Photograph of bride courtesy Index Stock.

ISBN: 0-312-97933-9

Printed in the United States of America

St. Martin's Paperbacks edition / December 2002

10 9 8 7 6 5 4 3 2 1

BROKEN
VOWS

PROLOGUE

THE clandestine meeting in the secluded hotel parking lot had gone without a hitch. Years later, he would tell investigators that somehow he'd managed to appear casual about the whole thing, even though inside he was secretly terrified.

As he drove away from the other car, he could feel the weight of the cash stuffed inside the envelope he'd been handed. It was nothing compared to the weight that was now dragging on his soul.

This seventy-five-hundred-dollar payment was only the first he would claim. Much more money would be coming his way if, in five nights' time, the killing he had just agreed to went down as planned.

It was a short drive back to his apartment complex in Cherry Hill, New Jersey. The Landmark Towers certainly are landmarks, not for their plain white brick architecture and rows of cluttered cement balconies, but for the fact that, at eighteen stories apiece, the giant ugly boxes soar above the rest of the dull landscape where the New Jersey Turnpike and Interstate 295 cut a swath down through what a century before had been unending apple orchards and farm fields in Cherry Hill Township.

The Landmark buildings loom directly above the cloverleaf where I-295 intersects Route 70, and from their upper floors it's possible to look westward along the length of Route 70's seemingly endless line of traffic lights, strip malls, fast food franchises, car dealerships, furniture stores, hotels, gas stations, and even the Garden State Park horse-racing track, to the point eight

*miles beyond where the Ben Franklin Bridge rises over
the Delaware River and the Philadelphia skyline forms
a series of gray peaks on the horizon of neighboring
Pennsylvania.*

*Parked at the base of Landmark Building Two, he
couldn't have been less interested in the suburban
sprawl and the fall-tinged trees surrounding him on this
October afternoon. His attention was riveted on the envelope full of money which he was now supposed to di-
vide into halves. As he thumbed through it, he noticed
that many of the mixed bills inside were hundreds. Carefully he separated every one of those out and put them
into his pile, along with the clear majority of the rest of
the bills. He rolled up his larger, considerably more
valuable, "half" of the money and wrapped it in a
rubber band before shoving it into his pants pocket.*

*The remaining money he dumped loosely into a
brown paper lunch bag. It was time to go upstairs and
subcontract a murder.*

*As he stepped out onto the tenth-floor landing from
the elevator, he already knew he'd find his partner right
where he'd left him. It was still the middle of the day,
but his younger roommate never worked; in fact, he
hardly ever budged from in front of the television set
within the dingy apartment they shared.*

*He unlocked the door and strode in, calling out,
"Hey, Duce!"*

*They had started calling each other "Duce" after
they had seen the nickname used in a gangster movie.
Both of them badly wanted to be thought of as gangsters;
as tough guys; as anything other than a couple of
strung-out losers crawling back up from the depths of
drug and alcohol dependency.*

*Duce didn't stir from his lounge chair in front of
the TV.*

*The older man strode up behind the chair and up-
ended the brown bag above Duce's head.*

"*Here's our down payment for killing Mrs. Neulander,*" *he casually announced.*

Fives, tens, and twenties rained down onto Duce like confetti.

Startled out of his perpetual stupor, Duce took a moment to consider the pile of currency falling all over his head, his shoulders, and in his lap. Then he went wild. To Duce the couple of thousand dollars he'd just been showered with might as well have been a million.

"*Mother fucker! Mother fucker!*" *Duce shouted in amazed elation, scooping up the bills. "The fucker's serious then?*" *he asked, staring intently for confirmation.*

His roommate nodded.

"*Then that bitch is dead,*" *Duce replied, shaking a fistful of the money in his friend's face as his voice rose to a near scream, "THAT BITCH IS DEAD!"*

CHAPTER ONE

CAROL Neulander was an extremely busy person. If someone wanted to kill her, they'd have to find her first.

Carol was the mother of three children aged 18 to 24, and the wife of Fred Neulander, the founder and senior rabbi of Congregation M'kor Shalom in Cherry Hill, New Jersey, which made her the "First Lady" of the more than nine hundred families that comprised the M'kor Shalom synagogue's "family of families."

Carol Neulander was also a successful business-woman. She had begun a bakery right out of her home oven, and expanded it over the course of a decade to the point where, by the fall of 1994, it was a full-fledged bakery chain with two growing retail stores in the neighboring New Jersey towns of Audubon and Voorhees.

Even at age 52, with her career and social life well established, Carol's day-to-day comings and goings hadn't slowed down. Her schedule was a whirl of appointments and meetings, activities and gatherings. Business and personal trips took her constantly around Cherry Hill and to the surrounding suburban and rural New Jersey townships. She also ranged frequently into the city of Philadelphia nearby and farther on up the Atlantic coast to New York City.

Carol's close friends regarded keeping up with her as a challenge, but if they left a message on her answering machine they would soon hear back, perhaps as she took a few minutes to call from one of her bakery's locations. Often she would call from the car phone in her dark Toyota Camry as she drove from one appointment to the next.

Standing just over five feet tall, the 136-pound Carol was never an imposing woman, but she had a straightforward take-charge manner and she made her presence felt wherever she went. Her inherent decisiveness was tempered by a kindness and warmth that seemed to radiate from her. With well-groomed auburn hair, expensive but tasteful jewelry, and large, dark eyes, she seemed to fill up the space around her. Carol was energetic and striking and had her own complex life that consumed most of her waking hours, but she liked to take the time to understand and interact with the people she was dealing with throughout her day. It was this genuinely caring nature of hers that had endeared her to so many people over the years, and it was a characteristic which many people felt she shared with her husband Fred.

As a couple, Carol and Fred Neulander were a matched set and a walking contrast at the same time. Not much taller than Carol at five-foot-four, Rabbi Fred Neulander was a solid wall of muscle in a suit jacket, or on some days just a dress shirt and bow tie. Fred was as sharp and as charismatic as any successful politician, and could be just as arrogant and irritating. He was undeniably dynamic, he oozed self-confidence, and he had a reputation for bringing people together and making sure things got done. Now, at age 54, he was the living embodiment of the community of M'kor Shalom, which he had created by sheer force of will. It was a community that had revolved around him for over two decades, during which he had played a pivotal role in almost all of the major milestones and events in the combined lives of thousands of people. To many of the congregants for whom he had spent a lifetime being God's messenger, Fred Neulander was the next best thing to the Boss upstairs.

M'kor Shalom, which in Hebrew means "Source of Peace," was itself a monument to Fred's electrifying effect on other people. It had rapidly grown to become the largest Reform Jewish synagogue in southern New Jersey, but Neulander had founded it on nothing more than a vision when, in 1974, as a young assistant rabbi at Temple Emanuel, Fred led what was in effect a palace *coup d' etat*.

Standing in the front room of a friend's home, the young Rabbi Neulander had gathered together a small handful of potential defectors and spoken forcefully about what he thought a progressive synagogue should be like, and how he would do things differently if he were in charge. It was his own mix of Reform Judiasm— a blend of traditions that he felt needed to be adhered to in order to keep true to Jewish spiritual and cultural identity, but at the same time, a profound willingness to experiment and to add the best elements of modern secular culture to the worship services and, more importantly, to the day-in, day-out life of the synagogue. He wanted M'kor Shalom to be a community, not where people escaped from daily life to visit the traditions of their dead ancestors, but a living place where they carried on their lives in conjunction with their friends and their faith.

Captivated by Fred's heartfelt message, the handful of couples who were present agreed on the spot to put up the money for the new venture. Eighteen families initially followed Rabbi Neulander out of Temple Emanuel and began M'kor Shalom more as an ideal than as an institution. The first services were held in a house borrowed from a real estate agent; the High Holy Days were celebrated at the Holiday Inn. Eventually a small warehouse in Mount Laurel, New Jersey, was divided into a sanctuary for the congregation and a Hebrew school for the children. It was an experiment operating on a shoestring and held together by Fred Neulander's forceful personality, but it had an undeniable warmth and a strong core of faith—and soon it had a waiting list to join.

In the early years of the new synagogue, Fred Neulander was a blur of activity: officiating at weekly Sabbath services, presiding over bat and bar mitzvahs, visiting the sick, manning the phones at the crisis hotline he'd helped create, teaching adult classes in Hebrew and the Torah. By his side throughout was Carol, caring and gracious where Fred was inspiring and gregarious.

Just as M'kor Shalom was a blend of different aspects of traditional and modern Judaism, the Neulanders themselves were a blend of Old World and New World backgrounds.

Carol had been born Carol Toby Lidz, the daughter of a wealthy button manufacturer in New York City's fabled Garment District. She had grown up on a sweeping estate in Hewlett Harbor, Long Island, with her sister and two brothers, where they were served by a butler and doted over by a governess.

Carol's upbringing on the manicured ocean-side lawns of coastal New York stood in sharp contrast with the early years of Fred Jay Neulander, who grew up in a rough-and-tumble section of Albany.

Neulander's immigrant parents owned a dry-cleaning business that his father struggled to run while his wife stayed home and cared for Fred, their only child. The Neulanders' surroundings were humble, but they had a profound love of learning and literature, both of which they instilled in Fred at an early age. They also took great pride in the fact that six successive generations of the Neulander family had produced rabbis, the most recent being Fred's uncle.

Fred Neulander and Carol Lidz's very different worlds would collide on a blind date in 1963. Fred was a senior at Trinity College in Hartford, Connecticut. He was studying religion and philosophy in a sophisticated environment that was new to him, but which he none-theless adapted to wholeheartedly. Carol was a junior at Mount Holyoke College in South Hadley, Massachu-setts, where she was studying psychology. It was an era when girlfriends wore their boyfriends' college pins, and soon Carol was "pinned" to Fred. An engagement fol-lowed and they were married right after their graduations in 1965.

It was a standing family joke that the prospect of having Fred, who could manage to look either like a distinguished businessman or a truck driver, depending on how he was dressed, as a son-in-law had terrified his future in-laws. Carol would slyly tell the story of how her father had turned to her as she stood in her wedding dress—just moments from walking down the aisle—and whispered hopefully to her, "I can still get you out of this."

At first the newly married couple stayed in New York, moving to Queens, where Fred earned a degree in Hebrew literature and was ordained as a rabbi in 1968 at the Hebrew Union College Jewish Institute of Reli-gion. It was his pursuit of a graduate degree at Dropsie University that moved the couple to the Philadelphia area. Three years after their marriage, Fred had found the position as an assistant rabbi at Temple Emanuel in Cherry Hill, New Jersey, and he and Carol had moved to an apartment in that expanding suburban township.

In 1975, the year after Fred defected and began M'kor Shalom, the Neulanders purchased a modest but nice two-story Colonial house on a quiet side street in the Wexford Leas section of Cherry Hill, and began rais-ing a family.

Cherry Hill, and most of western New Jersey, had once been rolling farmland punctuated by woods. But over the years it had become increasingly bisected by artery roads taking advantage of the growing suburban sprawl. The new grid of paved roads brought a cycle of boom development that in turn required even more roads until, by the time the Millennium hit, it seemed like every franchise that had ever advertised in North America finally stretched cheek-by-jowl down the length of Route 70.

In the 1960s, residential developers swept through Cherry Hill and built hundreds of houses practically arm's-length apart on winding little roads and cul-de-sacs that were carved out of the remaining farm fields with all possible expediency. Sprinkling in as many Colonial and Federal architectural details as they could think of along the way, the home designers tried to keep some reference to the history-steeped neighborhoods of Philadelphia, located just a few miles to the west, where the nation had been born. Then they tried to make up the difference by giving the tangle of brand new streets a series of particularly unlikely but historic-sounding names. These ranged from the merely improbable ("Gatehouse Lane" and "Candlewyck Way") to the overly imaginative ("Society Hill Boulevard" and "Buckingham Place").

With his own reputation as a charismatic spiritual and cultural leader well established, and his congregation steadily growing and prospering, it soon was time for Fred Neulander to lead M'kor Shalom to a more permanent location. In 1991 Rabbi Neulander guided the synagogue's swelling membership out of the converted warehouse to a piece of land on the Evesham Road in southeastern Cherry Hill, only a few miles from his own house.

The new complex of cream-colored buildings with their orange standing-seam metal peaked roofs sat beside one of the region's artery roads. The collection of buildings was a testament to how firmly the community had taken root during the two decades Fred Neulander had been at the helm. It was the eighth synagogue to be established within Cherry Hill, where a third of the

70,000 residents are Jewish, but it was now also the largest.

At its heart, any religious congregation is a reflection of, and is in fact all about, the families that make it up. By 1994, when it was said that M'kor Shalom had over 4,000 members, what they really meant was that 930 families considered it the hub of their spiritual and social life.

For so many of those who belonged to M'kor Shalom, Carol, as the wife of the beloved senior rabbi, was practically a member of their own extended families. The congregation greeted her with affection and admiration when she walked through the hallways. They enjoyed her insights and her sharp sense of humor. They shared stories about their own lives and their families with her.

Each Friday evening as worship services were about to begin, the congregation took note as Carol entered and sat in her accustomed place near the front of the sanctuary. But within the peaceful walls of M'kor Shalom, amongst the hundreds of congregants who watched Carol Neulander's comings and goings, there was at least one person who was planning to murder her.

CHAPTER TWO

FORTY years of rain will do wonders for even the most forced landscaping scheme, and by October 1994, the homes on Highgate Lane where the Neulanders lived were dwarfed by a neighborhood's worth of tall trees. All the rakes and leaf blowers in the Wexford Leas section of Cherry Hill couldn't keep the fall leaves from forming a billowing layer of color across the manicured lawns. On the winding side streets, children rode bicycles and put up Halloween decorations in windows, in bushes, and hanging from trees as they anticipated the approaching holiday.

Carol Neulander saw all the hustle and bustle of her neighborhood as she drove to and from her home. Her week was usually filled with dozens of different business and personal errands: visiting M'kor Shalom synagogue, shopping with her sister and sister-in-law, seeing friends, working at her bakery company, participating in a variety of neighborhood associations, civic groups, women's clubs, charities, and other worthwhile projects.

But on Tuesday afternoons, Carol's route was predictable, and on this Tuesday, October 25, 1994, she was right on schedule.

On Tuesdays Carol was foremost a businesswoman, and she spent the mornings and early afternoons at the Classic Cake Company store in Voorhees, the township neighboring Cherry Hill. And then, like clockwork, she attended the weekly business meetings for the company's management staff.

There's a substantial Jewish population in the New

Jersey suburbs east of downtown Philadelphia—
throughout the region for that matter—and it didn't take
long for Carol to realize that there was a need on both
the wholesale and the retail side for cakes and other
pastries that met traditional kosher requirements. In
1982, Carol began the company by baking kosher cakes
in her oven at home and filling orders for local restaurants. Soon she enlisted the help of her original business
partners, Judy Stern and Lynn Rothernberg, and founded
the cute little boutique bakery in a storefront in Audubon, New Jersey.

It started out as a niche market, but Gentiles quickly
discovered her array of delicious cakes, cookies, and
other baked goodies, and soon Classic Cake was marketing holidays like Passover and Easter side-by-side in
their window displays.

In 1987, Carol had sold most of her ownership
shares in the business to 31-year-old Richard J. Price, a
baker and cake decorator. Price had joined the company
in 1984 and quickly become the head baker, but it was
Carol who had the mind for business details. Even after
the sale, she stayed onboard as the manager of the growing company.

By 1992, after a decade of Carol's close and astute
guidance, Price had opened a second Classic Cake bakery in the large Eagle Plaza strip mall in Voorhees, and
the company's payroll of bakers, sales clerks, and truck
drivers was expanding towards four dozen employees.

Classic Cake's weekly business meetings took place
at the Cherry Hill home of the company's human resources director, Ronald "Arky" Helprien. Although they
began shortly before the close of business each Tuesday
afternoon, there was almost always enough to talk about
at the gatherings to keep things going for three or more
hours.

Once the meetings ended, Carol drove straight back
to her home at 204 Highgate Lane in the suburban south-

eastern corner of Cherry Hill. There she would usually make dinner for herself and whoever else was home.

Cherry Hill is certainly considered a safe township. So far, there hadn't been a single homicide there in 1994. But like any suburb that is only a few minutes' drive from a major urban area—especially one like Philadelphia, which includes several free-fire zones on its outskirts—it's always a good idea to take basic precautions to avoid becoming a victim of violent crime.

In that regard Carol Neulander was making one big mistake. Following the Tuesday afternoon management meetings, Carol had gotten into the habit of taking home the day's cash receipts from the two bakery branches. It felt like an okay thing to do. After all, Carol was certainly trustworthy, and it beat having to stay at the bakery after everyone had left for the day doing tedious busy-work. As long as it was kept a closely held secret, and Carol deposited the money in the bank the next morning, it seemed that there was nothing to worry about.

Although Carol and her partners didn't view it in these stark terms, what it meant was that a suburban housewife was driving home on a regular basis with anywhere between 5,000 and 15,000 dollars in cash in her purse, which she then counted out on her dining room table.

In effect, she was a much better and easier target than the rows of convenience stores and gas stations out on Route 70, just two minutes' drive from Highgate Lane. Over the years, those places had been robbed more than once for gains that were limited to a few hundred dollars at a time. With only a standard household door lock between her and the world, Carol was safe as long as no one figured out the secret of her Tuesday night routine. But if the wrong people ever figured out what she was so casually doing in her dining room, then, truthfully, she was a sitting duck.

Being the mother of three young adults, the wife of a rabbi, and the manager of a business, Carol Neulander was certainly a busy person, and she had long since learned to juggle a schedule and make the most of her time. As afternoon gave way to evening on the night of October 25, 1994, Carol was trying to maximize her drive home by using the time to make a call on her car phone to her daughter, Rebecca Neulander–Rockoff. Rebecca, now 24, was the oldest of the three Neulander children. Married and working as a hospital administrator, she had moved to nearby Philadelphia and kept in extremely close touch with her mother, usually by phone conversations that typically lasted up to an hour. These daily mother–daughter chats were a ritual the pair had developed years before, and when Carol pulled into the driveway of her home at on Highgate Lane, she stayed in the front seat for a minute winding up the call.

The Neulander residence wasn't large, but it had four bedrooms on two floors. With its yellow brick facade on the ground level and beige yellow clapboard upper story with wooden shutters and a sloped asphalt shingled roof, it was kind of a quiet mash between faux Colonial and 1960s builder's catalog hardware. The thick row of bushes clumped along the sidewalk in front of the house, and the grass and moss around the big trees at the edge of the small lot were all nicely kept.

On most evenings it was certainly possible to encounter someone out for a walk on the small sidewalk that wound its way down the street in front of the Neulander residence, but now darkness had fallen, and on this night a cold wind was gusting, making it so much more inviting to stay inside.

So when someone suddenly rapped loudly on the car's driver's-side window right next to Carol's head, it startled her, bringing her conversation with Rebecca to a brief halt. Glancing upward, and still cradling the car phone to her ear, Carol rolled down the window to speak to the large, burly man in a windbreaker standing beside her in the driveway.

"Hello! I have a package. I have something I'm going to drop off for the rabbi. Is he home?" asked the stranger. He had given his name with a sort of humble nod when he greeted her, but it was something completely common—like John, or maybe Jim—and since Carol was already distracted, she hadn't caught it.

"No, he's not," Carol replied, holding up her hand to indicate he should wait a second as she kept speaking into her car phone. "Why don't you come into the house?" Carol invited. Then she turned her attention briefly back to finishing her call to Rebecca so she could get out of the car.

On the other end of the phone line, Rebecca could hear snatches of her mother's conversation with this strange messenger. Given the late hour and the darkness that had fallen outside, she didn't like the sound of it.

"There's somebody here. I shouldn't be surprised," Carol reassured her daughter, adding, "Daddy told me to expect him."

Carol was used to strangers needing to get in contact with the rabbi for any number of reasons. Over the years she had taken numerous messages, and the occasional package, for him. Carol thought nothing of this visit, but there was something about it that Rebecca still didn't like. She asked her mother to call her back as soon as the messenger left, just to let her know that everything was all right.

Rebecca may have sensed the danger, but her mother entirely missed the gravity of the stranger's presence. To Carol, he seemed to be a bit of a harmless bumbler. In reality, his purpose was deadly serious. As he followed Carol inside the Neulander residence, he was preparing to commit a devastating act of violence— but moments after he stepped through the front door, he realized that things weren't going according to plan, and he began to get very worried.

Doing his best to appear nonchalant, he swept his eyes around the entrance hall and the front rooms on either side of the house, looking hard for something he had fully expected to see, something that, to his terrible surprise, wasn't anywhere in sight.

He'd spent years telling anyone who would listen that he was one smooth customer when it came to high-pressure covert situations, but the truth was that he had just made the rank amateur mistake of simply assuming that the object he was looking for would be sitting somewhere obvious in the residence.

He hadn't prepared a back-up plan, and now, as he struggled to develop one on the spot, panic was beginning to grip him. He knew that as soon as he and Carol had walked inside the house, his accomplice would have started working his way through the bushes to the corner of the residence. He also knew that as his accomplice lurked in the shadows and clutched his lead pipe, watching the front door for a signal, he would be getting increasingly jumpy as the seconds ticked away.

This wasn't going to work, and he had to get it back under control before his accomplice came bursting through the door and wrecked any chance of salvaging this plan and trying again on some future evening. He needed to stop the clock. He needed to buy time to think.

He turned to Carol. "Umm, can I use your bathroom?" he asked. It was the best ploy he could come up with on such short notice.

Smiling like the gracious hostess that she was, Carol pointed him through the kitchen to the first-floor bathroom at the back of the house.

As he walked through the kitchen towards the bathroom, he took a good look at the kitchen table. There was nothing on it and that cinched the matter. The small burgundy-colored item that was so critical to his plot was nowhere to be seen. Now he just needed to get quickly and safely back out of the house without arousing any suspicion on Carol's part.

When he emerged from the bathroom he pulled a plain white envelope out of his windbreaker and handed it to Carol. "Please give this to the rabbi when he comes home," he asked, trying to sound as breezy as possible as he slid his large frame towards the front door and freedom.

He was just inches from getting out of the house when, once again, something that he hadn't prepared for blind-sided him. Instead of just setting the envelope down on the antique bench in the hallway and leaving it for the rabbi to open when he returned, Carol shoved her fingernail under the flap and tore it open.

Puzzled, Carol stared into an empty envelope.

"There's nothing in here," she pointed out, looking up at the big man for an explanation.

"Ah, um, I must've picked up the wrong envelope at home," the stranger stammered sheepishly.

Again Carol urged him to just wait. The rabbi would be home soon and he could give his message in person, no problem.

The stranger couldn't stand much more of this. He was hovering by the door and incredibly nervous about what could come flying through it if he waited any longer. He wanted to leave, and leave fast.

"No! I really have to go," he insisted, adding, "Someone's waiting for me in my car. I'll get it to the rabbi later." He backed out into the night, pulling the front door firmly shut as he went.

"Let's get out of here," he hissed at his crouching accomplice. The pair rushed back to their waiting car just beyond the thick row of bushes that bordered the sidewalk in front of the house, and sped off down the quiet suburban streets.

Inside the house, Carol shrugged off the odd encounter and tore up the empty envelope, tossing the pieces into a wastebasket.

She picked up the phone and called Rebecca back to let her know that there was nothing to worry about. As she related the silly tale of the misplaced message to her daughter, Carol laughed and added, "The very strange thing was that he needed to use the bathroom."

CHAPTER THREE

IT was on the night after Halloween, exactly seven days after the first attempt, that the plan to kill Carol Neulander finally succeeded.

Like the week before, it was a Tuesday. Carol had spent the day working at the Voorhees location of Classic Cake until just before 4:30 P.M., when she once again drove to Arky Helprien's house for the weekly business meeting.

Carol had left that meeting shortly after 7:30 P.M., and as soon as she arrived at her own residence she picked up the phone and called Rebecca for their usual chat. It was in the middle of that call that once again there was a sudden knock, this time right on the front door.

Carol was standing in the formal dining room near the front of the house, and she padded out towards the entrance hall in her socks. Cradling the portable phone to her ear, she leaned forward and looked out through the large oval stained-glass window in the center of the door.

Although she really knew nothing at all about the large man standing under the glare of her porch light, she recognized him at once. His last brief appearance at the Neulander residence had been sufficiently comical that she had mentioned him in subsequent family conversations. She had also given him a nickname. To Carol, he was simply "the Bathroom Man," and the fact that he had been in the house once before was enough to prompt her to open the door on the chilly night of

November 1, 1994, and invite him in out of the cold.

Leaning into the phone, a surprised Carol told Rebecca, "Oh! It's the bathroom guy!"

As the Bathroom Man shuffled inside, Carol just assumed he must have returned with the message for her husband that he had tried so absent-mindedly to deliver once before. The fact that the previous visit had also been right after a meeting with the Classic Cake staff on a Tuesday evening escaped her. Rebecca, listening to the few snatches of her mother's front-door conversation that she could make out from her end of the call, had also forgotten that point.

In fact, what little of the conversation that Rebecca Neulander–Rockoff could hear over the phone between her mother and the Bathroom Man sounded perfectly ordinary.

"Hi," Carol said as she swung open the door.

"Hi. It's me again," a male voice replied cheerfully.

Rebecca heard her mother say, "Well, he'll be home soon. Why don't you wait?" and then a moment later she heard Carol add, "Well, don't leave him outside. It's cold. He can come inside."

Rebecca wasn't sure what her mother was referring to, but Carol had correctly guessed, based on what the Bathroom Man had said about needing to get back to his friend in the car at the end of the previous visit, that he once again had traveled to her neighborhood with a companion. However, when Carol glanced out the door, she couldn't actually see the car or anyone else, because this time they had parked two houses away where Market Street, a short connector street only a few car lengths long, came into Highgate Lane from Wexford Drive.

In the shadows of the Neulander home, Duce, the Bathroom Man's accomplice, was doing his best to stay out of sight as he crept up to the house and tried to get an angle where he could see in through the windows without being spotted. Dressed in a black sweatshirt and black sweat pants, Duce hovered just outside the door so he could keep one eye on his partner and the other on the old gray junker of a car they had left relatively exposed on the quiet street corner.

"I'll be right off the phone, have a seat in the living room," Carol suggested to the Bathroom Man as she began to wind up her call with Rebecca. Only half paying attention to her new house guest, Carol pointed off to her right.

The Bathroom Man took a slow step in that direction, but he didn't move far. He could see Duce's dark shadow lurking just outside the oval window in the door, and he wanted to stay where Duce would be able to see what was going to happen next.

After assuring Rebecca that things were fine, Carol said good-bye and placed the portable phone down on the antique bench just inside the front door. These phone calls had been a nightly ritual between mother and daughter for years, but, unbeknownst to either of them, the last one had just ended.

Like Carol, Fred Neulander had a regular Tuesday evening routine. His revolved around the synagogue, where he had a round of evening meetings and classes. Carol was convinced that the Bathroom Man had stopped in to speak to her husband when he got home, so it was just a matter of finding the unexpected guest a comfortable place to sit down and wait for the rabbi's arrival.

Still standing in the entrance hall, Carol motioned for the Bathroom Man to come along with her. "Why don't you follow me into the sun parlor?" Carol suggested as she walked past him toward the living room.

Behind her the Bathroom Man was pulling a short length of lead pipe out of his clothing.

As Carol took her first step into the front room, the Bathroom Man suddenly placed his left hand on her shoulder and, with his right, he smashed the pipe down

hard on the back of her head. The force of the impact
knocked Carol's glasses off her face. She staggered forward in shock with blood welling from her lacerated
scalp. The Bathroom Man gave her a forceful downward
shove onto her knees and turned back for the front door
just a few feet away. He was halfway to it when he heard
Carol fall with a thud onto the carpeted floor behind him.

"Why? Why?" Carol moaned loudly, but the Bathroom Man's attention was focused on getting the front
door open and finding Duce.

"Come on, come on, come on, get the fuck in here!"
the Bathroom Man hissed at the black-clad figure waiting outside.

Duce strode into the home, confidently took the pipe
from his older friend, and headed for the woman lying
curled up in pain and shock on the floor of the living
room.

The Bathroom Man waited squeamishly on the
porch steps, but even from there he could still hear the
long sickening series of thumps as Duce brought the pipe
crashing down repeatedly on Carol's head. It took all of
about thirty seconds, but to the Bathroom Man it seemed
more like three hours.

When a dozen blows had been struck on Carol's
fractured skull, the Bathroom Man grew impatient and
started back towards the front room to get Duce moving.

"Let's go! Let's go!" he called out.

"Okay!" Duce answered as he walked calmly back
into the entrance hall.

From the bloody pipe that Duce had gripped firmly
in his hand it seemed obvious, but the Bathroom Man
still needed to assure himself that Carol Neulander was
indeed dead. However, as he walked back into the living
room that he had left less than a minute before, nothing
had prepared him for the surreal scene that now confronted him.

What had moments before been a neat and orderly

space was now completely transformed into a horrific spectacle. He had expected to see a dead victim, but not like this. Carol's blood seemed to be everywhere throughout the room. A large pool of it was spreading out on the white carpet surrounding her head, and the whipping action of the pipe had flung even more of it outward in a series of arcs that had spattered clear across the room. The patterns of blood droplets stretched ten to fifteen feet in places across the floor, the glass coffee table, the window ledge, the walls . . . even the ceiling.

The Bathroom Man bent down to examine Carol's crumpled form. Lying on her side, she had managed to draw her hands up in a futile attempt to protect herself from the vicious assault. Her eyes were closed and her mouth was rapidly filling with blood and other fluids. All the Bathroom Man could hear was a sound like air hissing from a tire as it escaped from between her bloody lips. It sounded final.

Standing on the edge of the carpet, his victim dying right in front of him, the Bathroom Man couldn't bring himself to budge from the spot. The whole thing had him transfixed. He kept staring and staring at Carol Neulander's shattered body, trying to comprehend what he was seeing.

Duce grabbed the Bathroom Man's hand and shook it.

"What are you doing?" Duce shouted. "Let's get the fuck out of here!"

The Bathroom Man tore his eyes off the bloody living room and strove to pull himself together. There was a method to this madness, a careful plan, and so far it was on schedule, but he and Duce needed to take care of one more important detail before they could flee the Neulander residence.

Once again the Bathroom Man began to look around the home's first floor for the critical item that he had missed the previous week. This time he spotted it almost immediately. On the other side of the entrance hallway from the living room was the formal dining room and there, sitting on top of the table, was Carol's purse. Pulling it open, he spotted what he had been searching for— a burgundy-colored wallet.

The Bathroom Man heaved a sigh of relief and stuffed Carol's wallet into the pocket of his windbreaker. Seven days earlier he had thrown the entire murder plot into sudden reverse and nearly tipped his hand—all because he hadn't been able to spot this item. That oversight had given Carol a one-week reprieve. But now all the loose ends appeared to have been cleaned up, and that made it high time to get clear of the house.

Tossing the rest of the purse onto the living room carpet so that it would be found a short distance from their victim, the pair took one last look at Carol's still-bleeding body and rushed out the door into the night.

It was a straight shot back to the gray car parked on the corner of tiny little Market Street and, unlike the night before, when the area had been teeming with trick-or-treaters, no one was out on the sidewalks to see them. They had come and gone completely unnoticed.

With every car length they put between themselves and the bloodied living room, they began to feel better. They rode on in silence through the darkened suburban streets, glimpsing brightly lit front rooms and the blue glow of television sets. They passed fragments of smashed pumpkins on the pavement and neatly manicured shrubs and trees with ghostly sheet decorations hung from their branches. It would only take a minute— a couple of simple turns—to get back to Route 70 and the anonymity that the increased traffic there would afford them. At first the Bathroom Man was relieved to see the traffic light at the end of Old Orchard Road as he approached. If he could get out of this subdivision, out of his bloodied clothing, and on with his schedule, then his alibi would be airtight, and no one would be the wiser.

The intersection was looming closer and closer, but in an instant, his rapidly lightening mood was snuffed clean out and replaced by a burst of adrenaline and sheer stark terror. There, parked squarely ahead of him on the other side of Route 70, two Cherry Hill Police Department cruisers were drawn up alongside each other. The cops had the cars facing in opposite directions so their driver's-side windows were just inches apart, and they could chat. Now, just a few yards away, the Bathroom Man and Duce sat under the glare of the intersection's red light and waited . . . and waited. The Bathroom Man's pupils had gone wide in the dark, his knuckles were in a white death grip on the steering wheel, a dead woman's wallet was in his pocket, and a blood-covered pipe was at his feet. Next to him was a blood-soaked passenger dressed head to toe in black, and nothing he could say to himself was preventing his nervous system from shifting into full alarm.

The seconds seemed to tick away like hours on melted Salvador Dali clocks, but still the red glow reflected off his car and the two nearby cruisers. The Bathroom Man tried to be casual as he looked at the Saab dealership across the street and let his eyes wander over the single-story red-brick medical office buildings on either side of him. Still the red light lingered on.

When he looked over at Duce, he noticed that the younger man was busy squinting hard in an effort to get a better look at the cops.

"Don't stare at them," the Bathroom Man said through clenched teeth.

"Be cool," Duce sniffed.

But right now the Bathroom Man was anything but cool. The mere presence of the police was burning a hole through his panicked brain like a laser. His breathing was becoming ragged, and his hands gripped the steering wheel like he was trying to snap it in two.

Alarmed, Duce began to wonder what his unhinged partner was about to do. "Be cool, be cool, be cool," Duce began to mumble over and over.

Finally, when the agony seemed like it would never end, the light snapped green.

With all deliberate care, the Bathroom Man pulled gently into the intersection to make his right turn in what he hoped was the most non–attention-getting manner possible. A couple seconds later he turned right again, this time into the large, well-lit parking lot of a Clover department store. It wasn't until he was safely in a space out of sight from the cruisers back at the corner that he allowed himself to slowly unclench every muscle in his body.

Their close call behind them, the pair checked the time. It was going on 9 P.M., and it was high time that they put their endgame into motion.

Parked a couple of spaces away was a used white 1982 Pontiac Bonneville that the Bathroom Man had purchased a few days beforehand. The plan called for Duce to take the Bonneville and pick up his girlfriend before driving right back to the Landmark Building. Duce lived the kind of sedentary lifestyle that made it a stretch to think that anyone would care about his specific whereabouts this evening, but in the unlikely event that someone did ask, Duce was prepared to tell them that he had been home the whole night watching television. Those who knew him would have no reason to doubt the claim.

The Bathroom Man had another appointment, but first he had to clean up the last items on the checklist from the Neulander residence. He pulled a cheap duffel bag up to the front seat and dropped in the twelve-inch pipe they had just used to kill Carol. Duce's blood-stained sweatshirt, sweat pants, and sneakers went in next. Even though he didn't think he had gotten any of

Carol's blood on him, the Bathroom Man also stuffed his windbreaker into the bag as a precaution.

Next the pair turned their attention to Carol's burgundy-colored wallet. Opening it, they got a bit of a shock. There was only about 150 dollars inside. They had been expecting a hundred times that amount.

Carol had pre-signed the top check on the pad of checks, and the rest of the wallet was packed with credit cards, but the pair weren't interested in anything that could be traced. Disappointed, they split up the cash and tossed the wallet into the bag on the floor of the car.

Duce clambered out of the car and headed across the parking lot to the white Bonneville while the Bathroom Man checked his watch. It was 9 P.M., and so far the evening was going like clockwork, but now he needed to put the finishing touches on his own alibi.

Putting his old gray car back into motion, he shot eastward straight down Route 70 before taking the right-hand split onto the Old Marlton Pike. Five minutes later he slid into the parking lot of the tiny 7-Eleven on Main Street in the town of Marlton, three miles from the Neulander household.

Standing under the fluorescent lights in the convenience store, the Bathroom Man poured out four cups of coffee and carefully fixed on the plastic covers. He had a well-known routine on Tuesday nights, and now more than ever, he needed to keep to it in case questions were ever raised.

Back in the car, it only took a couple more minutes to reach his destination, and as he drove past the chocolate-colored Marlton Post Office and pulled into the parking lot behind the municipal building next door, he allowed himself a self-satisfied smile. "Maybe this is going to work after all," he thought.

The irony of his alibi was tremendous. He walked past car after car with New Jersey Police Association stickers on the windshields and down the three concrete

steps to the battered gray metal door just inside a ply-
wood shed attached to the back of the building. Someone
had scrawled "Slam hard to lock" in black marker next
to the neatly stenciled words "Evesham Township Police
Department" that were in the center of the rusting portal.

Seconds after he pressed the row of black buttons
on the silver box beside the door, the electronic lock
buzzed open and the Bathroom Man strolled inside with
his cardboard tray of coffees. Walking swiftly down the
small corridors with their battered white wood paneling
and oddly-stuccoed ceiling tiles, he called out greetings
to the dispatchers and cops on duty as he worked his
way back to the offices of the Detective Bureau.

"Hey, bub, you're late!" detectives jibed in welcome
as the Bathroom Man started handing out the steaming
cups of coffee to the night shift. With a nervous grin he
glanced at the clock. It was only 9:12 P.M. He wasn't
more than seven minutes off his usual Tuesday night
arrival time, so he knew it was just a joke. "Well, Jeez,
I've been out back buzzing for like five minutes," the
Bathroom Man retorted. With that, the conversation began to drift on, and as it did, relief began to flood
through the Bathroom Man. It was here, sitting in a room
surrounded by police detectives less than a half-hour after he had bludgeoned a woman to death, that for the
first time in days the Bathroom Man was finally beginning to feel safe.

CHAPTER FOUR

LIKE his wife Carol, Rabbi Fred Neulander had a full schedule this Tuesday, November 1, 1994.

In the late afternoon on this fall day, he had returned from M'kor Shalom to his residence at 6 P.M. to make dinner for himself and his oldest son, 20-year-old Matthew. Matt was now a medical student at Rutgers University in nearby Camden, but was still living at home with his parents while he served part-time as an emergency technician with the Cherry Hill Emergency Medical Service for the second year running. Matthew's younger brother Benjamin, 18, had recently left to become a freshman at the University of Michigan, so Matt was the only one of the three Neulander children who was still around most days, and he liked to arrange to have dinner with his parents before he left on his twelve-hour ambulance shifts.

Matt and Fred had bustled around the kitchen eating a pizza that Fred had brought home with him, and by 6:30, both men were out the door heading to their respective obligations.

Running a synagogue with 4,000 members and a school with a thousand children enrolled is a full-time business. There were also the religious ceremonies and cultural aspects that Fred Neulander was responsible for, but M'kor Shalom was operating smoothly, and there was a younger assistant rabbi and an experienced staff who helped with many aspects of the synagogue's day-to-day life. Rabbi Neulander had recently returned from a six-month sabbatical, although it wasn't much of re-

turn, really—he had just hung around town for six
months and grown a ponytail, to the chagrin of some
and the amusement of others. Still, it had been a break,
and when he returned, he'd managed to distance himself
from some of the hands-on aspects of the synagogue that
had pulled at his time in the past.

Assistant Rabbi Gary Mazo had taken on much of
the adult Jewish studies, and taught classes back at
M'kor Shalom on Tuesday evenings. On this particular
night, Neulander had decided to take a walk around the
complex and see how things were going. He had spoken
to some members of the congregation and their guests
who were attending a weekly Alcoholics Anonymous
meeting in one of the conference rooms. He had shown
some non-Jewish visitors the *bimah* in the sanctuary, the
raised altar-like dais where the sacred Torah scrolls were
read and other ceremonies performed during worship
services, and chatted with them about Israel. He had
dropped in on choir practice and strolled through,
greeted the whole group, and chatted with some individual members. Between making several phone calls about
synagogue business from his office, he had also sat in
on two different sessions of Rabbi Mazo's classes.

It was a long evening at the synagogue, but the rabbi
had met a lot of friends and was able to leave shortly
after 9 P.M. He waved to the rent-a-cops helping with
traffic and security at the busy center as he drove out
onto Evesham Road and turned for the short drive home.

When Fred Neulander pulled up to 204 Highgate
Lane that Tuesday evening at 9:20, things still appeared
perfectly normal. Carol's car was parked where he expected to see it. The "extra" car that his son Matt had
left there was parked in its accustomed place next to
Carol's. The front door was unlocked, but that wasn't
unusual either. Over the years, Fred and Carol had both
become increasingly lax about remembering to lock it
when they were at home.

There was nothing outside the house to suggest it was anything other than a typical Tuesday evening. But it only took Fred a couple of steps through the door to realize that something inside his house was terribly, terribly wrong.

Carol's sock-clad feet were visible, sticking out towards the entrance hall from the living room.

"Carol?" Fred called out.

Carol didn't answer.

As he moved forward instinctively to take a closer look, it was the floor surrounding Carol's body that showed Fred in a glance the full horror of what had transpired there within the past hour.

Carol Neulander had long before selected a pristine white carpet for the family's front room. It was the stark contrast between that bright white surface and the pool of blood that had soaked into it around her head, framing her strangely pale white face, and the radiating spray patterns of blood clear out across the room, which spoke of the ferocity of the attack that had been carried out.

Fred stepped back from the horrific scene into the entrance hall and fumbled for the portable phone that Carol had set down when she hung up with Rebecca. Hands shaking, he punched three buttons and waited what seemed like an eternity as it rang.

"911. State the emergency," the female dispatcher ordered.

"Hi, howyadoin?" Fred stammered reflexively, and then slowly, his voice twisted by agony, he continued, "I, I, Ahhh, I just came home and my wife is on the floor and there's blood all over. I, I, I don't know what to do."

During the seven-minute call that followed, as police cruisers ambulances, and paramedic vans raced through the suburbs to Highgate Lane, Fred Neulander would never think to mention to the dispatcher what he thought had just happened in his house. Based on what little information he gave her, the dispatcher assumed that Fred's wife might have committed suicide.

Dispatchers are trained to "handle" the callers—callers who, in many cases, are right smack in the middle of one of the worst experiences of their lives. The important thing is to stay one step ahead of the situation and think what needs to happen next, and also anticipate what else could go wrong. That's hard to do when you have to rely on information coming from someone who is edging towards hysteria.

Emergency calls are not social events. The 911 dispatchers who take them certainly care a great deal about the people on the other end of the phone, but their calm, detached manner of questioning and instructing callers is a piece of trade-craft developed through bitter experience. Commiserating with the caller's sense of horror, or sympathizing with their situation, or even trying to reassure the caller that things will be all right might all seem like polite or heartfelt reactions, but dispatchers have learned that all these things can be recipes for disaster during an emergency call.

Dispatchers are constantly walking a fine line, on the one hand trying to get the maximum information out of a caller about what is really going on at the scene, while at the same time trying to steer the caller away from a phenomenon known in the trade as the "re-freak." In a re-freak, a caller who has been dealing reasonably and calmly with the dispatcher suddenly realizes the enormity of what is underway, and panics all over again.

A hysterical caller is useless to the dispatcher, useless to the person they are trying to help, and frequently even a danger to themselves. The matter-of-fact, almost bullying, manner that dispatchers often adopt on 911 calls is a deliberate psychological tool designed to keep the callers focused on the dispatcher and not on the trauma.

There are many truly bad things that can happen

when a dispatcher loses "control" of a caller. One of the worst—and it does happen from time to time—is on suicide calls. A caller comes home and finds that a loved one has taken his own life, and, after several minutes spent in shock, he can spiral down into a fit of grief and remorse and then suddenly seize the same weapon and turn it on himself.

Dispatchers who think they might be dealing with a suicide call are very interested in determining whether a weapon was used, where that weapon is now, and in distancing the caller and others from that weapon as expeditiously as possible. The dispatcher who took Fred Neulander's call on November 1, 1994, repeatedly asked him about the location of a possible weapon.

"Okay. Are there any weapons around her, sir?" the dispatcher crisply demanded.

"I can't. I don't know," Fred moaned.

"Does she appear to be breathing?" she continued.

"No, no, there's blood all over," Fred repeated.

"Okay, we'll send somebody down," she replied firmly.

"No! Wait a minute. I've got another problem. My son is an EMT." Fred tried to explain, his voice a drawn-out wail.

It had suddenly hit Fred that his son Matthew, whom he'd been having dinner with in this same house just three hours before, was now on duty at Cherry Hill EMS over on Burntmill Road and 3rd Avenue on the other side of town. There was a good chance that Matt and his crew would be dispatched on this very ambulance call. Fred didn't want Matt to have to pronounce his own mother dead.

"We'll send somebody down. Calm down, sir," the dispatcher intoned.

"Wait a minute. Now, he's gonna hear, he's gonna hear this call, call. He's an East Side EMT," Fred pleaded.

"I have to send somebody down, sir," the dispatcher calmly replied.

"Ah, ah, oh, God," Fred fumbled.

"Calm down. Hold on a second."

What Fred and the dispatcher didn't know was that while Matt Neulander's crew was in fact not the ambulance that got tasked as the primary responder to the Highgate Lane call, Matt had indeed heard the message go out that someone was seriously hurt at his residence; he and the rest of his crew had run to their rig and were now racing down Route 70 trying to beat the world back to his house.

Numerous police and paramedic units were also signing onto the air and the dispatcher put Fred on hold while she talked to the responding units, trying to clarify directions to the house that, in the dark, could look much like the homes around it.

In the white noise of buzzes and clicks on the muted phone line, Fred Neulander's breathing became more and more ragged as he waited for the woman's voice to return. It was another thirty seconds before she came back on the line.

"Okay. Sir?"

"Where, where have you been?" Fred cried, his voice now a distraught whisper.

In the background he could hear the faint wail of sirens coming through her radios as confused police officers began asking for a better idea of what had happened at the scene. If this was a suicide, then how had it been carried out? Echoing their uncertainty, the dispatcher tried to clear this point up with Fred.

"Do you see *any* weapons around her, sir?" she asked again.

"No, I don't see anything. I don't see a *thing*!" Fred practically spat.

"She's just on the ground, and there's blood all over the place, correct?" the dispatcher repeated.

"She's in the living room, and there's blood all over everything," Fred agreed, sighing at the enormity of it.

"She's in the living room? Okay, hold on one second," the dispatcher leaned away from the phone and turned to her police microphone. "He's alone and he found her on the ground. There's blood all over the house. She's in the living room," she told police.

"Breathing?" an officer asked in the background.

"I don't know," the dispatcher replied.

"Sir. Can you tell if she's breathing?" the dispatcher asked, coming back to Fred again.

"What?"

"We're on the way, sir. Can you tell if she's breathing?"

"I can't tell anything. Do I touch her, or should I do anything? Oh, my God. There's blood all over. Do you want me to touch her?" Fred whispered, his voice trailing off to silence.

"Excuse me?" the dispatcher asked.

"Do you want me to touch her?" he repeated, louder.

"Now, now I want you to just calm down, I want you to calm down, okay? That's what I want you to do," the dispatcher replied.

"Hello?" Fred croaked out.

"Mmm, yes?"

"What do you want me to do?" Fred sighed, not really listening.

"I want you to just calm down, and you cannot see any weapons, am I correct?" the dispatcher asked again.

"I can't see anything."

A series of loud clicks began to fill Fred's phone line.

"Hello. Are you still there?" the dispatcher asked.

"Yes. That's our call waiting," Fred sighed.

"Okay. Just sit down and stay with me until the first officer gets there," the dispatcher told Fred, adding, "It's 204 Highgate Lane, right? The Neulander residence."

That startled Fred, who practically shouted back, "How do you know that?"

"When you dial 911, it automatically comes up here," she replied matter-of-factly.

Fred started to sob.

"Are you okay?" the dispatcher asked.

"My wife's on the floor," he responded incredulously.

There was another pause as Fred tried to collect himself. "I don't know what to say. . . . Should I touch her? Should I not touch her?" he finally wondered aloud.

"Just leave everything the way it is, sir, and stay on the phone with me until the first police officer gets there."

Fred began sobbing louder and gasping for breath. "Ah! Oh!"

"Sir?" the dispatcher sounded concerned.

"Yes?"

"Do you need an ambulance? Are you all right?"

"I'll be all right. How would you think? I, I can't, oh, Jeez. . . . I don't know what 'all right' is . . . There's blood all over everything," Fred moaned, beginning to gasp louder. "Oh, Jeez. Ahh. She's not moving. She's not breathing. Ah, Jeez."

"You say she's not breathing?" the dispatcher asked again.

"I don't think so. She's not moving."

"You don't think she's breathing?" the dispatcher repeated.

"No, ma'am. I don't think so. Where's the officer?"

"The officer will be there momentarily. He's on the way."

Fred broke into coughing sobs.

"Hold on one second," the dispatcher said as she turned back to her radios.

"Can we protect my son? How do we protect my son?" Fred continued, picking back up on his worry about Matthew hearing this emergency being dispatched.

"Hold on one second."

A loud buzz crackled down the phone line.

"You still there with me, sir?" the dispatcher asked.

"Yeah," Fred sighed. A moment later, he added, "The door's open. I can hear sirens on Market Street."

"As soon as the first officer arrives, I'm going to advise you to hang up and go talk to them," the dispatcher instructed.

"The door's open. I'm here waiting for them. Do I go outside and wait for them?" Fred wondered.

"Just stay on the phone with me, sir. Take it easy."

"Okay. Thank you."

"Just calm down," the dispatcher said firmly. "It's not going to do anybody any good if you're upset and something happens to you, all right?"

"Yes, but I'm in my home, though . . . I'm um, um . . . I can barely understand," Fred whispered.

"You got a chair there or something nearby that you can sit down on?" she asked.

"I'm on the steps."

"Excuse me?"

"I'm on the steps," Fred repeated referring to his front porch.

"Okay. You're on the steps. You are seated? Okay, because we are going to have a medic come and check you out, because you don't sound too good either."

Confused, and still worried that Matt might be assigned to this call, Fred tried to clarify his concern. "But my . . . do you hear . . . my son? Do you understand what I'm saying?"

"I understand exactly, sir. But we, we have nothing to do with the, with the, with the EMTs and we [don't] dispatch them from here. Camden County dispatches the medics and the ambulances."

"Oh, God, oh, my God. Oh, my God . . . Ohhhhh," Fred moaned.

The dispatcher keyed her police radio and asked, "Is anybody there yet?" to the responding cops.

Fred could hear the first police units turning onto nearby Wexford Drive, but then they seemed to pass by the turnoff that would take them to his house.

"Jesus, they can't even find the place," he cried.

"The officers are there, sir?" asked the dispatcher.

"They're running . . . I'm going outside," Fred replied.

"Don't hang up the phone," she advised him. In the background, confused officers began asking for a cross street as a reference point, but then realized where they had overshot the turn before they could complete the thought. "What's the nearest . . . okay. . . . The first officer should be there, sir . . . advise him the door is open," the dispatcher began to tell Fred.

"I'm outside," Fred replied. In the background the dispatcher could hear an officer on the radio saying, "We've got the caller on the lawn."

"Okay, you stepped outside?" the dispatcher asked Fred. "Okay, you are on a portable phone, then, I gather. . . . Okay, do you see the officer there, sir?"

"Yeah, he's coming," Fred sighed.

"Okay."

"What do you want me to do now?" Fred asked passively.

"Hang up the phone, speak to the officer," the dispatcher replied calmly.

Fred turned to the first arriving patrolman and asked the same question. "What do you want me to do?"

CHAPTER FIVE

THE minutes and hours after Rabbi Neulander placed the 911 call from his entrance hallway were a blur of activity. With each moment that passed, more people seemed to arrive on Highgate Lane in either an official or personal capacity, and the normally quiet street began to teem with people.

Fred had picked up the phone and called for help at 9:22 P.M. The first Cherry Hill Police units began arriving at 9:29 P.M.

It took just one look for police to determine that they were at the scene of a homicide and not a suicide. It was obvious to the officers and detectives arriving at Highgate Lane that Carol Neulander had been savagely beaten to death right on the spot.

Matthew Neulander and his ambulance crew had raced through the streets from their station in the Deer Park section of Cherry Hill but another squad from Ashland Ambulance had beaten them to the scene. The local paramedic service, essentially highly trained doctors with specialized life-saving skills that go way beyond what can be done by regular EMTs such as Matthew, had also been dispatched to this call and had arrived a minute earlier, but as Matt pulled up to the house he saw something that made his heart sink. The paramedics had already climbed back into their big specially rigged sport utility vehicle and shut their strobe lights off. They were now pulling away from the Neulander house, not rushing inside. This didn't bode well for the status of the victim.

As Matt approached, he could see through the front

windows that there were police officers inside the house with guns drawn. Behind the bay window to the right of the front door a large cluster of officers were staring down at something on the living room floor. He ran for the entrance, but a fellow EMT who knew him stopped him on the front porch and steered him towards his father, who was at the end of the driveway. Matt asked repeatedly what had happened, but all Fred could tell him was that he had found Carol lying there when he walked in.

"Is she dead?" Matthew implored.

"I don't know," Fred replied.

A moment later an EMT came outside and confirmed that Carol was deceased. Matthew walked down the street in anguish, the red and blue strobe lights of a dozen emergency vehicles pinging off all the quiet tree-shrouded homes around him as the evening's bitter cold wind blew dried leaves down Highgate Lane.

If this same tragedy had struck almost any other night of Matthew's young adult life, he would have been equally bereft by his mother's sudden, senseless death, but on this particular night he realized there was something else that he needed an answer to, and he needed it quickly. Returning to the driveway, Matthew Neulander approached his father and began to pepper him with rapid-fire questions about what had just happened. It had been three hours since they had shared a pizza together and narrowly missed their mother's return to the house. Matthew wanted to know where his father had been, and he wanted to take a good look at his father's clothing. He was surprised at the immense relief he felt when his cursory survey confirmed that there was no blood visible anywhere on Rabbi Fred Neulander.

Fred had been anguished during his 911 call, but now, standing in front of his house as the investigation into his wife's murder began to ramp up to full speed, Fred was becoming remarkably calm and collected.

Whatever Matt would ask him, Neulander's response on this night was always the same: "Everything is going to be okay."

As more and more patrol officers and detectives arrived at the scene, word spread like wildfire amongst the Neulanders' wide circle of friends, many of whom were connected to the municipal government in Cherry Hill, that something had happened to Carol.

One of the first to arrive at the house was Cherry Hill Mayor Susan Bass Levin, who, as one of the M'kor Shalom congregation, had known the Neulanders for fifteen years. "The entire community mourns the Neulanders' loss," Levin told the *Courier-Post* later that evening. "Carol was very active both in the neighborhood community and the temple's community. She was a very caring and giving person. This is a terrible tragedy." Even as midnight approached, the number of the Neulanders' friends who came to the scene would swell to nearly fifty people.

One of those friends picked up Rebecca from her apartment in Philadelphia and drove her through the darkened streets to Cherry Hill. She arrived to find her childhood home surrounded by a growing contingent of marked and unmarked vehicles in what now looked like a scene from a police drama.

Sitting on the bench inside the heated ambulance parked in his driveway, Fred Neulander talked to his children and to friends as they tried to console him and make some sense out of what had happened.

A mile away, Rabbi Gary Mazo had arrived at his own home in Cherry Hill at the same time Neulander had arrived back at his. Mazo had grabbed a beer out of his refrigerator and was preparing to watch an episode of *NYPD Blue* when a close friend walked through his front door with the real thing. "Carol's dead," his stunned friend announced, so distracted by the horror of what had happened that he hadn't bothered to knock as he entered the Mazos'.

Rabbi Mazo arrived on Highgate Lane to find that police had cordoned off the Neulanders' yard with yellow crime-scene tape and were already dusting the front door for fingerprints. He found Rabbi Neulander in the back of the ambulance with his head buried in his hands, and tried to comfort his colleague. Neulander asked that Mazo arrange to recite a *vidui* for Carol, a traditional Jewish confession for the dead. He also asked Mazo to retrieve the family's address book from the house and call his youngest son Ben at Michigan State and tell him what had happened.

Rabbi Neulander obviously couldn't be left to arrange and officiate his own wife's funeral, so Mazo and his wife Debbi Pipe–Mazo, also a rabbi, began immediately to make plans for what was clearly a major tragedy in the history of their synagogue.

Mazo asked detectives to let him into the house to perform the *vidui* and prayers for Carol. They wanted to accommodate him, but told him to be patient; it was going to take time to process the body and the front room for evidence, and until that was done no one else could go inside.

While the crowd gathered outside, detectives looked around the rest of the house and marveled at how untouched, how pristine, everything inside appeared to be. Meanwhile, in the living room, forensics experts started their excruciatingly thorough examination of Carol's head and the space immediately surrounding her body.

They noticed numerous lacerations to Carol's scalp that were still obvious under her blood-matted hair. The coroner would later determine that she had been struck a dozen times in the head, most likely with a tire iron, and that six or seven of those strikes were parallel to each other, suggesting that the victim was not moving, or at least not moving much, when they were inflicted.

The careful examination of the body turned up small traces of a thick substance in Carol's hair that looked like it might be grease. This further heightened the coroner's suspicion that the weapon used was a tire iron.

There was also evidence of severe blows to the backs of Carol's hands, indicating that at some point she had placed them behind her head to try to protect her skull from the terrible beating. One of her fingers had been nearly severed by the strikes against it. Despite the ferocity of the blows to her brain, the forensic examination revealed that those were not what had actually killed her. In a final indignity, Carol had choked to death on her own vomit before she could succumb to her head injuries.

Carol was lying almost underneath the edge of the glass-topped coffee table wearing a blue pantsuit with a floral printed top and a matching blue vest. Her clothes hadn't been hiked up or removed, and it didn't appear that her assailant had made any effort to search her person. The diamond engagement ring and the wedding band she had worn for the last twenty-nine years was still on her finger. Around her neck was a favorite gold necklace with six diamonds inset along its center, and on her left wrist there were still several gold bracelets and an expensive watch.

Aside from Carol's body, there was almost nothing at the murder scene for detectives to work with. Nowhere in the whole scheme of the Highgate Lane house was there anything to suggest that Carol had been killed by more than one person, and whoever had killed Carol had taken their weapon with them. Two drops of blood were found just inside the front door on the hardwood floor of the entrance hallway. That simply suggested that the weapon had been dripping with blood when the killer walked back outside. But, beyond the graphic murder in the front room, there was nothing unusual about the house itself. Nothing appeared to have been moved,

searched, or disturbed. There was no evidence of forced
entry, the murderer hadn't left anything of his own behind at the scene. A careful sweep of the property didn't
come up with any fingerprints, bloody shoe prints, or
even footwear impressions. No trace evidence of any use
had been transferred over to Carol's body during the
course of the assault.

Over time, Fred Neulander and his children would
verify that nothing appeared to have been stolen from
anywhere in the residence . . . nothing except for Carol's
pocketbook.

Carol's purse was found lying just a few feet from
her body on the white living room carpet. It looked like
it had been tossed a short distance either by Carol or her
assailant, and a quick check of the contents revealed that
her burgundy-colored wallet was missing.

To the uninitiated this immediately suggested that
Carol had been the victim of a robbery. Some small-
time criminal or drug user desperate for money had rung
her doorbell, bludgeoned her to death, and disappeared
into the night with her wallet. However, to the experienced homicide detectives arriving at the scene, this explanation felt all wrong.

Taken purely at face value, the crime might have
been a relatively simple home-invasion–style robbery
gone bad. Even then, it would still be a rare and weird
one. The perpetrator would have taken some real risks,
given the proximity of many potentially vigilant neighbors on the peaceful street. Furthermore, a lot of luck
would have to be involved in picking a house and finding only a lone victim at home at the time. There was
also the inexplicable rationale behind beating Carol to
death when knocking her out or tying her up would invite a much less intense investigation. Still, it could, just
maybe, have been as senseless and random as it seemed.
But when Rebecca Neulander–Rockoff arrived, she immediately went over to detectives and explained to them

what little she knew about "the Bathroom Man" from her phone conversation earlier in the evening. She told the officers that this had been his second visit to her mother's house.

That changed everything. Detectives couldn't yet be absolutely certain that the Bathroom Man and the murderer were one and the same, but in a heartbeat this person had become their prime suspect. Even though they knew so little about him, they immediately realized several key facts. First, he had come to the house and specifically mentioned the rabbi as the reason for his appearance when he introduced himself to Carol. This was no randomly selected home invasion carried out on a whim. Somebody had known who the Neulanders were, and deliberately come to their house. Second, he had been there once before and then come back. If this were a simple robbery, targeted at grabbing Carol's purse, by some desperate character who figured that a rabbi's wife was more likely than some other housewife to carry cash, then the robbery would have gone down the first time. Detectives knew that a return visit meant that something more elaborate was at work here.

If the Bathroom Man had indeed intended to rob Carol, then all that he had taken was her wallet. He hadn't taken the other expensive jewelry that she was wearing. He hadn't ransacked the house—in fact, there was nothing to suggest he had even wandered around it looking for additional valuables. But if it was essentially a targeted purse-snatching, why had he also pounded Carol to death with some kind of weapon?

Rebecca's tip to the police about the Bathroom Man moved the investigation one giant leap forward, but there was still so much that left detectives frustrated. Beyond his ridiculous nickname, Rebecca had absolutely no idea who the Bathroom Man was. She also had no idea what he looked like, what kind of car he drove, where he was from, what he did for a living, what his supposed message had involved, and certainly no idea why he seemed to know the identity of Rabbi Fred Neulander.

Right off the bat, detectives had made the connection that, in addition to being the rabbi's wife, Carol was also a successful businesswoman in her own right. And they soon learned that she was in the dangerous habit of bringing substantial amounts of cash home with her from the bakery. That fact opened up a much more reasonable explanation as to why Carol might have been the target of a serious robbery attempt. A housewife, even a wealthy housewife, with some cash in her pocketbook is one thing, but a businesswoman who's in the habit of lugging around $15,000 in her purse is quite another. If the Classic Cake cash receipts were the motive behind this, then it was an inside job of the first order; supposedly almost no one knew about this activity. It now looked like Carol could have been killed by a very close associate from Classic Cake or by someone there who was tipped to the secret. However, Carol would have recognized everyone even remotely associated with her own business, so if that robbery scenario was correct, the Bathroom Man had to be at least one step removed from whoever had set the plot in motion.

In addition to the robbery theory, there were other, slightly less obvious, possibilities that were nonetheless very much in the minds of the investigators. In that regard, Fred Neulander had two strikes against him. Fred was both the "finder" and the spouse of the victim. Even if detectives knew nothing else about him, those two facts would each make him a murder suspect unless and until he was ruled out. Simple analysis of decades' worth of solved crime statistics has made it clear that people who find murder victims, and people who are married to murder victims, frequently turn out to be responsible for their deaths.

All these thoughts were on the detectives' minds as they began talking to the gathering knot of bewildered people in the Neulanders' driveway. The more they had a chance to talk to the family members and friends, the more they learned about Carol and Fred Neulander. The more they learned, the more they felt they smelled a rat.

Police are in a business where they expect to be lied to almost as a matter of routine. Any beginning patrolman investigating something as minor as a fender-bender quickly learns that he can expect the parties involved in an incident to present the facts of the situation in the most self-serving, non-incriminating manner possible. Historical revisionism and convenient lapses of memory occur with astonishing speed when it's in the self-interest of an individual who's trying to get his side across to police. These little twists and bends on the absolute truth are something police learn to consider as part of the background noise of their day. But murders are special cases. When somebody has been murdered, all bets are off. Polite decorum and expectations of privacy cease to exist. There is literally nothing that a homicide detective can't ask someone. And they have every reason to believe that people cooperating with a homicide investigation should be willing to give them the absolute truth. The stakes in a murder investigation are too high for petty vanity and face-saving omissions, and detectives are especially interested in who decides to lie to them under those circumstances. That's because murderers seeking to avoid capture can never really give a completely honest account to detectives. They have to lie about either their whereabouts at the time of the murder, or their knowledge of the circumstances of the crime, or, at a minimum, about their true feelings towards the victim. Somewhere, somehow, they are going to be forced to fudge the truth of some aspect of the situation, perhaps on something major, perhaps on something seemingly insignificant. That's why the mere existence of an inconsistency, the slightest hint of a lie, is incredibly meaningful to homicide detectives. Lying to

48   ERIC FRANCIS

detectives, even to avoid embarrassment, is to invite intense and sustained scrutiny of the most gut-wrenching order.

Before the clock hit midnight on November 1, before Carol Neulander's shattered body had even been lifted from her living room floor, the homicide detectives assigned to investigate her death began to feel that Rabbi Fred Neulander was lying to them, and they very much wanted to know why.

CHAPTER SIX

DETECTIVES and police officers had immediately begun knocking on doors and canvassing neighbors up and down Highgate Lane, Market Street, and the half-dozen homes on the Pembroke Court cul-de-sac right across from the Neulanders'. No one remembered anything suspicious in the two-hour time frame between 7 and 9 P.M. that authorities were interested in. Next door, the Neulanders' neighbors, the Mitchards, had noticed Fred and Matthew through their kitchen window bustling around with their dinner around 6 P.M., and they had noticed that Carol's car wasn't there at the time. In the following hours, they had moved on within their own home and were watching television by the time Carol did return. The Mitchards hadn't seen her come in, nor had they seen anyone else or any unusual vehicles in the time period after Carol must have returned.

The question of motive was as disturbing to area residents as it was to police. People don't get mugged in their homes, and it was hard to fathom why even a home-invasion robbery, unlikely as it was in this neighborhood, would have necessitated Carol being bludgeoned to death. Several of the homes immediately around the Neulanders' had burglar alarms, but many others didn't, and up until now, the most prominent fear had been what could happen if a home was left unattended and burglarized—not armed robbery and/or murder of homeowners.

Two hours after his father discovered his mother's body, Matt Neulander was briefly interviewed by Detec-

tive John Long and Investigator Arthur Folks of the
Camden County Prosecutor's Office as he sat in his ambulance in front of his house.

The investigators wanted to know if there had been
any recent conflicts within the Neulander household. Already traumatized by his mother's violent death, Matt
was noticeably reluctant to start trashing people's perceptions of his parents' long marriage; however, he did
have a very clear memory of some disturbing events that
had transpired only forty-eight hours before. In fact, in
the two decades that Matt had observed his parents, this
past weekend was the first time he remembered seeing
any serious cracks appear in their marriage.

Fred and Carol had left for the weekend to visit
relatives in New York. Matt had been at home when
they returned on the night of Sunday, October 30.

As soon as Carol walked into the house, Matt could
tell that she was quite upset, and it quickly became apparent that she and Fred had been having one hell of an
argument on the ride back home to New Jersey. Carol
pointedly said to Matt that his father had something important to tell him. When Matt looked to his father for
an explanation, Fred remained silent. Carol stepped back
into the void his father was leaving in the conversation
and told Matt that Fred had decided he was leaving.
Confused, Matt at first took her to mean that he was
planning some sort of a trip. "No, he's going to be seeking a divorce," Carol clarified.

Matt was floored by this completely unexpected turn
of events, and was still thinking about its implications
when his mother returned later in the evening. Carol said
she had just had an extended conversation with Fred,
and told Matt that "Everything is going to be all right."
Matt Neulander took this to mean that his parents had
gotten over whatever had sparked this rift, and things
were getting back on track, but a short time later Matt
encountered his father, and Fred seemed to feel that the

opposite was true. He wouldn't tell Matt what his dis-
agreement with Carol was about, but he did tell him that
he should "prepare for the worst."

This sudden downturn in his parents' relationship
was still very much on Matt's mind when he received a
phone call from his mother about 4:30 P.M. on the day
she died. Carol had called him on her car phone and
mentioned that she had just pulled into Arky Helprien's
driveway for the weekly Classic Cake meeting. Carol
wanted to reassure Matt that she and Fred had resolved
their differences from the other evening, and they now
planned to jointly receive marriage counseling to prevent
this from happening in the future.

Encouraged by the seeming upturn in this tempest,
Matt had tried to kick-start a conversation about his parents' problem over the pizza he'd shared with his father
that evening. Fred wasn't in any mood to discuss the
matter, and just brushed off Matt's attempt at a discussion.

Hours later, when Matt Neulander heard that his
mother had suddenly been murdered in her own living
room, he couldn't help but wonder whether there had
been another argument that had escalated between his
parents. Had his father killed her?

Matt told the detectives that when he arrived at the
house and spoke to his father, he'd looked closely at the
rabbi's clothing, and had been relieved to see that there
wasn't any blood on him.

Detectives had also looked closely at Fred's clothing
and hands, and they too had noted the lack of blood.
Their take on the matter, however, was a bit different
from Matthew's conclusion that the lack of bloodstains
automatically exonerated his father. If Fred Neulander
had been covered in blood spatters, police would have
been deeply suspicious, but at the same time, they would
have understood if he literally had some blood on his
hands. This was his wife of twenty-nine years, not a

corpse he had stumbled across in an alley, and detectives would not have been surprised if he had in some way touched her body. But Fred hadn't touched his wife at all. He hadn't checked for a pulse, he hadn't gotten down on the blood-soaked carpet for a close look at her face to see if perhaps there was any hope that she was still breathing. The fact that he hadn't approached Carol raised a question in their minds. That said, they also had to admit that anyone objectively looking at Carol, at the massive bloodstain around her on the carpet and the ghastly white color of her skin, would probably have correctly concluded that she was dead, even if they didn't want to believe it.

Matt's revelation that Fred Neulander and his wife were right in the middle of a difficult period in their relationship, that divorce had been mentioned as a possibility for the first time just two days before, gave the investigators much to think about. Having learned that things between the Neulanders might not have been what they seemed, Long and Folks broke off the impromptu interview. They thanked Matt and told him they would soon pick back up on their line of questioning down at the Cherry Hill police station once everyone had a chance to regroup.

By this time, the section of Highgate Lane out in front of the Neulander residence looked like an episode of *Law & Order*. Ambulances, marked and unmarked police cars, and crime-scene equipment vans were parked everywhere, and cops, neighbors, and friends were milling about trying to make some sense out of what had happened to Carol.

Rebecca climbed on board the ambulance in the driveway to be with her father, who was still sitting on the patient bench under the bright surgical lights in a slight refuge from the chaos outside, and Detective Long and Investigator Folks followed her in for a brief interview with father and daughter.

Rebecca was distraught, but she remembered clearly her conversation with her mother at about 8 P.M. that evening. She described the arrival of "the Bathroom Man" during the call, and how she could hear her mother invite him inside. She also noted the passing reference her mother made to someone who seemed to be accompanying the Bathroom Man.

She described what she remembered of the Bathroom Man's previous visit to Carol, which Rebecca had also heard pieces of over the phone connection, but she wasn't able to remember precisely what day that first visit had occurred. Her guess was that it had been about two or three weeks beforehand.

Rebecca described the stranger's request to use the bathroom, the empty envelope, and the fact that her mother had mentioned Fred telling her to expect a package to be delivered in the near future.

When Rebecca wrapped up her description of the Bathroom Man, the detectives turned to the rabbi and to Matt, who had also climbed back into the ambulance at that point. They asked what the rabbi knew of this Bathroom Man and his package or message. Fred put his arm around Rebecca, looked down at the floor of the ambulance, and said softly that he had no knowledge of any such delivery.

"Did Carol tell you about the empty envelope, or show it to you?" the detectives asked.

"No," Fred replied.

How then, they wondered, would Carol have dealt with such an empty envelope?

"She would have torn it up and thrown it out," Fred stated matter-of-factly. The detectives made a mental note that Fred hadn't even tried to come up with another solution or explanation for what might have become of this potential piece of evidence.

Was there anyone, the detectives asked, who made deliveries of letters or packages to the rabbi on a regular basis? Fred explained that he was on the board of trustees at the Cooper Medical Center hospital, and normally, before the board met each month, a packet of material would be dropped off at each of the board members' houses. The detectives wound up the interview in the ambulance and told the three Neulanders to meet them again in a few hours down at the Cherry Hill Police Department.

The forensics team began to wind up their work in the living room at about 2 A.M., and detectives called for Rabbi Mazo to come inside so he could perform his rites over Carol's body. Mazo got as far as the entrance hallway, which was now coated in black fingerprint powder, and saw Carol's feet sticking out on the living room floor, and some of the blood. Detectives, reacting to his look of utter horror, decided to send him back out to wait again, saying they would bring Carol out to him. Relieved, Mazo waited another quarter of an hour before they brought out the black zippered body bag and placed it solemnly on the lawn while Mazo recited the *vidui* and a memorial prayer.

It would be another hour before detectives were able to find and retrieve the address book for Mazo. He and Cantor Anita Hockman drove back to M'kor Shalom and looked up the number of a local rabbi in Michigan and had him go and wake up Benjamin Neulander in his dorm room. Mazo didn't want the 18-year-old to be all alone at 3 A.M. when he heard of his mother's death. After the other rabbi arrived, Mazo called and told Ben what had happened.

"At that moment all of my rabbinic training felt utterly, totally useless," Mazo later wrote.

No one was going to get any sleep this evening anyway, so at 1:30 A.M. on November 2 the detectives resumed their interview with Rebecca over at the police station. An hour later they re-interviewed Matt and at

3:30 A.M., it was time for another interview with Fred Neulander.

Fred told the investigators that he had spent most of the day at M'kor Shalom, and had last spoken to Carol on the phone at her workplace at the Voorhees Classic Cake location in the Eagle Plaza at approximately 3 P.M. He said that the purpose of his call was just to say, "Hi! I love you, I'll see you tonight." He said that there was also a brief mention by Carol that she had gotten hold of a rug cleaner and perhaps that person was going to be in the house that afternoon to work on the carpets.

Since Carol was off to her usual weekly business meeting and wasn't expected home until about 8, Fred explained that he had come back to the house about 6 P.M. and made dinner for himself and Matt. Then he returned to the M'kor Shalom temple where he had attended to various business around his synagogue for just over two hours.

"I was at the synagogue and I saw some people, I made some calls, I did some work, because my wife always goes out on this Tuesday night, and we don't get enough nights together, so I try to do my work on Tuesday nights as well," Neulander said.

Neulander explained again that when he had returned home at 9:20 P.M., he had walked in through the unlocked front door of his house. "When I walked into the foyer, I could see that she was lying on the floor, so I just threw my stuff, the green raincoat and a brown quilt bag and my keys . . . I just threw it on the ground and then I went over to her and I just looked, and it was so repulsing and frightening to me—that's when I called 911. I didn't touch her. I don't know if I was playing in your job," Fred said to the detective, "but you don't touch a body and, I don't know, I just, it was very scary for me, and I didn't know anything, I didn't know what to do. What I really wanted to do was to get a blanket and cover her, but I didn't.

"I dialed 911, and I just kept saying, 'What do I do? Should I cover her?' I asked the question, 'Should I touch her?' and the woman on the other end of the line said, 'Just wait for the officer, wait for the officer, wait for the officer,' so I didn't touch her, but I did move out of the foyer and, quite frankly, I, I, I couldn't go into the room. I, I looked once and, ah, I was, it was so horrible I just couldn't stay in the room, so I stayed in the foyer and then I opened the door and then went outside and I was, and I was on the portable phone and I, you know, I, I don't know which officer it was, but he said to me, 'Who would do this?' " Fred recalled.

Was there anyone who would wish harm to Carol because she was the wife of a rabbi? detectives asked. Neulander said that he had gotten an anti-Semitic hate letter in his mail at the synagogue over a decade beforehand but nothing that would suggest he was being stalked by a neo-Nazi or the like. Occasionally congregants had gotten upset with him over the years. "Sometimes people want something and I just can't do it," Fred explained. "They want a particular date for a particular occasion and I don't have it free, and they get kind of upset at that, but, you know, that's it. There's been no ongoing hostility. There's no enemy as far as I know. I'm just bewildered by this."

Asking about the possibility of a robbery, the police questioned Fred about his wife's jewelry. He described the scalloped gold necklace with the half-dozen diamonds that she usually wore, and he remembered that she had given him one of her gold bracelets just that morning because it had been bent and she wanted him to take it to a jeweler for repair. "It may still be in my pocket back at the house, I don't know," Fred sighed, apparently referring to his suit jacket.

The detectives asked Fred about Carol's habit of bringing home large sums of money from Classic Cake. Fred acknowledged that she sometimes brought thousands of dollars back home with her, but he said she didn't have any set schedule for that. He also said that he had tried to discourage her from doing so for her own safety. He said he had asked her to think about what would happen to the money if she were in a traffic accident or something on the way home.

Were there any problems between Carol and her associates at Classic Cake? Long and Folks wondered. Fred said he hadn't heard anything beyond the usual workplace issues that sometimes frayed nerves, but certainly there was no real tension between her and the rest of the managers.

The investigators delved into the issue of delivery people coming to the house. What could Carol and the Bathroom Man have been talking about when they seemed to indicate that Fred had told her to expect a package of some sort? Neulander said he really had no idea what they could have meant. "I don't remember anything like that," Fred said, adding, "I know, because I don't want people in the house. I have little enough privacy. And, you know, if deliveries are made, I would want them to be at the . . . deliveries are made where I don't, I don't want people around . . ." It was 3:30 A.M., after a harrowing night, and without sleep, Fred was beginning to meander in his answers, but he struggled to point out that, beyond the packets that came once a month from Cooper Medical, he wasn't expecting anything specific. "And I would never have said, you know, 'I want you to drop something off [at my house],' a delivery. I don't want to confound you, but it wasn't until tonight that something was said," Neulander added.

What, then, did Fred know about this guy who had shown up saying he had a message for him, and why would Fred have told Carol to expect someone?

"I heard nothing about it. The only thing I can, you know, the only thing I'm trying to put together is this, this bathroom guy," Fred began. "I don't know anything about that. Because she told me that this weird guy, she said he had something, I forget, and then he asked to use the bathroom, and then . . ."

"Hold on!" Detective Long interrupted. "She told you this before?"

"Yeah. She told me . . . I forget what she said," Fred struggled.

"What time? When did she tell you this?"

"Just last week when it happened. She said he had to use the bathroom, and she's very trusting, and she let the guy use the bathroom and then he went away."

"Why don't you go into detail on this discussion, how this discussion turns out?" Long pressed.

"All my wife said was, this guy had this thing, this, some kind of note, and, ah, he was kind of weird because he asked to go to the bathroom, and that's it. There was nothing in the envelope, so she tore it up and threw it away. That's, that's all she said," Neulander concluded.

"Did she mention that the guy was there to deliver a package to her or to you or . . . ?"

"She said that, something, she said to me that, yes, she had a package for me, it came to the house, and that's, that's all."

"Did she ever show you the package that he, ah, delivered?"

"No. That was the whole conversation. She didn't seem upset about him, and I wasn't upset at all."

Neulander couldn't remember the precise day that Carol had said the Bathroom Man had first visited, but Long continued to probe around about the incident.

"What was your response when she said all this to you?" he wondered.

"It was nutsy," Fred replied. "You know, sometimes people do drop things off, but they usually leave them in the mailbox."

"Did your wife seem upset by this individual? Did

you think it was strange, or was it upsetting to you?" Long asked.

"It wasn't at all upsetting to me," Fred replied. "It was kind of strange, but she just passed it off, so I just passed it off."

"What gave her the impression that he was weird?" Long wondered.

"I didn't ask her," Fred replied.

"I have a question for you. It's an awkward situation, this being your wife's death, but would you be reluctant to tell us if there were any problems between you and her? Would you fear that we would look at you differently?" the detective asked.

"No. I told you there were the normal kinds of bumps, disagreements about the kids, those kind of things," Neulander said.

Arthur Folks followed up. "There were no marital problems? Everything was kosher?" and then, realizing who he was talking to, Folks thought better of the phrase. "Excuse me, it's the expression that everything . . ."

"Yeah, everything was kosher," Fred responded wryly. "We had never been to a marriage counselor, we have had arguments, like, I imagine, the same things I hear about in my office, but no crisis intervention, no violence or domestic abuse."

Detective Joseph Vitarelli of the Cherry Hill Police Department joined the interview and returned to the topic of the Bathroom Man. "My main concern is that she never offered a physical description of this character who came into the house and asked to use the bathroom. We don't have very many details here, what's, what . . ."

"She was virgin. She was very trusting," Neulander responded.

"We know that," Vitarelli replied.

"It was just, you know, in my job there are so many nutty, well not nutty people, but unusual things that happen, unusual conversations that I have requests about, people calling in the middle of the night for their crises, so I'd say we run into an awful lot of stuff. I guess our level of what we think is really strange is probably not the same as other people's. It was just that he asked to use the bathroom, and that's that. I've had notes before left in my box that people don't sign and, you know, they want me to do something, and all kinds of things."

Detective John Long began to steer Neulander onto the state of Fred's relationship with Carol. "My wife and I would have been married twenty-nine years this December, and I had known her for about three years before that," Fred recalled. "We met when I was a senior in college, so we've been a part of each other's lives just about my entire adult life, ever since I was twenty-one and, you know, other than the normal bumps and twists about how we don't spend enough time, two-income houses, two-income families, it's, you know, I was very lucky to have her. She was a terrific partner."

"There are some personal questions we have to ask you," Detective Long noted.

"I understand. I understand," Neulander said.

"Did your wife have any relationships outside the marriage?"

"I don't," Neulander replied, shaking his head.

"Did you have any relationships outside the marriage? No problems whatsoever?" Long continued.

"No," Fred replied.

"And how did you consider your marriage?"

"Good. Great," Fred responded.

"And there was no conflict between your wife and any other family members?"

"No, as a matter of fact, just by sheer coincidence we saw most of the family Sunday at a birthday party for an aunt. Carol has a brother and two sisters, and all eight of us were together last night," Fred explained. "That was in north Jersey, in South Orange, at the home of my brother-in-law. His wife had lost her father, and we were there for what we call a 'shiva'—after a death we all gather together—and I made the remark that Carol's mother was dead, but I remarked how lucky she had been in central Jersey, and in this day and age when everything is falling apart, all four of her kids were happily married, all ten grandchildren were healthy, and everybody lived within two hours of Carol's mother, and she was just a very lucky lady." He added that they had driven home on Monday evening and returned to Highgate Lane about 11 P.M.

As the sun came up over Cherry Hill on the Wednesday morning after the murder, investigators once again stepped under the yellow crime-scene tape and began scouring the Neulander property in the improved light. Borrowing ladders from a Cherry Hill fire truck, they climbed up on the roof and took a good look. They poked around the trees, grass, and bushes. The Neulanders' lot was small—most of the houses in Wexford Leas are so close together that you can practically stand between two of them with your arms outstretched and touch them both—but there are plenty of tall trees towering over the area, and fall leaves covered the ground. Detectives literally turned over each leaf and then rummaged through the Neulanders' trash cans and recycling bin, as well as those at nearby properties. They also carefully examined the three cars that were parked in the driveway. They looked at everything they could look at, but for all their thoroughness they were having as little luck finding anything useful outside of the house as they had inside.

Back at the police station, the detectives had decided to turn their attention to the staff of the Classic Cake Company.

Over the noon hour on Wednesday, the police scheduled an interview with Richard J. Price, 31, of Audubon. Price had known Carol for a decade. He'd first

come to work for her in 1984, two years after she had
founded her bakery, and he had quickly risen to the position of head baker. By 1987, he'd wanted to purchase
the business from Carol and Judy Stern, but he didn't
have enough capital to buy it all at once, and besides,
he knew that it was Carol's business acumen that had
kept Classic Cake growing. Price worked out a deal
where Carol stayed on as part of the business, even
though he was gradually taking over as owner. The tech-
nicalities of the financing were known only to a handful
of people, and the public was just told that Price had
purchased the company and retained Carol as manager.

Price told the detectives that the weekly management meetings had been a regular feature of his and
Carol's lives for over a year now, and at the November
1 session the day before, Carol, Price, Helprien, and the
current head baker, David Spillane, and head decorator
Gary West had been present. The meeting had begun as
scheduled at 4:30 P.M. and revolved around general business issues of little note. At 7:30, Price became the first
of the five managers present to leave the gathering. He
drove over to the new bakery branch in Audubon, which
was being renovated, and then over to the store in Voorhees. Price said he arrived at the Voorhees branch at
about 8 P.M.—his sister was already there and could
vouch for his presence—and that he stayed there until
about 9:30, at which point he drove home, arriving back
there at approximately 10 o'clock.

Price said he didn't learn about Carol's death until
he arrived at the Voorhees bakery the next morning and
Gary West told him that there had been a death on Highgate Lane in Cherry Hill. Price drove over to the Neulander residence, where he learned that it was indeed
Carol who had been killed.

When asked, Price said he had never heard or seen
any indications of any marital strain between Carol and
Fred.

The detectives wanted to know about the large amounts of cash that Carol was known to bring home with her from these weekly meetings. Price acknowledged that Carol frequently took the money home because there wasn't enough time to count it during the day. He said Carol would return the next morning and give him an accurate count of the receipts and inform him when a deposit would be made. Price told the officers that he didn't think there was anyone besides himself who knew that Carol brought the cash back home. Furthermore, he told the detectives that the previous evening had not been one of those occasions. All of the bakery's money from November 1 was accounted for and locked in the safe back at the store.

Price told the detectives that Carol was actually the cornerstone of his company, and without her the business might well fail. When Price became emotional and started crying, the police decided it was time to stop the interview.

Next up, the detectives interviewed Classic Cake's head decorator Gary A. West, 43, of Glenside, Pennsylvania. West worked out at the Voorhees branch of the business, and he told the police that he had known Carol for about five years. He had been the third person to leave the management meeting, behind Price and then Spillane, and he had gone directly home from the gathering to meet with his friend John Loesch. West had no clue why Carol had been killed, and was not aware of any problems she was having with her family or anyone else. His brief session with the detectives was quickly concluded.

In his interview, head baker David Spillane, 33, of Lindenwold, New Jersey, gave the same details of Tuesday night's business meeting, and expressed the now-familiar bewilderment at Carol's death, but he was able to add one thing that was of great interest to the detectives. The day before Carol died, she and Spillane were both at the bakery branch in Voorhees. Carol had casually asked him, "How are you doing?"

"I'm fine," Spillane had replied, and then out of courtesy, he asked her the same question back.

Carol sighed, "Fine—other than my husband is not speaking to me." Spillane wasn't sure what to make of the remark, and let it drop.

Later on Wednesday afternoon, it was Assistant Rabbi Gary Mazo's turn to sit down and be formally interviewed by the detectives. The thirty-year-old junior rabbi not only lived nearby in Cherry Hill and worked with Neulander, but, not surprisingly, he and his wife had been close friends with both Fred and Carol for over a decade. Mazo unhesitatingly described Neulander as his mentor; the very reason Mazo had moved to western New Jersey and M'kor Shalom was to be near Fred and learn from him before someday taking on his dream job of a smaller congregation on Cape Cod.

Mazo didn't have any clue about relationship problems within the Neulander family, and voluntarily provided police with an alibi for his boss, whom he revered. Mazo, an avid toy collector, taught confirmation classes for Jewish teens at M'kor Shalom every Tuesday evening from 7:30 to 8:10, and then again from 8:30 to 9 P.M. He distinctly recalled Fred stopping in on his first class at about 7:40 for approximately twenty minutes before leaving to make some phone calls. It had been years since the senior rabbi had bothered with the classes, and Rabbi Mazo and the students had been delighted to see him. Rabbi Neulander came back into Mazo's class again at about 8:45, and stayed until it finished at 9. Mazo recalled that he and his wife Debbi left M'kor Shalom together at what he guessed was around 9:20 P.M., and at that time, Fred was still in the building.

On that Wednesday the police also got hold of Kevin Halpern, 46, a fellow resident of Cherry Hill, and president and CEO of the board of trustees for the Cooper Medical Center in Camden. Halpern's office routinely prepared a packet of documents and letters that the board members would need for each monthly meeting on the fourth Monday of the month. The packets were put together a few days in advance and were hand-delivered to each board member's house. Halpern told police that the deliveries were made during regular working hours between 8 A.M. and 4:30 P.M., and he agreed to have his office provide investigators with the names and routes of the delivery personnel who had been working the past couple of weeks. Halpern couldn't think of anything else about the Neulanders or his delivery operation that would be of use to the investigation.

The investigation into Carol Neulander's murder was in its early phases, and there were still so many unanswered questions that hadn't been looked at yet. But of all the people who had been interviewed, and all the clues that police had come across, the one person whose answers didn't seem to fit with the rest of the information that was known during that first week in November was Fred Neulander. Detectives decided they needed to take a much harder look at the senior rabbi.

CHAPTER SEVEN

NEWS reporters and photographers had begun arriving on Highgate Lane within minutes of Fred's 911 call. It was clear to them that this was going to be a story of major importance to the community, and of interest to the whole Philadelphia area. Like the police, they were up the rest of the night working feverishly trying to figure out what had happened.

Shortly before noon on Wednesday, Camden County Prosecutor Edward Borden and Cherry Hill Police Chief William Moffett were ready to try to answer some of the hundreds of queries the press had put in seeking information, and they stepped up to the microphones at the Cherry Hill municipal building and faced the phalanx of television cameras and journalists.

Borden and Moffett ended up largely confirming what the reporters had already figured out: that someone had entered the Neulander residence the night before without having forced entry, and then beaten Carol to death with multiple blows to her head using some kind of a blunt instrument.

The officials said that no weapon was recovered, but there were signs of a violent struggle. Borden told reporters, "There are a number of substantial leads we are pursuing. We have a lot to go on."

Moffett worked to reassure Cherry Hill residents, many of whom were interpreting Carol's murder as a random attack, that police patrols throughout the neighborhood around Highgate Lane were already being increased. "This investigation will be going forward full force," Moffett said, adding, "An incident like this doesn't take place too often, especially in Cherry Hill."

Tantalizingly, the officials tossed in a few other details that were new to the public. They explained for the first time that robbery could well be the motive, because Carol was known to carry home large sums of cash from her bakery business, and that the Voorhees branch of Classic Cake had apparently been the target of an abortive armed robbery attempt less than a month prior, on October 3. "We are looking into the relationship between the store burglary and the incident last night," Borden explained. "There is circumstantial evidence that points to the theory that robbery was the motive here."

Borden also announced to the public that they wanted to speak to two local brothers named Dan and Frank Spanolia about Carol's death. The Spanolias had just been paroled from New Jersey State Prison two months before, and had a history of breaking into homes in the Cherry Hill area where they lived. Borden made the questioning of the pair seem routine. "They are on intensive supervisory probation. We've been alerted by neighbors about them. Attention to them is part of the investigation. I wouldn't classify them as particular targets of investigation," Borden said. In fact, the Spanolias would eventually be questioned and dropped from the investigation's pool of suspects.

While town officials were talking to the press, the religious leaders over at M'kor Shalom were tearfully making preparations to bury Carol. It was an extraordinarily difficult funeral to prepare for, because those in charge of setting it up had all been especially close to the victim. They had to put aside their own grief and make arrangements on behalf of the Neulander family and the larger congregation to which Carol had been so central.

Jewish tradition calls for a swift burial after death, if possible within twenty-four hours, but with the criminal investigation and the need to autopsy Carol's body for clues at the medical examiner's office on Wednesday, her funeral had to be pushed back to Thursday morning, November 3.

Because the congregation was in absolute shock, members had started spontaneously gathering at M'kor Shalom early on Wednesday morning. Although it wasn't strictly in accordance with Jewish tradition, Mazo and the other clergy who were assisting him decided to go ahead with a special memorial service for Carol that evening, in part because the body wouldn't be released from the coroner's office until at least the next day.

A thousand members of Congregation M'kor Shalom turned out on Wednesday night for the memorial. Near the beginning of the service, Rabbi Mazo looked out over the sanctuary and noted to those gathered, "We should not be here. This is not how our world is supposed to work."

Hovering over the bewildered congregants was the haunting question of 'Why?' Police had released very little information at that point, but it was clearly understood that Carol had been savagely beaten by an assailant, and the word around town was that she had actually put up a fierce struggle against her attacker. Many of those who attended were learning for the first time about reports that Carol had carried home a large amount of cash from her business, and in all likelihood she had been followed home and killed during a robbery.

At the end of the service, several minutes of silence were observed before Cantor Anita Hockman's voice drifted in over the stillness with the final verse of one of Judaism's most solemn prayers for the dead, the Mourner's Kaddish.

Someone had killed Carol, but they had also attacked her friends, the congregation she loved, and indeed, the township of Cherry Hill, which was not used to this kind of senseless violence in their tranquil midst.

"This is what you expect to see on 'Action News' and not in your neighborhood—and especially not to a family so community-oriented," the Neulanders' next-door neighbor Jack Mitchard told the local *Courier-Post* as he raked leaves from his lawn a few feet from the crime-scene tape next door.

M'kor Shalom Congregational President Sheila Goodman issued a statement on behalf of the synagogue to reporters who had gathered there to cover the memorial. "Our synagogue is grieving as a family for the Neulanders," Goodman began. "Carol and Fred have been the heart of our synagogue. We'll miss her terribly. We loved her very much. She was a wonderful person. Carol was always there when she was needed."

Rabbi Richard Address, a fellow M'kor Shalom congregant and the regional director of the Reform movement's Union of American Hebrew Congregations, expressed much the same sentiment to the press gathered there that evening, telling a reporter from the *Jewish Exponent* newspaper, "She was a lovely, wonderful human being. It's a horrible, horrible, horrible, horrible, unspeakable thing."

On Thursday afternoon, over 2,000 people attended Carol Neulander's funeral. M'kor Shalom's funerals usually took place at the graveside or the funeral home, but Carol was afforded the rare honor of a funeral right in the sanctuary of the congregation she had played such a pivotal role within for the past twenty-one years. The receiving line to speak to and console Carol's family stretched out the doors of the synagogue and half a mile down Evesham Road.

After the psalms and prayers and eulogies had been spoken and countless tears cried at M'kor Shalom, the funeral procession drove the ten miles to neighboring Pennsauken, New Jersey, where Carol was laid to rest under an evergreen tree on the perimeter of Crescent Memorial Park Cemetery. Her ground-level black-and-gold headstone, adorned with a small metal turtle, read simply "Beloved wife and mother."

As Carol was being buried in the Jewish cemetery in the next town, police were holding another press conference in Cherry Hill. Although the investigation was still running largely on coffee and adrenaline, the detectives had gotten a chance to gather together and do a quick sift through the important clues from the first twenty-four hours, which experience has shown again and again is usually the most critical time period in any successful homicide investigation.

Camden County Prosecutor Borden was still signaling a robbery as the likely motive, noting that Carol's purse and an unspecified amount of cash had been taken, but he added that Carol's death did not appear to be connected to other recent burglaries that had occurred in her general neighborhood.

Police also said that they had received a tip that a dark-colored car, possibly a Buick Regal or a Chevrolet Monte Carlo, had been seen in the area between 7 and 9 P.M., and that they wanted to talk to whoever had been in the car as potential witnesses, not necessarily as suspects.

Of all the interviews they had done so far, the police had gotten their most useful information to date from Rebecca Neulander. Her phone call to her mother gave them what was in all likelihood the near exact time of the murder, because it was hard to imagine a scenario in which "the Bathroom Man" wouldn't have commenced his attack within a minute or two of the time Carol had hung up with her daughter.

Because Rebecca knew about the Bathroom Man's previous visit, police were able to establish that Carol was the known, intended target of whatever was going on here and not a random victim, and Rebecca had picked up on the slight reference to another person having accompanied the Bathroom Man on both occasions.

Police didn't tell the reporters present where they were getting their information or why they had reached those conclusions, but the officials did stress that Carol's murder looked targeted.

"Based on a careful search of the crime scene, interviews with a number of people, and a thorough review of Mrs. Neulander's movements on the day of the murder, we do not believe that the attack was a random one," said Borden, adding, "We believe that her attacker planned to victimize Mrs. Neulander individually and did not simply choose her home by chance."

Even while the synagogue had been focusing on its preparations for Carol's unprecedentedly large funeral, questions were arising about how to arrange for her shiva, the Jewish equivalent of the Catholic wake. Given that Carol had been murdered right there in the very room in that family home where the shiva would normally take place, the first thought was that it would have to be moved. However, Fred Neulander wouldn't hear of it. It was his house, it was Carol's house, and even the fresh horror of what had happened couldn't cancel out the memories of the happy times they had shared there over the years. The shiva would take place at 204 Highgate Lane.

On Wednesday afternoon, just hours after police had released control of the house back to Neulander, Fred walked through the front room with a contractor, pointing out the renovations that needed to take place by the next evening. Although he still appeared to be in a daze, Fred explained how he wanted the carpet, with its horrible bull's-eye stain, torn out and the walls and ceiling repainted.

Many of those attending over the next several nights were quite disturbed by the prospect of holding the shiva in the same room where someone had killed Carol, especially since the hasty redecoration had failed to entirely eliminate all traces of Carol's blood from the walls. Still, many of them commented on the courage and the fortitude it had taken the rabbi to press onward in the aftermath of such a deep violation of his home.

CHAPTER EIGHT

SOME of the friends who visited the Neulander household as Fred, his children, and Carol's relatives observed the shiva had to ask themselves an uncomfortable but lingering question: Was it in any way possible that the rabbi had killed his wife?

Fred had been the one to find her body upon his return home, and he had been married to her for decades. In another time, both of those facts would have tended to eliminate him as a suspect, but in this era of ubiquitous murder-mystery television shows, the one principle the public knows for certain is that things are not always what they seem.

The police were busy asking themselves the same question.

The main problem with any speculation that Fred Neulander might have killed Carol was that, by all accounts, there was no way he could have killed anybody on Highgate Lane during the time frame in question. The two oldest concepts in murder investigation are motive and opportunity. Even supposing that Fred had some motive, he wouldn't have had an opportunity to have driven home and killed her between 7 and 9 P.M. that Tuesday. He said he'd been at M'kor Shalom the whole time, and there were several reliable people who could vouch for his having been there. Come to think of it, there were actually dozens and dozens of people who could be counted on to place him firmly at the synagogue that night. But as investigators began to look at just how truly airtight Neulander's alibi was, they suddenly began to see a problem with it.

The trouble wasn't that Fred's alibi for the time surrounding the murder wasn't good. It was great. It was excellent. In fact, it was practically the Mother of All Alibis. Fred had attended Mazo's evening class sessions not once but twice that night, thus insuring that even more people had seen him and that they could specifically remember what times he had been there. When he wasn't sitting in with Mazo, he was on his office phone calling other people who would remember speaking to him at approximately the time of the murder. If the detectives wished to double-check, those same calls were also creating an electronic record that could verify the times he was at his desk that evening down to the second. And then there was Fred's surprise appearance at Cantor Anita Hockman's choir practice that evening. Hockman had been at M'kor Shalom for thirteen years and had long ago made it well known that she didn't like to have her rehearsals interrupted. Neulander rarely ever bothered to visit the choir practices, but on November 1 he hadn't just looked in, he hadn't just stood in the back and watched for a moment, he had strode in mid-note, like a celebrity, practically high-fiving the choir members on his way down the aisle, as he greeted Hockman and paused to talk with several people. Hockman later described Neulander's visit as "very rare" and noted that "he was very upbeat. He really stopped the action."

There are plenty of perfectly innocent people on this planet who simply don't have witnesses to verify their whereabouts at a particular time and location, but Rabbi Fred Neulander was having no such problem. As detectives began to consider the far-fetched possibility that a rabbi might have hired someone else to kill his wife, the fact that Fred Neulander had practically run a victory lap around the M'kor Shalom complex on that Tuesday evening was beginning to strike them as suspicious.

To decide if there was anything actually noteworthy about Neulander's almost too-good-to-be-true alibi, detectives would first have to figure out if there was any reason why Fred would want Carol out of the picture.

As with all high-profile murder cases, unsubstantiated rumors began to swirl like snowflakes in the wake of Carol's death, and both police and reporters were bracing themselves for the onslaught. Of the hundreds of wildly speculative theories that get pumped up from a "What if . . ." to an "I just heard from somebody who knows . . ." in a single trip around a water cooler, the truth is that all of them are dead wrong . . . except perhaps for one. Finding that one correct needle in the haystack of constantly multiplying misinformation is what makes both sound investigation and good journalism so very difficult.

Reporters can pretty much guarantee that before any major case is over, they will have been taken aside by at least one person who will earnestly tell them not to overlook the possibility that space aliens might be involved. Many more people will also tell them theories that question the sexual habits, sexual orientation, and sexual appetites of every single person connected to the case. The rumor mills' ability to imagine any number of permutations in the relationships amongst the figures in a murder case is nearly infinite. Passion and jealousy can lead to murder, so those with badges and those with spiral-bound notepads have to pay at least some attention to the stories; there is, after all, always the chance that there's something to them.

In the Neulander case, the first and loudest sexual rumor out of the box was that Rabbi Fred Neulander was actually quite the Casanova.

It was an edgy but obvious inside joke to make about the silver-haired rabbi with the intense blue eyes— "Fred's a real babe magnet"; "He's always out having lunch with gorgeous women"; "Neulander's the Playboy Rabbi." It seemed like a harmless shot; truthfully, what were the odds? Besides, since Neulander had an iron-clad alibi, if you were to believe that any marital infidelity was behind Carol's murder, you would also have to believe that Rabbi Neulander was capable of hiring a hitman to kill his wife of nearly thirty years.

The affair rumors dogging Fred Neulander in the days after his wife's murder looked like the usual kind of idle talk that can emerge in the wake of any sensational case. The only difference was that this time the rumors were true.

Fred Neulander did have something that he very much wanted to keep a secret. For the past year and a half he had been having daily sexual romps with a tall and slender, feisty and elegant redhead who was not only a prominent member of the M'kor Shalom congregation, but was also well known to hundreds of thousands of talk-radio listeners in and around Philadelphia.

Elaine Soncini was the news director and host of the morning drive-time show on WPEN-AM in Philadelphia. Her name was everywhere, and she hobnobbed with the newsmakers and bright lights throughout one of the largest cities on the East Coast. And just about every day of the week, the striking forty-eight-year-old and Rabbi Fred Neulander met in her well-appointed house in Cherry Hill, usually at lunchtime and, some days, again in the evenings.

Fred had been at Elaine's for their usual assignation over the noon hour on November 1. He had taken care to pull his car all the way into her garage when he visited so the distinctive "clergy" sticker on the back windshield wouldn't be noticed.

Soncini was a rather recent widow and, although her friends had no idea that she and Fred were having an affair, those few who knew the details of the basic friendship she shared with him had reason to be deeply touched by it.

Soncini had been married for twenty-two years to Ken Garland, another well-known radio personality in the city of Philadelphia. Garland had been an on-air fixture, having spent thirty years broadcasting to the City of Brotherly Love. For the last five of those years, Ken and Elaine had co-hosted their morning show together, before, in the early part of 1992, Garland had been diagnosed with leukemia and begun a slow and painful decline towards his death in December of that year.

Soncini was a Catholic and Garland a Jew, but their unconditional love for each other was captured in the words of their favorite Cole Porter song, the one that mentions one and one becoming two. Soncini would sing the words softly as Garland died in a Cherry Hill hospital room with Garland's son Doug by her side. In the room watching silently as Garland passed away was Rabbi Fred Neulander.

"I want to help you," Soncini remembered the strong and handsome rabbi saying as he wrapped his powerful arms around her that afternoon. "Let me comfort you."

Two days later, Rabbi Neulander would officiate at Garland's funeral in front of a large and prominent crowd of Philadelphians gathered at a Cherry Hill funeral home. It was a gathering that included many accomplished public speakers, but Neulander was memorable among them for the drama and gravity that he brought to Garland's passing. "There are poets who will never reach what could be said. There are musicians who could compose and it would be inadequate. There are philosophers who could never catch the soul and essence," of the man who was now gone, Neulander intoned.

Remembering Ken, Soncini stood and cut a striking figure in her tailored black suit and high heels. "I love

you, Ken, on this earth and thereafter," she concluded at
the end of her eulogy.

It was later, at the cemetery, after the coffin had
been lowered into the ground and as the mourners were
slowly filing away, that Rabbi Neulander, his black yar-
mulke pinned to his elegant head of silver steel-wool
hair, turned to Elaine Soncini and asked, "Can I call
you?"

A week had passed when Neulander invited Soncini
out for lunch to see how she was coping. Not feeling
like going to a restaurant so soon after Ken's death, Soncini instead invited the rabbi to dine with her at her
Cherry Hill home. Soncini had inherited over a million
dollars from her husband, and her lifestyle was not in
jeopardy, but she was disillusioned about religion and
was searching for answers in the wake of Ken's passing.
Over a whitefish salad, they chatted and then continued
the discussion in her comfortable front room. Neulander
seemed profoundly interested in helping Soncini through
her loss.

"When he presented himself to me, there was a
sweetness about him, a civility about him and intelligence and compassion and understanding, and all those
qualities that you look for in a human being and a spiritual leader," Soncini would tell *The Philadelphia Inquirer* years later.

When Neulander stood to leave that afternoon he
suddenly turned to Soncini again. "May I kiss you?" he
asked.

The answer was yes, and soon the pair were making
love at Soncini's house during the noon hour nearly
every day.

"It was heart-stopping, goose bumps, take off your
clothes in the hallway and go right upstairs without saying a word. It was a wonderful, powerful attraction,"
Soncini told the *Inquirer*.

It wasn't always over lunch that Neulander and his

fiery mistress met. Sometimes he would return in the early evening—never later since Soncini had to get up early to be on time for her break-of-dawn radio show.

On one occasion, Soncini even ended up having sex with the rabbi in his office at M'kor Shalom. Although the deadbolt on his door was locked, Soncini later said she had been "very uncomfortable."

The two had more in common than their sex drives. They liked to talk about philosophy, the theater, music, and history on their afternoons together. They also liked to talk about religion, and Fred carefully explained the tenets of Judaism to Elaine as the months went by. Captivated by Fred and his sincerity, Elaine began the process of converting to the Jewish faith. They would spend more time together during the day than many married couples could squeeze from their schedules. Elaine would later recall hours of Hebrew lessons from Fred as they both lay naked in her bed.

The Cherry Hill police and Camden County detectives were hearing these rumors and keeping their eyes open for confirmation, but at first they didn't have any proof. They had already asked the rabbi point-blank about any affairs, and he had flatly denied that there had been any. At first the police simply moved on; they had no specific reasons to doubt the rabbi on the matter. However, they did realize that his version of his recent relationship with Carol in the days before the murder had contrasted sharply with the account given by his son Matthew.

It took a couple of weeks, but detectives eventually got hold of copies of the Neulanders' phone records stretching back several months before the murder. They were mainly interested in seeing who might have called Carol during the daytime, when Fred usually wasn't home, in the hopes there might be a clue worth pursuing. There were a lot of records to sift through—the house phone, Carol's car phone, Fred's office phone—but when they did, police soon noticed something unusual. There were scores of calls to a single number in Cherry Hill and to the WPEN radio station in Philadelphia. The numbers were Elaine Soncini's, and detectives decided to pay her a visit. Why, they wondered, was she getting so many calls from the Neulander household? Was she a friend of Carol's?

Soncini told the detectives that she was actually a close friend of the rabbi. She explained that Fred had been helping her recover her faith in the wake of her husband's death, so much so that she was now a member of his congregation. Detectives wanted to know if that was it or if perhaps their relationship was closer than that. That was it, Soncini insisted.

The detectives thanked her for her time, and left. They went back to their station and took another look at the facts surrounding Soncini. Ken Garland had died in 1992 and the "recovering widow" bit didn't seem to square with the volume of calls they were seeing eighteen months later. Especially intriguing was that these calls seemed to be coming from Fred to Elaine's home and not the other way around. If this relationship was so platonic, then why weren't these calls going anywhere near where Carol might reasonably be expected to pick them up?

The detectives decided to watch Elaine for a bit, and in early December 1994 they began to drop in on her at home and at work to ask her these and other probing questions in order to see how she reacted. Soncini was already being wracked by her own doubts about Neulander's potential role in his wife's death, and she too was beginning to question whether or not she was the motive for a murder. Scared by her possible involvement, and facing increasingly frequent visits from increasingly skeptical detectives, Soncini began to cave. A few days later, accompanied by two of her lawyers,

Elaine walked into the police station and sat down to tell detectives how her affair had begun.

Fred Neulander's affair with Elaine Soncini was a clear transgression, not only of his marriage vows to Carol, but also of the position of trust he held with M'kor Shalom and within his extended religious community. But police soon discovered that it wasn't the only affair he'd had.

There had been at least one with another member of the congregation who had converted to Judaism and actually received marriage counseling from Neulander at one point. Another woman came forward and told police that Neulander had met her once in a diner after he answered her personal ad. She said the rabbi had asked her to accompany him to a Red Roof Inn that afternoon, but she had only just met him and was already turned off by lewd remarks he had made during their lunch.

This was a side of the rabbi that the police hadn't seen previously, and now they wanted to know how much else they might not know about this pillar of the community.

CHAPTER NINE

THERE was one person detectives thought could be shedding more light on what had been going on: Assistant Rabbi Gary Mazo.

Mazo and his wife and fellow rabbi, Debbi Pipe–Mazo, who now served as staff chaplain at the University of Pennsylvania's hospital, had been close friends with both Fred and Carol Neulander for over a decade. Debbi had grown up in Cherry Hill, and was a member of Congregation M'kor Shalom before she and Gary had even met as college students at Brandeis University. She had introduced Mazo to Fred Neulander, and the younger man, like so many others, had been entranced by Neulander's magnetic personality.

The two couples had kept in touch, and the Neulanders had even traveled to Israel to visit the Mazos when they were rabbinic students there. Gary Mazo considered Fred Neulander his mentor, and in June of 1990, when the position of assistant rabbi at M'kor Shalom had come open, he had applied and was thrilled to be accepted.

At first, things had gone well, but as 1994 began, Neulander had been encouraged by the M'kor Shalom board to take a six-month sabbatical. After Neulander reluctantly agreed, everyone assumed that he would do what rabbis usually do on such occasions: go to Israel, study something profound, maybe even write a book. Fred Neulander astonished the leadership of his synagogue by basically hanging around Cherry Hill the whole time and keeping on with his preferred regime of weightlifting and racquetball. The only new thing he seemed to do was grow a ponytail. He still wandered into the synagogue offices just about every day to get his mail. No one knew that the rabbi was seeing Elaine Soncini each day, so his decision to stick around made no sense. There was speculation that the rabbi was having some sort of mid-life crisis.

When Neulander did return to the job mid-year, he was somewhat half-hearted about picking up where he had left off, and he began to get especially critical of Mazo. The younger man put the escalating hostility down to growing pains in their mentor/student relationship as he came into his own as a rabbi. Mazo started quietly looking for another job as the leader of a smaller congregation of his own.

Then came Carol's murder, and suddenly Mazo was the de facto leader of a dazed and deeply wounded institution.

Shortly after the funeral, homicide detectives began asking routine questions of Gary Mazo. He was both a close friend and a business associate of the Neulanders, so he was a logical person to speak with about the circumstances surrounding Carol's death.

Mazo was thirty years old at the time, but he still considered himself something of a beginner in his religious career. Used to much gentler handling within the closed walls of M'kor Shalom, he was not doing well under the scrutiny that the real world was suddenly putting on him. Detectives felt there was a lot more that he could be telling them, and they kept dropping by to talk. Their mere presence at the synagogue began to give him stomach aches.

"The anger that raged within me toward the police was exceeded by what I felt toward the prosecutor's office. There was no respect for me as a rabbi, or for the synagogue and our need to heal," Mazo later wrote. There was also no explanation as to who had beaten

Carol Neulander to death in her own front room, and detectives weren't inclined to back off just because the topic made an assistant rabbi queasy.

The detectives told Mazo that Carol's death felt like a "hit" to them, not a robbery. They began to ask him probing questions about Fred Neulander's personal life. Scheduled to go down to the police station and give a formal statement, Mazo became sufficiently nervous that he met with Neulander the day before.

Neulander told his younger associate what he thought the police had as the working theory of the crime and how he thought the questioning would go. Then, for the first time, Neulander told Mazo details about his personal life that he had never shared with him before, presumably centering on his history of extra-marital affairs.

Even though Mazo was the junior partner in this arrangement, he was a full-fledged member of the clergy, which meant that for purposes of the discussion they were now having, Neulander had to be afforded a "clergy/penitent privilege" for the information that he was conveying. There are only a handful of legal relationships where one person can legitimately withhold another's information from the court system because of an overriding privilege against testifying. The main ones are attorney/client privilege, doctor/patient privilege, spousal privilege, and to a lesser extent the "shield laws" that protect reporters from having to reveal their sources and unpublished notes. Hours before he was supposed to talk to the police to see if he could be helpful in solving the homicide of a woman he had considered a close friend, Mazo had just been put in a tremendous bind by Fred Neulander.

He didn't do well at his interview the next day. He was incredibly nervous, and the detectives were convinced that he was holding back information that they very much needed to hear. Mazo left the station with the impression that police felt he was in collusion with his senior rabbi, which, given the difficult position Neulander had placed him in the day before, was somewhat true. If Neulander had been truly penitent, he could have told some or all of the same information to his young colleague at any time during the decade he had known him . . . not just hours before he wanted Mazo to keep it from the police.

Rather than resent the position he had just been placed in by his mentor, Mazo seemed to reserve much of his anger for the investigators, and especially for the press.

"Even more intrusive and more unethical were some of the media. Over time I learned more about how to deal with media—and unfortunately, I also learned to despise many members of the profession," Mazo the clergyman wrote, adding, "They showed little regard for the fact that we were real human beings dealing with complex emotions."

In his book *And the Flames Did Not Consume Us*, about his experiences in the aftermath of Carol's murder, Mazo praised a reporter who agreed not to quote him by name in print, saying that she "understood the aims of the synagogue." On the previous page of the same book, Mazo condemned the unattributed "leaks" from police officers who had the same relationship with other reporters.

Confronted by a bewildered congregation searching for specific answers to the worst tragedy in their shared communal experience, Mazo launched a series of sermons specifically condemning "*lashon hara,*" a Hebrew phrase meaning "evil talk."

In the end, for all of Rabbi Mazo's condemnation of the media and their habit of lifting up rocks to look underneath, it would be the press that had won the day. When the Neulander case was finally cracked open, it would be because a lone reporter had stayed with it for years and tracked down every available piece of "*lashon hara*," and finally figured out what the police could not. She would lead them to Carol Neulander's murderers, and one of them would turn out to be a person whom Rabbi Mazo had sat with for hours in his own office trying to help think of theories that would "solve" the crime.

CHAPTER TEN

IN the first cold months after Carol's murder, the public could see little of what was happening within the investigation, and the first flurry of leads that had poured into the phones at the Cherry Hill Police Department slowly dried up.

Police had looked everywhere for the dark-colored car that had been seen leaving the area, but finally admitted to having drawn a blank.

Many possibilities had been quietly ruled out, but the investigation was still not getting the kind of break that it needed in order to put the case on the fast track towards a solution.

As 1994 drew to a close, friends of Carol Neulander, frustrated by the lack of an answer to the tragedy in the seven weeks since her death, put up a $35,000 reward that they hoped would entice someone to come forward with another piece of the puzzle.

Fred Neulander was also doing some quiet digging of his own. He had hired a private investigator—who happened to be a member of his M'kor Shalom congregation—named Leonard Jenoff to poke around and see if he could find anything. Jenoff was considered a bit of an odd-ball, but he was known to have had experience working for the Central Intelligence Agency, and he volunteered his time at the synagogue. A fellow smoker, he often joined the rabbi out back for a quick puff when they were taking breaks at M'kor Shalom. Jenoff knew a lot of police officers around the region, and as the weeks progressed he would get to know the press assigned to the case as well. Over time he would become something of an informal spokesman for the rabbi's innocence and an advocate for the theory that Carol Neulander had been robbed by someone who had discovered she often carried home large sums of cash from her bakery.

Meanwhile, Camden County Prosecutor Edward Borden, Jr., had scheduled a rather routine news conference to announce the creation of the reward fund. But it was something else he said to the gathered press corps that nearly pushed the $35,000 right to the bottom of the next day's stories.

The reporters present had heard all the rumors around Cherry Hill, and they wanted to know who the police suspected had killed Carol. Several of them asked point-blank if Rabbi Neulander could be characterized as a suspect in his wife's death. "We're not ruling him in or out. We don't have a list of suspects," Borden said, adding, "A lot of people have been questioned. Of course we've talked to family members in the case."

Borden added that he felt it would be unfair to Fred Neulander to say that, just because he hadn't been eliminated as a suspect, he was therefore the focus of the investigation. "There are many rumors I've heard," Borden commented, speaking carefully. "Most of them—ninety-eight percent—have no basis in fact, and are terribly destructive and harmful."

Public officials who don't want to be bitten later by a "hard quote" that turns out to be wrong often give cloudy answers to highly specific questions. Reporters return the favor by putting the responses they get through a kind of weighing process. It seemed to the press corps that if Borden did not really consider Rabbi Neulander a suspect, then he would have said something much firmer to that effect, even if he left the door to that possibility slightly ajar. The fact that he seemed to be putting the needle of suspicion right on the split as neither in nor out was taken as the equivalent of saying there was a 50/50 chance that Fred Neulander was the killer.

The nuances may have been there in Borden's statement, but headlines have to be short and to the point. "Cops Don't Rule Out Anyone, Even the Rabbi," read the front page of the next morning's *Philadelphia Daily News*. The *Trentonian* cut it even closer with just six words: "Rabbi Among Suspects in Wife's Death."

Afterwards, Borden was furious about what he characterized as the twisting of his words out of context. He said it was unfair to take what he'd said to mean that Rabbi Neulander was the prime suspect, when he thought he had plainly stated that no one was ruled in.

"It is unfair and not justified by our investigation for the press to focus on Rabbi Neulander," Borden told the *Jewish Exponent*. "I cannot control how newspapers may misinterpret me . . . how they skew things."

Rabbi Mazo was one of the first to step up and criticize Borden, saying, "I think the prosecutor's office knows absolutely nothing. Since they know nothing, they look everywhere. All that does is fuel unfounded, vicious gossip. It's *loshen hara*, plain and simple. There's a need to invent a story. It's just ugly. There's no foundation for it."

Many other rabbis in the region joined in the chorus of condemnation for the stories, and in expressing their support for Neulander.

Marcy Partnow, a long-term member of M'kor Shalom told the *Exponent* that she and the other members were still standing behind their senior rabbi. "My heart goes out to him," Partnow said to the paper. "Aside from dealing with the tragedy that happened to his wife and the breaking up of a nuclear family and trying to bring his children back to normalcy, I am particularly aghast that he has to also deal with rumors about his integrity."

Across town at Temple Beth Sholom in Cherry Hill,

Rabbi Emeritus Albert Lewis also stood by Neulander, telling the *Exponent*'s reporters, "I cannot express my feeling of revulsion at the rumors. All I can say is, I am disgusted with people's looking for answers and taking the most bizarre kind of approach." Lewis continued, "It's upsetting to us that a colleague could be subjected to this kind of slander. When you have no proof of anything, you have slander. Those two things are totally counter to Jewish life and Jewish law. To me, it's revolting."

Matthew Neulander also deplored "all the rumors and the whispers" about his mother's murder, adding, "I wish my father would give me the freedom to lash out and speak about these ridiculous rumors."

Matthew said that the police had not led family members to believe that their father was a suspect. "The very idea is ridiculous," he said.

Despite the support from his colleagues, it would take only four months for the rumors swirling around him to catch up to Rabbi Neulander and wreck his career.

On February 22, 1995, local newspapers reported what had already been in the wind around Cherry Hill. An unidentified official confirmed to reporters at the *Courier-Post* that investigators viewed Fred Neulander as a definite member of the suspect pool.

The official described the evidence linking Neulander to his wife's murder as circumstantial, and reiterated that robbery still remained a real possibility. However, the official said that the robbery angle was being pursued separately from the investigation that was now focused in on Rabbi Neulander.

At almost the same moment as the story hit the papers, the M'kor Shalom board of trustees announced in a letter mailed to the 930 families in its congregation that Rabbi Neulander would be taking an indefinite leave of absence from his position "to seek counseling and be with his family."

Once again Prosecutor Borden was ticked off by the reports, but he reiterated that he would not be drawn into stating who was and wasn't a suspect in the ongoing case.

Borden also denied television reports that the investigation was leaning toward the theory that Neulander had hired a hitman to kill Carol—a theory that placed his remarkably airtight alibi for the night of November 1 in a new context.

A couple days later, Borden's office announced that a "full-scale inquiry" would be launched to search out the source of the leaks. Nothing can destroy the morale amongst local police quite like having the county prosecutor's office sic an internal affairs investigation on the department, but the Cherry Hill police gamely assigned officers to phone reporters and ask where they had gotten their information. The calls were pretty short, as the reporters immediately invoked New Jersey's press "shield law" that is designed to prevent exactly that sort of probe.

The history of exhaustive efforts by busy officials to find out who gave reporters *incorrect* information could be slipped inside a fortune cookie, so the fact that Borden was angry enough to start a full-scale leak hunt was a sign to the press that they were barking up the right tree. Reporters decided to probe even further into Rabbi Neulander's activities in the days and months preceding his wife's death.

Suddenly all of the sly jokes and knowing winks about what a smooth customer Neulander was with the ladies seemed to be less of a metaphor about the Rabbi's personal charisma and more of a real possibility.

Working backwards, reporters reasoned that any member of the clergy who might have somehow been mixed up in the murder of his own wife could also be capable of cheating on her—after all, Judaism (and all other mainstream religions, for that matter) is pretty specific in its condemnation of both.

Things began to snowball and on Sunday, February 26, 1995, just four days after Neulander announced his leave of absence, nearly 800 members of the M'kor Shalom congregation gathered for a special session seeking to learn more about what the rabbi's decision meant. The word in the hallways was that Neulander was only planning on being gone until June, but the group was stunned by what happened next. Congregation President Sheila Goodman read out a new letter from Neulander in which he said he was resigning his position as their senior rabbi. Neulander's letter announcing that his resignation was effective immediately floored his staunch supporters at the synagogue and, adding insult to injury, in the letter Neulander for the first time publicly made veiled references to his romantic relations with women outside his marriage.

In the letter, which the board had already received that Thursday, Neulander cited his own personal need to grieve and heal in the company of his children. "Quite obviously I had nothing to do with my wife's death," he wrote, but he continued that the "media frenzy" had released "information and misinformation."

He said that reports had "revealed information I am not proud of" and "behavior that brings no honor to me" which in turn "had the effect of crushing my spirit and bewildering and enraging this congregation." The press took those words as tacit confirmation of the rumors that had been whirling about the rabbi's extramarital affairs.

Neulander concluded his letter, "Because of my conduct, because I feel that my grief and my healing are incomplete, and because the media appetites are not sated, I don't feel I can serve you as I would wish and as you deserve."

Grown men were crying throughout the crowd by

this point, and several people stood to defend Rabbi
Neulander, angrily accusing their board of abandoning
him in his hour of need.

The crowd went completely still as Rabbi Richard
Address—who at the time was head of the regional
council of Reform Jewish synagogues—then stood and
spoke of his meeting with Fred the week before, in
which Neulander finally decided that the best course was
to leave his post. "We spoke of all the events that have
surrounded these tragedies and his own personal anguish
and those of his children, and his own searching for
strength, and frustration in light of all the maelstrom that
has developed," Rabbi Address told the gathering. "At
one point at the end of the afternoon and at the end of
these discussions, Rabbi Neulander acknowledged to me
that 'for the best interests of my congregation, I have to
move on at this time.' "

Fred didn't attend the gathering, but his son Matthew was there and told the crowd, "His behavior was
an indiscretion, and he feels so terribly that we could
have to suffer for it. . . . His actions were beneath the
way a rabbi should act. I don't know whether or not he
wanted to resign. I don't know whether he feels supported. I would doubt it. Anyone under these circumstances would feel alone." As some members of the
audience began to sob, he went on, "I ask if you can
find it within your hearts to continue to support him. He
needs us. Dad spent twenty-one years here. He gave his
life to this place," Matthew said. "There are twenty-one
years of services, twenty-one years of lectures, twenty-
one years of classes, meetings, counseling. I'll tell you
what a tragedy is," he continued. "A tragedy is if all that
went to waste, if he didn't teach any of you compassion
and forgiveness. The real tragedy is if you didn't remember all he's done for you, if you didn't remember
he's just a human being, no more, no less . . . and he's
really hurting right now. I ask everyone here just to think

what Dad did for all of you," Matthew Neulander said, concluding, "Just keep that in a special place in all your hearts."

Afterwards, in an interview with the Associated Press, M'kor Shalom's vice president, Linda Angstreich, said, "I think everyone in the synagogue is saddened by this. But we are a strong organization and we will survive."

"Anyone who could have seen his face and lived through those first twenty-four hours with him after she died would know he couldn't have had anything to do with her death," Associate Rabbi Gary Mazo told the *Bergen Record* afterwards.

After the meeting, dozens of crying congregants streamed up to the *bimah* at the front of the sanctuary and hugged Rabbi Mazo and Cantor Hochman.

Carol's death had a profound impact on the congregation as a whole, and in an unusual move, M'kor Shalom had started holding a daily "*minyan*" memorial prayer service for Carol at the synagogue, as well as making crisis counselors available to members.

Clearly, M'kor Shalom was still actively grieving Carol's loss, and was even raising funds to install new stained-glass windows in the synagogue in her memory, but Rabbi Neulander's resignation would signal a parting of the ways, and the congregation slowly began to drift away from its increasingly controversial founder.

In an interview later that same week with the *Jewish Exponent*, Rabbi Mazo told reporter Marilyn Silverstein, "Our heritage taught us that in times of crisis, we've always emerged stronger—but different, with a different vision and a different focus. This synagogue will change," Mazo said, "but based on everything Fred gave us, it will only grow, it will only flourish. I think it's going to come out okay. I think it's going to be strong and healthy. It's just going to be different."

The brutal murder of their rabbi's wife had not only

hit the adults at M'kor Shalom, but also the 740 students in the religious classes that children attend from kindergarten through their confirmations, usually at age sixteen.

Camden County Victim–Witness Advocate Linda Burkett, 45, was also a member of M'kor Shalom, and she went with Assistant Rabbi Mazo and M'kor Shalom Hebrew School Principal Yossi Afek to speak to the students and teachers, bringing ten members of her crisis intervention team with her.

The students wanted to know how God could let a rabbi's wife be murdered, and if someone like Carol could be killed in her own home, a home which had a *mezuzah* (a small Hebrew prayer scroll symbolizing God's protection for those who dwell in a Jewish household) by the door, then they wondered what would keep their own parents safe.

The counselors assured the children that it was normal to experience a bewildering mix of emotions following a traumatic event, and that someday soon life would return to normal in their community. "That's really what M'kor Shalom is all about," Burkett told the *Jewish Exponent*. "It's a family that helps one another when people need help."

CHAPTER ELEVEN

DURING the summer of 1995 Fred Neulander dropped largely out of the public eye. Still living in the house on Highgate Lane, he passed his time reading and writing on small projects and did volunteer work with various Jewish charities in the neighborhood.

That relative tranquillity would disappear in August when Camden County prosecutors made public that they were considering the possibility that Neulander had hired a hitman to kill his wife. Acting Camden County Prosecutor Joseph Audino told reporters that the idea that Fred Neulander was somehow behind Carol's murder was "one of the better theories" the investigation had going.

The next day, Assistant Camden County Prosecutor Jim Conley confirmed that detectives were investigating whether Fred Neulander had hired a hitman. Conley noted that the unidentified hitman might have visited the Neulander residence two weeks before he returned and murdered Carol.

The officials began to give reporters much more detail than ever before about the circumstances surrounding Carol's murder on November 1, and for the first time the public learned of the existence of "the Bathroom Man" and his previous visit with the empty envelope.

Cherry Hill Police Chief William Moffett said his investigation had been unable to find any area businesses that had had any deliveries scheduled for the Neulander residence on either November 1 or the time approximately two weeks before.

"There's a very strong possibility that this Bathroom Man was the killer," Acting Prosecutor Audino said, adding, "The question is, why was he sent? He was not a regular delivery person."

For the first time, Audino also picked up on Fred's airtight alibi for the two-hour window of time in which Carol's murder took place. Audino noted that several M'kor Shalom officials had told investigators that it was actually unusual for Rabbi Neulander to have been there on a Tuesday evening, and that Neulander also drew an uncharacteristic amount of attention to himself and his presence that particular evening. "That gives us some pause," Audino noted to reporters.

Chief Moffett also mentioned that there had been many anonymous calls to the police hotline set up to gather information on Carol's murder, and said that some had been particularly valuable to the investigation. "It's clear from those calls that there are people out there that know a lot more than what they already have reported. Those people need to get in touch with us again," Moffett urged the public.

Fred Neulander wasted no time calling his own press conference later that same afternoon in Camden, New Jersey, at the offices of new lawyers, Jeffrey C. Zucker and Dennis Wixted. With Zucker at his side, Fred read a prepared statement to reporters.

"The thought of killing my wife is both inconceivable and repulsive. Despite my cooperation with this investigation, including interrogations by the police, I came to find myself labeled in news accounts as a suspect, and have had to endure reading various accounts attributed to sources both unnamed and irresponsible, which by innuendo, speculation, and gossip link me somehow to Carol's death," Fred stated, continuing, "These past ten months have been a bewildering and painful time, with multiple losses for me and my family. Now, the Camden County prosecutor says that I have knowledge of what happened. To the prosecutor I say this: I categorically deny that I murdered my wife or arranged to have her killed. I ask that you devote your time, resources, and energy to solving this brutal crime, rather than indulging in speculation and calling it reasonable and logical." Neulander concluded, "I could not live with my conscience if I were responsible in any way for Carol's death, and I am not."

Zucker also denounced the prosecutor's office for zeroing in on his prominent client. "I don't know if by naming him as a suspect they hoped to find a witness, or expected Rabbi Neulander to get down on his knees and say, 'You've got me,' " Zucker wondered. "Otherwise, if they had any concrete evidence, I suspect they would have indicted him or arrested him. At least then he could answer it in court, and I am fully confident he'll be exonerated."

The hitman theory had landed Neulander right back on the front pages of the Philadelphia press, but the latest firestorm was just beginning. The next round would come the day after Neulander's defiant press conference, and it would also begin on the front page—this time of the *Philadelphia Daily News*.

Interestingly, the smaller *Daily News* would actually end up scooping its rival, *The Philadelphia Inquirer*, even though the *Inquirer* had originally been way out ahead on this piece of the story.

Six months earlier the *Inquirer* had gone looking for Neulander's mistress, and had managed to uncover Elaine Soncini's identity. The *Inquirer*'s reporter had confronted Soncini, and Elaine had reluctantly agreed to be interviewed, but on one condition. The understanding was that the *Inquirer* would hold the story back from publication and would only run it in the event that police officials publicly identified Soncini. She was hoping that the investigation would take another approach and that her relationship with Neulander would stay in the realm of hallway gossip and not news.

But on August 17, 1995, the *Philadelphia Daily News* was told by law enforcement sources that Soncini and Neulander had been having an affair, suggesting a possible motive for Carol's murder. The *Daily News* reporters, unaware of and not bound by Soncini's agreement with the *Inquirer*, quickly began preparing a story about the affair. They met with the manager of WPEN and explained that Soncini had a chance right then and there to get her side of the story out, but their piece was going forward with or without her. After meeting with her manager, Soncini decided to go ahead and speak to the *Daily News*.

Even though they were now being burned by their competition, the *Inquirer* held to their agreement with Soncini and continued to sit on their story. Because they had stuck by their word, Soncini sat down again with the *Inquirer* the next day and did an expanded interview with them, as well as with a Philadelphia news television station.

During the week that followed, Acting Camden County Prosecutor Joseph Audino angered Soncini's camp when he acknowledged to reporters that Soncini herself had been in the pool of suspects considered by police as the potential killer, although he downplayed the significance of police interest in her as such, saying that, beyond the obvious implication of being Neulander's mistress, there was little to suggest that she had done anything.

"She's not a big suspect, but she is one of the theories. We don't know that she didn't hire someone to do it, so we have to consider it. She certainly has a possible motive. But we have nothing linking her to this," Audino told the *Courier-Post*.

"She is not a prime suspect, but there is always a possibility,"

Audino added in a separate interview. "She had a motive. She was his girlfriend. We are not ruling anything out in this case."

Still, it ticked off Soncini's attorneys, who put out a statement reading in part, "The comments by Prosecutor Audino are undeserved as Ms. Soncini has done everything asked of her by law enforcement." And eventually Soncini herself spoke up about the implication, saying she had tried to help the investigation because "I was looking for the truth, too. What I did was have a relationship with a married man, period," Soncini said. "They know I had nothing to do with it."

In the series of interviews she had given over the weekend, Soncini said that the affair with Fred Neulander had lasted nearly two years, continuing on for several months after Carol died. But she said she finally broke it off in February 1995 when she learned that the rabbi had been cheating on her with another woman.

Soncini told the *Daily News* how she had met Neulander in the wake of her husband's death. "He said he wanted to comfort me. He said he wanted to console me," Soncini told the *Daily News* in a story that ran on Friday, August 18, 1995. "I was at the weakest and most vulnerable moment in my life. I was suddenly alone in the world. I really felt that God had brought someone to me."

Soncini had been raised a Catholic, but with her faith in God shaken to its core by her loss, she had ranged further for spiritual answers and fallen into Neulander's powerful orbit.

"Why don't you tell your boss, God, to come through these doors?" a skeptical Soncini had challenged the rabbi.

"Maybe," Fred Neulander responded, "I'm His messenger."

Under Neulander's tutelage, Soncini would study Hebrew and eventually convert to the Jewish faith.

That same Friday afternoon, Soncini appeared on a news television program in Philadelphia and stated that following Carol's death, Fred had met with her and told her to hire a lawyer whom he recommended. Elaine said that Fred asked her to deny the affair if police ever asked about it. Soncini added that she had done nothing of the sort.

"He suggested that what I say was that he was my rabbi, and that we had buried Ken, and the whole Judaism affiliation, and leave it at that," she told *The Philadelphia Inquirer*.

When Soncini did eventually meet with detectives, they told her that the investigation's working theory was that Fred had hired a hitman to kill Carol, at least in part so that he could continue his affair with her. "If in fact he did it because of me, without my knowledge, it is reprehensible and repugnant to me," Soncini said in her newspaper and television interviews. "That in itself is horrifying. How do I live the rest of my life knowing that I could be the possible motive?"

On the question of whether or not she herself thought Fred had arranged to have Carol killed, Soncini said she really didn't know the answer, but she did have several damning context clues that she was able to add to the circumstantial evidence in the case.

Soncini told reporters that though she had not drawn any personal conclusions about Neulander's possible involvement in Carol's death, "I wanted to know. I wanted to know so I could go on with my life." She agreed to wear a wire over to Neulander's residence and talk with Fred about the killing so that investigators could tape any incriminating statements he might make. Neulander agreed to meet with Soncini at his home, but the sting was canceled when Fred spotted a television news van parked outside and called off their meeting.

Most importantly, Elaine said that she and the rabbi had truly been in love. In the summer of 1994, when she became tired of sneaking around, she had given Fred an ultimatum: "If you cannot leave your wife, I will leave you," she'd said. She remembered Fred's reply: "Trust me, we will be together. Everything will work out by your birthday." Elaine's birthday was in December. As November began, Carol was dead.

Soncini remembered Fred being concerned about what effect a divorce would have on his position as senior rabbi, something he had spent his whole life working to create at M'kor Shalom, and what might happen to his finances.

Soncini told *The Philadelphia Inquirer* that Neulander had professed his love for her and talked of divorcing Carol, but at the same time, he was afraid it would cost him his carefully constructed career in the only vocation he had ever known. "He talked a lot about the fact that he wanted to leave," she said, adding, "He was talking to people about whether it was possible to do this" without having to give up his position as senior rabbi. "Some people said it would be Okay; others said it would not be Okay."

Fred's problem with a potential divorce was twofold: it was bad enough to be a rabbi who was in the position of leaving his wife shortly before their thirtieth anniversary, but any divorce proceeding against Carol could also be expected to dredge up his history of affairs, and that could cost him dearly in terms of both his settlement with Carol and as far as his position was concerned at the synagogue. He might be able to stay on as a divorced person, but not as an adulterer. Of course, that was exactly the problem that ultimately did force his resignation from M'kor Shalom four months after Carol was killed.

Still, for all his concerns, Soncini herself had assets of about one million dollars, and she had offered to help Fred financially if he would divorce Carol and join her.

Fred's response to Elaine was that he foresaw a "tumultuous autumn."

She said that Neulander had dreamed of violence befalling Carol, and once even had said to her, "I wish my wife would just be gone, or just disappear." Soncini said her response was, "You better not be thinking what I think you're thinking." Neulander didn't reply.

Speaking about the night of Carol's murder, Elaine said that usually on Tuesday evenings, Fred would return to Soncini's home to see her again, but on Tuesday, November 1, 1994, he had told her earlier in the day that he "forgot again" that there was a class he needed to attend at the synagogue.

For all the time and intimacy Elaine and Fred had shared, which Soncini at one point described as having been "like a marriage," Elaine told reporters that she now regarded Fred Neulander as a "controlling, manipulative, destructive person."

Soncini's bombshell revelations were a massive blow to the image of a respectable citizen unfairly scrutinized by police that Neulander's lawyers had spent the previous day issuing from their Camden offices. Now they were in the awkward position of neither confirming nor denying Soncini's account of the situation. Zucker characterized questions about the affair as revolving around Neulander's personal morals and ethics, but dismissed any notion that they had bearing on whether or not he killed Carol. "In no way does this change our client's statement about the murder. He did not kill his wife, nor was he involved in her slaying," Zucker said, adding, "It's a personal business thing . . . unless someone is saying it was a motive, but that is absurd."

The following Monday morning Soncini took to the airwaves on her own program for the first time since the scandal had erupted on the front pages of the Philadelphia press. She gave an on-air apology to her listeners for her romantic involvement with Neulander. "I have made some errors in judgment. Unfortunately, these errors in judgment have made their way to the public forum," Soncini said. "If in any way this has caused you discomfort or pain, I am truly sorry. I hurt more than anyone, because I have to live with my mistakes every day—not just in my heart, but on television and in the newspaper."

Not surprisingly, Soncini's devoted listeners sided with her, and jammed the switchboards at WPEN offering their support.

Soncini ended her weekend of interviews by expressing the age-old hope of those suddenly thrust into the spotlight of scandal: by having come clean and told what she knew, maybe she could put the issue to rest and move on with her life.

It was a fond hope, but it was not to be. In a case characterized by its escalating series of public flare-ups, Soncini would soon become embroiled in another romantic scandal, this time involving the Cherry Hill Police Department.

After Soncini initially began cooperating with the investigators who were probing Neulander, officials had become concerned that if Elaine really was the reason for the murder, she herself might end up as the next victim. In December 1994, she was quietly assigned a twenty-four-hour-a-day police guard detail. One of her chief bodyguards was Cherry Hill police officer Larry Leaf, 47.

Leaf had been with the Cherry Hill police for a quarter-century, and was a member of the surveillance team that had initially been assigned to keep an eye on Fred Neulander in the days immediately after the murder.

Spending considerable time together, Leaf and Soncini quickly became friends, and soon became romantically involved. By January 1995, the couple were talking about an engagement, and on June 9, 1995, they were married. Leaf moved in with Soncini at her Cherry Hill residence. This was not what the Cherry Hill police command staff had meant by round-the-clock protection, and Leaf was forced to resign when his superiors learned of the relationship. Supervisors had sympathy for Leaf's plight, and they allowed him to total up his unused holidays, sick leave, and vacation time from the past twenty-five years and use it so that it pushed him over the August 1 deadline when he would have been eligible to retire anyway. Soncini and Leaf soon began making plans to relocate to Florida to establish their new life together, far from the painful memories within Cherry Hill.

Cherry Hill Police Chief William Moffett subsequently minimized Leaf's role in the Neulander investigation and insisted that his relationship with Soncini had not compromised the case.

CHAPTER TWELVE

WHILE the public was learning more than he—and they—had ever anticipated about his sex life, Fred Neulander was largely spending his time out of sight at his home in Cherry Hill. Friends said he was busy writing a book, although he wouldn't tell anyone what it was about. On Sabbath days he would quietly attend an elegant old synagogue in the Society Hill section of Philadelphia. It had once been an Episcopal church; Neulander had told Soncini before they broke up that he liked the atmosphere in the historic building, and also the fact that he could blend in and pray merely as one of the congregants.

Zucker was busy defending Neulander in the press and pointing out that Fred still had many supporters and sympathizers from his own community who were convinced that their former rabbi could never have arranged any harm to Carol. "He's attempting to cope with the horrible tragedy and get on with his life," Zucker said. "The guy has lost his pulpit, and the community is abuzz about whether or not he's involved with a hitman and other ridiculous things."

The public got their best in-depth look at Fred Neulander's life when *Philadelphia Magazine* published a lengthy article in their October issue by writer Carol Saline, who had formerly been a member of the M'kor Shalom congregation, and who had known the Neulanders for years.

In it, Fred Neulander admitted his affairs, but denied plotting to kill his wife. "I made mistakes, errors in judgment that I would never make again. I have deep regrets that I've hurt people," Neulander said, but he added, "the idea that the police want me to come crawling in and say, 'You've destroyed my life, so I might as well confess to a crime I didn't do' is absurd."

He also said that he didn't recall comments attributed to him by Elaine Soncini that she shouldn't call off their affair because "something was going to happen by the end of the year."

In the course of three separate interviews with Carol Saline, all of which took place with his lawyers present, Fred Neulander finally gave an explanation for why he had initially lied to investigators about his extramarital affairs. "The night of the murder, the police had asked me about adultery. I was embarrassed and afraid of what might happen if it came out, so I lied," Fred admitted. "When I arrived for fingerprinting, adultery came up again with some intensity. I lied again, and that's when I realized these guys are looking at me. I'd better get a lawyer. As soon as I did, I told him to tell the police the truth."

Neulander said there were days when it was hard to get out of bed and keep going in the wake of all the scrutiny directed at him by the police, the media, and the "bloodsuckers" amongst the public who doubted his innocence.

Saline also interviewed Rebecca Neulander–Rockoff, who said that she stood by her father, even in light of his marital infidelities. Rebecca said that when she first heard authorities reveal the affairs, "I was really angry and confused. I thought what he did was awful, but it wasn't my role to play judge and jury. . . . He's had a lot of losses. I didn't want to be another one."

In November 1995, something popped up on the radar that most people following the Neulander case had forgotten was even a possibility. A killing had taken place in Teaneck, New Jersey, with enough similarities to Carol Neulander's death that authorities there suggested the same murderer might have been responsible.

Investigators in Bergen County began conferring with Camden County detectives to see whether the killing of businessman Howard Lewis earlier that month might be linked to Carol's death the year before.

Lewis was the wealthy co-owner of the Sealy Mattress factory in Paterson. Like the Neulander killing, Lewis had been surprised at home by two men—one of them wearing a cartoon mask—when he returned from work, and he had been beaten in the head with a blunt object. Unlike the case in Cherry Hill, Lewis had been gagged and blindfolded with duct tape before his assailants dragged him to an upstairs bedroom where they also gagged and tied up his 86-year-old wheelchair-bound mother.

Police in Bergen County believed the Lewis killing was similar to an attack two weeks beforehand in Englewood Cliffs, New Jersey, where the owner of several bagel shops was attacked in his garage by two men, one of whom was wearing a wolf mask. The victim, who survived, was beaten around the head, and his attackers made off with a thousand dollars in cash.

When authorities sat down together and went over the details of the November 8 slaying of Lewis and compared it to the Carol Neulander murder, they found enough substantive differences that they came away from the meeting doubting any connection, even though there were some superficial similarities between the two homicides.

Six months later, in April 1996, the Central Conference of American Rabbis, an organization of 1,750 North American Reform rabbis, meeting at their annual convention in Philadelphia, voted to suspend Rabbi Fred Neulander for a minimum of two years. The group said they were reacting to Neulander's acknowledgment of extramarital affairs, not to suppositions that he might be a suspect in the murder of his wife. The move stopped far short of a defrocking procedure, and the gathered rabbis said the suspension was meant to encourage repentance, not merely to act as punishment.

Once again, little seemed to be happening in the investigation, but every now and then a new detail from the case would make the news. At one point Neulander's attorney Jeffrey Zucker revealed that he had been approached by Jim Conley, the head of the Camden County Prosecutor's Homicide Unit, asking if Fred would be willing to take a lie detector test regarding his involvement in Carol's murder.

Zucker said he had rejected the request out of hand, arguing that the inexact tests are only as good as the person administering them. However, in September 1996, it was revealed that Neulander had voluntarily taken a polygraph test after all. It had occurred in December 1994, a month after Carol was killed, and Neulander had not done well on it. Sources said the test indicated that Fred was being deceptive when he denied hiring a hitman to kill Carol.

Newspapers quoted people familiar with Neulander's test as saying that he passed the question "Did you kill your wife Carol?" but when asked "Did you have your wife killed?" the response indicated an emotional reaction suggesting deception. In a widely quoted remark, one of the anonymous sources supposedly said that Neulander's response "was off the charts."

Defense Attorney Zucker wasted no time in decrying the reports, saying that the test, which had been administered by Neulander's previous attorney, Edward Fitzpatrick, was unreliable because Neulander had been taking stress medications at the time. Zucker also disputed that Neulander had been asked about hiring someone to kill Carol. He added that the mere fact Neulander was willing to take the test in the first place indicated his innocence.

At the time, Fitzpatrick had not requested a written report. Instead, polygrapher Paul K. Minor of Fairfax, Virginia, had discussed the results with the attorney verbally.

Once again, it was Neulander's private investigator, Len Jenoff, who stepped forward to explain the rabbi's innocence to the press. Jenoff said that the questions where deception had been indicated had to do with Neulander's denial at the time that he had extramarital affairs. "He was trying to keep the affairs secret," Jenoff told the *Courier-Post*.

For almost three years, despite the flurry of scandalous revelations towards the end of 1995, progress on the Neulander case had moved at a crawl. Prosecutors, who continued to feel that they were within striking distance of solving the case, kept going over and over their files looking for ways to break it open. Actually, many of them felt sure they had solved it within hours of Carol's murder, but they were still far away from an arrest.

It's one thing to suspect that someone hired a hitman, it's entirely another to prove it beyond a reasonable doubt. Prosecutors were hemmed in by the very seriousness of the crime. In New Jersey, soliciting murder-for-hire is a capital offense, and officials knew they would have to do better than just a strong supposition when it came to convincing a jury that they were justified in seeking to execute a member of the clergy.

By September 1997 prosecutors decided the time had come to kick-start their investigation and convene a grand jury to look at what they felt was damning circumstantial evidence linking Fred Neulander to his wife's death.

A dozen subpoenas began to issue to the players in the tragedy, and once again the story was pulled back into the local news cycle.

Elaine Soncini would get one of the first subpoenas

to appear, as would Rabbi Gary Mazo and Neulander's oldest son Matthew, who had completed his stint as an emergency room technician and was now a freshman at the New Jersey School of Medicine and Dentistry in Piscataway.

Neulander's attorney Jeffrey Zucker was upbeat about the coming investigative session. "We really welcome the opening of a grand jury because it's always been our client's position that he had nothing to do with this," Zucker said. "He is as much a victim as anyone else. Perhaps a grand jury will get to the bottom of whoever is responsible for this horrible murder."

The grand jury met four times during the month of September, talking to some people for just a few minutes and others for hours on end.

One of the more colorful characters who got subpoenaed to appear before the grand jury was Neulander's friend and M'kor Shalom smoking buddy, Leonard Jenoff. He would be called back three separate times to answer the grand jurors' questions.

Len Jenoff was something of a wild card in the whole proceeding, but he was well connected amongst the police and the FBI in the New Jersey and Philadelphia areas. Fred had actually hired Jenoff the day after Carol's murder to help find the killer, and when he received his summons to testify, Jenoff was quick to defend his rabbi's innocence. "I'm glad it's gotten to a point where there's activity in this investigation," Jenoff told the *Courier-Post*. "I am hopeful that by bringing in numerous witnesses, including myself, we can shed light on this case."

Jenoff dismissed the notion that Neulander had hired anyone to kill Carol, noting that the case clearly appeared to have been a robbery. "She carried home large sums of money from the bakery she was associated with," Jenoff said. Although prosecutors had since said that none of Classic Cake's money was taken during the murder, Jenoff insisted that Carol had taken home $5,000 that evening, and that it had been stolen. Jenoff insisted that his research to date had shown no evidence that Neulander had anything to do with the crime.

Jenoff also advanced another theory, albeit cryptically, to reporter Marilyn Silverstein of the *Jewish Exponent*. As he got back on the elevator to return to the closed courtroom, Jenoff turned to Silverstein and said that in addition to the robbery motive, a "possible organized-crime theory" had surfaced. "Russians or Israelis. That's all I can say," Jenoff whispered before the doors snapped shut.

In addition to Jenoff, there was another new face before the grand jury. It was a long-time friend and racquetball partner of Rabbi Neulander's named Myron "Pep" Levin.

At 71 years old, Levin liked to describe himself as an "entrepreneur," but reporters preferred to describe him as an "ex-felon with reputed underworld ties." Whatever the truth of those alleged mob connections, Levin had been convicted and jailed for a multiplicity of criminal activities. It all began when the price of silver spiked sharply upwards in the 1960s; the value of the silver that was then contained in US coinage actually began to exceed the value of the coins themselves. The Treasury's solution to this problem was to stop putting actual silver in the coins, but Levin's was to put together an illegal smelting operation. By the time Levin was caught, he had melted down millions of dollars' worth of coins and earned another nickname—"King of Silver"—for his efforts.

Released from jail for that enterprise, Levin went right back for two more years in the 1970s when the feds discovered he was running a scam to illegally obtain and then illegally sell US food stamps. Over the years he was also convicted of tax evasion and conspiracy to commit arson for a Baltimore torch job in which one of the arsonists died and another was severely burned.

In his hour before the grand jury, Levin made quite an impression. He told the jurors that just weeks before Carol was beaten to death, Fred Neulander had asked him if he could help arrange to have Carol killed.

Levin said that he and Neulander were playing their usual game of racquetball at Gold's Gym in Cherry Hill when Neulander threw down his racquet and said, "I wish I would come home one night and find my wife dead on the floor."

Levin told the grand jury that Neulander was worried that if he divorced his wife, it would cost him his position as rabbi at M'kor Shalom. Levin said his reply to Neulander was that the rabbi was crazy, and added that he didn't really think Neulander was serious until he heard the news of Carol's murder.

Zucker wasted no time disputing Levin's account before the grand jury, calling his testimony "blatantly false" and adding that Neulander "never made such a comment. He says it's ridiculous."

Shuffling out of the grand jury session, Levin refused to talk to the gathered reporters, but his attorney, Jaime Kaigh, brightened things up when he told the press that he was "fairly certain" that Levin wasn't actually a target of the investigation.

By October the grand jury had finished its probe and moved a step closer to issuing an indictment. Camden County's new prosecutor Lee Solomon announced that he was making progress and was confident the crime would be solved after all.

While the grand jury was wrapping up its session, M'kor Shalom was being forced to evacuate its buildings due to a bomb threat that was phoned in by someone who specifically mentioned the grand jury proceedings. Camden County Sheriff's Department Bomb Squad personnel and dogs swept the buildings, and even though nothing suspicious was found, police remained in the synagogue right through the evening to guard congregation members attending various classes.

Back at M'kor Shalom, Rabbi Gary Mazo, as well as other rabbis in the region, began complaining about the timing of the grand jury probe, which coincided with Judaism's holy High Holidays. Some even went so far as to accuse *The Philadelphia Inquirer* of being anti-Semitic because it put the story on the front page during the same holiday period. Given the large number of religious holidays that are on the Jewish calendar, at least the orthodox one, it was a fairly easy conspiracy theory to advance, and prosecutors dismissed it out of hand.

The grand jury had met four times to consider Carol Neulander's death, but no indictment was issued at the end of their session, and disappointed prosecutors continued to sift through what leads they could for any new information. When 1998 rolled around, there were still no charges pending in the case.

It would take nearly the full year, but all of that would change early one morning in September.

CHAPTER THIRTEEN

WITH nearly four years' worth of investigation, rumors, and leaks played out time and again in the headlines, it seemed that if the authorities ever did develop enough evidence to bring Fred Neulander to trial, it would eventually be announced in the form of a grand jury indictment. But on the morning of September 10, 1998, Fred Neulander was arrested for murder in a day-long scene that looked more like a breaking news story than the potential resolution of a cold case.

Neulander, now 57 years old, had driven barely three blocks from his home when police pulled his car over at 9:15 A.M. and slapped him in handcuffs on an arrest warrant charging him with being an accomplice to murder and conspiracy to commit murder.

Reporters were already gathering outside the Cherry Hill police station when Neulander was led inside in his striped shirt and blue slacks. It was the first time he had been photographed in cuffs, but by mid-afternoon, when he appeared before Superior Court Judge Linda Rosenzweig at the Camden County Hall of Justice, his transformation was even more startling.

Neulander was led into the courtroom wearing the orange prison jumpsuit and white canvas high-top sneakers that just screamed "Felon!" when pictures of his appearance were later shown on television and in newspapers. With his bound hands out in front of him, Neulander watched emotionlessly and stayed silent throughout the entire arraignment procedure as prosecutors laid out before the judge their probable cause for the charges.

Camden County Prosecutor Lee Solomon outlined the circumstantial case against Neulander, saying that the rabbi clearly had a motive to get rid of his wife in order to continue a string of illicit affairs, for if Neulander had simply divorced her, he would have risked his job.

Solomon didn't name Elaine Soncini during the hearing, but no one was in any doubt that he was talking about her when he said that Neulander's mistress had over a million dollars in assets and was putting pressure on Neulander to either marry her or break off the relationship. Solomon said that Neulander had told Soncini "to trust him, that their problem will be solved by December 1994."

Solomon also told the judge about Myron "Pep" Levin's statement that Neulander wanted to come home one day and find his wife dead on the floor and wondered if Levin knew anyone who could arrange for that to happen.

"We do not allege that he, of his own hand, committed that murder," said Solomon. "We allege that he conspired to have her killed and played the part of accomplice in that murder." The charges carried a sentence of life in prison with no parole for at least thirty years, but they also left open the option of seeking the death penalty.

Solomon also said that, far from being a regular occurrence, Neulander had only started attending the Tuesday night classes at his synagogue two weeks before the murder. To detectives it looked like the work of a man bent on establishing an alibi for what he knew was about to happen.

Even though the evidence against Neulander was completely circumstantial, Solomon characterized it as "both compelling and overwhelming." But looming over the case was the fact that if the murder had been a hit, where were the hitmen? The police had spent years looking at everyone Neulander might have contracted for such a job, but they still had no idea regarding identities of the Bathroom Man and his even more mysterious colleague.

Zucker entered a not guilty plea to both felony charges on Neulander's behalf and listened as Judge Rosenzweig set bail at $400,000 and ordered Neulander to surrender his passport. Later it would be suggested that an attempt by Neulander to renew his passport had prompted his sudden mid-ride arrest that morning.

By 7:30 P.M., his attorneys had posted bail for Neulander and he walked back out the doors of the Camden County Jail.

It had certainly been a dramatic day in the ongoing saga and, in the opinion of the defense attorneys, the whole thing had been far more dramatic than was necessary. Zucker thought the whole cops-and-robbers traffic stop and arrest smacked of showmanship, a way for prosecutors to ensure that his client showed up on the evening news in a bright orange jumpsuit, rather than just giving his attorneys notice and letting Neulander appear in court to voluntarily answer the charges.

"The real question is, why now?" said an angry Zucker. "What is different today? It's the same old song. If this is such an overwhelming case, why haven't they indicted him?"

Wixted, a former criminal prosecutor in Camden County, said the whole thing also struck him as a circus. "To let us surrender wouldn't be good press," he noted.

The decision by police to swoop in and arrest Fred Neulander as he was driving through Wexford Leas came as a surprise to most who had been following the case closely, not the least of whom was Matthew Neulander, now 25 years old and in his second year as an honors student at Robert Wood Johnson Medical School. Matthew spent the day watching his father's arrest unfolding on television from his apartment in Franklin Township out in Somerset County, New Jersey.

"It's been a lousy day," Matthew Neulander told reporters who reached him. Speaking about his mother, he added, "She was my best friend. I have never met anyone as warm, gracious, and kind in caring for her children as my mother was.

"I'm concerned about my brother and sister," Matthew continued, referring to Rebecca and Benjamin, who had both since moved to Massachusetts (a few months before, at his graduation from the University of Michigan, Ben had put his mother's initials on his mortarboard). "It's hard for them, being so far from home."

"It was such a pitiful, sad sight," Matthew told Nancy Phillips of *The Philadelphia Inquirer*. "He was led out there like a common criminal."

Out of the three Neulander children, Matthew was alone in beginning to express doubts about his father's innocence in the wake of all the damning revelations that the past four years had turned up.

Watching his father arraigned for his mother's death was "painful to the point that I can't even describe," Matthew told Phillips, adding, "Nothing in the world would make me happier than to find out someone else did this. But if one word describes me, I'm a realist, and I have to look at all possibilities."

Matthew Neulander said that he could see compelling arguments on both sides of the questions revolving around his father, but he concluded, "In my heart of hearts, I don't believe that he did it. Maybe I'm clinging to it stupidly. It's the best that I can do."

As it had the Neulander family, the sudden arrest also whipsawed the emotions of the already battered M'kor Shalom congregation. So many there had already suffered so much emotional pain over the past years as they tried to keep an open mind about the accusations against a rabbi who had been regarded with heartfelt love and respect for so long.

"The death of Carol Neulander has been a great loss for our congregation and especially for our family," said spokeswoman Sharla Feldsher in a prepared statement. "The passage of time without any closure has prevented the wounds from healing."

"It just kind of shakes my belief in who you can trust," said Diane Steinberg, a member of the synagogue in an interview reported by the Associated Press. "How can you have faith in any person that you know when a person you adored, felt was a kind, good person, can be involved in something like this?"

"He's upset and disappointed," defense attorney Jeffrey Zucker said of Neulander after the arraignment. "I think it's horrible that they charged him. I don't believe the guy had the slightest thing to do with this."

"This case is wrapped with a tissue of supposition, opinions, and theories out of *True Detective*," said attorney Dennis Wixted.

With prosecutors alleging that the mysterious "Bathroom Man" was actually a hitman hired by Neulander, it fell once again to his loyal friend, private investigator Len Jenoff, to point out to reporters the absurdity of the scenario. "I don't believe the rabbi is capable of that," said Jenoff. "He's a good man."

Jenoff reiterated to reporters outside the courthouse that the weird comings and goings of the Bathroom Man sounded much more like an incompetent robber than the work of an experienced underworld hitman.

Again, Jenoff advanced the theory that Carol had been carrying cash home from her bakery and in doing so had made herself a target. "No hitman goes to the house twice," Jenoff scoffed to reporters. "This is not a professional hit."

On Friday, October 23, 1998, Neulander's defense team suffered a pair of setbacks when Superior Court

Judge Linda Rosenzweig refused to order an evidentiary hearing to see whether the overall case lacked probable cause, and also refused to use speedy trial provisions to force prosecutors to rush their developing theories of the murder back before another grand jury.

"It's tough to defend someone until we have something to defend," Zucker argued. "They've had four years to get this together. Why can't they tell us what they have?"

An interesting side note to the proceedings occurred two months later, on Friday, December 18, 1998, when Myron "Pep" Levin filed a complaint saying that Neulander swindled him in a deal involving a Torah that Levin was donating to M'kor Shalom. Levin had commissioned Neulander to actually purchase the sacred scrolls, which contain the first five books of the Old Testament, so that Levin could then donate them to the synagogue in memory of his late wife.

This was a new one as far as the annals of crimes were concerned. Torahs are not something one can just order up from a print shop. The sacred scrolls are usually handwritten by an orthodox Jew, usually in Israel, and the individual pieces are carefully handsewn together. When the scrolls become unusably worn, they are retired, but still venerated as holy objects. Most Torahs belong to congregations, though some are in private hands—many were taken by the Nazis during World War II and subsequently released onto the international collecting market, including some that were damaged or contained errors. Just as with works of art, the Torah scrolls are valuable to collectors and it is not unknown to have them stolen. In fact, in the 1980s there was a rash of Torah thefts from a dozen synagogues in the Philadelphia area, including M'kor Shalom. A drug-addled Jewish man with ties to the Torah collecting market was eventually identified and charged, and all the missing scrolls were recovered and returned to their congregations.

Levin's complaint said that the Torah Neulander sold him in 1994 for $16,000 contained errors and was actually worth about $3,000.

The case started as a complaint lodged by Levin with the Cherry Hill Police Department after an expert scribe declared that the Torah Neulander had purchased for Levin was faulty. The case ended up being charged as theft by deception.

"He cheated me," Levin told *The Philadelphia Inquirer.* "He told me it was a very fine Torah, and it turns out to be junk. He besmirched the memory of my wife."

Zucker countered that the first Neulander had learned of a problem with the scrolls was when Levin had written him a letter about them in 1997, and suggested that anger over the alleged incident might have motivated Levin to make up the damning quote about Neulander wanting his wife dead.

"This is one of the most absurd, ridiculous accusations that I have heard in my entire career as a practicing criminal defense lawyer," said Zucker. "There would have been no reason in the world that Fred Neulander would have bought an inferior product."

CHAPTER FOURTEEN

ON Monday, January 11, 1999, Fred Neulander received another piece of bad news. A Camden County grand jury had finally decided to issue a two-count indictment charging him with the same accomplice to murder and conspiracy to commit murder charges that the police had stopped him with on the street.

The indictments spelled out the belief that Fred had been acting with "a person or persons unknown" to arrange Carol's murder, and for the first time prosecutors revealed on the record that they would not be seeking the death penalty. The sticking point on that decision seemed to be the circumstantial nature of the case and the fact that the hitman or hitmen had not been identified by investigators. It was going to be an uphill fight for prosecutors to convict the rabbi based only on a few statements he had allegedly made, and on the ongoing affairs. A jury could be counted on to be especially wary of convicting on a death penalty case even with much more solid proof. The prosecutors were apparently acknowledging that hesitation when they decided to keep the whole game in the 30-years-to-life arena.

Back out in front of the courthouse defending the rabbi was his friend Len Jenoff, who had spent so much time interviewing associates of Neulander and poking around Cherry Hill looking for clues that would exonerate him.

Jenoff characterized Neulander as "guilty as sin" when it came to adultery, but he once again insisted that that didn't mean the rabbi had planned, or even wanted, to find ways of getting rid of Carol. "There's no evidence he hired anybody to kill his wife," Jenoff said. "They have no case. He's innocent."

Neulander had been living in a strange purgatory halfway between accusation and exoneration for over four years. His suspension in 1995 by the council of rabbis essentially meant that he wasn't welcome at their gatherings and wouldn't be placed with a new congregation until the suspension was lifted. But it didn't mean that Fred Neulander was anything less than a rabbi in the eyes of the religion itself. He had still kept busy writing curricula for educational field trips and tutoring some of his friends' children.

Neulander had even performed several marriages and funerals for close friends who still firmly believed in him as their rabbi. But as the indictment came down from the grand jury, events were already moving past Neulander in the lives of his former congregation. The simple passage of time was beginning to heal some of the wounds that the lack of an explanation or official resolution had not.

Many within the religious community around Cherry Hill kept fervently hoping that a better explanation, one that left their rabbi out of the crime, would suddenly appear, yet with each new development Fred Neulander only seemed to be mired further in a cloud of dark suspicion.

In an interview with reporter Marilyn Silverstein of the *Jewish Exponent*, Rabbi Gregory S. Marx, religious leader of Congregation Beth Or in Spring House, New Jersey, called the news of Neulander's grand jury indictment "terrible" and "a *shanda*"—a Hebrew word meaning *disgrace*.

"I think that it's a terrible day for the American rabbinate. It's sad for our people," said Marx. "I see no good coming out of this. I want justice to be served. I really do," the Reform rabbi said, "but I think this is going to be a very painful journey for the community."

Rabbi Mayer W. Selekman of the Temple Sholom in Broomall, Pennsylvania, who had attended the seminary with Neulander three decades before, still urged the community not to make up their minds until all the facts were in. "I love him. He has been a dear friend, and the presumption of innocence must prevail," Selekman said to the paper.

Back at Congregation M'kor Shalom, the four years that Assistant Rabbi Gary Mazo had put in as leader of the bewildered organization were drawing to a close. Mazo had always dreamed of being the leader of a smaller flock on Cape Cod, and now there was such an opening. He quickly made plans to move his family north.

In his place, filling the formidable and yet utterly confusing legacy left by Rabbi Neulander, would be Rabbi Barry Schwartz of Amherst, New York, a suburb of Buffalo. The 40-year-old Schwartz, also the father of three children, was familiar with New Jersey, having grown up in the Hudson Valley, and he had developed a reputation as an environmental activist who liked to grow his own organic vegetables and donate them to food pantries for the poor. He would become the first leader to officially take over M'kor Shalom as a new senior rabbi in its twenty-five-year history, and that would put him at the helm of a synagogue that, even despite the unprecedented scandal of which it was the epicenter, had grown to the point where it was now the largest synagogue in southern New Jersey, with almost a thousand families in its congregation and a thousand of their children in the affiliated religious school.

After Mazo left his toy-packed office at M'kor Shalom, he would make his way back into the news for taking a strong stand on including gays and lesbians in his Cape Cod congregation. Mazo told Jewish newspapers that he felt there was nothing within the Reform movement's teachings that excluded homosexuals, and he said he was prepared to officiate at same-sex commitment ceremonies on the order of marriages.

While others moved on with their lives, on March 15, 1999, Fred Neulander was back in court for his formal arraignment on the grand jury indictments. This time he was able to forgo the bright orange jumpsuit and instead appeared in a conservative blue suit and maroon tie, appearing much more relaxed and even jovial during the short, seven-minute-long process.

After entering pleas of not guilty on Neulander's behalf, the defense attorneys asked for more time to go through the 4,000 pages of evidence that the prosecution had turned over to them, and Judge Rosenzweig granted an extension through July.

Attorney Wixted told the court that he was considering whether or not to ask for a change of venue in order to try to get away from the vast amount of pretrial publicity that had centered around the case in Cherry Hill.

Wixted also said that he wanted an opportunity to investigate the prosecution's witnesses, including the colorful Myron "Pep" Levin.

When reporters cover high-profile court cases, there always seems to come a moment when, despite the best efforts of everyone involved, the defendant and the press all end up in the same elevator together. That happened this day and, reporters being reporters, they tried softballing Neulander a question about whether he would be commenting on the day's proceeding. Neulander didn't take the bait and instead rode in stone-faced silence down to the lobby level while a million unspoken follow-up questions whirled in the minds of those standing shoulder-to-shoulder with him on the uncomfortable journey.

When everybody got back out in front of the courthouse, defense attorney Zucker did take questions despite the icy wind blowing through Camden's streets, and he hotly disputed notions that Fred would find a way to cut a deal. "There will be no plea bargain in this case. The rabbi has always asserted his innocence, and you can bet this case is going to trial. Quite frankly, I don't know why they indicted the man," Zucker added. "There's not one thing [in the grand jury discovery] I've read that I hadn't read before in the newspapers. I think the whole case—as far as I know—is a 'he said, she said.' "

Zucker said that Neulander was looking forward to getting the case to trial. "He's anxious to get this behind him. He knows he's innocent, and he wants to be exonerated."

In April 1999, defense lawyers sifting through numerous boxes of discovery records that had been turned over by prosecutors were ecstatic when they came across a tape of a telephone call that Elaine Soncini had made to Fred Neulander. The call, taped shortly after Carol's death, was a set-up arranged by police to see if Soncini could catch Neulander admitting his involvement in Carol's murder. Instead, Neulander had professed his innocence, and adamantly denied any role in the killing.

"She called Fred and tried to dupe him into talking about this," Zucker said in an interview. "It's a great piece of evidence for us, because he denied it."

While the legal system worked its way onward, other aspects of life in Cherry Hill began making strides back toward normality. The once-thriving Classic Cake Company had teetered without Carol at the helm, and by January 1999 financial problems that had developed in the wake of her death finally caught up with the company.

On January 5, 1999, the Audubon, Cherry Hill, and Voorhees locations closed their doors without warning. A short time later, the company was bought out by two couples with ties to M'kor Shalom who had also had experience in the restaurant industry. By May 1999 the Cherry Hill location had reopened and Classic Cake started to climb back into business. Eventually it would grow even larger and open several more stores than it had the first time around.

CHAPTER FIFTEEN

THE prosecution had a theory that hitmen had killed Carol Neulander, but didn't have them identified. All along, the defense attorneys representing Fred had insisted that the case the prosecutors were putting together was big on generalizations and innuendo, but light on specific proof.

Cheating on one's spouse is a moral lapse, not a crime—not even for a rabbi. Having what others might view as a motive for murdering someone is nowhere near the same thing as actually acting on that motive. As a story narrative, the quotes and circumstances the prosecution had found were certainly enough to focus an investigation towards Fred Neulander, but without an actual hitman—or something that constituted conclusive evidence that one had existed, such as a signed contract—it was hard to see how a jury could be convinced that a man who could have hundreds of people stand and testify to his good moral character was guilty of these charges.

Confident that the prosecution was right on the edge of over-reaching, Zucker and Wixted decided in June 1999 to see if they could get the indictment against Fred Neulander thrown out of court.

One of the oldest jokes in the legal profession is that a skilled prosecutor can get a grand jury to indict a ham sandwich, so just the fact that the defense thought the prosecution's case was thin would not be enough to get it dismissed. A defendant faced with a weak case against him can still expect to go through a trial before being

Carol Neulander
(*Courier-Post*)

Rabbi Fred Neulander, accused of arranging his wife's murder so he could continue adulterous affairs (Court TV)

The Neulanders' suburban home in Cherry Hill, New Jersey where Carol was beaten to death (*Eric Francis*)

Matt Neulander, oldest son of Fred and Carol Neulander (Court TV)

Rebecca Neulander, who spoke to her mother on the phone moments before Carol was murdered, testifying in court (Court TV)

Congregation M'kor Shalom in Cherry Hill where Fred Neulander was senior rabbi (Eric Francis)

Congregation M'kor Shalom (Eric Francis)

Assistant Rabbi Gary Mazo had to take over the synagogue after revelations of Rabbi Neulander's affairs forced his resignation (*Courier-Post*)

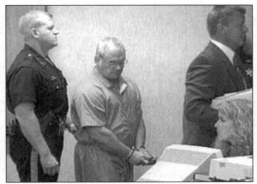

Fred Neulander handcuffed and being led into court after he was first arrested on murder charges in August, 2001 (Court TV)

Fred Neulander in court (Court TV)

Fred Neulander waits at the defense table as the jury is sent back in to resume their work on the sixth day of deliberations (Court TV)

Len Jenoff (Court TV)

Paul Michael Daniels   (Court TV)

The Landmark apartment building on Route 70 where Jenoff and Daniels were roommates (Eric Francis)

Elaine Soncini, radio talk show host and mistress of Rabbi Neulander (Court TV)

Myron "Pep" Levin testifies in court about Fred Neulander's alleged desire to have Carol killed (Court TV)

Nancy Phillips, reporter for the *Philadelphia Inquirer* (Court TV)

Attorney Wixted makes his opening statement as Judge Baxter presides on the bench (Court TV)

Camden County Prosecutor Lee Solomon (left) and First Assistant Prosecutor James Lynch (right), who conducted a withering cross-examination of Fred Neulander (Jose F. Moreno — *Courier-Post*)

Neulander's trial attorneys Jeffrey Zucker (left), Mike Riley, and Dennis Wixted (right) successfully defended Rabbi Neulander at his first murder trial (Tina Markoe Kinslow — *Courier-Post*)

exonerated. To really have a chance of pre-empting a trial, Neulander's team would have to show more than simple over-eagerness on the part of the grand jury. They would have to show misconduct or malice on the part of the prosecutor's office.

While Neulander sat between his attorneys and watched quietly for most of the ninety-minute session, Wixted launched the first shot, alleging that press coverage which had resulted from the extensive leaks that had apparently come out of the prosecutor's office and the police departments made it impossible to get a fair trial.

Wixted also asked the court for nearly twenty more pieces of evidence that had been gathered, including an interview that a police investigator had reportedly conducted with Joey Merlino, the reputed boss of the Philadelphia–South Jersey Mafia, about whether or not Neulander had approached organized crime figures looking for a hitman. Merlino denied any such contact in an interview with a Philadelphia television station.

Wixted also wanted all correspondence between Neulander and Soncini that the police had collected, and all of the Cherry Hill Police Department's documents regarding former officer Larry Leaf, who had ended up marrying Soncini after taking guard duty more seriously than his department intended.

Finally, Wixted also wanted all the records the police had on their contacts with Myron "Pep" Levin.

One of the more creative forms of prosecution misconduct that the defense alleged was that the leaks of embarrassing information, and even Neulander's sudden arrest on September 10, 1998, had all been timed to coincide with Jewish holidays.

Citing news accounts of information in the Neulander case that had been covered on or near the High Holidays, Wixted accused the prosecutor's office of selectively releasing embarrassing facts about the rabbi to the news media. "Things seem to happen around the High Holy Days. We don't think that's fortuitous," Wixted told the judge, adding, "We think the entire manner in which this case has been conducted has been for the purpose of destroying and humiliating a man you may very well not be able to convict."

By October 1999, the case was drifting towards a trial sometime in 2000, but the defense was still pressing to have the charges tossed out, and was needling the prosecution for more details of their investigation. Neulander was now sporting a new beard and mustache, but little else had changed about his strange life in limbo.

First Assistant Prosecutor James Lynch disclosed that new leads had been gleaned from inmates in jail, but, as with most jailhouse rumors, it was way too early to tell if there was anything to them.

One of the inmates who had been talking to prison officials said flat out that Neulander had offered him a contract to kill Carol. The second one reported that his former cellmate claimed to have killed Mrs. Neulander during a robbery. The problem with the second rumor was that the cellmate in question had since died. Part of one of their tales also involved misconduct by a Cherry Hill police officer. Prosecutors didn't seem too excited by what they were hearing; it looked like another case of bored inmates trying to cook up ways of getting favors or reduced sentences. After all, every hearing and interview they had to give at least meant a break in their day, or perhaps even a brief trip out of the jail. Inmates had been known to go to elaborate lengths for far less attention.

Defense attorneys also learned that a source interviewed by the Cherry Hill police had reported that a member of the John Stanfa organized crime family was somehow mixed up in contracting Carol's murder.

Another report the defense wanted looked into stated that $10,000 in cash was missing from a drawer in the

Neulander household. There had been several conflicting reports in the wake of the murder that money had been missing either from the house or from the bakery, but detectives and prosecutors continued to insist that audits of the business and other financial checks had failed to turn up any evidence to support the rumors.

CHAPTER SIXTEEN

In the six years that the Neulander murder had been on the books as an unsolved case, it had been punctuated by any number of sensational bombshells. But by far the biggest was dropped on May 1, 2000, when police in Cherry Hill announced that they had finally identified and arrested "the Bathroom Man."

He had been there all along, right under their noses, 7in their police stations, amongst the M'kor Shalom congregation, at the rabbi's house, palling around with investigators, chatting with witnesses, dining with reporters, and doggedly defending Fred Neulander's innocence at every opportunity . . . and now, wracked by a guilty conscience, he had come forward and confessed. He was Len Jenoff.

Jenoff would tell police a harrowing tale of deceit, betrayal, and murder, packed with details that only the murderer could have known. He would give up his fellow hitman, his roommate and friend Paul Michael Daniels. Most importantly, he would tell prosecutors what they had long suspected, that the whole murder had been set in motion by Rabbi Fred Neulander, who'd wanted Carol dead, and wanted the hit to look like a robbery. Jenoff would give police all of this and more in the days and weeks that followed, but as dire, as complete, and as damning an account of Neulander's involvement as Jenoff spelled out—as sure as it seemed that Fred Neulander was going straight to jail, if not to the execution chamber—Jenoff would also inadvertently sow the seeds of doubt about the one key premise of the murder: that

Fred Neulander actually had anything to do with it.

As much as it seemed that Jenoff had slammed the door on Rabbi Neulander and thrown away the key, it would turn out that Jenoff, in fact Jenoff's very personality and propensity for exaggeration, would leave that iron door open just a crack, and that crack would let the light of reasonable doubt shine in on the case.

Jenoff had begun to unravel psychologically almost from the first moment of the murder. He had told all kinds of people what a tough character he was; he had implied that he had been trained in all sorts of dark arts involving spy craft and espionage. To hear him tell it, he was the next best thing to James Bond, but the simple truth was that killing Carol Neulander had tormented his soul.

It ate at him, it gnawed away, it was both the horror of it and the shame of being the bad guy. It was also the simple fact that Jenoff couldn't keep a secret, at least not this secret, for years on end.

Jenoff badly wanted to tell somebody what had happened.

In February 1995, Jenoff's charade of being an investigator looking to clear Neulander of suspicion intersected with *Philadelphia Inquirer* reporter Nancy Phillips.

Like many residents of the Philadelphia area, Phillips was also Jewish, and that played some part in why Jenoff trusted her, but beyond that, Jenoff simply felt an affinity, a basic friendship, towards the hard-charging reporter. That didn't keep him from initially wasting huge amounts of her time by sending her on a few wild-goose chases, but even though Phillips found much of Jenoff's hints and suppositions about the Neulander murder to be far-fetched, he got enough things right—and he was close enough to Neulander himself—that she kept in touch with him as a source.

After months spent trying to lead Phillips astray with

psychics and other highly dubious leads involving mob
assassins and international intrigue, Jenoff began to get
serious. He told her that he knew a secret about the case
and that this secret was eating away at him.

In her account of the pivotal meeting, which ran in
The Philadelphia Inquirer, Phillips described how, two
years to the day after Carol had been killed, on November 1, 1996, Jenoff invited her to his "office" in the
Landmark Towers apartment complex. The office turned
out to be half of his bedroom. Jenoff wanted Phillips to
like him, to trust him, and he showed her pictures of
himself from over the years, and photos of his son
Marty. As he chain-smoked in the cramped bedroom,
Jenoff spoke of not only wanting to help his friend the
rabbi, but also of some lingering anger with Neulander
over unpaid bills . . . and something else.

As Phillips recounted in her story, "He pulled his
chair closer to mine and leaned forward. Suppose hy-
pothetically, he said, that the rabbi had told him there
was someone he wanted harmed and asked whether Jenoff knew anyone who could do that. Suppose that Jenoff
gave him the phone number of someone who might do
that. And suppose that he later learned that Carol Neulander was dead, and feared that he had unwittingly been
involved in the crime."

Jenoff had been a friend of the rabbi for some time,
and the two took cigarette breaks together and walked
in the small patch of woods behind M'kor Shalom. Jenoff told Phillips that the rabbi, who had heard Jenoff's
ongoing tales of being a spy, asked if one of Jenoff's
two roommates, a pharmacist named Richard Plum,
might be able to obtain chemicals that could be used to
kill someone without leaving a trace. Jenoff also said
that the rabbi had talked about eliminating enemies of
Israel.

Phillips wasn't buying all of the details, but she
came away from the meeting believing more and more

that Jenoff knew something much more specific about what had happened to Carol Neulander, and that in time he might tell her.

Jenoff's conversations with Phillips were always held off the record. At one point, he told her, "I'm sitting on so many secrets that before I can reveal them I may need a prosecutor's immunity."

Phillips was meeting with Jenoff nearly every day, racking up expense reports for the *Inquirer* in diners and restaurants over coffee and lunch, and listening to Jenoff describe his problems with Judaism and how his religion had long made him feel unworthy. It was charismatic Fred Neulander who had finally made him feel welcome in his own faith, who had persuaded, had practically ordered him, to come to worship services on a regular basis and be part of the synagogue community.

Jenoff, his life out of control, his self-esteem shot by years of lies, deception, and failures in everything from his career to his marriage, ravaged by alcoholism, and drifting without an anchor, had clung to Rabbi Neulander and his promise of salvation within a community and culture that cared for him, and which was his by birthright. Jenoff loved Neulander, he worshipped the man, he told Phillips, he would have done anything for him, anything he asked, he would literally have died for him, and then . . . one day . . . the rabbi asked Jenoff for a favor.

Phillips was a sharp reporter and she knew enough to be profoundly skeptical of some of Jenoff's stories, including his elaborate tales of service as a CIA agent.

Real spies don't go around telling people they're spies. After all, that's where we get the term *secret* agent. Normal people don't give it a lot of thought, but it's amazing how many fakers, flakes, and psychics have heard of the CIA's long-standing policy of neither confirming nor denying who is or was an agent for them. That allows a lot of wild claims to fly under the radar unchallenged. If you claim you are a Congressional Medal of Honor winner, there's a list available that can be checked. But claim you were a CIA agent, and who's to say you weren't?

Jenoff didn't just hint about his CIA connections in dark barrooms. In 1998, he marched right through the front door of Rutgers University in Camden on more than one occasion and lectured the political science students on his training and the missions he carried out for the agency. He told the students that both he and his father were long-time spooks with "the company" in Langley, Virginia.

When word of these exploits was finally made public, the Central Intelligence Agency decided that enough was enough as far as Jenoff was concerned, and CIA spokesman Mark Mansfield issued a rare public dismissal of Jenoff's claims. "We normally don't comment, but we decided to part from that policy in this case," Mansfield said. "This individual has never been employed by the CIA."

Phillips also got a close look at the signed photograph of Ronald Reagan that Jenoff carried around in his wallet. On it, the Gipper had apparently written that Jenoff was "a loyal friend and a comrade in arms." Phillips compared the handwriting to President Reagan's. It didn't match. It did, however, look an awful lot like Jenoff's penmanship.

Jenoff claimed to have worked with the CIA in Vietnam when he was in the Army. His Army records claimed he had been a cook in the reserves who was never deployed overseas. Phillips found all this and more, but still felt that Jenoff knew more than he was saying.

During the time that he was meeting regularly with Phillips, Jenoff had also met and fallen in love with an Episcopalian woman who became his third wife in a ceremony officiated by Rabbi Neulander in August

1997. The marriage took place in Neulander's own front room, just inches from where Carol had died.

Jenoff and his new wife sent Phillips vacation postcards from Mexico, and later, holiday cards, and he introduced Phillips to his son Marty. Jenoff started to think of Phillips as a sister figure, even though she was firm that she was there as a reporter.

By December of 1998, Jenoff was becoming more insistent that he had something major he wanted to tell Phillips. Then one day, in a remorseful discussion in his new home in Collingswood, New Jersey, Jenoff told her that he had arranged to have Carol Neulander murdered.

"I can't believe I'm telling you this. I've held this in for so long," Jenoff told Phillips. "You don't know how close I've come to telling this to you so many times. Please don't hurt me with this, Nancy. I can't ruin my life. I may have to take this to the grave."

Phillips left the Jenoffs' house in a double bind. She had agreed to keep these conversations off the record, which meant that there was little she could do with the information. And at the same time, she was now "in the loop" on a murder, so, if Jenoff had second thoughts, he might decide to "take back" what he had said by harming her as well.

The best solution to both problems, Phillips decided, would be to try to coax Len Jenoff into telling the authorities what he had just told her.

Over the following months Jenoff continued to trickle out the information about what had happened. It was clear that a full confession was going to burst out of him one way or another. He started by giving her the initials of his fellow hitman: PMD. Eventually he gave her a complete name: Paul Michael Daniels.

In January of 2000, Jenoff told Phillips that the rabbi had been tracking her stories and considered her an enemy—to the point that Neulander suggested that Jenoff lure Phillips into a sexual relationship in order to wreck her credibility.

Phillips had spent years wondering whether Jenoff was really even worth the effort to cultivate as a source. Even with that question clearly answered in the affirmative, she had spent more months maneuvering through a complex minefield of journalistic and legal ethics, when suddenly she began to seriously wonder if her very life wasn't in danger.

Phillips explained in one of her *Philadelphia Inquirer* articles: "In February, Jenoff and Daniels made an unannounced visit to my office. Jenoff had called earlier in the day to tell me he was meeting Daniels for lunch and asked whether I wanted to come along. I was frightened, and I declined. So I was startled when the two men arrived. Jenoff introduced me to Daniels, and asked me to join them at a nearby restaurant. I said I was too busy. He then handed me an envelope and asked me to give it to my rabbi. The envelope was empty."

Phillips instantly saw the creepy parallel between Jenoff's action that afternoon and Carol Neulander's experience six years before, when the receipt of an empty envelope had been followed by a deadly attack one week later.

Jenoff kept calling Phillips. He would tell her that his secret was keeping him up nights, that he had hoped for years that he would just die, and it would all go away.

Then in late April 2000, Jenoff called once more, and Phillips agreed to meet him for lunch at a Cherry Hill restaurant. He told her that he had decided to confess to authorities, probably during the next week.

Phillips took another big risk and agreed to ride with Jenoff for a close look at a couple of spots in Philadelphia that he said were linked to Carol's murder. As the pair drove down Route 70 and got closer and closer to the looming Ben Franklin Bridge, Phillips asked Jenoff if he wouldn't feel better just taking the turn toward downtown Camden and meeting with County Prosecutor Lee Solomon. Jenoff agreed, and Phillips called Solomon on her cell phone to arrange a meeting over coffee at a restaurant a few minutes from his office on Market Street.

There at the Weber Colonial Diner in Audubon, a nervous Jenoff worked his way through a fruit cup and drank coffee as he met with Phillips, Solomon, and homicide investigator Martin Devlin for three hours and explained his involvement in Carol's death. Jenoff was a long-time police groupie, and had been hanging around the Neulander case from its inception, so Jenoff and the two officials were acquainted with each other. Investigators hadn't previously focused on him as a suspect, in part because he didn't seem to have any direct connection with Carol Neulander. Jenoff explained that when Neulander had hired him, he was simply told he was going to kill "an enemy of Israel" who had to die for the good of the Jewish state.

During his initial confession at the coffee shop, Jenoff said two things that he would later admit were false. First, he said that he had had no idea until the very last moment that the victim was to be Carol Neulander. Second, he said that he had planned the details of the killing for months. "It was my Entebbe," Jenoff told the small gathering, likening it to the intricate raid on the airport in Uganda in 1976 where the Israeli Defense Forces rescued a planeload of hostages from terrorists.

Those discrepancies weren't critical, but they did point out a habit of Jenoff's: even when he was trying to tell the absolute truth, he couldn't bring himself to avoid either embellishment or self-flattery.

Solomon and Devlin thanked Jenoff at the end of the meeting, and told him they would need some time to think about what he had said, and to check out the details. Phillips' editors at the *Inquirer* also decided to hold off on publishing the story, even though the off-the-record hurdle had been cleared. Like the officials, they were still not certain whether Jenoff's confession actually amounted to the truth, or was simply a deranged story from someone with a serious personal problem.

The authorities spent just over a week checking the details that Jenoff had given them with what they knew about Carol's murder. They quickly became confident that after all their years of searching and wondering, they finally had their hitmen. Despite the enthusiasm that had now reinvigorated the dormant investigation, there was one more hurdle that had to be cleared before police could start making formal arrests.

Jenoff had confessed, and he'd implicated Daniels, but prosecutors realized that all the physical evidence from the murder was long gone. From a legal standpoint, there was absolutely nothing other than Jenoff's say-so that tied Daniels to the crime.

To get around that deficiency, the investigators decided to try a sting. Detectives picked up Jenoff, now 54, and Paul Daniels, now 27 and living in an apartment in Pennsauken, and brought them in to the Cherry Hill police station. Jenoff, wearing two concealed police microphones, was left in a holding room with Daniels, where he carried out a theatrical discussion with his dazed younger friend, telling him that it was the rabbi who had given their names to police and gotten them hauled in for questioning. At first, Daniels was reluctant to tell the police anything, saying over and over that he didn't want to go to jail, but finally—when Jenoff continued to insist that only an immediate confession would prevent the rabbi from sticking them with the blame, and getting off scot-free—Daniels agreed to join Jenoff in admitting to the killing.

In separate interviews with groups of detectives, Jenoff and Daniels began telling their stories, stories of lives that had slid far off the rails and then collided head-on with the life of a woman whom neither man had spoken to before they showed up at her house to kill her. After the long, twisted, and bizarre tales were told to the detectives, and the tape recorders in the nondescript interview rooms were clicked off, Jenoff and Daniels were lodged overnight at the Camden County Jail pending their arraignment the next day. They would both be charged with murder and conspiracy to commit murder, and ordered held without bail pending the trial of Rabbi Fred Neulander.

Neulander had been scheduled to go on trial in June, but this new development was obviously a show-stopper. It was clear that the trial would have to be moved back several months, and that when it did resume, Fred Neulander would be facing the death penalty . . . making him potentially the first member of the clergy to be executed in New Jersey's long history.

CHAPTER SEVENTEEN

To the public watching the case unfold in the headlines, it looked like Len Jenoff had ruined any chance Fred Neulander had of saying he wasn't involved in Carol's death. After all, this was a confession, not a tip; and how could Jenoff have known these insider details if things hadn't happened the way he was now reporting? Normally, that line of reasoning would make for an open-and-shut assumption of truthfulness; however, the main problem with the confession was that it was coming from Len Jenoff, and six years after the fact.

It would have been one thing if Jenoff had confessed six hours after the murder, when few other people knew the specific details of the crime scene. However, Jenoff was a private investigator, and even though he worked out of his bedroom with the aid of psychics, he still had managed to gain solid access to just about everyone involved in the case, including Fred Neulander. On the one hand, what he was saying sounded very much like the inside scoop from a hitman who had been there, but on the other hand, he'd had six years to insert and embellish any details he wanted to add, and make them fit with the facts and the time-line.

Neulander's defense would ultimately hinge on the question of who was the bigger liar: a religious leader who was willing to have sex with his mistress right in his office at the synagogue he'd worked decades to build and consecrate; or a man who carried around a forged note from the President of the United States and liked to imply that he had killed communists in Nicaragua for the CIA, even though the closest he'd ever gotten to the region was a vacation in Puerto Vallarta, Mexico.

Both sides of the Neulander case knew that Len Jenoff was not an inherently credible person. He had lied about any number of things over the years, he had exaggerated even more, and his record as a private investigator was checkered with numerous run-ins with the legal system and private firms, because he had repeatedly pushed the limits of situational ethics into the red zone.

Hitmen don't usually get a receipt for their services, so even if Jenoff testified that Fred Neulander had hired him to kill Carol, it was still going to require more proof. Normally a jury might take someone's word for something like that—after all, why would they lie? But with Len Jenoff, lying seemed to be part of the territory. What he had to say about Neulander's actions and motive certainly looked compelling as narrative, but to a jury, it had to be compelling beyond a reasonable doubt. And there were lots of reasons people might doubt Len Jenoff.

Wixted and Zucker wasted no time in zeroing their sights in on Jenoff's record of past transgressions and exaggerations.

Len Jenoff was a poser and a fraud in most of his dealings, and he had admitted to killing a woman he didn't know for idiotic reasons. But even though a lot of people had cause not to like him, in May 2000, there was a point where a careful look at Jenoff's background revealed a reason, if not to sympathize with him, then at least to understand how he had gotten to be quite so pathetic.

Jenoff had been born and raised in Atlantic City, New Jersey. Once the playground of Philadelphia society, with the famous Boardwalk that had been immortalized along with the city's streets in the game Monopoly, the city had plunged through a harrowing cycle of decline with the advent of commercial air travel. The upscale tourists who once flocked to the Jersey shore spent decades jetting off to even more exotic destinations, leaving an economic vacuum in what had once been their premier vacation spot. But Atlantic City surged back to life almost overnight following the 1976 referendum in which New Jersey voters decided to legalize gambling there.

Jenoff went to school at Monmouth College in central New Jersey, but hadn't graduated. In September of 1966, the height of the Vietnam War, he joined the Army Reserves, cooking for them one weekend a month until he was honorably discharged from the service in 1972. In the meantime, he began a meandering career that sometimes involved detective work and sometimes didn't. Beginning as an insurance adjuster and claims investigator for Tremotion Union Insurance in 1966, he moved on a year later to work at a company called International Data Processing Institute on North Broad Street in Philadelphia. After that, he sold Yellow Pages advertising for a Bell Atlantic contractor called National Telephone Directory for two years.

It was while he was working at NTD that Jenoff met and married his first wife in March 1970. She was an Irish Catholic with a five-year-old son from a previous marriage. This first go at the altar would end just four and a half months later in a messy divorce.

Jenoff's parents didn't like the sound of the sudden and acrimonious breakup, and they urged Len to get out of Philadelphia and rejoin them down in Baltimore while things settled down. So in July of 1970 he moved in with them to get a new start. He lived there right up until his second marriage in December 1972. Jenoff and his second wife eventually had a son, Martin, and this period would be one of the more stable in Jenoff's rather chaotic life. His father got Len a job in the company that he had founded, the Data Processing Institute of Baltimore, which taught students key punch data techniques in the earliest days of the computer revolution. Len quickly became a vice president. While working in the office building which housed DPI, he later told police, Jenoff befriended a lawyer in another office who, he claimed, unbeknownst to him, was an associate of a Jewish underworld figure. Jenoff said that he ended up being a paid informant for the Baltimore Police Department Intelligence Unit during those years as he passed information on about the men's activities and associates. Jenoff stayed with DPI for four years until his father died in January 1975.

Jenoff began once again to drift through jobs, selling pharmaceuticals and then x-ray film to hospitals for G.A.F Medical X-ray. In 1978, with a one-year-old baby at home, Jenoff got another job, this time with Arcata, a microfilm manufacturer, who moved him back to New Jersey to cover their sales territory there. A year later, in 1979, with his background at his father's computer company, Jenoff landed back in Philadelphia with a job as sales director for Control Data Corporation in Philadelphia at 15th and Walnut downtown.

By this time, gambling had been legalized in Atlantic City, and in 1980, Jenoff came down with a case of casino fever. He told police that he had befriended several casino executives. "It's not what you know, it's who you know that gets you the good jobs there," Jenoff noted, and sure enough, when the opportunity arose, his friends at the Golden Nugget gave him a call and got him in at the Playboy Casino in Atlantic City. Eleven months later, Jenoff changed jobs across town and began working at the Resorts International casino. Five months later he was out the door again.

Jenoff was finally going into business for himself, and, armed with a New Jersey state junket license, he began putting together the bus and airline package trips to Atlantic City that fuel the huge river of cash that flows onto Boardwalk every day. The streets might all still have the names from the Monopoly board game, but any accurate reflection of modern values in Atlantic City would have to be about building hotels and casinos—not houses and hotels.

As an independent licensed junketeer, Jenoff spent several years earning a respectable living and working for himself, gaining commissions on every graying head he packed onto a bus and rolled into the doors of a casino. He was enjoying his longest period of career stability to date, but it all came apart in a squeal of brakes on Route 73 in Maple Shade on a warm night in the summer of 1986.

Jenoff recounted the incident a decade later to Cherry Hill homicide detectives. "I was coming home late, I can't recall from where, and there was a small car, like a real small Pinto, with, I believe, three kids in it, all eighteen years old," Jenoff began. "I was heading southbound on Route 73. They were coming northbound and their car became disabled. They started pushing it into the northbound lane. They were wearing dark clothes. The car had no headlights. I didn't see them until it was too late. I hit them head-on, and immediately took the life of an eighteen-year-old kid," Jenoff whispered.

The Maple Shade Police Department, the New Jersey State Police, the Burlington County Prosecutor's Office, and the state Department of Motor Vehicles all took a hard look at Jenoff's role in the fatal accident, and all exonerated him, Jenoff said. He was never charged with any wrongdoing. But the official clearance didn't help Jenoff. He sought counseling the next day, and he also started drinking. The counseling didn't seem to help with the pain and anguish Jenoff felt—but the drinking did, and soon he was imbibing heavily. He drank every day, and his once stable job began to become erratic; his work suffered, his wife suffered, and Martin had to put up with a father who was drunk for at least some portion of every day.

The death had obviously been nothing more than an accident, so clearly not Jenoff's fault that he had never even been charged in connection with it. But still, by all accounts, it had shattered Jenoff's life.

Jenoff's neighbor at the Cypress Court condominium in Marlton was Joe Alfieri, a printer, who remembered Jenoff coming over for the next three years and crying about the boy's death. Jenoff tried several times to reach the boy's parents and express his regret for what had happened, but when he was rebuffed, he spiraled further and further into guilt and depression.

The junketing business was too time-consuming for someone who was drinking heavily, and it soon slipped away. Jenoff drifted back into private detective work and kept getting paychecks. For four years, between 1988 and 1991, he worked odd jobs for Holmes High Tech detective agency in Northfield, New Jersey. His bogus CIA connections had helped earn him the job with the firm, which was run by an ex–New Jersey state trooper. But as the 1990s dawned, it became clear that Jenoff was anything but consistently sober, and he was fired.

Jenoff continued drinking, and his marriage began to disintegrate. Week after week Alfieri would print another batch of business cards as Jenoff careened from one unsuccessful attempt to restart his life to another.

Jenoff's drinking went from bad, to worse, to out of control, and in 1991, his wife had had enough. She left with their son in a separation that Jenoff later recounted to detectives as having had as much to do with Judiasm as it did that he was a drunk.

"My wife had come from a rather religious Jewish family. Conservative, bordering on orthodox," Jenoff explained. "She was certainly conservative, leaning towards orthodox, and in the Jewish religion, it's very much shameful or frowned upon if you become an alcoholic or a drunk, and I'm sure she was getting her ears full from her parents and her brother about how I couldn't keep a job because I was always drunk. My son, who was in his early teens, always saw me drunk and always throwing up. I tried selling cars, but I couldn't keep a job. She'd had enough, and basically, when she left me, she said that I was just a very sick Jewish drunk, and I became a disgrace to her and her family."

With his wife and son back in Maryland and living with her mother, Jenoff stayed in Marlton and wandered alone through what had been their four-bedroom house, continuing to drink his time away as bills piled higher and creditors began to systematically shut down the components of his crumbling life.

He didn't pay the mortgage, and the house went into foreclosure. He didn't pay Bell Atlantic, and they shut off his phone. He didn't pay his utility bills, and they shut off his gas and electric power. Jenoff had a driver's license, but his car was towed. He had visitation rights, but no means of going to see his son a state away.

It was December of 1991, and at age 46, Len Jenoff knew that he was at rock bottom. But when people would listen to him, he would tell them that he had once worked for the CIA or the FBI, and some measure of respect for the rumpled figure in front of them would be restored.

Jenoff's life drifted and meandered along, but no matter where it took him or how he strove to correct past mistakes, he couldn't bring himself to drop the CIA story. It was the only part of his past he really felt proud of—even though it wasn't true.

"I never had a life," Jenoff later explained to detectives. "I never had a career like my older brother. I have a brother three and a half years older than me, you know, immediately developed a career with insurance and got respected. He climbed up the ladder. And I was always

job to job. I felt always, my whole life, like I was worthless. I had no self-esteem, no self-respect, and I created
this whole, like, new identity for myself. A fantasy identity, and I was pretty good at doing that. I knew the right
buzzwords and I knew how to have documentation that
made it look like I was real."

Jenoff had been going to Alcoholics Anonymous
meetings, and he told his friend that he wasn't happy
with his having become a "Jewish drunk," but he didn't
think his religion had been there to support him when
he was down.

Jenoff was trying desperately to get into Oxford
House—a rehabilitation and treatment center—but he
needed five hundred dollars to pay for admission to the
program. He approached Jewish Family Services, who
interviewed him, rejected his request, and then, adding
insult to injury, suggested that he go see Catholic Charities for the money. Jenoff later told the story to Richard
Hyland, an attorney he knew who happened to be Catholic, and who thought the whole thing was amusing. "I
didn't think it was funny. It made me very resentful toward my religion and my people, to the point, where I
said some pretty profound things, like 'Fuck my religion,' and that upset him [Hyland], so, unbeknownst to
me, he went to two Jewish people that were of influence,
a doctor and an attorney, and they were on the Board of
Directors of Jewish Family Services, and when they
heard the story that my own people rejected me and sent
me to the Catholics, they went ballistic and said, 'Go
back to JFC,' and that time they gave me the five hundred," Jenoff told the police.

In March of 1992 Jenoff had gotten into Oxford
House. His financial life was still in shreds, but in a rare
stroke of good luck, a lawyer who had befriended him
helped Len sell his house, avoiding a nasty foreclosure.
With that lingering issue cleared up, Jenoff slowly began
to return to the working world. He started with a mini-

mum wage job at Denny's, exchanged that job a few
weeks later for a stint behind the wheel as a cab driver
in Gloucester County, and then began working as a bill
collector for $6.50 an hour. That was big money com-
pared to what he had been making, but six months later,
he started working for a company called Legal Concepts,
serving subpoenas and surveying accident scenes, and in
that way he returned to the world of private investigation.

In June 1993, Jenoff obtained a New Jersey private
investigator's license and began working for additional
attorneys' offices as "Len Jenoff Associates," a licensed
and bonded detective agency.

Jenoff may not have had a particularly successful
life except on paper, but, as he explained to investigators
years later, the lie became his truth.

"I created a pretty good résumé. It was a reality. I
became that person, I mean, I'd even stopped using
'Leonard.' It was *Len* Jenoff, former CIA. I believed it,"
Jenoff told detectives shortly after his arrest for Carol's
murder. "I believed it, and I got the whole world to
believe it. When I started my own business around 1995,
I created this nice résumé, and every time I got a new
law firm to hire me, I would add them on the law firm
list on my résumé, and it mushroomed to the point that
I probably had seventy-five nice law firms that have been
giving me work up until last week."

Some of the jobs went well, but others questioned
Jenoff's tactics, and one attorney fired him on the spot
when Jenoff proposed sending a man who claimed to
have a bad back a disguised package full of bricks. The
attorney told Jenoff that he was looking for the truth,
and didn't want to hurt the man if he really did have a
back injury.

Every time Jenoff started to pick up little pieces of
his life, he seemed to run afoul again of his religion. In
Oxford House, someone who was trying to be helpful

brought him a book about dealing with Judaism and issues such as drug, alcohol, and sexual abuse. The friend thought it would probably be uplifting, but when Jenoff read it, he discovered that the book, which he said was sanctioned by the Reform movement rabbis, basically said that God didn't listen to the prayers of alcoholics. "It was stuff that just, like, made me more ashamed, and made me feel like I was a worthless piece of shit," Jenoff said. "Jewish people didn't want to lend me the five hundred dollars of their own free will. I was pretty much saying, 'The hell with my religion,' you know, 'I'll give up Judaism.'"

Then one day, out of the blue, Len Jenoff received a phone call that would literally change his life forever.

Jenoff had complained to his lawyer friends that he felt let down by Judaism, that even though he had spent ten years paying dues at a temple when he was married, the rabbi had had little interest in him. Friends picked up on his deep conflict about being a Jew and how much it meant to him, and explained his situation to someone they thought could help.

When Len Jenoff met Rabbi Fred Neulander, he was simply in awe. After a lifetime spent out of synch with his religion and on the fringes of society, Len Jenoff suddenly felt as welcome as any upstanding member of the congregation.

Years later, sitting in a room surrounded by detectives in the Camden County Prosecutor's Office as he confessed to murder, Jenoff would remember the fateful phone call he picked up that day in the rehab center. "I get a call and the man identifies himself as Fred Neulander. 'I'm the rabbi at M'kor Shalom.' He said he understands that I'm kind of, like, hurting, and I have a lot of Jewish issues, and, I remember he didn't ask me, it was like he demanded that I be in his office on Wednesday at 9 A.M. And he told me where this place was. I know it had to be after July of '92, because I bought this old piece-of-shit junk car so I was able to drive to M'kor Shalom. I had never been there my whole life.

"I never had any relationship with any rabbi before, even when my former wife and I paid dues for ten years. The most I would get with any rabbi was five minutes, 'Hello, good-bye,' I never had a rabbi hug me or spend more than ten minutes with me," Jenoff explained to the detectives.

"I show up at nine A.M. at M'kor Shalom. Four secretaries were sitting there, they knew of my arrival. They offered me coffee. They were nice to me. I waited maybe five, ten minutes, and I was sitting there looking down this long hallway when I see this man come out, kinda short. I can't recall what he was wearing, but he wasn't wearing a jacket, 'cause it wasn't like I felt intimidated. He, maybe had on a shirt and tie or bow tie, but he walks up to me, says, 'I'm . . .' he didn't say *Rabbi*, he said, 'I'm Fred Neulander,' and he gave me, like, this warm handshake. I started like getting chills, like, 'Cool!' you know, and he said, 'Come on back, we'll talk for a while,' and I remember him saying to one of the four secretaries to hold all calls. . . .

"I had this secret I kept all my life. To me it was like a sin." It was a secret that had haunted a man who would spend so much of his life haunted by secrets. Only his mother, father, and brother knew it, but Leonard Jenoff had never been bar mitzvahed.

Most Jewish males are bar mitzvahed at age thirteen; it's a ceremony that signifies a boy has become a man in the eyes of the Jewish faith, and Jenoff felt that much less of a man for having skipped his. He didn't dare tell his secret to his religiously conservative second wife, and he made a major effort to ensure that their son was properly bar mitzvahed. The ceremony is both a solemn event and usually accompanied by a lavish celebratory party, and Jenoff wanted to make sure his son Marty had the full package. Even though he wasn't making his regular mortgage payments at the time because of his drinking, Jenoff went out in June of 1990 and put a second mortgage on his family's house at 22 percent interest to get the extra $10,000 he needed to throw a big bar mitzvah party at the Cherry Hill Inn.

"I was obsessed with my son preparing for his bar mitzvah," Jenoff confessed to the detectives. "I was giving him what I never had, but I never told him or my wife why. I had that shame that I couldn't read Hebrew. I carried that shame with me and now the Rabbi Neulander pulls me back into this office. It was really a neat office. He tells me to sit down and relax, but I'm sure he took, he made me feel comfortable and at first he was sitting behind this huge beautiful red desk with neat ornaments and stuff, and I'm sitting on the sofa . . . then after a while he would come over and sit next to me and hold my hand and, this might sound stupid, I'm certainly not gay, but it was like instant love. This man just knew how to push every button,'cause I was so . . . I had nothing in my life, nothing in my life. My wife had left me in disgrace, took my son away from me. Never bar mitzvahed. I was a Jewish alcoholic. I had no money, no job. I was physically hurt. I did, from being drunk and falling down, I had physical hurt."

Neulander started putting Jenoff's shattered self-esteem back together piece by piece. He told Jenoff, to Len's great relief, that the bar mitzvah ceremony was actually something that Judaism had only developed as a tradition four or five hundred years before. None of the biblical Jews had been bar mitzvahed and Neulander said that Jenoff didn't need to be so worked up about it either. Still, he knew it was important to Len, and he got him enrolled in the Hebrew classes it took to participate in the ceremonial reading of the Torah scrolls. Eventually Jenoff went through the ceremony, finally crossing a deep mark of personal shame off of his lifelong list of things to worry about.

The rabbi was a busy person, he was an important person, he had a fancy office and a staff, but he made time for Len Jenoff. He invited him to sit and chat with him, he listened intently as Jenoff spun his usual fables of unloading arms off planes on remote jungle airstrips for the Nicaraguan Contras, and crawling through Vietnamese rice paddies with the fabled Studies and Observations Group. If Neulander doubted any of these *Men's Adventure* tales, he never let on.

"It seemed like a minute, but it was like three hours. When I walked out, I realized it was like noon, and he's walking out the hallway, showing, walking me to the door, he's now hugging me. I'm like twisting, turning in my head thinking that if I had paid the previous rabbis hundreds of dollars, I couldn't have gotten three hours from a rabbi," Jenoff told the detectives, adding quickly, "It sounds terrible. This sounds very terrible, and I know this is going to offend a lot of people. So, forgive me, but see, sometimes with the Jewish religion you almost have to like pay for what you get, like I've been to a lot of church services. They'll pass the basket. You got a buck, you got a five . . . The Jewish religion's different. You don't give every service. You write checks out every quarter, and your amount of check almost determines how much of a relationship you have with the rabbi, and respect . . ."

Unlike Christian churches, which are in the habit of passing a plate down the pews and hoping for the best, synagogues typically have a much more stable financial structure. The synagogue's board figures out an annual budget and then assesses membership dues to each family that belongs. With his life and finances in tatters, Jenoff couldn't contribute his share, but Neulander not only waived his fee, he practically ordered Jenoff to sit unapologetically in the front row each Friday evening

Sabbath service, and to participate in the life of the congregation as a full-fledged member.

"... here this guy was hugging me and giving me time like I was a million-dollar donor. I just immediately felt cap, cap, captuated," Jenoff struggled for the word.

"Captivated?" a detective offered.

"Captivated by this man's charisma, already, he started treating me like a good person," Jenoff continued.

"Okay, so it was pretty heady stuff for a first meeting?" the detective prompted.

"Yes, sir," Jenoff agreed, adding, "He would sit next to me on the sofa, and he said to me, almost like demanding, 'I know you have no money, but you are part of this congregation. I want you to come on Friday nights. I'll introduce you to people. I will start helping you,' and he started telling me that I am, I, I'm as much, I'm as Jewish as the people, and he would point, like," Jenoff mimed Neulander's firm demeanor, waving his finger, "'I'm as Jewish as the people that give a million dollars a year, which I had trouble accepting, but he started immediately building my esteem and said, 'I want to see you Friday nights, and at least once a week, you call and make an appointment for counseling, and I'm not looking for one penny from you.'"

The three-hour meeting with Rabbi Neulander in 1992 was in many ways a new beginning for Len Jenoff, but at the same time, he missed his biggest opportunity to truly make a break with his past. Before the first meeting between the two men ended, Jenoff had once again compulsively trotted out the same old stapled-together patchwork of lies about his past as a CIA agent who had spiraled over the abyss in his personal life, in part because he had been asked to do dire, unspeakable—and unspecified—things for his country.

During his confession at the prosecutor's office in May 2000, Jenoff would still remember it vividly. "I'm there. I'm confessing to this man about not having a bar mitzvah and how I can't speak Hebrew and, yet, now I'm lying 'cause I, I, it's the only thing I knew how to do, saying that my alcoholism was caused by my CIA career," Jenoff said.

Senior Investigator Martin Devlin pressed the point with Jenoff: "Did you tell him, when you lied to him, did you tell him that you had done terrible things for the CIA?"

"Yes," Jenoff sighed.

"Did you tell him you had done murder for the CIA?" Devlin continued.

"Yes."

"Did you tell him that you were involved with covert operations for the CIA against other countries?"

"Yes, specifically Iran–Contra," Jenoff said, adding, "I said that I was like one of the big shots."

"And why did you tell him that?" Devlin wondered.

"I remember when that was going on I was reading about it, and it was just, like, something where I got a lot of those books, like when the Tower Commission report came out in the Oliver North story, and it was like I could talk the talk, you know," Jenoff explained, adding, "I would never say, like, I knew Colonel North, but I was one of the key people."

"Well, let me ask you this," Devlin continued. "While you were telling him these, these lies, and this was just during the course of a conversation, the first meeting–type conversation, but he made you feel comfortable enough and you were in awe of him . . . and you told him these lies. In your opinion, was he buying it?"

"Oh, yes. Oh, yes," Jenoff replied.

"And when you told him you did murder for the government, what did he say on the first meeting?" Devlin asked.

"He never said anything verbally, but he would, like, look at me and, like, shake his head like he was listening to everything I said, but these were lies. I had never, you know, robbed or murdered anybody," Jenoff said.

"Right. Okay, so after you left there and he had told you he had wanted you there every Friday night and at least once during the week, did that happen?"

"Yes," Jenoff answered.

"Okay, and the relationship got stronger?"

"Yes, sir."

"And the, uh, the feelings you had for him grew?"

"Again, I'm homosex . . . uh, I'm *not* homosexual," Jenoff began haltingly.

"Right," Devlin reassured him.

"But I fell in love with this man," Jenoff continued.

"Okay. All right."

"I had lost my father already," Jenoff tried to explain, adding, "And I never had a close relationship with my brother. He became like my rabbi. He even said, 'I am your rabbi.' He was my rabbi and my father and my confidant . . . everything wrapped up in one."

"And the truth of the matter is, at that particular time in your life, you had no one . . . and your wife and your son were in Baltimore," Devlin noted.

"Right," Jenoff sighed. "She had divorced me by then, and what was even more shameful, I forgot to mention, on the actual divorce documents, like, Cause of Divorce said 'habitual drunkenness,' and that was so shameful—habitual drunkenness—especially when I found out the legal definition of it is, drunk every day for three hundred and sixty-five days a year."

Although few people paid much attention to Neulander and Jenoff together, the mere fact that Neulander had devoted considerable time to such a sad case, and worked hard to welcome him into the Jewish community, would not have surprised the rabbi's friends and supporters in the least. This was exactly the Rabbi Neulander they knew, a caring, patient, powerful presence who loved his community and thought the best of people. If the rabbi took pains to help even Len Jenoff, then that was no less than what those who had come to admire Fred Neulander so deeply would have expected.

For nearly two years after they first met, Fred Neulander made time to be a genuine friend and mentor to Len Jenoff. Jenoff began to feel like a responsible person again; his business grew, and he moved into a new apartment with a pair of roommates he had met in the Oxford House rehab center. Butted up against the New Jersey turnpike and Route 70, the Landmark Towers weren't the most prestigious address in this affluent township, and the young schizophrenic loner named Paul Michael Daniels wasn't the most engaging of companions for the gregarious and fanciful Jenoff, but it was an apartment that he could afford, and he took pride in being able to make the regular payments.

Jenoff felt a deep loyalty to Neulander, and he was amazed by the rabbi's continued generosity towards him. He also felt increasingly beholden to the man who had gone out of his way so many times to help him over various hurdles that most people could breeze right past in their lives, but which, to someone in Jenoff's struggling circumstances, were major events—like parking tickets:

"I was still, like, drunk. I was collecting welfare and food stamps from Cherry Hill Township, and I was going to Alcoholics Anonymous regularly," Jenoff remembered. "In March of 1993, we had this AA convention at the Cherry Hill Hilton, and somehow I inadvertently parked my car half into the handicap space, and I come out and I get this hundred-dollar handicap parking ticket. Somehow I was talking, the next day or something, to the rabbi that I got this hundred-dollar handicap ticket, and he didn't say nothing. He just listened to me. A few days later I'm talking to him, and he hands me an envelope, which I still have to this day. He always would use green felt-tip pens, and it said something like, 'Dear Lenny—Be careful where you park,' and there was a hundred-dollar bill in there. I naturally took the hundred-dollar bill, but I still have that letter. All of this was like, 'My God! Look what this man's doing for me!'

"He was my father, my brother, my best friend, my confidant, and he's giving me self-respect and self-esteem. I'm going to the synagogue on Friday nights and he has me sit in the first row. When it was his night to do, like, the sermon, he always had this thing, there's a Jewish expression called '*shtik,*' routine, where he would come in almost like a, uh, uh, comedian and he would start shaking hands, kissing the babies, holding the babies, and there were people he would want to point out. I was sitting there, and he would lean in, and none of these Jewish people knew me, but when he started leaning in shaking my hand and hugging and kissing me, all these rich Jews looked at me like, Wow! I must be important. You know what that did to my ego? Huh? You know, it's like I was looking at all these people like, 'Your rabbi knows me!,' " Jenoff recalled, still honored by the impression that Fred Neulander had gone out of his way to make on Len's behalf.

Neulander smoked, but he didn't want the kids in M'kor Shalom's school programs to look out the window and see him standing behind the buildings taking a drag on a cigarette, so he invited Jenoff to accompany him on walks through the woods behind the synagogue complex on Evesham Road. On their walks, Jenoff would inevitably keep up the fiction that he had trapped himself into on the very first day the men had met. Jenoff told Neulander that if it hadn't been for his drinking and his association with the Iran–Contra scandal that had caused such a headache for the Reagan administration, he could have been one of the CIA's directors, not just a lonely alcoholic. Jenoff lamented that it was a shame that at age 46, someone with his depth of experience and record of service to the nation would never be taken back into the fold at the Central Intelligence Agency.

Jenoff told the detectives when he confessed that he was convinced the rabbi bought every word of it. Neulander's trust and interest in what Jenoff had to say was apparently one of the reasons Jenoff found it so hard to stop lying. Jenoff valued this new friendship too much to risk admitting that he had been lying from day one.

In all the reading he had picked through over the years about the CIA, looking for tidbits that he could appropriate for his own fantasy persona, Len Jenoff had seen any number of items about the CIA's counterpart in Israel—the Mossad.

One day, in one of their walks through the woods, the Mossad came up in conversation, and it occured to Jenoff that the covert agency could be a new home for him. He turned to Neulander and asked if the rabbi knew anyone connected to the organization, perhaps among influential Israelis living in Philadelphia. Jenoff said that Neulander's reply was that yes, he did know such people. Jenoff then suggested that, once he got his life back together, maybe he could interview for a position with that organization. He later recalled to detectives that Neulander said something could happen, given Len's extensive covert background.

Why either man would think that a former CIA agent would need a suburban New Jersey rabbi's help to make contact with Israeli intelligence apparently wasn't brought up; Jenoff simply claimed that Neulander expressed enthusiasm for the idea.

From the moment this version of Jenoff's story was released, Neulander's attorneys vehemently denied that their client had ever said anything of the sort to Len Jenoff.

Taken at face value, the alleged conversation that Jenoff laid out for the detectives during his confession sounded almost comical, but in the months and years to come, people's lives would ultimately hinge on the bizarre exchange.

First of all, the simple fact of the matter was that Len Jenoff hadn't worked for the CIA. He hadn't even swept the parking lot at the Langley, Virginia, headquarters building, and this would have been immediately evident to the Mossad.

Second, the notion that rabbis are likely to have contact with the Mossad just because they have a strong affinity for Israel is as plausible as assuming that Episcopal priests are likely to have connections within Britain's MI-6.

What also made the conversation, as Jenoff described it, particularly dubious was that any real former CIA agent would have known that working with the Israeli intelligence service without the CIA's prior permission would be illegal in the extreme. When former US intelligence agents go to work here at home for other governments' intelligence services, even those belonging to governments who are friends and allies of the United States, it's not called "a second career"—it's called spying, and is prosecuted by the FBI's Counterintelligence Division to the fullest extent of the law. Try the same stunt overseas, and you are a double agent. The only real difference is that you get tracked down and handled by the CIA's very own counterintelligence officers.

These prohibitions don't just apply to former CIA agents. Any ordinary American citizen could be prosecuted for espionage, if not treason, if they slipped so much as one classified US government document to even the Canadians.

If Neulander did casually suggest that he could get Jenoff a job with the Mossad, then the rabbi was effectively asking him if he'd like to join up with a very small fraternity of traitors that includes convicted Israeli spy— and former American citizen—Jonathan Pollard, who is currently serving a life sentence in a federal prison for abusing his position in the US Navy to obtain classified information for Jerusalem.

Despite the inherent ridiculousness of the discussion, Jenoff insisted that in late 1993 and early 1994, he and Rabbi Neulander began a series of conversations about whether or not Jenoff loved Israel enough to join the Mossad.

Then one day it happened. Jenoff later described to the detectives what he recalled as the turning point: "I said I would do anything in the world to work for Israel and Mossad, and one day we—I'll never forget this— we were smoking, and he looked at me and we were walking, but he took me, he kind of, like, grabbed my elbow and made us stop walking, and then he looked at me very sternly. He said, 'Would you die for the state of Israel?' And I said, 'Yes.' And we took a few more steps, a few more puffs on our cigarettes, and he stopped me and he looked at me again. He says, 'Would you kill to defend the state of Israel?' And I said, 'Yes, you mean, Rabbi, you mean like working for Mossad?' And he said, 'Yes.' And I said, 'Yes then I would.' "

According to Jenoff, it was a simple yes to a question that would forever alter his life. "So what happened was, when I said yes to killing or dying for Israel, he then kind of like tapped my forearm and looked at me and says, 'Well, then maybe you can do it—do me a favor one day.' And I remember, as clear as it was yesterday, I said, 'Anything I can do to repay you, Rabbi, and that's where he left at that conversation."

When 1994 began, Rabbi Neulander would do Len Jenoff another major favor—one that Len pointed to with great pride amongst his circle of recovering alcoholic friends. Jenoff told Neulander that it was ironic that he and the other Jewish Alcoholics Anonymous members were spending each night of the week in different churches that gave them space. Jenoff asked if it would be possible for the group to meet once a week at the synagogue. Neulander met with the M'kor Shalom board, and soon had approval to let Len's AA group meet weekly in one of the conference rooms. Jenoff was bowled over. Instead of giving them some folding chairs in a corner of a church basement, M'kor Shalom gave them a board room with padded seats, air conditioning, and an eighty-cup coffee urn for their use.

Jenoff remembered it as being around March 1, 1994, after the AA meetings were up and running each Tuesday night, that Rabbi Neulander once again brought up the possibility of Jenoff doing him a favor. "Right around when we got the AA and, man, I'm hooked, uh, hooked on this guy. He said, 'Remember our talks about the Mossad and our talks about Israel?' and I said, 'Yes?' He said, 'Remember I asked you if would you die or kill for Israel?' I said, 'Yes.' He says, 'Do you mean it?' and I said, 'Yes. Did you mean it?' and he said, 'Well, I have a problem.' I said, 'Can I help you, Rabbi? What can I do for you?' "

According to Jenoff, Neulander began to talk about "a person" who was "an enemy of the state of Israel." At the same time, Jenoff said, Neulander began giving him the names of people he could see in Philadelphia who would eventually get him into the Mossad. According to Jenoff, the rabbi didn't link the two items directly, and Jenoff got the impression that the person Neulander had in mind was more of a threat to the local Jewish community than to Tel Aviv per se. Allegedly, Neulander implied that if Jenoff could handle this local threat, it would impress the Mossad agents and improve his chances of being recruited. Jenoff said that Neulander implied he should " 'show these people you have balls and I know they'll take you,' or something like that."

The pair continued their conversation as they walked and smoked their way through the woods. Jenoff said the rabbi became more and more specific about what had to happen to this enemy of Israel. "He said that this person has to be stopped, has to be stopped, and I'm looking and I'm shaking my head in agreement, and he said, 'Now, remember those stories you told me of what you did with the CIA? Do you think you could remove this person?' and I said, 'What do you mean by "taken care of"?' He said 'You know—like removed.' I said, 'Removed like with prejudice?'—it's, like, an intelligence term—and he said, 'Yes. Taken care of—killed.' And I said, 'If I can.' All of a sudden, now, I'm getting scared, 'cause now he's calling my bluff on all my tough-guy lies."

Jenoff told the detectives that the pair walked on, and kept smoking for a couple minutes until suddenly Neulander stopped Jenoff again. Staring intently, Neulander said, "Am I scaring you?" Jenoff covered for his internal turmoil. "Oh, no." "Am I talking to the wrong man?" Neulander pressed. "He was like baiting me, and at that point, I was afraid to say yes, 'cause, I was afraid to say, 'Yes, you're talking to the wrong man.' I, I had owed the man, this rabbi so much," Jenoff would later confess, continuing, "And I was still, like, I was, 'Here I'm still bullshitting about this fucking agent, secret agent shit.'

"He said, 'Should I continue with the conversation? Am I talking to the right man?' And I said, 'Yes. You are talking to the right man,'" Jenoff later recalled.

Jenoff said that Neulander left the conversation there, but said they should talk again in a few weeks' time. In the meantime, Jenoff said, Neulander gave him the names of some people he could talk to who were connected to the Mossad.

But for somebody who liked to tell people that he was a secret agent, Jenoff had a remarkable inability to keep his mouth shut. As Cherry Hill Investigator Devlin later led Jenoff through questioning, Len admitted that he'd told several people that his rabbi was busy hooking him up with a new job in the Mossad. In fact, in those heady days during the summer of 1994, Jenoff was not only telling close friends about his efforts to join a foreign intelligence service, he was busy telling friends of his who were police officers. He even went so far as to tell an FBI agent in Baltimore!

Jenoff told Devlin and the other detectives that his FBI agent friend had been very interested in Jenoff's new career choice and met with Len two or three times to discuss it. It never occurred to Jenoff that he had told the very people who spend their days trying to root out foreign spies on US territory that he was in the process of interviewing for a job with a foreign intelligence service. The fact that his FBI friend was curious about who the rabbi had put Jenoff in touch with was hardly surprising.

Jenoff said he met the "Israeli tough guys" who were supposedly connected to the Mossad in the Blue Moon Jazz Club in Philadelphia, as well as at a club owned by several Israelis called Delilah's Den.

Jenoff later told Cherry Hill investigators that on two occasions his FBI friend had decided to tag along and meet Len's new friends. In fact, several days after the murder of Carol Neulander, Jenoff's contact in the FBI called and wanted to collect some more information about Fred Neulander, but Jenoff, "scared to death," said he had nothing to say, and hung up on the agent.

CHAPTER EIGHTEEN

THE whole Mossad pantomime seemed to fade as the summer of 1994 dragged on. But a few weeks later, Jenoff said, Neulander was back to the topic of "eliminating" this mysterious enemy of Israel. Slowly, according to Jenoff's confession, the rabbi became more specific. The target was going to be an Israeli woman who was out to destroy the rabbi and the local Jewish community.

Jenoff told Devlin that Neulander began asking about how Jenoff would kill this woman if he were with the CIA. Jenoff began to spin tales of dribbling antifreeze in drinks and a chemical called resenic acid that he had heard would be untraceable after death. The antifreeze idea was from a newspaper article he had read in Baltimore, and the acid idea was taken from the babblings of an elderly drunk he had met at an AA meeting. The rabbi allegedly liked the acid idea, but Jenoff first said he would need a few weeks to obtain it, and later told the rabbi that he couldn't get any.

Jenoff told Devlin that he was already committed to the "assassination" when, in August 1994, he eventually learned who was to be the target. Jenoff said that Neulander had waved him over to his Acura one day and said, "Let's go for a ride." The rabbi drove over to Wexford Leas and pointed out his house on Highgate Lane—which Jenoff had never seen before—and told Jenoff that the person to be killed was Carol.

"He never told me why. He just told me that it was something evil, something that she could destroy his life.

Totally destroy his life and in destroying his life, she would, in fact, be destroying the Cherry Hill Jewish community. That she was a very evil woman," Jenoff told detectives.

"Did you say anything to him like, 'Well, I thought it was for Israel?' " wondered Devlin.

"I said that and he kind of looked at me and I remember once even like, like it was a love tap on my cheek, like 'Believe what you want to believe, but you're in it too deep to say no,' and I was scared," Jenoff replied.

Jenoff said that Neulander offered him $30,000 in cash to kill Carol, with a large payment beforehand and the rest of the balance to be paid afterwards over a period of three months. Jenoff had never been introduced to Carol, but he had seen her on a number of occasions over the years at the synagogue. Jenoff said the rabbi had always taken care to put him and Carol on opposite sides of the congregation during services.

As Jenoff described the plot, when he was unable to come up with a suitable poison, the rabbi began to drive elements of the plan forward himself, urging Jenoff to get on with it. Stalling for time, Jenoff told the rabbi that he needed to wait until the longer nights in the winter gave adequate cover for the attack. Reluctantly, Fred agreed, and Jenoff continued to work on the plan.

Tuesday nights were agreed upon, Jenoff claimed, because Jenoff always had AA meetings at M'kor Shalom, and Neulander, as senior rabbi, could basically wander wherever he wanted and make sure as many people saw him as possible.

It was at this point that Jenoff asked Neulander to assure him that he wasn't killing for the wrong reasons. "I had heard rumors that they called Fred Neulander 'the Playboy Rabbi.' I heard it, but I never believed it. So, when he eventually told me this was his wife that was to be killed, I looked at him and I said, 'Swear to me,'

I remember we were outside the back of the synagogue by the incinerator and I said, 'Swear to me that this is not about another woman,' or, I used the profanity, uh, cunt. And he swore to me it was not about any other woman. It was about something much, much more important than any other woman. And I said, 'Are you seeing any woman?' I had no knowledge about these other women. 'Are you seeing anybody else? Do you love anybody else?' And he looked at me with a straight face and said, 'No, I am not.' " Having cleared up the moral issue, Jenoff continued with his plans for killing Carol.

Jenoff said that Neulander became relentless in his desire to get the scheme underway. He proposed having Jenoff shoot him and Carol as they left a Broadway show in New York, killing Carol and only wounding him, but Jenoff no longer owned any guns and begged off the scheme because he would need an unregistered weapon.

Neulander then allegedly told Jenoff that Carol was in the habit of going to the New Jersey Mall in Short Hills with her sister-in-law, and perhaps Jenoff could make her murder look like a mugging out in the gigantic mall parking lot. Jenoff said the idea was to find the car by its license plate, hide inside, and kill Carol when she came back, making it look like a botched mugging. "I said, 'Well, what if the sister-in-law is with her?' and he said, 'Well, you kill that bitch, too . . . then you kill them both.' "

Another scheme Jenoff remembered being kicked around was gunning down Carol in the parking lot outside her monthly meeting of a charity board at Camden City Hall. Neulander allegedly told Jenoff that if they made it look like a drive-by shooting, then minorities would be blamed.

"Every time we discussed this, New York, Short Hills, he kept coming back to his house. Do it in his house. Do it in his house," Jenoff later explained to detectives, adding that Neulander eventually showed him a sketched diagram of how the interior of the four-bedroom residence was laid out. "Why?" Devlin wanted to know. "Because he said to me the last place people would think I'm having my wife killed is in my own house. And I said, 'But,' the only expression I could think of is, 'you don't shit where you eat.' I said, 'Why do it in your own house? What if your children are home?' I didn't know like his children's routine. He said, 'Well, that's just the point. On Tuesday night my son Matthew would be driving the EMT ambulance that night.' He says it would look so heinous that 'nobody would even think that I could have done that, you know, in my own home with my offspring, with my son possibly being there.' "

Jenoff said he and Neulander eventually arrived at the plan to murder Carol in the house and take her pocketbook full of money, making it look like a robbery gone awry. The key was not to slit her throat or break her neck or shoot her, nothing that would suggest a professional killing. "Neulander said, 'I want it to look, like, sloppy, a fucking sloppy, uh, like, uh, like a drug addict came into the house to steal her money,' " Jenoff confessed to Devlin.

Jenoff had already undergone one soul-wrenching experience, having caused the death of another human being, albeit in an accident, and despite all his planning, this time he didn't think he could go through with it by himself. Rather than simply back out of the treachery, Jenoff said he decided to subcontract the deal and hire his own hitman. He naturally turned to his nearly child-like roommate. When Jenoff had first met him three years before at Oxford House his name had been Paul Michael Gately. Paul had bragged that he was a tough guy, that he and his brother had been in the Westies gang and that they had killed people.

At the time, Jenoff was getting ready to move out

of Oxford House into an apartment in the Landmark building with another roommate, but Gately's mother and stepfather practically begged Jenoff and his friend Richard "Big Rick" Plum to get a three-bedroom apartment and include Paul in the mix, saying that they would guarantee his rent. They thought Paul was a good kid who could stay clean and sober if he was around the right people. Jenoff and Plum both actually liked Paul, so they took him in when they got their place on the tenth floor of the Landmark.

It was a charming combination. Len the recovering alcoholic spent his days telling Paul all about his dubious exploits as a CIA agent, and Paul the recovering drug addict returned the favor by telling the man he had taken to calling "Uncle Len" questionable tales about his days killing people in New York as a hitman for the Westies. For some inexplicable reason, Jenoff, of all people, said he actually believed what his paranoid schizophrenic younger friend was telling him.

Finally, Jenoff, who had often told his roommate about his good friend Rabbi Neulander, asked if Paul, who by now had changed his last name to Daniels, wouldn't like to earn some extra money by hurting someone. At first Jenoff described the victim as an Israeli vending machine operator, and then as some other important business person, and eventually as a woman who was bothering the rabbi.

Living on welfare and food stamps, Daniels was delighted with the opportunity to make some extra cash. "He said, 'No problem,'" Jenoff later recalled. "But I said, 'I can't do it. You have to do it. You have to physically kill this woman. I'll take you there. Line it up. And, you know, be the alibi, and he said, 'OK, I'll do it.'"

Jenoff told Devlin that Neulander didn't want to meet the second hitman, he didn't even want to know his name. Paul Daniels had been to some of the AA meetings at the synagogue, and Jenoff had pointed out the rabbi on some occasions, but had never introduced the two. It was only about three weeks before the murder that Jenoff told Daniels that it was the rabbi's wife, Mrs. Neulander, who was to be the target.

Paul Michael Daniels didn't need a grand scheme involving nation states to induce him to kill. He was in it for half of the money. Actually, he was in it for one-fourth of the money, because Jenoff cheated his young friend by saying the total was to be $15,000, not $30,000. That brought Daniels' payment for killing Carol Neulander down to $7,500.

Things were on track for the murder the night of Tuesday, October 25, 1994, and on October 20, Jenoff met the rabbi in the "overflow" parking lot for the Sheraton Hotel. It was their agreed-upon "secret location" for the exchange of the money, and the rabbi handed Jenoff an envelope stuffed with mixed bills totaling about $7,500.

That Tuesday, Len opened the AA meeting at 7 P.M. and closed it at 8 so that everybody would see him. Jenoff told detectives that he spoke briefly to the rabbi before the meeting began and Fred told him, "I'm going home to have dinner with Matthew. Then I'm leaving, coming back here. When I go back home, she better be dead."

Jenoff told investigators that in preparation for Jenoff's October 25 visit, Fred Neulander had disabled the porch light at the front of the house to ensure that it would be as dark as possible when Jenoff knocked.

Jenoff told the detectives that it was critical to the robbery plot that he find the burgundy-colored pocketbook that Carol carried with her. He said the rabbi had told him to look for it on either the antique bench just inside the doorway or on the dining room table. When he hadn't seen it on his way to the bathroom, Jenoff had panicked and called off the hit.

The detectives wanted to know about the murder weapon. Jenoff said it was a solid piece of metal about eight to twelve inches long that he thought had been the center of a dumbbell. He had found it propping open a door on the loading dock at the back of his Landmark Apartments building.

After the abortive attempt to kill Carol, Jenoff said that he and Daniels went their separate ways as planned, and he drove over to the Evesham police station in Marlton like he always did after Tuesday AA meetings, and visited a long-time friend of his who was a detective there.

Jenoff said that the next morning he got a call from the rabbi, who didn't sound pleased. They agreed to meet back at their secret location in the Sheraton parking lot.

"He was waiting there, and I pulled up my car next to him, and he's signaling for me to get in his car," Jenoff remembered. "I got in his car and he looked over at me. I was in the passenger side and he grabbed me by the arm and squeezed real hard, and he looked at me and his face was cherry red. His eyes were bulging like he was going to kill me. I never saw him look at me like that. I never saw this anger. And he put fear into me. And he, I can't recall his words, but he was like, 'What happened? Why wasn't it done? I went home and she, you know, gave me a bunch of shit about this empty envelope and the porch light being out.' "

Jenoff said he was too nervous to recall the part about the missing pocketbook, and he just ended up telling Neulander that he and Daniels had gotten bad vibes and just left.

"He said, 'Well, you're in too deep. You're as guilty as me. You better get the job done, or I will kill you. And if you don't think I can have you killed, then test me. The job will be done, or you're dead. There are no more Tuesdays after next Tuesday,' " Jenoff claimed.

The next Tuesday began the same as the previous week's. Jenoff arrived around 5:30 P.M. to start making the large volume of coffee needed to keep the AA meeting rolling. A short time later, smoking a cigarette out by the incinerator behind M'kor Shalom, Jenoff was joined by Neulander, who told him he was going to grab a pizza and go home and eat it with his son Matthew before the latter went on ambulance duty. He mentioned that he would make sure he was seen by a couple of the hired security officers who were watching the synagogue that evening, and by the members of the choir when he returned. "I said fine, right after the meeting, Bam! Five after eight, I'm out of there," Jenoff recalled.

Then things began to go awry. The meeting got underway and two friends of Jenoff's, a school teacher in Mount Ephraim and her boyfriend, who was an FBI agent, unexpectedly showed up. Some time before, Jenoff had issued the couple a standing invitation to drop by on any Tuesday to meet the rabbi. Jenoff had essentially forgotten about inviting them until suddenly, on November 1, they appeared.

But as soon as the meeting was over at 8 P.M., Jenoff took his friends to the M'kor Shalom sanctuary and found Rabbi Neulander. He introduced the three and stayed about fifteen or twenty minutes, much longer than he had wanted. But, Jenoff said, eventually he saw Neulander give him a significant look, and he excused himself, driving his white car to the Clover store parking lot to link up with Daniels, who had his old gray junker.

The pair cruised by the house to confirm that Carol's Toyota Camry was in the driveway, and then parked. As they were about to get out, Daniels threw in a new wrinkle. "I remember, Paul had said to me, because of all these, like, mob movies, he gives me this lead pipe and says, 'You bring her down. I want to see you do it,' or 'You bring her down, then I'll come, I'll finish her.' "

Jenoff took the pipe and knocked on the door. Carol answered and the murder went off as planned this time, right down to the discovery of the pocketbook—only instead of the $15,000 in cash they had been led to expect, the wallet contained about $150. Still, Jenoff said, they were confident that Neulander would pay for the killing one way or another, and didn't give it much thought beyond the initial puzzlement.

Jenoff kept his usual Tuesday evening appointment with his close friend, the detective at the Evesham Township Police Department, and while he was there, the murder weapon, the pocketbook, and the bloody clothes remained in the car parked among the police cruisers out back. Jenoff always got to the station between 8:55 and 9:05 P.M., and his punctuality had become something of an inside joke. But on the night of the murder, he came in the door about 9:12 P.M. At the time, he used the excuse that he had been ringing the buzzer out back for several minutes before anyone heard him and let him in the building.

After midnight, as he was driving towards Philadelphia, Jenoff swung behind the Pep Boys auto parts store opposite the Cherry Hill Mall and tossed the duffel bag with the murder weapon and the clothing into a large metal recycling Dumpster, making sure to bury it down with the batteries and other junk on the bottom so that it wouldn't immediately be visible if someone looked inside.

Next, Jenoff drove over the Ben Franklin Bridge into Philadelphia and made the first hard right turn onto 4th Street. He then drove up to 42nd Street on his way to Spring Garden, where he spotted an alley with another set of large Dumpsters. He parked and tossed Carol's pocketbook up over the lip of the tall Dumpster and immediately drove back to the Landmark building in Cherry Hill.

Jenoff later told Devlin that he'd nearly had a heart

attack when he got to the Evesham police station in
Marlton the week after the murder. The Neulander murder had been all over the news, and his detective friend
started ribbing Jenoff that he had been several minutes
late the previous week, and saying that he was going to
tell the police that Jenoff had set the whole thing up and
had blood on him when he dropped by that fateful Tuesday. Jenoff did his best to laugh along with the joke, but
he nearly died of fright at the same time.

Jenoff didn't see Fred Neulander again until the funeral, when the hitman got in line with the rest of the
people coming up to the grief-stricken rabbi to pay their
respects. "After a long wait I got up to the rabbi and I
shook hands with the family, and he then embraced me
and I went to hug him, and he pulled me in, he pulled
me in where, like, my ear was, like, face-to-face, cheek-
to-cheek, and he said everything was all right now, or
everything will be all right now, and then he gave me,
like, a consoling double pat on the back," Jenoff remembered.

Remarkably, Jenoff also went to Carol's shiva and
sat in on the ceremony of mourning for the deceased for
the next three nights—in the very front room where he
had killed her.

"I believe it was the second night. We were sitting
on the sofa in that casual living room, because it had
been all re-done, new carpet, new wallpaper, and there
were so many uniformed police officers there, so he said,
'I'll walk you out to your car,' and when we got out by
his garage, he hugs me good-bye and he puts an envelope in my pocket. When I got in my car and drove
away, I looked in. I can't recall exactly if there was
another five thousand or seven thousand dollars in
there," Jenoff said.

Jenoff said he gave the bulk of the second payment
to Daniels because he didn't want to have him nagging
to get paid, and Daniels didn't know the extent of the

full amount anyway, so it was easy to just take care of him. Daniels would later tell investigators that he used the money to buy drugs and entice women back to his apartment.

Since Neulander had "hired" Jenoff to investigate Carol's murder, he was able to launder out the rest of the payments through checks written by his lawyer for services rendered. In fact, it was really the balance on the murder itself that he was paying for, Jenoff said. The process took two and a half more years to complete, in a series of checks that ranged from $200 to $800 at a time.

During Jenoff's confession, detectives wanted to know to whom else besides themselves he might have confessed his role in Carol's murder.

Jenoff said that a couple of months before, in February 2000, his wife had come home unexpectedly and found Jenoff crying uncontrollably as he sat on the couch in his living room. Len said he had often cried over the murder, but always when he thought no one was around. He said that when his wife asked what was the matter, and caressed him, he fell apart and said, "Fred's guilty," and she started crying as well, although she didn't press further as to Len's involvement.

Len also explained about his relationship with *Philadelphia Inquirer* reporter Nancy Phillips, saying that he had met her before his present wife and had something of a crush on her. He liked to hang out with her and talk about the case, and he liked to run parts of his usual voodoo CIA résumé past her. Phillips picked up on the hints that Jenoff dropped, both deliberately and unintentionally, that there was actually something more that he knew, and as his conscience torqued him, he began to divulge more and more, relying on Phillips' commitment as a reporter to protect sources speaking off the record.

"It was professional, but then she became like my sister," Jenoff explained. "She kept assuring me that anything in the world I would tell her was protected by the First Amendment, you know, the freedom of the press, that she wouldn't be, she can't be compelled to tell the authorities.

"Well, you have to understand, I met my wife, and when I met my current wife, then I couldn't keep the secret in, it was killing me. The guilt. The shame and the guilt. Should I have come to the authorities? Yes. But I was deathly afraid, deathly afraid, but yet it was burning inside me for somebody to hear me and know, so I felt safe with this woman. And when we originally met, I wasn't married, kind of had a crush on her and nothing went of it, but I had this fantasy or crush, and I started trusting her, and telling her, but with lies, like half truths, half lies. And then we continued on as friends. Then I got married to my wife and then, I'd say about three or four months ago, I started telling (Phillips) more truths and less lies, but always with some lies. She kept, I'd say about two months ago, she kept saying to me, 'Let's drive into Camden, let's drive into Camden,' you know, 'You'll solve this, you'll solve this.' Saying stuff like that, be a hero, you know, by coming forth."

Devlin wanted to know why Jenoff hadn't come in and told the cops much earlier instead of putting the whole county through a wrenching six years of speculation and expensive effort.

"I was afraid, Marty," Jenoff replied.

"Afraid of me?"

"No. I was afraid, well afraid of you, afraid of Mr. Solomon."

"Well, why would you be afraid of me?" Devlin asked.

"Well, because I was afraid that, well, you know, 'cause we had met six years ago, give or take, and I kind of knew I couldn't lie to you, you know, I can tell the whole world my bullshit stories, but you saw through me, and I was afraid of that, and I was afraid that this true story that I told you tonight, how I met the rabbi and how he controlled my mind, I was afraid you guys wouldn't believe it. But Ms. Phillips, when I told her that story, she said, 'Lenny, it's believable, 'cause this is what he's done to all those women, all the other people. It is believable. Solomon and them will believe you. It's the truth.' "

Devlin pointed out that as of the previous week when they all met in Weber's Diner in Audubon, Jenoff had still been lying to Phillips, telling her and the investigators that he hadn't struck any of the blows against Carol, and didn't even know in advance that Carol was to be the target. "Yes, I wanted to tell her the truth, but I was afraid to tell her every detail, so I added some salt-and-pepper lies," Jenoff admitted.

Referring again to the meeting in the diner, Devlin pushed Jenoff to admit that he had still lied about some of the details of the killing. "At that meeting you told us that you were involved in the murder of Mrs. Neulander," Devlin began.

"I was involved in it, and orchestrated that murder," Jenoff agreed.

"But, you told us also that, at that meeting, that you didn't know it was Mrs. Neulander."

"Right. I lied. I told you like ninety percent truth. Still couldn't tell it all," Jenoff admitted.

"You did lie about the fact that you weren't physically involved as far as beating her to death, that you set it, that, well, Neulander set it up, you, you carried the plan out and you got this Paul Daniels . . ."

"Right, and that was true, except at the last minute, Paul said I had to hit her once," Jenoff interjected.

"And the other lies you told—and you have told for the last six years, right?—are you telling us now that what you've told us here, at this time, in front of your attorney and in front of the Cherry Hill detective and myself, that this is the truth, the whole truth, and nothing but the truth?" Devlin asked.

"Yes, sir. It is," Jenoff said as his confession ran its course.

"Tonight, and—What you put on this tape, every word of this is true. Correct?" Devlin pressed.

"True, you know, to the very best of my memory and recollection, you know, some details, yeah, I could remember tomorrow or next week, but what I've said tonight is the truth that my involvement, Paul Gately, Paul Daniels, about how the rabbi hugged with me and convinced me, and Israel and Mossad, the whole, everything he did for me, falling in love, you know, everything was the truth."

One of the most interesting features of what Jenoff, and eventually Daniels, would tell police over the weeks surrounding his confession was that Jenoff seemed to be slanting his admissions in ways that minimized his own role in the killing.

On the one hand, here he was confessing to murder. On the other hand, he first had told Nancy Phillips that he was the middle man and then that he was the architect of the killing. Then, when he first met with the cops, the story was that he had waited outside while Daniels did the actual killing. Next he told investigators that he'd struck the first blow, but Jenoff said it was still Daniels who had done the heavy bashing. But even then, Daniels said later that Jenoff had gone back in and given Carol a final whack to make sure she was dead. Jenoff said that he hadn't hit Carol very hard, hadn't hit her very much. Daniels said he just hit her three or four times. This didn't square with what was left of Carol's head. Somebody had smashed her skull with anywhere from seven to twelve blows that were hard enough to repeatedly fracture it and splatter her blood all over the front room—right up and over the lampshades and onto the

ceiling. Someone was being far too modest about their
level of viciousness.

If Jenoff wasn't telling the whole truth about the part
that was indisputable—that someone had pulverized
Carol's head in a bloody frenzy right in her front room—
then why should Jenoff be believed about other elements
of his story, such as being invited by the rabbi to join
the Mossad? After all, whatever he'd said had happened
in the bars and nightclubs of Philadelphia sounded much
more like the meanderings of a fantasist with an interest
in spy stories than a serious attempt to make contact with
foreign intelligence. If Jenoff was lying about the Mossad connection, or if he simply had trouble in his own
mind telling the difference between reality and a fantasy
world of make-believe, then why should he be believed
when it came to his story about Carol's murder? Jenoff
had direct access to the key figures surrounding Carol's
death, and he had six years to find out and think about
the details. He claimed to have killed her with his own
hands, but he had an indisputable history of lies and
exaggerations, and of describing things in a manner that
made him the victim and minimized his own responsibility: His brother had overshadowed him and made him
feel inferior; the teen he had accidentally driven over
made him drink; his wife had dumped him and taken
away his self-esteem; his religion had let him down and
made him feel worthless. And now his rabbi had put
him up to murder.

Investigators had to view Jenoff's entire confession
with a grain of salt. They also had to consider the possibility that somewhere in the months that Neulander and
Jenoff had known each other, the rabbi may have let slip
some mention of the fact that Carol often brought home
the bakery receipts on Tuesday evenings. What if the
whole thing really was the robbery attempt that Jenoff
had stood on the courthouse steps for years and pro-
claimed it to be?

But investigators had to admit that there were several circumstantial items that became very hard to explain if Jenoff and Daniels had thought up a scheme to rob and kill Carol Neulander on their own. For instance, why would Jenoff bother to tell Daniels that it was anything other than a home invasion and murder? Daniels didn't know Rabbi Neulander; he'd agreed to go rob and kill Carol just to make money.

Second, why make two trips to the house? Why not rob Carol the first night? Even if he couldn't see the pocketbook, Jenoff could have killed Carol and searched for other valuables in the house. Plus, the "robbery" on November 1 didn't result in a large take of cash, so if Jenoff had been surveilling Carol on his own initiative, it was a complete failure.

The prosecutors and detectives looking over Jenoff's confession felt that he was telling the truth, at least the basics of it, and Daniels' confession just served to back him up even further. But Neulander's besieged defense attorneys immediately set out to find every possible instance where Jenoff had invented things, altered stories in subsequent interviews, or evolved his facts to fit new scenarios. If they were going to defend Fred Neulander from the death penalty, they were going to have to convince a jury that killing Carol Neulander and saying that Fred had contracted the murder were two entirely different things—or at least that there was a reasonable doubt.

CHAPTER NINETEEN

In October 2001, after weeks of elaborate jury selection, the rescheduled trial of Rabbi Fred Neulander got underway in Camden County. It had taken since August to sort down from a pool of over a thousand potential jurors to just fifty-eight qualified candidates. The extensive questionnaire given to those initially selected for screening had wanted to know everything, from their feelings about the death penalty to how they felt about Jews in general and what sort of bumper stickers they might have on their cars. It would take several more days while the attorneys on both sides narrowed the fifty-eight selectees down to the final twelve jurors and four alternates.

It was a short walk through the back hallways each day from Neulander's plain cell in the Camden County Jail to Courtroom 33 in the adjoining Camden Hall of Justice. Both modern, chocolate-brown brick buildings wrap in a tall wedge around a street corner in the middle of Camden's small, edgy downtown. Philadelphia was less than a mile away across the Delaware River, the historic World War II Battleship USS *New Jersey* was anchored near the end of the street, bright yellow busloads of school children rumbled by every few minutes on their way to the New Jersey State Aquarium, and around a few corners, students were busy on the comparatively serene campus of Rutgers University's law school.

Inside Courtroom 33 there were no such distractions. There were only thirty seats for members of the public on the wooden pew-like benches and they would have to cram in shoulder-to-shoulder with eighteen members of the press. Both Neulander, his defense team, and the prosecution would have to share different ends of the same L-shaped table. Superior Court Presiding Criminal Judge Linda Baxter and the sixteen jurors would get the best seats, complete with cushions and armrests.

Charged with capital murder, felony murder, and conspiracy to murder, "Mr. Neulander," as the judge had insisted he be called in order to avoid imparting any religious overtones to the strictly secular proceedings, now faced the possibility of execution by lethal injection if the jury found him guilty.

If he was found guilty during the "guilt or innocence phase" of the trial, but not sentenced to death during the "penalty phase," then Neulander would face some very murky math when it came to potential prison sentences.

Because Carol had been murdered in 1994, the sentencing rules that were in effect back then would have to apply to Fred. This meant that if he were given maximum sentences on all three charges, some of which ranged potentially up to life in prison, his actual term would not exceed 30 years without parole. And even that potential sentence would be less the year and half he had already spent in prison awaiting trial since his bail was revoked in June 2000.

On Monday, October 15, 2001, almost seven years after he had found Carol's body in his living room and dialed 911, Rabbi Fred Neulander, now 60 years old, sat behind the defense table and listened as prosecutors began their opening arguments in a case they hoped would result in his death.

Prosecutor James Lynch turned to the jury of nine women and seven men and began. "This was a man, ladies and gentlemen, who had it all," Lynch said, gesturing towards Neulander, who was sitting just a few feet away in a dark suit between his attorneys. "He's a man who had the respect and admiration of his peers and his congregation. He had the love and support of his family. But it wasn't enough for this man."

Lynch said that Fred Neulander had used his position as the senior rabbi and his contacts with vulnerable members of his congregation to find both lovers and killers, depending on his needs. Neulander, he said, wanted badly to continue his relationship with sexy and wealthy Elaine Soncini, and had therefore masterminded a plot to kill his wife of nearly thirty years. The rabbi and Len Jenoff had figured out "how to do it neat, how to do it clean, and how to keep suspicion off Mr. Neulander," Lynch said, continuing, "This was no burglary, ladies and gentlemen. They came into this house to kill. She opened the door to her killers. A series of blows rained down upon her head. They came to kill, and they carried out their purpose."

Lynch explained to the jurors that in a short while they would get to listen to the 911 call Fred had made the night Carol was beaten to death, and he urged them to note how Neulander, in Lynch's opinion, seemed more concerned with keeping Matt out of the crime scene than with getting medical attention for Carol.

"This is a man who fell victim to his own needs," Lynch said. "This is a man overwhelmed by lust, greed, arrogance, and betrayal. As a result of those qualities and those characteristics, he involved himself in the murder of his own wife. He planned it. He plotted it. He paid money to have it carried out."

Attorney Jeffrey Zucker began the defense's opening argument in front of the jury with his core point, that proof of adultery was not proof of murder-for-hire. "Fred Neulander may be a person who betrayed, a person who disappointed. But that is not what he's on trial for. You're going to find out that there are a whole lot of gaps in this case," Zucker promised the jury.

"There's no question Fred Neulander was unfaithful,

no question he carried on an affair," Zucker continued. "He betrayed his family, his wife, his three children, his synagogue, and his religion. But it's one giant step from adultery to murder."

Zucker also began to lay the foundations for doubting the key prosecution witnesses. He wanted the jury to consider that even if some of the less-than-flattering things that witnesses like Len Jenoff, Elaine Soncini, and Myron Levin said about Fred Neulander were true, that they all might have their own individual reasons to have fabricated the critical parts of their damaging testimony.

Zucker said that in Jenoff's case it was because Jenoff, "a sick, demented person who is desperate for money," had long since lost his ability to tell the difference between what had actually happened in his life and what he so desperately would rather have happened. "This is a man who, by his own admission, could not sift out truth and fantasy," Zucker said. "His whole life was a fantasy."

Zucker told the jury that he would lead them on a tour of Jenoff's elaborate fantasy life, including his claims to have been a CIA operative during the Iran–Contra Affair, who eventually received a pardon for his role in the scandal from President George Bush.

"You will also hear the concern the rabbi expressed to Jenoff when he told him, 'I'm concerned for the security of my own home. I don't have an alarm, and my wife brings home large sums of money from the bakery and she always leaves the doors unlocked,' " Zucker said as he strode towards the jury, flagging the defense's alternate theory of why Jenoff could have wanted to kill Carol.

Zucker said that Jenoff had made up details that implicated the rabbi because he was smitten with reporter Nancy Phillips of *The Philadelphia Inquirer*. Jenoff wasn't really having an intimate physical relationship with Phillips, he wasn't on his way to being her boyfriend, but he thought he was, and that was why he put together a juicier story, Zucker explained.

"What kind of person comes to a diner to confess a murder and brings a *Philadelphia Inquirer* newspaper reporter with him instead of a lawyer?" Zucker asked the jury. "That kind of person is Len Jenoff."

As for Myron "Pep" Levin, Zucker said that Levin was a career criminal, someone who had done any number of bad things without regard to who they hurt or what the consequences were. Peppy had made millions melting down US coinage, which is public property. He had been involved in an insurance fraud where a man, albeit one of the arsonists, had died. He was someone who hadn't had a bad thing to say about the rabbi until police told him that Neulander appeared to have defrauded him on the purchase of the Torah. Then, suddenly, on the third time he was interviewed by detectives, Levin remembered a conversation where Neulander supposedly said he wanted to find his wife dead on the floor some night.

Zucker also wondered about Elaine Soncini's statement that Neulander had called her after the murder to discuss what to tell police about their relationship. Zucker said that Soncini might have thought she was a suspect when the police first arrived at her door; after all, jealous mistresses have killed before. He also revealed that some of what had gotten Cherry Hill police officer Larry Leaf drummed out of the force was not just that he had fallen in love with a witness, but that he was caught going through the Neulander case files, which he wouldn't normally have had access to. What, Zucker wondered, might Leaf have shared from those files with Soncini, and how might that have influenced her testimony at the time? "Her statements get more and more detailed against Neulander the further she went along," Zucker said.

Zucker also took a shot at the quality of the crime-scene investigation on the evening of November 1, 1994. He told the jury that a sharp knife was found beneath a davenport cushion while the family was sitting shiva about three days after the murder. Apparently it had been missed during the police search of the living room. Zucker claimed that it was also discovered that Carol Neulander's purse was actually missing much more money than the $150 that Jenoff had testified to, but Cherry Hill police didn't learn of this until later.

The first real piece of evidence the jury considered was the tape of Fred Neulander's 911 call.

As the courtroom hushed and strained to listen, the dial tones of a man frantically punching keys could be heard from the speakers, and then suddenly the quiet drawn-out voice of a man in anguish wondering what he should do. His wife was on the floor covered in blood, and she wasn't moving.

Sitting between Wixted and Zucker, Neulander frowned, ground his teeth, and chewed on his thumb while listening to the playback of his seven-minute call. His children and Carol's family members sitting near the front of the court reacted with pained looks as the dispatcher and Fred discussed the amount of blood and the fact that Carol didn't appear to be breathing.

Standing after it was over, Zucker said the tape demonstrated that Fred Neulander was innocent. "It's either an Academy Award performance or the horror and terror of a man who came home to find his wife beaten and bludgeoned on the floor," Zucker told the jury.

On the second day of the testimony, things quickly got to the heart of the case. Elaine Soncini, who had traveled back from Florida, took the stand first, and her riveting testimony would become by far one of the most closely watched portions of the entire trial, which was being broadcast nationwide on Court TV.

Wearing a dark brown suit that set off her perfectly groomed red hair, Soncini, now 53, looked almost regal as she spoke for nearly five hours in the sexy low voice that had become so familiar to Philadelphia in her twenty-four years on the air there.

Sitting just a few feet from Fred Neulander, Soncini had to delve into several of the most embarrassing and terrifying moments of her two-year turn as "the other woman" in the rabbi's marriage.

As all three of Neulander's children watched from their seats in the small courtroom, Soncini recounted one of the closest calls she'd had with Carol—and Carol's children—during the months when Elaine was sleeping with Neulander on a daily basis. The rabbi had set up what appeared to be a chance meeting with him and Matthew at a local deli, where Soncini would then join them for lunch. Soon after Elaine got there, Carol also showed up with Rebecca. Then, to compound the awkwardness, Benjamin happened upon the group with several of his friends. Soncini said she felt like crawling under the table, but managed to hold herself together as the family chatted away around her. She even ended up buying lunch for the gathering.

Soncini didn't look at Neulander as she testified, especially when she described what had originally attracted her to the married cleric. She said that in some ways Neulander was like her husband, Ken Garland, whom the rabbi had watched die in the emergency room.

Both men were "geniuses," according to Soncini, and both had a masterful command of the English language. "I thought he was brilliant," she said. "I thought he was extremely articulate, very expressive—superior to most anyone I had ever met. He was the world to me." Neulander sat with his back against the wall at the defense table and scribbled notes intensely on a yellow legal pad before him, while Soncini spoke of her initial admiration for him.

Soncini said that she had been searching her soul and questioning her faith in the wake of her husband's untimely death, and she considered it a sign from God when Neulander came into her life.

Elaine testified that she and the rabbi had first consummated their relationship on Christmas Eve, 1992, at her house on Embassy Drive in Cherry Hill, within two weeks of her husband's death.

"I was not the grieving widow," she admitted. She also knew that she was betraying another woman's trust in a three-decade-long marriage that had produced three children. Soncini said she entered the affair with open eyes and "my own lack of moral character."

"He said I was much more like the soulmate he would have liked to have," Soncini testified. "He told me I was the most special woman he had ever met." Fred called Elaine up to ten times a day, exchanging expensive gifts along the way. And they started sending each other sappy little love poems. "The rabbi was a wonderful writer," Soncini said. "He would write me poetry, I would write him poetry . . . love letters, beautiful love letters."

During the first year of the relationship, Soncini testified, she had tried twice to break it off, and had dated other men. Coming back from one of those dates, she found a message on her answering machine from Fred. "Look for the blue rose," it said. She found it the next morning tucked under the windshield wiper blade of her Lexus.

Elaine bought Fred lavish presents: custom-tailored shirts and sport coats, several Wittnaur wrist watches, shoes, a teddy bear, a briefcase, a leather jacket, a tuxedo, a porcelain statue of Moses, and hundreds of music CDs. She bought him the gift membership at his racquetball club. He used her gift certificates to purchase a $700 television set, a stereo system. She gave him a Mont Blanc pen that wrote in his favorite green ink. Fred gave Elaine jewelry, a large reading pillow, a silver pin that had belonged to his mother, which he said "was his most prized possession," an umbrella, and sexy underwear.

By the summer of 1993 the couple were getting together almost every weekday over the noon hour, again on a few weeknights, and again on the weekends. Elaine had felt so strongly about her new, albeit illicit, relationship that she converted to Judaism. But being the other woman was grating on the vivacious Soncini. She testified that by mid-1994 she was putting pressure on Fred, saying that she would phase out their relationship by the end of the year if he didn't leave Carol for her. In response, Soncini said that Fred had insisted they would be together by her birthday on December 17.

Elaine said that dreams became a topic between the two in 1994, when she mentioned to Fred that she had been having some nightmares. He claimed that he was suffering from them as well, she recalled. "He said he was having bad dreams, that violence was coming to Carol," Soncini said. During the same conversation Neulander told her he thought "It was going to be a tumultuous fall."

Soncini testified that Neulander talked of wanting badly to be with her, but not knowing how he could engineer a divorce with Carol and retain his post as senior rabbi, or even how he would start over with another career. Soncini offered to pay his rent for an apartment and let him use her car, but he still had trouble committing to what was obviously going to be a complex and nasty divorce. "He said to me that he just wished that she were gone—poof, just gone," Soncini testified, adding that he had also said, "I wish her car would go into the river."

Beyond wishing that Carol was just not a part of his life, Elaine said that she never heard Fred Neulander specifically criticize Carol or disparage anything in particular about her. In fact, he said repeatedly that she was a good mother. But, she testified, "he never told me he loved her."

On the Tuesday Carol was murdered, Fred, as per his normal routine, had come to Elaine's house right at noon and had left as usual around 2:30 P.M. to go back to the synagogue. She thought he might have called her again at dinner time and again early in the evening "to say goodnight," since she went to bed just before 8 P.M. each evening in order to get up for her radio show, which began before dawn each morning. It was hard for Soncini to remember the specific calls, because she got so many of them from Fred during an average day. He would start calling her some days as early as 3:45 A.M.— when she got up to go in to work—and would frequently call her from his home, if necessary standing in a closet to avoid detection.

There was one major difference about Fred Neulander's schedule on Tuesday, November 1, 1994, that Soncini did remember. On Tuesday and Thursday nights, Carol Neulander usually volunteered to help with AIDS babies over in Camden, and Fred usually returned to Soncini's for another visit. But on November 1, he said he "forgot again" about a class that he needed to teach at M'kor Shalom. He'd had to beg off on his visit just one week before for the same reason.

It was at her desk as the news director of WPEN-AM early on the morning of November 2, 1994, that Elaine Soncini learned that Carol Neulander had been beaten to death. A friend, who had no idea that Elaine was having a torrid affair with Fred Neulander, called to let her know that a major story had been breaking overnight. When she realized what she was hearing, Elaine screamed. Unable to tell anyone about the pain that she felt, Soncini had to take to the air when the music ended, and, fighting back tears, she told Philadelphia about the murder. When the microphone clicked off at the end of the newscast, Soncini threw up.

Neulander called Soncini an hour later, around 8:30, saying that he had just left the Cherry Hill police station. "He asked me if I was frightened," Soncini said. "He was afraid he was going to lose me and lose his children . . . he said he wanted justice for the murder of his wife."

The first time Elaine ever entered the Neulander household was in the week after Carol's murder, as one of the mourners at her shiva, she testified.

Less than two weeks after Carol was murdered, Soncini said, Neulander had called her into his office at M'kor Shalom and promised he would marry her "as soon as appropriately possible."

"Trust me, when God closes a door, He opens a window," she remembered the rabbi saying.

Soncini told the jury that Neulander also showed her a small piece of paper on which he had written the letters "N Y Y" and "ASAAP." He explained that he had written it while thinking, "Did I think God was going to punish me? No. Do I love you? Yes. Will I marry you? Yes. When? As soon as appropriately possible."

Soncini said that her relationship with the rabbi was immoral, and she accepted responsibility for it, and that she ended the affair when she learned that Neulander was suspected of having arranged Carol's murder. Elaine also added that she ultimately began to fear for her own life. After being questioned by detectives on December 5, 1994, Soncini told the court, "I was afraid Fred Neulander might kill me, as a matter of fact, because I didn't know what had transpired" at the Neulander house on November 1, 1994. "I was afraid of everything. I didn't know what had occurred the night of the murder. I didn't know where I was in this relationship."

Zucker zeroed in on Soncini's claims of being afraid for her life in the wake of Carol's death, wondering why, if she really thought that Fred might be planning to kill her, she had continued their sexual relationship.

"Have you ever been involved in taking acting lessons in New York?" Zucker asked sarcastically. Soncini replied that she had taken a few as a seventeen-year-old when she was growing up in Philadelphia.

On the cross-examination, Soncini admitted initially lying to police when she told them during a December 5, 1994, interview that she had not been having an affair with Fred. She said part of the reason was that she had a morals clause in her radio contract, and she feared an affair with a married rabbi involved in a scandal would get her fired.

She also implied to the detectives that her understanding was that Carol had been having an extramarital affair. She later said that was a lie that she had invented herself. "I wanted to protect Fred," she explained. "I was hoping Fred was not involved." Why then, wondered Zucker, did Elaine come forward with her own lawyer on her third police interview, and admit to their ongoing affair?

"A man with whom I was having a two-year relationship has a wife who was brutally murdered, and I am the other woman," Soncini replied. "Something terribly wrong is going on, and I didn't know what." She said that Neulander rebuffed her attempts to ask him about Carol's death. "I wanted to know [whether] this man for whom I had such great regard could have been involved in something like this," Soncini said. "I had dishonored his wife in life, and I was not going to dishonor her in death."

The last time Fred and Elaine were intimate was early in December, when Neulander stopped by her home to light a Hanukkah candle with her. After she told him to stop calling and seeing her, he wrote her letters. In one of them he took issue with her suspicion that he had had something to do with the killing. "The thought of my being a murderer or instigator is repugnant," Neulander wrote.

Questioned about her relationship with Patrolman

Larry Leaf, Soncini testified that she had simply fallen in love with the officer when he showed up as part of a two-man guard detail (Soncini didn't know it at the time, but they were also there to keep her under surveillance).

Leaf returned five days later, just hours after the security detail had ended. He was off-duty and asked Soncini out. It quickly became a sexual relationship, and in June the couple were married.

During her cross-examination, Soncini said she had never realized that her new husband had been the focus of an internal affairs disciplinary procedure for having accessed her file. (Cherry Hill officials had said that Leaf, who was falling in love with Soncini, just wanted to assure himself that he wasn't dating someone who might have killed Carol.) Soncini took a philosophical stance on her decision to marry her one-time bodyguard. "For whatever my weaknesses as a human being, I like being part of a couple," she sighed. "Larry was the first really good thing that had happened to me in years. He was just a decent guy."

Zucker asked if her interest in Leaf at the time had had anything to with his ability to supply her with information. "It had nothing to do with the fact that he was involved in the investigation?" Zucker asked.

"Oh, no," Soncini replied. "It was in spite of the fact."

As Soncini ended her testimony, Zucker once again turned to the jury box and reminded the jurors that Neulander was not on trial for adultery.

On Wednesday, the third day of the trial, it was Rebecca Neulander–Rockoff's turn to testify about the events on the night her mother died. Now 31 years old and living with her husband in Connecticut, where she still worked as a hospital administrator, Rebecca returned to Camden County for testimony that set the time frame for the events on the night of November 1. She also told the jury about the cryptic snippets of Len Jenoff's conversation with her mother that she was able to hear during both of his appearances at Highgate Lane.

Rebecca described how she and her mother had talked every day on the phone, and met together at least once a week. "We were very close, like best friends," she testified, and then she went into detail about their final phone conversation. Rebecca remembered that the call had begun around 8 P.M., but then it was interrupted about twenty minutes later when a visitor arrived at the Neulander household. "Oh, it's the bathroom guy!" she remembered Carol Neulander saying as she answered the knock on her front door.

After her father discovered her mother's body, he had called Rebecca in Philadelphia and said that there had been an accident; she needed to come to the house as quickly as possible. When a friend drove her to Cherry Hill, she arrived to find her dad alternately wandering the driveway or sitting in the back of an ambulance. "I would describe him as quiet, just very quiet and hurting," she recalled. She remembered sitting beside him in the back of the ambulance, talking to police and telling them about the Bathroom Man and his empty envelope the week before, and how her father had told police he knew nothing about a planned delivery to his house.

Zucker asked Rebecca about her mother's habit of bringing home cash from the bakery. Rebecca said she recalled the amounts ranging from $5,000 to $20,000, and added, "I told her I didn't think that was prudent. It's not safe to travel with that kind of money, or to keep it in the house."

Following Neulander's daughter, Camden County Medical Examiner Robert Segal explained to the jury his examination of Carol's crushed head on November 2, 1994. Displaying graphic color photos of the injuries found during the autopsy, Segal showed how a blunt instrument tore into Carol's head, breaking her skull and injuring her brain. Segal's examination found evidence of a dozen separate blows, including a series of six or seven wounds that were "all parallel and all clustered," indicating that they were delivered while she was down on the floor and not moving.

During Segal's testimony, Fred Neulander leaned forward on the defense table, his jaw set and eyes glistening at times.

The afternoon's testimony centered around Myron "Pep" Levin, now 76, who had played racquetball with Neulander over the years. Levin had been having a rough year, but his performance on the witness stand still managed to live up to his "Peppy" nickname that he had earned decades before as a youth playing baseball in New Jersey. Levin had suffered a heart attack earlier in 2001, and then a stroke during a follow-up double by-pass operation, but he made it to the witness stand to report some of the most damaging direct quotes that would be attributed to Neulander during the course of the trial.

Court officers had to pin a wireless microphone on Levin so that everyone could hear his gravelly voice, and he sweated profusely on the stand, frequently having to brush his face with a handkerchief during the hour he was testifying, but Levin resisted all offers to break during the proceeding so that he could rest or get water. At one point, when Judge Baxter told the attorneys that she was allowing extra latitude in the questions because "we are dealing with a seventy-seven-year-old man," Levin drew a laugh when he shot back "I'm seventy-six, Your Honor."

Levin, now in the outdoor advertising and billboard business, raised eyebrows when he said that he had voice, reading, mobility, and memory problems in the wake of his heart complications, and he had trouble remembering quite what the past crimes for which he had been convicted were. However, as dim as his memories of his own criminal past may have been, Levin said he still clearly remembered Rabbi Neulander making a remark about wanting his wife dead.

Aside from Jenoff, the fanciful hitman, Levin was the only witness in the trial who claimed to have heard Neulander express unequivocally that he wanted to have his wife killed. But at the time, Levin said, he basically thought Neulander was joking.

Levin testified that he was also one of the few people who knew that Neulander was having various affairs; Neulander would invite the women he was seeing to watch him play racquetball, and, Levin added, Neulander would inevitably win when his girlfriends were there to watch him.

Testifying about the incident involving Carol, Levin first turned to Judge Baxter and asked "if it is all right to curse" in court. Baxter said he should do so if it was part of what had been said at the time.

Levin said that at the end of their match one afternoon in mid-1994, just two or three months before the murder, Neulander slammed down his racket and said, "I wish I could get rid of my goddamn wife and have her killed on the ground when I go home someday."

Neulander wanted to find somebody who could "get rid of" Carol for him. "Do you know anybody?" Levin remembered the rabbi saying. He also "asked me if I could do it," Levin told the jury. "I said, 'Are you fucking crazy? Are you nuts? Get the fuck out. Fred, you've got a lovely wife. Stick with her. Forget you even said that to me. I've had my problems in the past. I don't want more in the future.' "

A bit frail and unsteady on his feet, Levin nonetheless came across as feisty during his testimony, drawing laughs from the court on several occasions with his blustery remarks, including once when he challenged a lengthy question by Zucker, saying, "What's your point?"

When Zucker resolutely cross-examined Levin, noting that he added more and more expletives to Fred's alleged quote each time he testified, the elderly felon sparred right back. "There was no lying in anything," Levin insisted, adding loudly: "Let me get that clear to you."

Zucker noted that Levin had not told any version of this racquetball story to the police during his first two interviews, but by the time he did so before the grand jury in 1997, there had been a new development. Levin had learned that Neulander had purchased a sub-standard Torah with the $16,000 Levin had given him years before.

When prosecutor Lynch came back and asked Levin if he had in any way decided to implicate the rabbi because he had learned of the Torah swindle, Levin replied, "That is so sick."

Levin said that initially he didn't think the remarks at the racquetball game were relevant to what had happened to Carol. "I didn't think it had any bearing on it," Levin said, adding that police were focusing on him right after the murder. "They thought possibly I did it," he said.

Zucker asked Levin how he felt about the fact that the Torah Neulander had arranged to purchase on his behalf—so that Levin could donate it to M'kor Shalom in memory of his deceased wife on the occasion of his grandson's bar mitzvah—was actually worth less than a fifth of what he paid for it.

"I was had," Levin said.

Did that bother him? Zucker wondered.

"Very much," Levin replied. "It still does." But Levin said the apparent Torah fraud had not affected his testimony against Neulander, in part, he said, because "I've wasted more money than he ever had in his life."

The last witnesses on October 17, the third day of the trial, were M'kor Shalom's cantor Anita Hochman and congregation member Patsy Brandt. Both women told the jury that Neulander had taken them aside in separate conversations shortly after Carol Neulander was murdered and told them that he and Carol had an "open marriage," and that he had been seeing other women, including members of the M'kor Shalom congregation. Hochman said Neulander identified one of the women as Robin Gross, but she only learned that the second woman was Elaine Soncini later from friends of hers.

"He told me in this conversation that he and Carol had an agreement that they would give each other permission to go outside the marriage," Hochman said. "He said he essentially had permission."

Hochman said the "uncomfortable" December 1994 conversation was initiated by Neulander because he wanted her to hear about the situation from him first, in case it suddenly appeared in the media. "He said he was embarrassed," Hochman said. "His tone was . . . very apologetic."

CHAPTER TWENTY

On Thursday, October 18, the fourth day of the trial, Len Jenoff was scheduled to take the stand for the first of his much-anticipated testimony before the jury. But the day began with Matthew Neulander's account of the worst argument he had ever witnessed between his parents.

Fred Neulander, seated only a few feet from his son in court, looked especially nervous on this day, and people seated in the courtroom noted that his hands trembled as he poured himself a glass of water before Matt even began speaking.

Matthew Neulander, now 28 and a medical resident in Charlotte, North Carolina, testified that he was at home on the night of October 30, 1994, when his parents returned from a trip to see family members in North Jersey. "Pretty much from when they walked in the door I noticed there was a problem between the two of them," Matthew began. Both were in a white heat, and Matt suddenly realized his parents' marriage had gone "from fine to not fine."

"They had never fought to this extent before," Matthew recalled. At one point, when his mother asked the rabbi if he wanted a divorce, his father replied, "It's over, yes." A short time later, Carol went down into the basement and returned carrying suitcases.

Listening to Matt testify as he sat at the defense table, Fred Neulander appeared to be distressed. He fiddled with a red ballpoint pen while Matt continued on.

"Their relationship over the years had grown increasingly distant," Matthew testified. "They were clearly spending less and less time with each other, they were squabbling more and communicating in a less friendly way when they were in the house."

The morning after the bitter argument, Matt's mother seemed to feel better—"almost cheerful"—as she told him that she and his father were thinking about marriage counseling. Matt said that, although he tried over the course of the next two days to ask his father about what was happening, Fred's only reply was, "Time will tell."

Then there was the harrowing night of November 1, 1994. Matt had been at work with his ambulance crew for only a couple of hours when an emergency call was transmitted to the station at 9:21 P.M. for a person down and bleeding at 204 Highgate Lane. As he rolled through the streets of Cherry Hill heading towards his home, Matt testified, he could hear the radio chatter between the dispatchers and responding police units, and it didn't sound good.

"We heard a great deal of information, but it was confusing and contradictory." Dispatchers thought perhaps it was a suicide, maybe with a knife, maybe with a gun. At first it wasn't clear whether it was a male or a female who was down at the scene. "I don't believe I had ever heard the urgency and increase in intensity of the voices that were discussing what was going on at the house," Matthew testified. Although the call sounded serious, Matt said he was hoping it would turn out, as so many 911 calls do, to have been overstated by someone panicking at the sight of blood. "Bleeding calls are usually benign. Someone has cut themselves and can't drive to the hospital," he told the jury.

At first he was relieved to see that the highly trained paramedic unit had beaten him to the scene. But a moment later he was horrified when they shut down their strobe lights and pulled away from the curb. With even a minor injury, Matt knew the paramedics would have stayed a few minutes to help. "Their services were not needed," Matt said. "It was a bad sign."

Matt remembered turning to his father for answers after a fellow EMT had stopped him from entering the house and essentially carried him back down the driveway. "He appeared calm and collected, but he was not looking at me as I would expect, and he was not answering my questions," Matt said. "I got one response to all my questions. He said,'Everything is going to be all right.' "

Matthew said that several years after the murder, when he was subpoenaed by the investigative grand jury, he had immediately called his father, who had arranged to hire a lawyer for his son. But Matthew said that when he told his father he planned to hire his own lawyer what followed was the biggest argument the two men had ever had. Fred Neulander called the move "ungrateful and disloyal." He said he would withdraw his financial support for Matt, who was then attending medical school, if Matt didn't use the lawyer he had selected. Matt went ahead with his own choice of attorney.

Zucker started in on his cross-examination, pointing out that Matthew had never forgiven his father for cheating on Carol, and implying that police investigators had tried to convince Matt that his father was guilty. "Is it true that once you found out about your dad, you never had the same thoughts about him that you had before?" Zucker asked.

"Yes," Matt replied.

"Hasn't he always told you he wouldn't have anything to do with this?" Zucker asked.

"Yes, sir," Matt acknowledged.

After a break, it became time to hear what would probably be the most important witness in the entire case: the ever-bewildering Len Jenoff.

Jenoff shambled into the courtroom in his bright or-

ange Camden County Corrections jumpsuit and white
prison sneakers. As he took the stand, Jenoff had trouble
raising his right arm—his wrists were wrapped in
chains—but nevertheless, he swore to tell the whole
truth and nothing but the truth.

Now 56 years old, balding, and sporting a graying
beard and mustache, the huge Jenoff began by telling
the jury that he had suffered from a lifetime of low self-
esteem, depression, and self-admitted lies.

He had begun by lying about his graduation from
Monmouth College, when in fact he had dropped out
after two years, and he then began to develop his incredibly elaborate series of tales about being a CIA
agent.

He admitted he had forged a thank-you note from
Ronald Reagan, and lied about serving on a presidential
commission that investigated organized crime.

Jenoff walked the jury through his alcoholic spiral
into divorce and home foreclosure before telling them
how he had begun to question his faith as his life fell
completely apart. And then he testified about Rabbi Fred
Neulander.

"I felt like I was an unworthy Jew," Jenoff said,
"and he took all that shame away from me. I was overwhelmed by his graciousness."

But still Jenoff couldn't stop lying about the CIA,
and that was how the subject of killing people came up
in their conversations. "I wanted to impress the man,"
he admitted.

Jenoff remembered Neulander telling him that there
was an enemy in his midst who needed to be eliminated,
and said that doing the job could be an entrée into Israel's Mossad security service. "There was a person in
Cherry Hill that could destroy Israel, that could destroy
the Cherry Hill community," Jenoff recalled.

"He took me by the elbow and said, 'Would you
kill for the state of Israel? Would you fight and kill

against the enemies of Israel?' " Jenoff said. "I was almost afraid to say no with the stories I had told him about being a tough guy and killing for the CIA. I felt I had to say yes."

Jenoff told the jurors how Neulander eventually revealed the enemy's true identity. "He said, 'The woman you said you would kill is my wife.' He was saying she was an enemy of Israel," Jenoff testified. "I wanted to know details. He said, 'There's no need to know details. Either you are the man for the job, or you are not the man for the job.' "

Jenoff said he asked the rabbi flat-out if the real reason was that Neulander was seeing another woman. "He looked at me and swore to me that it wasn't; his wife was about to destroy him," Jenoff said. "He said, 'I'll pay you thirty thousand dollars if you kill my wife,' " Jenoff said, turning to Camden County First Assistant Prosecutor James Lynch and pointing over at Fred Neulander sitting at the defense table. Neulander stared back at him. Jenoff added, "Unfortunately, sir, I said yes. And I did."

Why, Lynch asked, would Jenoff do such a thing?

"I was kind of broke. I wanted the money, and I wanted the job with Israel. It was the darkest day of my life, but I took that man's promise of thirty thousand dollars, and that was from Fred J. Neulander, and I killed his wife for that promise of thirty thousand dollars." Neulander rocked slightly in his chair while Jenoff was speaking, and looked at the floor.

Jenoff detailed the various plots he considered to kill Carol, but he said the rabbi wanted it done at his home.

Watching Jenoff testify, Neulander shook his head as if in disbelief at what he was hearing.

"He kept coming back to that he wanted it done at his home, and he wanted it done on a Tuesday night," Jenoff continued. "We talked about a pistol," Jenoff said. "The rabbi thought if she was killed that way, it might look too professional. He wanted it to look like a burglary." When Jenoff said he wanted additional help in the killing, he said Neulander's response was, "You can look for someone to help you, but it's your responsibility and you're paying him out of your money. I'm not giving you a dime over thirty thousand dollars."

Jenoff testified about the aborted first attempt: "I knew Mr. Neulander was going to be very mad at me because he was totally expecting to come home and find his wife dead on the floor. I knew I was going to catch hell the next day." When they met in the parking lot of the Sheraton, Jenoff said that Neulander was hopping mad. "His face was red, his eyebrows were raised. He was absolutely furious . . . I'd never seen the rabbi so furious ever, ever, ever." Jenoff said the rabbi insisted the murder had to occur the next week. " 'You better do it next Tuesday. There are no more Tuesday nights.' " If he didn't kill Carol in seven days, Jenoff said that Neulander had threatened, " 'You'll be dead. I'll kill you. And if you don't believe me, just try me.' "

In the hushed courtroom, Jenoff choked back sobs as he told how he had actually killed Carol Neulander the next week. Jenoff said that when Carol answered the knock on the door, he'd said, "Hi, it's me again," and then he waited until she ended the phone call with her daughter before he struck her. He said he hadn't planned on being the one to hit Carol, but that Paul Daniels had insisted that he start the attack so that they would both be equally involved. "She turned her back to me," Jenoff said, his voice breaking. "I put my left hand on her shoulder. I pulled out the lead pipe, and I whacked her in the back of the head." He said he heard Carol ask, "Why? Why?" just before he handed the pipe to Paul Daniels to finish her murder. "I heard thumps," Jenoff said, trying to hold himself together as family members sobbed. "It seemed like forever." When he went back inside to confirm that Carol was dead, "I didn't touch her, but bent over. She was lying on her side," Jenoff said. "I heard a noise. It was like the sound of gurgling, regurgitation, like a hissing."

Fred Neulander stared intently at Jenoff as he testified, and in the back of the courtroom the Neulanders' three children held hands and cried as they listened, Rebecca resting her head on Matthew's shoulder as she sobbed.

Jenoff said he had collected the second payment for Carol's murder from Neulander when he stopped by to pay his respects at her shiva. From then on, the balance of payments was made through Jenoff's private investigator business. "He could basically hire me to help investigate who killed his wife," Jenoff said. "And that way he could pay me for investigative services, but it would really be for murdering his wife."

Neulander had originally told him that it would take two more months to pay him the balance he owed on the murder, but it soon stretched to over two years, Jenoff said, in part because the murder investigation the police had launched was carefully going over the rabbi's financial records. "I didn't think that was reasonable, but at the same time, I had no choice," he explained. The payments decreased from a range of $800 to $900 at a time down to about $100 or $200 a pop right through 1997, Jenoff said.

Beyond the money, there was one other favor that Jenoff had asked of the rabbi. Three years after the murder, Jenoff had fallen in love with an Episcopalian woman, and he wanted Neulander to perform a traditional Jewish wedding for him. Initially, he said, Neulander "was not happy" about officiating at a mixed wedding where the spouse hadn't converted to Judaism. "I simply said to him, 'Fred, you're talking to me. Don't give me any shit,'" Jenoff said.

The rabbi consented, and Jenoff was married for a third time on August 10, 1997, by Neulander, who performed the ceremony in his own front room, right where Jenoff had clubbed Carol to death three years before. The rabbi's gift to Jenoff and his new bride was a wedding cake from the Classic Cake Company. Jenoff broke into sobs when prosecutors showed the jury enlarged snapshots of his wedding and the elaborate three-layer frosted white cake sitting inches from where Carol had died.

When Myron Levin appeared before a grand jury and started recalling that Neulander had spoken of wanting Carol dead, Jenoff said that an infuriated Neulander had called Jenoff and asked if he could kill Levin, perhaps with a stun gun powerful enough to stop the elderly man's diseased heart. "He said Pep had become a traitor, a turncoat," Jenoff said. Neulander was also angry at Camden County Prosecutor Lee Solomon. Jenoff said Neulander had told him that he thought Solomon would block efforts to indict the rabbi out of courtesy to a fellow Jew, and had been livid when Solomon convened a grand jury probe.

Finally the whole thing had begun to wear away at Jenoff's conscience, and, even though he still considered Neulander "my very good friend, my personal rabbi, and my mentor," he had begun bit by bit to tell Nancy Phillips what he had done. "It was a vile, despicable, animalistic act. It was like a cancer inside of me, this murder that I did. I did evil. I wanted it to come out," he testified. Jenoff said his relationship with Phillips had always been "professional and friendly" and explained why it was her he first chose to tell about the crime: "I was burning inside because I had done something so terrible, and that was not like me, and I had to get it out."

Defense attorney Dennis Wixted began his cross-examination by picking up on the central point about Leonard Jenoff—how could anyone believe specific details from a man who had spent a lifetime fabricating

208 ERIC FRANCIS

fictional stories to supplement his mundane past?

Deriding Jenoff as "super-secret squirrely Lenny," Wixted hammered down on him, asking him to explain how he had gone about manipulating the facts while all the while trying to give them a veneer of truth.

Wixted showed Jenoff the photograph of former President Reagan on a horse with the glowing thank-you note "to Len Jenoff, an old friend and comrade in arms," scrawled on it with the President's signature supposedly below. Jenoff admitted to forging it.

Holding up Jenoff's application for a New Jersey private investigator's license, Wixted read off item after item from Jenoff's résumé, each one false. "It's a fraud, but not a complete fraud," Jenoff insisted.

"You took a real person and put him into a fictitious situation," Wixted pointed out. "You would create conversations that never happened. You took something real and true and turned it into a fictitious [event], correct?"

"Yes," Jenoff replied.

It was hard to figure out what was real on the form. Jenoff had written that he was a former CIA agent, that his father was former CIA, that he had been on the President's Commission on Organized Crime, that he had been the vice president of the Playboy Casino Hotel in Atlantic City, that he had worked in the casino intelligence division of the New Jersey State Police, and that he had been assigned to the organized crime division of the Baltimore Police Department.

Jenoff admitted that none of those items were anywhere near true. He said that once he had been involved as an informant in a prostitution sting, and his only major job in the casino industry had been to dress up as an Arab sheik for a Smothers Brothers stage show.

There would be many more questions for Jenoff as the trial progressed, but Thursday's session was winding up and there would be a long break until testimony resumed the next Tuesday. Wixted wanted to leave the jurors with four days to think about other possible scenarios beyond the one that Jenoff had just so graphically spelled out for them over the past forty-five minutes.

Wixted returned to the idea that Jenoff might have found out that Carol carried home large sums of cash, and planned the robbery, enlisting Daniels' help on his own. "You took advantage of Mr. Neulander, and he never paid you anything, and you robbed Mrs. Neulander," Wixted said. "The only one who really knows if anything really happened is you, right?" Wixted asked, continuing, "You were the one who robbed and killed Carol Neulander, weren't you?"

"Absolutely," Jenoff replied. "On orders of your client."

The day's testimony would end a minute later with one of the few shows of emotion by Fred Neulander the entire week. As Jenoff admitted to Wixted that he had once described Carol Neulander as "a cunt," Fred Neulander covered his face with his hands at the defense table.

CHAPTER TWENTY-ONE

WHEN the trial resumed for its second week on Tuesday, October 23, Jenoff, who, with his oversized wire-rimmed glasses looked like a large orange owl behind the small witness stand, was back answering questions while Wixted once again tried to prove that Jenoff could have robbed Carol of his own accord. Jenoff inspired some basic sympathy as Wixted, the tall, tanned, broad-shouldered attorney in a sharp suit, argued for six straight hours that the notion of an abject heartfelt confession by Jenoff might well be something of an oxymoron.

Wixted suggested that perhaps all the payments Fred Neulander made to Len Jenoff Associates for investigative service were for just that—Len's investigative efforts—and not secret payments for Carol's murder.

Jenoff, however, said that he had done very little actual private detective work for the money, and that what he had done was just plain silly. He had hired a psychic to draw up a sketch of the real killer and taken it around and shown it to reporters and police. He had hung out in the parking lot of the Classic Cake Company and taken photographs of "potential suspects." He took pictures of the interior of Neulander's home. He had basically hung around the investigation and chatted up the cops and the participants, something he did for free most weeks when he wasn't "working" anyway. "The whole thing was a farce," Jenoff said. What then, Wixted wanted to know, were the payments for? "I earned them when I killed Mrs. Neulander," Jenoff said, adding,

"Your client was paying me cash for killing his wife at his behest. He gave me eighteen thousand dollars total. If I submitted a bill to you for twelve thousand dollars for the balance, you would've wondered what the hell it was for."

Jenoff also stood by the truthfulness of his confession to reporter Nancy Phillips, or at least the sincerity of it, because he had to admit that several of the key details that he told Phillips—and later prosecutors— were not accurate.

Wixted suggested that Jenoff could have gotten many of his details about the killing and the circumstances surrounding it from the media and from his own interviews with family members and others close to the investigation. Jenoff countered that he was "like a bubble about to burst," and that he would have confessed with or without Phillips' help. Looking back, he said he probably should have talked to his lawyer, Francis Hartman, first, and not a reporter, but he said it would not have changed his decision, explaining, "Regardless of what Mr. Hartman [would have] said that day, I had to confess."

Admitting to having had a crush on Phillips at one time, Jenoff said he came to regard her more as a sister. Despite that, he had actually tried to call Camden County Prosecutor Lee Solomon on April 27, 2000, in order to arrange to turn himself in. "At that time I was ready. I would have met him right then and there and confessed," Jenoff said, but when he called, there was no answer. Instead of calling again, the next day he turned to Phillips, and after lunch he had her call Solomon.

Phillips did tell Jenoff that going to the police and turning himself in would make him a hero, Jenoff acknowledged, but he said that wasn't his reason for confessing. "She said that, but I didn't believe her," Jenoff said to Wixted. "Admitting to a murder would make me a hero? I don't think so."

But Wixted kept pointing out that Jenoff seemed as interested in being part of the action and part of the story as he did in getting paid. If Jenoff truly was drawn to the media spotlight like a moth to a flame, then that would suggest an alternative reason for his decision to confess. Wixted pulled out a letter sent to his law office by Jenoff's attorney, Francis Hartman, demanding payment for Jenoff's work as a private investigator. "This is not just about money," Hartman wrote. "It's about his recognition and respect."

Jenoff himself made a similar point when he described a conversation he allegedly had with Neulander about his outstanding balance. "He kept insisting he had no more money to pay me," Jenoff testified. "I said, 'Well, then, at least include my name in the book you're writing.'"

If Jenoff was so interested in bursting forth with the truth that he could no longer contain himself, why then, Wixted asked, did he lie again and again as he sat with coffee and a fruit cup at Weber's Diner and told Prosecutor Solomon and Homicide Detective Martin Devlin about his involvement in the murder? "I was trying to confess," Jenoff explained, "but at the same time, I was trying to minimize my participation."

It wouldn't be until after he had entrapped Daniels on a tape, a tape in which Daniels reminded Jenoff that he had struck the first blow, that Jenoff came forward and told investigators that he too had a direct role in killing Carol Neulander.

Daniels had been picked up and brought to the Camden County Prosecutor's Office on May 1, 2000, where, not knowing that Jenoff had already confessed, he was left to wait alone with Jenoff in an interview room. Jenoff was wired for sound, and he tricked Daniels into discussing his role in the murder. Jenoff's tactic was to tell Daniels that it was Rabbi Neulander who had been talking to the cops and who had suddenly turned them in.

The polite, almost shy, Jenoff on display in the witness stand stood in stark contrast to another side of Jenoff that the jury got to hear when attorneys played the profanity-strewn tape in which he had entrapped Daniels the year before.

The jury listening to the forty-five-minute tape first heard detectives wiring Jenoff up for sound with two tape recorders, one disguised as a pager, just to be on the safe side. "I think you're liking this too much," chief investigator Martin Devlin can be heard joking as he gets Jenoff set for the sting.

Then Jenoff and Daniels are placed together in an interview room, where Daniels thought he was waiting to be questioned by police. It is really his friend, the man the rudderless Daniels had taken to calling "Uncle Lenny," who is doing the questioning.

"They know because they've already talked to Fred," Jenoff assures Daniels. "I wouldn't be surprised if he's thirty feet away from here giving us up." Jenoff suggests to Daniels that they tell the police all about Neulander's involvement. "He hired me, I hired you," Jenoff prompts, "We both went in there that night. When we left that house, she was dead."

Daniels is initially wary of talking to police, but Jenoff keeps urging him to get out ahead of Neulander's supposed confession. "You're not ready to admit the truth, huh, Paul, no?" Jenoff prompts. "Don't fuck me, Lenny," Daniels responds, "because I, because I ain't going to jail today." Jenoff replies, "We're both going to jail today."

Joining in the theater, detective Devlin can be heard walking in and warning the pair, "Both of you guys are telling different stories," suggesting that they need to get their account straight, before stomping out with a slam of the door. When Devlin leaves, Daniels starts to complain that police think he, and he alone, was responsible for bludgeoning Carol Neulander to death. "They think that I was the only one at the house . . . that I hit Mrs. Neulander with the pipe," Daniels mumbles. "That motherfucking rabbi set us up," Jenoff counters, adding, "You and I are going to be in jail, and he'll go back to his four-hundred-thousand-dollar house."

Daniels still doesn't want to come clean, telling Jenoff again and again, "Don't break down. Don't break down." But Jenoff keeps insisting that if it looks like the rabbi is going to skate out on them, that they should have a pact to speak to prosecutors and sink Fred Neulander. "What's wrong with you? You always trusted my judgment before," Jenoff wheedles. "I don't want to cut no deal," Daniels mutters over and over.

As the session wears on, Daniels starts to cave in to Jenoff's pressure, but he says he doesn't want to end up taking a 15- to 20-year prison sentence if he talks. "Yeah, if we keep our mouths shut and get convicted 'cause of Fred's say-so," Jenoff counters. "Now that we have the opportunity to tell the truth, let him take the hundred-year rap, let him get the chair . . . the question is [whether] we go to jail for twenty years or maybe five.

"We'll say he hired us, and I hired you," Jenoff continues. "Then they'll work with us. We'll set him up. Then they'll know that we turned him in. Then they'll know he hired us. Well, he hired me."

Daniels finally agrees to go along with Jenoff, but he still doesn't like the fact that Jenoff seems to be saying that Daniels and only Daniels actually attacked Carol Neulander. The younger man didn't realize that Jenoff had already confessed to the cops, but had lied about not being in the house at the time of the killing.

"You gonna tell them you were there with me?" Daniels asks.

"Yeah, I'll tell them I was there with you," Jenoff replies. "I'll tell them he approached me, paid me, and I hired you, that's the true story, on my own. I hired you. You went in and did it, and drove away."

Daniels still doesn't think that sounds like Jenoff is saying that he too had hit Carol Neulander with a pipe. "You did it too," Daniels reminds him.

Jenoff says he will say that he had pushed Carol down or tripped her. "I tripped her, and she hit her head on the coffee table. . . . I was scared. Anyway, we're both in it together. We walked out. I remember one thing, remember I had left, you were still there, and I was wondering what was taking so much time," Jenoff suggests, adding a moment later, "I pushed her down and you finished her."

"All right, we both did it," Daniels says.

"I'm as guilty as you," Jenoff responds. "Remember, you said, 'This is the knockout punch,' and you smacked her one time," Daniels insists.

At several points in the tape the jury heard Daniels at first express reluctance to confess to police, but then give in when Jenoff insists it was either them or the rabbi.

"They said that you gave me up," Daniels tells Jenoff in one exchange.

"They're lying. Now is the time to give him up," Jenoff replies, referring to Neulander.

Daniels doesn't like the haste. "I say we wait," he counters. When Jenoff presses harder, Daniels practically pleads with him not to tell on him or the rabbi: "I ain't ready for that. I ain't ready for that, Uncle Len," Daniels says, suggesting instead that they talk to Neulander themselves first.

Jenoff agrees that if they end up avoiding arrest that afternoon, they should drive over to visit Neulander that evening. But "If we get arrested, we give him up. . . ." Jenoff persists.

"All right, fuck him," Daniels says.

"Okay, buddy, fuck him," Jenoff says, picking up on Daniels' capitulation. "Remember, we both walk, we visit him tonight. We're locked up, we both talk. We burn that fucker, okay?"

"All right, all right," Daniels agrees again.

"Give me your forehead. I love you," Jenoff says, planting a kiss on the younger man's head like a scene from *The Godfather*.

"I love you, man," Daniels replies.

With the tape over, Wixted concluded Tuesday's questioning by sarcastically grilling Jenoff on his motives. "Wouldn't it be fair to say that, as you think about things, your version gets better and better for the state?" Wixted asked.

"No, sir," Jenoff replied. "You've sworn to God a lot of times and not told the truth, haven't you?" Wixted continued.

Jenoff replied, "I'm telling the truth today."

Wixted took pains to point out to the jury that Jenoff's tortured conscience hadn't forced the hitman to give himself up during the six years when he teased reporters and detectives with dozens of wild theories. Nor had he confessed when he visited with top officials in New Jersey's Division of Criminal Justice in 1996 and urged them to begin a grand jury investigation; it had certainly not intervened eighteen months later when Jenoff spent days testifying before the investigative grand jury, where he had lied under oath while knowing the whole time that he was the killer. "I knew I had to lie. I tried to answer the questions so I would not be arrested," Jenoff said, adding a short time later, "I was covering up for the rabbi."

Wixted also probed for ongoing changes within Jenoff's story. There was no mention of Neulander having given Jenoff a diagram of his house in Jenoff's original statement, nor had he said Carol's last words were

"Why? Why?" How then did those items happen to come up in his court testimony over a year later? Wixted wondered. "I remembered that after the statement," Jenoff answered.

Wixted asked right out if Jenoff was embellishing his testimony to the jury now seated before him.

"No, sir, I swear to God I'm not," he answered. "I'm telling the truth now. This week I'm telling the truth."

"Have you lied under oath?" Wixted asked. "Not many times," Jenoff replied, but he acknowledged that on past occasions, "I have lied under oath."

Wixted wanted the jury to consider that Jenoff could quite possibly get extra consideration and a reduced prison sentence if his testimony helped the prosecutor's office sink the rabbi.

"Isn't it better for your deal if Neulander is convicted?" Wixted asked. "Your deal and your future are on the line here."

Jenoff nodded. "My future."

Since the plea bargain in exchange for his testimony against the rabbi had reduced the charge against him from first-degree murder to aggravated manslaughter, Jenoff's maximum potential sentence would be thirty years. However, the minimum for the same sentence was ten years, which meant that Jenoff could be eligible for parole as early as 2003. "I'm hoping for the minimum," Jenoff acknowledged.

Wixted also implied that Jenoff was embellishing how close a friend the rabbi had been over the years. He picked up on Jenoff's testimony that Neulander had singled him out in the front row of the synagogue and made a big fuss over him during services. Wixted suggested that Jenoff had simply shown up early to get a front row seat because he knew the rabbi was in the habit of walking by there with his wireless mike as he greeted people each week. "You wanted to be seen by the people being hugged and kissed by the rabbi, but you really

were not singled out?" Wixted asked. Jenoff acknowledged that there were many people in the front rows
whom the rabbi hugged and kissed each week.

Wixted also got Jenoff to admit that anybody could
have joined the rabbi on smoking breaks outside M'kor
Shalom. But Jenoff took issue when Wixted questioned
just how secret a location the Sheraton parking lot could
really have been. "People could have seen us," Jenoff
admitted, but he added, "They just wouldn't have heard
him asking me to kill his wife."

Returning to the question of the Mossad recruitment
that Neulander had supposedly dangled in front of Jenoff, Wixted got the hitman to admit that one of the contacts was simply the Israeli Consulate in Philadelphia,
something anyone could just look up in the phone book.
Jenoff then testified that the rabbi's other advice on joining the Mossad was to " 'Have your passport ready and
lose some weight' so that I would be more attractive [as
an agent] to the Israelis."

The Mossad angle got loopier by the minute. Jenoff
testified that when the rabbi introduced him to two men
named Leo and Moishe, Jenoff started discussing ways
to purchase nuclear weapons and chemicals used in their
production. Then Jenoff decided to meet with his friend
the FBI agent to see if discussing smuggling US nuclear
weapons technology to a foreign country "might cause
me problems legally."

Wixted just stared at Jenoff with incredulity and
asked if he had volunteered to take a polygraph test with
the FBI to show whether or not he was telling the truth
about the Mossad. Jenoff said he'd declined the opportunity because he was already busy plotting Carol Neulander's murder.

Bringing up Jenoff's time in prison for the past year,
Wixted asked him if he remembered telling an inmate
named David Beardsley that the murder was part of a

robbery and that Rabbi Neulander had nothing to do with it.

"I remember Beardsley saying that to me," Jenoff replied.

Wixted asked if Jenoff had ever said that it was only himself and Daniels who were solely responsible for the crime.

"Absolutely not," Jenoff replied.

Minutes later there was an exchange between Wixted and Jenoff in which Jenoff added onto the end of a comment that it was all Neulander's idea to kill his wife. Wixted angrily shouted back, "We didn't need you to give us a commercial about Mr. Neulander's guilt, or did you just volunteer that because you want to hammer home to the jury that this man's guilty?"

Jenoff shot right back, "I know the man's guilty, sir."

"When you lie, does your nose grow?" Wixted retorted, continuing in a sarcastic tone, "How can anyone tell if you're lying or telling the truth? No jury can ever know when you are telling the truth or lying, because you do both the same way." Prosecutor Lynch objected to the question, calling it "insulting and demeaning."

"I believe now I am telling the truth and the judge and the jury will recognize that," Jenoff calmly replied.

Prosecutor Lynch appeared to agree as he made a tactical decision that surprised many courtroom observers. After a day and a half of Wixted's attempts to shred Jenoff's credibility, when it came time for Lynch to "rehabilitate" his witness, he skipped the opportunity for a cross-examination. "No questions, Your Honor," he noted. It was a bold gamble; Lynch would let Jenoff speak for himself.

CHAPTER TWENTY-TWO

THE prosecution's case had brought a sensational array of witnesses before the jury: Soncini, the coifed and contrite mistress; Jenoff, the remorseful hitman trying to do the right thing; Levin, the feisty elderly felon. But on the last day of the prosecution's case, the state would feature the one other person besides Carol Neulander who seemed to be largely a victim of the others in the tragedy that had befallen Cherry Hill on November 1, 1994.

Paul Michael Daniels, now 28 years old, would take the stand in his neon orange prison jumpsuit and appear as a pale zombie-like figure literally haunted by demons. For over a third of his life, Daniels had suffered from paranoid schizophrenia and bipolar disorders, and, despite being on a potent cocktail of four prescription antipsychotic medications that included Thorazine and Haldol, he was still hearing voices.

Seated under the fluorescent lights with his closely shaved head and wisp of a beard, Daniels would deliver his hours of testimony in a barely audible monotone. Despite his unearthly voice and his detached manner, Daniels' answers would come quickly and responsively to the questions he was being asked.

At first, Daniels had appeared downright dangerous and spooky when he was led into the courtroom, but as his testimony progressed, he seemed more and more to be merely a pathetic shadow of a person, more worthy of sympathy than fear. Halfway through the proceedings, when he tried to lean over at an angle to drink out of his water cup, Judge Baxter took pity on him and ordered deputies to remove his handcuffs. The pallid Daniels seemed unfazed by his new surroundings in the plain courtroom packed with people, but throughout his appearance he glanced repeatedly at his mother, Janet Daniels, who was seated in the second row of the public section.

Prosecutors walked Daniels through some of his childhood history of sexual abuse, drug use, and mental illness in order to give the jury a sense of what a shipwrecked, pliable individual he was when Jenoff, a man he trusted as a badly needed father figure in his dismal existence, cajoled him into taking part in a murder.

According to his attorney, Paul had been sexually abused by his biological father from the age of six onward. By the time friends and relatives realized what was happening, the deep psychological damage had been done. Still, as a younger teenager attending Lakewood High School in central New Jersey, it looked like Daniels might pull through and make it to adulthood intact. He was a popular, easy-going kid with green spiked hair and a penchant for body piercings, who took special education classes because his grades were way below par. Since the age of 12 he had been known to sneak out for a little marijuana, but his peers didn't think he was headed for trouble. Then, so the story went, a sudden breakup with a girlfriend sent the fragile youth, whose favorite game even in high school was still Candy Land, into a spiraling addiction with cocaine and heroin. His heavy drug use took all of his available cash, and by the time he was eighteen, he had left his Ocean County home for a life of petty thievery to support his heavy drug habits. All of this was soon compounded by a diagnosis of paranoid schizophrenia that began manifesting itself in his late teens, complete with voices that would tell Paul he should harm himself. Soon Paul was in and out of hospitals and couldn't stop using drugs,

especially cocaine, even when he was enrolled in two
residential drug treatment programs. He worked as a
busboy for a while, but it was strictly to get extra cash
to buy drugs. By the time he was in his early twenties,
friends who had known him from high school couldn't
even conduct a simple conversation with Paul because
he was so out of it. His newer friends, mostly met
through drug treatment programs, would describe him as
likable but easily led.

It was in the context of a life spun wildly out of
control that Paul's mother and stepfather were relieved
when their boy finally befriended somebody who might
bring him some stability. Fate had finally provided
someone who could fill the role of a caring authority
figure, which the troubled young man badly needed to
anchor his drifting existence.

What he got instead was Len Jenoff, who would mix
him up in the murder of an innocent human being, and
then sell him down the river into prison six years later.

The prosecutors wanted to show that, while Daniels
was in some sense an attorney's worst nightmare when
it came to credibility—he was a weird-looking, psy-
chotic, walking pharmacy who had confessed to killing
somebody sight-unseen for cash—he was still at least as
reliable a witness, if not more so, than Len Jenoff.

There had been some question initially whether
prosecutors would even risk calling Daniels as a witness,
but in the end they decided that even as bizarre as Daniels was, he could credibly tell what he had known of
the murder plot. Prosecutors hoped those details would
be sufficient to back up the main themes within Jenoff's
testimony.

In part, it was precisely because so much of Daniels'
personality had been pulped out of him by his dysfunc-
tional childhood and his mental illnesses that prosecutors
thought he would make a good witness. He seemed almost too child-like, too guileless to scheme, connive,

and lie. Daniel's lawyer, Craig Mitnick, described his client as so zoned out that he would answer questions in the simplest possible manner: by telling the truth. "I don't think he's capable of fabricating anything," Mitnick noted.

Getting past Daniels the person, the prosecution still had a big problem with his testimony as Daniels the hitman. It was Fred Neulander who was on trial here, not Len Jenoff, and everyone freely admitted that Daniels had never plotted with, talked to, or even met the rabbi except for two brief occasions: "two seconds" at an Alcoholics Anonymous meeting, and after the murder, when he and Jenoff had attended Carol's memorial service. Daniels testified that the rabbi had hugged him and quietly asked him if he was okay. Daniels said "Yeah," and asked Neulander the same question and got the same response.

"You took that to mean he was admitting he was involved?" Wixted asked.

"I think so," Daniels replied.

Initially Jenoff had just asked his gullible friend if he would like to make some extra money by harming someone. Then Jenoff had slowly escalated it into the planned killing of the wife of an "Israeli vending machine operator." Finally, Jenoff told Daniels that it was the wife of his rabbi friend that they were being hired to kill. Daniels said he spent the two large payments he received for his participation in the murder on "girls, clothes, and drugs."

"Did Lenny ever say to you he felt very bad about what he had done?" Wixted asked during his cross-examination. "Yes," Daniels said. "I said I feel the same way." At one point Wixted tried to get Daniels to acknowledge that robbery had been foremost on their minds when they drove over to the Neulanders', but Daniels insisted the intent was "not rob her, just kill her."

Daniels' understanding of why he had killed Carol Neulander was the same as Len Jenoff's, but that was because he had gotten all of his information directly from Jenoff, and only Jenoff. The fact that he fully believed Jenoff when the latter said their ultimate employer was the rabbi still didn't make it true.

Despite that major disconnect between Daniels and Neulander, the testimony formed a few of the smaller, more basic pieces of the puzzle—which the prosecution hoped Daniels would be able to verify—that could convince the jury that the circumstances surrounding the murder wouldn't have made any sense unless Jenoff was telling the truth.

Namely, Daniels could testify about the advance payment of several thousand dollars, and the large follow-up payment afterwards. The defense still contended that several thousand dollars had actually turned up missing from the Neulander household and from Classic Cake Company when audits were conducted months later; however, the prosecution had insisted there was no evidence to support the theory that any substantial sum of cash had been taken from either Carol or her house on that November night.

In order to believe the defense theory that Jenoff had thought the whole thing up himself, you would have to believe that the real motive on November 1 was robbery and not murder. In turn, you would have to believe that either Daniels was lying about what Jenoff told him, or that Jenoff had some reason to persuade Daniels that it was really a hit. Then you would have to believe that in order to make his hitman cover story credible, Jenoff had gone out and gotten several thousand dollars of his own money and showered it down on Daniels just for the pure theatrical effect of it all. It would have been a pretty extravagant and arguably pointless gesture for a man who was almost always broke and who was planning to commit an armed home invasion in order to get more cash. If it was just a robbery, why would he need to pay Daniels in advance, and then several thousand dollars again after it "failed"—and frankly, why would he even have needed Daniels along at all?

The defense's main argument in the wake of Daniel's testimony was that Daniels and Jenoff had differed on many of the small but key details of the murder. Daniels remembered taking two pipes into the Neulander house and Jenoff insisted they had shared just one. Daniels remembered Jenoff keeping the duffel bag and Carol's wallet for several days, hiding them along with the second pipe in the wooded area near the Landmark until things settled down. Jenoff insisted that he had gotten rid of everything the very night of the murder. Daniels also claimed to have only struck Carol twice on the head (he drew a wince from Fred Neulander as he calmly pounded the witness stand twice with his fist to demonstrate how hard he had hit her). But Daniels' two admitted blows coupled with Jenoff's one initial hit only accounted for three strikes. This was way short of the dozen or more indentations the medical examiner had found on Carol's skull.

The defense's main point about the discrepancies wasn't who was right and who was wrong, but rather that Daniels' testimony didn't actually match Jenoff's on matters that it seemed it should have. If Daniels was wrong about things like the number of murder weapons, then only Jenoff could be believed about the significant details of the plot. And the defense had already spent days pointing out that for the past thirty years, wherever Jenoff had traveled, a string of flaky tales had quickly followed.

The defense was now put in the unique position of having to convince the jury that, faced with a choice between the heavily medicated and notably confusable Daniels and the calm, polite, repentant Len Jenoff, that it was actually Jenoff whom they should believe was the crazier of the pair.

Now, having heard from the second hitman, it was time to hear from a second mistress.

Robin Gross Rappoport of Cherry Hill spoke for only a few minutes at the trial, but she said she'd had an affair with Fred Neulander beginning in 1992 or 1993 and ending around the spring of 1994, all of which overlapped the same time period that Neulander and Elaine Soncini were having their affair.

Rappoport said that the "personal relationship" developed after she decided to see the rabbi for personal counseling in 1992, as she considered whether to formally convert to Judaism.

Neulander did tell her that he was unhappy with his marriage, but when Rappoport asked him why he didn't just get a divorce, "He said a rabbi couldn't do that," she testified.

Once, while driving to a religious class at M'kor Shalom in 1993, Rappoport said she passed Carol Neulander in traffic, and then mentioned it to the rabbi when she got to the synagogue. "He said, 'Why didn't you run her off the road?' " Rappoport testified.

The prosecution wrapped up its presentation with Carol Neulander's sister, Margaret Miele, of Montclair, New Jersey. Miele had a unique take on Fred Neulander's demeanor in the wake of Carol's death, since she had spent decades working around people who suffered from severe traumatization. "I'm a medical social worker and spent thirty years dealing with people coping with severe illness and death, and so I think I have a pretty good sense of people's reaction. I found Fred's reaction unusual," Miele recalled.

Miele described the telephone call she got from Fred about 1:30 A.M. on November 2, a few hours after the murder. "He said they had a break-in, that things got out of hand, and Carol didn't survive. I didn't take it in,"

Miele said. "I didn't know what he was talking about. Then he said, 'Carol's dead.' He was totally calm and just kind of, like, 'I'm sorry, Midgie,'" she said.

The next day, when Miele saw Neulander, she said he "was totally, totally calm. I saw no signs of grief." She remembered talking to Fred during Carol's shiva. "We said,'How did this happen?' and 'Who could have done this?' and I said, 'I hope they find him soon.'" Miele said Neulander's reply was, "Oh, they'll never find the person," in what she said was an "almost cavalier" fashion." 'It could have been anyone. They're never going to solve this,'" Miele recalled Neulander saying, adding, "I was so taken aback."

Cross-examined by Wixted, Miele admitted that Fred Neulander had a "very controlled personality" and different people handle grief in different ways.

"The state rests," First Assistant Camden County Prosecutor James Lynch intoned after Miele concluded her testimony. It had taken seven years to get Carol Neulander's murder case into court, but it had only taken seven days for the prosecution to present their case that Fred Neulander was responsible for his wife's death all along.

As the session was ending and the crowd standing to move towards the courtroom doors, Carol Neulander's brother, Robert Lidz, and Rebecca Neulander–Rockoff walked over to Janet Daniels and embraced her. Daniels broke down in tears. "I'm so sorry," Daniels said to Lidz. He replied that the extended Neulander family shared her pain and hoped she would find some comfort. It was a reminder after a week of listening to treachery and deceit that not all people wish each other ill.

Next it was the defense's turn to make their presentation, and on October 29, they fired the first of many shots at the credibility of Len Jenoff by bringing in David Beardsley, his former cellmate.

Now serving a 20-year sentence for sexual abuse

and child endangerment, Beardsley took the witness stand sporting a black heart tattooed on his arm, and wearing distinctive red glasses. He testified that Jenoff claimed to have told his story to reporter Nancy Phillips because she had promised Jenoff immunity from prosecution if he came forward—and that as a bonus she would provide him with "a lifetime of [sex] and a Pulitzer Prize–winning book" if he confessed to the police. Jenoff bragged that he had traveled to Mexico with Phillips and that he was planning to start a new life with her once she raked in the money from the sensational book she was planning to write about the case, according to Beardsley.

Beardsley went on to allege that Jenoff had admitted Carol was killed during a botched robbery that targeted her: "he knew that the lady had a lot of money because she owned a cake business. He was hurting because he was financially strapped. He told me Mr. Neulander had absolutely nothing to do with it.

"After talking to Mr. Jenoff, I asked him outright, 'Don't you feel it's wrong to finger this rabbi man when he didn't do anything?' " Beardsley recalled. "He said, 'I gotta do what's best for me.' I said, 'Well, I gotta do what's best for the truth.' "

Oozing sarcasm, Lynch praised Beardsley's cannot-tell-a-lie sincerity. "It's certainly a commendable cause," Lynch agreed, striking a pose like one of the Three Musketeers with an imaginary sword and stabbing toward the wiry witness.

"I always tell the truth," Beardsley volunteered in response, adding that he was now writing Christian children's books (an interesting line of work for someone who will be under Megan's Law supervision for the rest of his life).

"Did you tell the truth, sir, when you told Mr. Jenoff that you hate Judge Baxter?" Lynch wondered.

Beardsley broke into a grin and replied calmly, "I never said I hate Judge Baxter."

Well, then, Lynch wondered, did Beardsley have any reason to hate the prosecutor's office that had just put him behind bars for two decades, and might that have influenced him to come downtown and try to undo one of their high-profile cases?

"I'm a criminal, you know," Beardsley began with a laugh. "I've never been fond of the prosecutor's office. I don't like the way they manipulate people. I don't like the way they use people and pay them to lie."

The next inmate up before the court to testify was James Patrick Keeny who had met Jenoff during prison AA meetings while serving a five-year sentence for check forgery. Keeny said that after just a couple of AA sessions together, Jenoff had started treating him "as if we were friends," and gone on to tell him that Carol only died after Daniels "went crazy" during what was supposed to have been a robbery.

Lynch cross-examined Keeny by repeatedly pointing out that the details he had given could have come from newspaper articles about the case that were published after Jenoff was arrested.

Other witnesses also breezed through the courtroom on that busy Tuesday afternoon, adding their individual pieces to the growing pyramid of doubt that the defense was constructing. Daniels and Jenoff's other roommate, Rick Plum, settled his large frame in behind the stand and recalled how he'd lived with the pair, but was not a close friend of either man. He did, however, see them on a daily basis, and he thought it odd that he didn't notice any uptick in the amount of money the pair had in the weeks before the murder when Neulander had supposedly paid them thousands of dollars. In fact, Plum remembered having to loan the pair some of his own money during that time period so they could make ends meet.

Reporter Nancy Phillips made a brief appearance in a striking blue outfit and high heels. Questions directed at her were confined to a narrow range of items that she had already printed in her articles. Her role before the jury was simply to read and verify what she had already written: that Jenoff had initially told her that the rabbi hired him to kill "an enemy of Israel," which he felt made it a justifiable killing; that he had claimed he hadn't realized that it was Carol Neulander he'd killed until the next day, when he heard news reports on the radio; and finally, that Jenoff had initially told her there had indeed been several thousand dollars in Carol's purse when he took it.

Hours later, Phillips would speak with her colleagues out in front of the courthouse and say that Jenoff's suggestions that he had some sort of romantic relationship with her were "outrageous lies, and I was offended by them." Her sister Jean, 31, who had flown in from Delray Beach, Florida, for the trial, put an even finer point on the matter by noting the contrast between her tall, attractive sister and the short, slovenly Jenoff: "It's not very plausible," she said. "When you look at her and you look at him . . . He's a dreamer."

Other defense witnesses testifying that Tuesday included: investigator Ann Prochorenko, who had infiltrated Jenoff's Weight Watchers group and testified that Jenoff's reason for wanting to lose weight was that the Neulander case was going to put him on television; private detective Willard Brown, who said Jenoff had told him that the Neulander case would be his ticket to fame, which would be payment enough for his efforts; and Fred Stahl, a M'kor Shalom security officer, who testified that the rabbi would often stop by the complex at odd hours and late in the evening. Stahl added that he didn't remember Jenoff being a regular attendee at Friday evening worship services. Attorney David Stefankiewicz testified that he had worked on an investigation

with Jenoff and remembered Len bragging that he had
a sexual relationship with a "knockout" reporter named
Nancy Phillips. Stefankiewicz testified that Jenoff had
described the blonde reporter by saying "You should see
this girl, on a scale of one to ten she's a fifteen."

Months before the trial began, a complicated series
of issues regarding Jenoff's discussions with the FBI
around the time that he was supposedly trying to join
the Mossad had been hashed out by several judges. The
problem was that the FBI didn't want to just hand their
files relating to Jenoff and his contacts over to the defense, citing any number of potential problems, including compromising their sources. The Bureau also
angered Judge Baxter by suggesting that she too would
need to undergo an FBI background check and be issued
a "temporary clearance" if she was to be allowed to review the files. Baxter, who was, after all, a judge, was
not amused by the implication and refused to play any
such games with the agents.

Eventually the Bureau relented and Judge Baxter
was allowed to look over the complete dossier, which
mostly consisted of a 68-page file from the Baltimore
office from the 1970s and an 82-page "Philadelphia File"
relating largely to Jenoff's allegations of Mossad activity
in that town. After studying the contents, Baxter agreed
that the heavily "redacted," or blacked-out, copies that
the FBI was willing to provide the defense were all that
they needed anyway.

Philadelphia-based FBI agent George Stukenbroeker
took to the witness stand on Tuesday, October 29, and
testified that Jenoff had approached him in March, 1994
saying that he had worked for the CIA running a front
company that shipped drug-making chemicals overseas,
and then as the vice-president of the Playboy Casino in
Atlantic City, where his assignment had been to "mix
with narco-terrorists." Jenoff told the agent that Rabbi
Neulander had asked him if he was "willing to die for

Israel" and was getting him mixed up with the Mossad. In June of 1994 Stukenbroeker wrote up a report for the FBI saying that Jenoff "apparently is worried that he is being manipulated, set up or guided into illegal activities."

Stukenbroeker continued to write a series of classified reports about his contacts with Jenoff during the summer and fall of 1994. As part of his investigation he called his counterparts at CIA Headquarters in Langley to verify Jenoff's claims of employment. The agency told him there were no records indicating Jenoff had ever worked for the CIA. Stukenbroeker confronted Jenoff with the CIA's denial and told him that the FBI couldn't work with him on sensitive counterintelligence matters unless he was willing to take a polygraph test to verify his story. Jenoff declined, offering as an excuse that he didn't want to risk disclosing any past illegal activities he had carried out on behalf of "the Company."

At first, Stukenbroeker's testimony to the jury in the Camden District Court seemed to offer little more than another affirmation of the already belabored point that Jenoff hadn't really been a CIA operative. But then Wixted asked Stukenbroeker to read two more brief sentences from one of his last reports on Jenoff, a report that had been written just a few weeks before Carol Neulander was murdered, and which had the potential to shake the prosecution's theory of her murder to its core.

As Wixted hovered nearby, Stukenbroeker read aloud from the witness stand: "On approximately 9/13/94, Jenoff said he had joked at the synagogue about security, upset some people, and the rabbi now seemed angry at him. On 9/23/94, Jenoff said the rabbi still seemed upset with him, and may have dropped him."

For anyone searching for a reasonable doubt with which to exculpate the rabbi, that information amounted to a bombshell.

Off all the witnesses that had been paraded before

the Neulander jury, Special Agent Stukenbroeker was one of the few who didn't have an ax to grind with Fred Neulander. His observations had been written down weeks before Carol was murdered, and years before Jenoff had been revealed as the murderer. Further, Stukenbroeker's information that the rabbi was so angry at Jenoff that their friendship might actually have been over came from none other than Len Jenoff himself.

The next day in the newspapers, there was almost no mention of Stukenbroeker's testimony, mainly because Phillips and the inmates made for far more colorful copy. But with Stukenbroeker the audience that really mattered—the jury—had heard right from a credible and neutral witness that Len Jenoff had suggested clear back in the fall of 1994 that perhaps he hadn't been under the spell of Fred Neulander after all.

If Jenoff and the rabbi did have a falling out in mid-September 1994, then there was nothing in the FBI records to indicate they had patched things up. Stukenbroeker testified that a month later, on October 14, 1994, just two weeks before Carol's murder, Jenoff told the agent that his relationship with the rabbi had "kind of died" and then, being Jenoff, he went on to suggest that instead of getting involved with Israelis he might instead soon be buying radioactive cesium from the Russian mob.

What Jenoff had told Stukenbroeker shortly before Carol was murdered suggested that Jenoff might have had an entirely different frame of mind, and thus a completely different motive, when he entered her house with a metal pipe. Jenoff clearly had a fragile ego when it came to being believed about his secret agent persona and if he had shot his mouth off about security at M'kor Shalom and been rebuked by the rabbi, who had admittedly told Jenoff that he was worried about the security at his house, then there were other sinister reasons why Jenoff could have made his own way to Highgate Lane.

If Jenoff's version of how he had been coerced into being a hitman was to be believed, then it was critical that the jury conclude he was indeed in awe of the rabbi in 1994 and would have done anything, even kill, out of blind loyalty. If Stukenbroeker's account was right, and Jenoff was instead angry and embittered after already having fallen out of the rabbi's good graces, then the key reason that prosecutors had put forward as to why Jenoff had agreed to kill Carol had been stood on its head.

The parade of rag-tag inmates and other supporting players was an interesting—and somewhat amusing—sideshow, but the star witness for the defense would clearly be Fred Neulander. Neulander signaled early on that he planned to take the witness stand on his own behalf. When he got there he would have to convince a jury that, whatever his faults and personal failings, he was, and always had been, one of the good guys. Or at least that there was a reasonable doubt about whether he wasn't.

CHAPTER TWENTY-THREE

ALL Fred Neulander had to do on Tuesday, October 30, 2001, was have a good day on the witness stand.

No one had come forward with a smoking gun; there were no instructions on how to kill his wife written in his hand, no carefully sketched diagram of his house; no bloodstained cash had been traced back to him; even the murder weapons were gone. And there were some doubts raised about the veracity of every major prosecution witness and major doubts about the two most important ones.

To walk safely out of Courtroom 33 a free man, all Fred had to do was be the opposite of the manipulative Machiavellian schemer he had been portrayed as by the prosecution; because for all their damning efforts, there had only been circumstances and surroundings, appearances and speculative deductions to tie him to a killing. The defense had called witness after witness to testify to Fred Neulander's personal magnetism and warmth, his erudite command of the language, the way he strolled the aisles of his congregation and made people feel welcome, made people love their religion, made people love being part of a larger community. As he took his place in the witness box in his dark pinstriped suit with his red-and-green–patterned tie, all he had to do was be nothing but a charming rabbi who may have sinned, who may have strayed, who may have had a mid-life crisis and gone way too far into temptation with other women. At the end of the day, at 60 years of age now, with a long history of public and community service behind him, he just had to be something other than the kind of person who looked and sounded like he might try to arrange someone's death and it would be a cakewalk across the line into reasonable doubt.

Instead, Fred Neulander spent the better part of two days stammering through contradiction after evident contradiction as Lynch paced back and forth and bashed his character apart like a piñata.

The tenth day of his trial had actually started well for Neulander as his own attorney Dennis Wixted put him on the stand for a series of questions about his background that were lobbed like softballs. Answering them was a breeze, and Neulander took the time to address himself directly to the jury.

Neulander had shown what appeared to be genuine emotion when he started to cry as he described coming home to find his wife lying dead on the floor of his house. "There was an enormous amount of blood," Neulander recalled, his low voice halting on the words as his face flushed. "I was terrified. I was frightened. I didn't know what to do."

Nearby, his children began to cry as well, Rebecca wiping tears from her eyes as her youngest brother Benjamin sunk his head between his knees.

Neulander went on to describe his wife as someone he had loved and admired as a friend, a mother to his children, and as a partner, but also as someone with whom the romance had disappeared from their relationship.

Together, Neulander and Wixted painted a picture of a twenty-nine-year marriage between a husband and a wife who grew over the years to be more "like brother and sister" than lovers, according to Neulander.

"Carol's business was very successful. My synagogue was moving very, very well, and quite frankly, that took up a tremendous amount of our lives. We began to have separate focuses," Neulander said, continuing, "The part that suffered the most was the intimacy," he said, adding that for years they had had "very, very infrequent sex."

Neulander said that both he and Carol had agreed that they could go "outside the marriage" in search of sex. It was an "open marriage" agreement that no one else had heard a thing about. Neulander himself admitted that as far as he knew, it was only he, and not Carol, who had ever taken advantage of this. Still, he seemed genuinely contrite and even humble when he described the arrangement as "arrogant," "selfish," and "embarrassing." "It was wrong," Neulander said. "It is wrong."

Neulander confirmed the affairs with Soncini and Gross and added, "I was selfish and arrogant, and I went beyond the bounds of marriage." In doing so, he said, he had betrayed many: "I betrayed Carol, I betrayed my family, I betrayed the community, I betrayed the synagogue, I betrayed my profession." But he denied that Soncini's threat to break off the relationship had given him a motive to contract Carol's murder. "No, no, never," Neulander said calmly when asked by Wixted about such a possibility, and he repeatedly said that he hadn't been interested in nor had he ever even considered seeking a divorce to marry Soncini.

Neulander also revealed that shortly after Carol was murdered, he had leveled with the leadership of M'kor Shalom and with his three children about his previous affairs, saying that he didn't want those closest to him to learn about them if the stories broke in the press.

Following Wixted's prompting, Neulander denied every significant element of the previous week's worth of testimony. He told the court that he hadn't given Soncini any pins that belonged to his mother, that he was absolutely certain that he'd never told his "semi-friend" Myron Levin that he wanted to find Carol dead on the floor some day, and he adamantly denied that there was anything unusual about his being at his own synagogue in the evening.

Wixted led Neulander down a laundry list of all of the charges that Len Jenoff had made against him, asking if he had done any of the things that Jenoff alleged in his testimony. Neulander answered back with a long string of "no"s and "never"s as he denied each element of the conspiracy that Jenoff had laid forth. What parts of the conspiracy Jenoff described were actually true? Wixted asked. "None of it," Neulander replied.

Neulander said that he and Jenoff had a "professional and smoking relationship," but he had only invited Jenoff to join the congregation because he was undergoing a "life crisis," and that the extent of their business together was that Jenoff had offered to improve the security system at the synagogue. Signaling a major piece of the robbery theory back to the jury, Neulander said that he had also discussed having Jenoff install an alarm system at his home, because his wife was in the habit of bringing back "a ton of money" every few nights from her bakery business.

Neulander acknowledged that Jenoff had brought up the topic of joining the Mossad in conversation, but the rabbi claimed that his only advice was to suggest calling the Israeli consulate in Philadelphia. "I couldn't" help him get into the Mossad, "I have no idea how. It's a terrifically secret organization," Neulander testified.

Following the murder, Neulander said he had hired Jenoff to work for him as an investigator to help solve the crime, but he said that when he hired his new defense lawyers, Zucker and Wixted, in 1997, they had urged him to dump Jenoff from the payroll. Initially he hadn't done so, but later they had insisted, and Jenoff and his sketches by psychics were shown the door.

"As you sit here today, sir, are you guilty or innocent?" defense attorney Dennis Wixted concluded.

"I'm innocent," Neulander replied firmly.

During the morning session, Neulander had played to the crowd, going into rhetorical flourishes and looking directly at the jurors to emphasize his sincerity. But moments after the lunch recess, the afternoon session began on a completely different note as Lynch used every moment of the three hours allotted to him to bore down into Neulander's previous statements to the investigators and the jury.

Neulander quickly forgot about the jurors and concentrated his attention on the relentless Lynch as the prosecutor stalked back and forth in front of the witness box. Neulander's face began to flush and his voice got less and less sonorous. Finally his answers faded almost entirely away as Lynch seemed to rip little pieces off of Neulander with each pass. Neulander's direct and elaborative style seemed to disappear behind a cloud of equivocation as he repeatedly said, "I don't deny it, but I can't recall it," as Lynch pressed his attacks home.

Rather than concentrate on the quagmire involved with Len Jenoff and the details of the actual murder, Lynch took an unexpected tack and aimed much of his firepower at Neulander's illicit relationship with Elaine Soncini. It made sense, considering that Soncini's affections were at the core of the prosecution's theory of motive, and Lynch pinned Neulander into the awkward position of having to acknowledge that he was either lying to the jury about how much he loved her, or he had been lying to her.

"You were grieving, heartfelt grief, but you still found time to share sexual moments with Elaine Soncini?" Lynch asked in one exchange.

Neulander waited a long time and then answered: "Yes."

Lynch played a message that Neulander had left on Soncini's answering machine saying that he loved her. If he didn't love her, then how did he explain the message? Lynch wondered.

"I wanted to continue the relationship," Neulander said.

Lynch hammered at Neulander's seemingly lax attitude towards solving Carol's murder. Why was he so disinterested in having the police find the killers? he wondered. Why had the rabbi lied to detectives about his affairs, when doing so was likely to impede the efforts to find the real killers? Just to avoid embarrassment? he wondered.

"Your personal interests were more important to you than solving the murder of your wife, correct?" Lynch pounded.

"Yes," Neulander replied, admitting that he had thrown police off the trail and wasted their time.

Lynch asked whether Neulander had written Soncini love poems as she had testified.

"I believe I did. I don't recall. I write poetry to a lot of people," said Neulander, adding that he was in the process of writing a book of poetry.

Neulander denied that he had given Soncini a pin that once belonged to his mother.

"Did you ever tell Miss Soncini that she was the most wonderful thing that ever came into your life?" Lynch asked.

"No," Neulander replied.

Lynch flipped on an answering machine tape that featured Neulander saying to Soncini, "Hi, this is your friend. I love you so much. . . . You are the most wonderful thing that ever came into my life."

"So, didn't you just tell this jury you never said that?" Lynch shouted.

"I made a mistake," Neulander said meekly.

"Did you say that?" Lynch pressed.

"Yes," Neulander acknowledged.

"Did you mean it?" Lynch asked.

"No," Neulander replied.

"You lied to her," Lynch stated.

"Yes."

Lynch pulled a letter off his desk written just two months after the murder in Neulander's favorite green ink, in which he wrote that a love like the one he and Soncini shared was given by God just once in a lifetime. Before he showed it to Neulander, he zeroed in even harder with his line of questions.

"You loved her?" Lynch asked.

"No. I cared for her," Neulander countered.

"Were you concerned she'd break off the relationship?"

"No, she could end it any time she wanted."

With that, Lynch whipped out the rabbi's letter, which read that their romance was profound, "a gift God permits so infrequently."

"You invoked the name of *God* in your relationship, didn't you, sir? Are those your words?" Lynch shouted.

"Yes," was the meek reply back.

"Did you mean them?"

"Yes," Neulander whispered.

"So you didn't love her before Carol died, but after, you loved her as much as you could?"

"Yes," the rabbi repeated in an ashamed voice so low it could barely be heard in the hushed courtroom.

Lynch seized back on Neulander's statement that divorce from Carol wasn't even a possibility and that he never seriously contemplated spending the rest of his life with Soncini.

"But when your wife died, it became a possibility?" Lynch shouted.

"It turned out that way," Neulander acknowledged in a whisper.

Lynch wondered why Neulander would use such language to Soncini if it was just a fling that either felt they could back out of at any time.

"I wanted the relationship to continue," Neulander said.

"This insignificant relationship with a woman you never loved, correct, sir?" Lynch sneered.

"It was just a relationship; that was what it was, and it wasn't going to go anywhere," Neulander replied.

Initially Neulander implied that he had never loved Soncini, but as Lynch began to read parts of the letter that Neulander had written, he admitted feeling "strong and powerful" emotions towards her, and said he did love her at the time, but he continued to insist that he had never considered either marrying her or divorcing Carol.

What changed between the time that he felt they had a casual relationship to the time where he wrote that their romance had been handed down from heaven above? Lynch asked.

"I don't know," Neulander responded quietly.

"Carol was dead. That changed, didn't it?" Lynch said sharply.

Switching rapidly among topics and looking for examples of hypocrisy, Lynch asked Neulander if he cared so much about preventing intermarriage amongst Jews and non-Jews, preaching several sermons about it over the years; and if Len Jenoff wasn't a close friend, and if he hadn't owed him a big favor, then why had he married Lenny to an Episcopalian right in his own front room?

Neulander said it was part of his way of putting his grief behind him. Turning to the jury on one of the few occasions during the afternoon when he seemed to be able to catch his breath, Neulander explained that Judaism teaches the importance of not "over-grieving" a loss, and to "choose life" by going on with life.

Neulander said he had been fully aware that the living room was where Carol had died, but, he added, "more importantly, she had lived in that house . . . I have memories of anniversaries and birthdays and treasure hunts and family and laughter and friends, and she was the centerpiece of those," he said, appearing to be on the brink of tears.

Neulander appeared to struggle with his emotions as he described the horror of the scene in his front room and the fact that he didn't want his children to enter the house and see their mother that way.

Lynch ended his session Tuesday with the very beginning of the case, the 911 call at 9:22 P.M. on the night of the murder. Why, he wondered, during the entire seven minutes that Fred Neulander talked with the dispatcher, hadn't he bothered to request an ambulance for his bleeding wife of twenty-nine years.

"I assumed she was dead," Neulander said.

"Were you sure?" asked Lynch.

"No," Neulander admitted.

"So, you wanted her to get immediate medical help?"

"Yes."

"And isn't that why you said, 'Send an ambulance to 204 Highgate Lane'?" Lynch said with biting mockery.

"What you wanted was immediate medical assistance to try to save your wife, right?" Lynch boomed, voice still dripping with sarcasm.

"I assumed she was dead," Neulander repeated. "I knew not what to do."

"Did you hold her?" Lynch countered. "Did you comfort her? Did you help her breathe? Did you tell her you loved her?"

"No," Neulander whispered.

Pointing out that Neulander was a rabbi, Lynch asked if he had prayed over her body.

Neulander said he was so "terrified" by the horrific crime scene that "I moved out of the room. There was so much blood," he said. "I couldn't deal with it."

"Is that all it was, was fear?" Lynch barked.

"Fear is a light word," Neulander replied.

It had been three hours of intense close-quarters courtroom combat and Judge Baxter gaveled the day to a close. As Neulander and Lynch walked back to their respective sides of the large shared table, both men looked battered.

On Halloween Day, Wednesday, October 31, 2001, Fred Neulander was back on the witness stand for the second and last day of his testimony in the trial.

Stung by Lynch's withering cross-examination the day before, Neulander was quickly back in a tangle with the prosecutor as the morning began.

Neulander quickly pointed out that he wanted to take back one of the things he had said the day before—that there was ever a point where he really loved Elaine Soncini. Neulander said he had thought about the letter he had written Soncini on January 4, 1995, just two months after Carol had been killed, saying that his relationship with Soncini was a once-in-a-lifetime gift from God. He said the letter was designed to keep their affair going, and was not deeply sincere. "I gave the wrong impression," Neulander said, "and I used the wrong words."

Lynch once again pounded away at Neulander's credibility.

"Do you believe . . . that the two persons who took your wife's life from her are in the process of being brought to justice?" Lynch asked.

"Yes," Neulander stated.

"What about the man who hired them?" Lynch asked.

"I'm innocent," Neulander replied.

"You're an innocent man with a bad memory?" Lynch queried.

"As to what?"

"As to your testimony yesterday," Lynch suggested.

"I'm not perfect. I don't have all the answers," Neulander said.

Neulander finally got off the stand. It had seemed so easy and so obvious: put the personable man of God up in the witness box and let him testify to human failings that most people have struggled with in one form or another, albeit probably more successfully in most cases, since the dawn of time. Have him admit to selfishness and even adultery, but show that he was not the kind of person to get mixed up in a murder plot. Instead, what the jury had seen was a man who appeared to be weaseling his way through a minefield of half-truths, spin, and self-inflicted deceptions. He still might not be a proven murderer, but he looked like far less than the forthright and contrite clergyman they might have been expecting.

Fred Neulander had spent the better part of two days slowly feeding most of his remaining good will and credibility through a tree chipper, but the best part of his defense was still that so much of the prosecution's case hinged on the jury believing that Len Jenoff's testimony was the truth.

Sure, Jenoff had lied for years—and then he had lied when he initially confessed; and there were questions about whether he had lied in his statements days later when he confessed some more; and there were discrepancies with Daniels' account that suggested somebody either had a terrible memory or was still lying a little bit—but the central premise supporting Len Jenoff's damning testimony against his rabbi was why anyone, let alone someone as self-centered and self-absorbed and grandiose as Len Jenoff, would confess to something as despicably evil as being a hitman if there wasn't any truth to it? The best explanation, according to prosecutors, was the one that Jenoff was giving, that there is some hidden portion of the human conscience that simply can't live with itself if it is sitting on information about something so heinous. Prosecutors wanted the jury to believe that Len Jenoff, a man who had never before felt compelled to correct a misstatement in the course of his adult life, had now been forced by some dormant portion of his own tortured inner-being to come forward, despite the dire consequences to his reputation, social standing, personal life, and even his freedom. Such is the power of truth and justice that it will shine its light outward through the darkest of nights and compel even the fallen to come forward and do the right thing. But now, as the Neulander case drew to a close, a surprise witness would appear on the stand and bring up the other irresistible force in the universe that might have compelled Len Jenoff to drop three decades of deception and testify in open court: Hollywood.

Late on the afternoon of October 31, 2001, with Halloween trick-or-treating only minutes away as the sun began to sink over the Pennsylvania horizon beyond the Delaware River, in the proverbial eleventh hour of the eleventh and final day of testimony in the Neulander case, James "Mickey" Rooney, 54, of Voorhees took the stand and raised the most direct doubts to date about the one thing that Len Jenoff claimed he was now doing right: telling the truth simply for its own sake.

Rooney was a home improvement salesman who had been a friend of Jenoff's for seven years, ever since they had both attended the same Alcoholics Anonymous meetings night after night in the churches and synagogues of Cherry Hill. Rooney testified that he had been scheming up ways to get Jenoff a book or movie deal about Jenoff's role, first in the mystery, and then, when Jenoff confessed, in the murder trial. Jenoff had told his friend, "Do what you can do," and had written a series of letters from jail to share ideas and check on the progress towards selling the rights to his story. Rooney had brought four of the letters that mentioned various media deals with him to court.

Jenoff had been presented in court as a man blinded by his love and admiration for a charismatic rabbi who led him unquestioningly into a dark pit of murder. For that transgression, Jenoff was supposedly now going to pay a heavy price: years behind bars, only to emerge some time in the distant future to ignominy, disgrace, and financial ruin. But Rooney said that in his conversations with Lenny, he got the impression that, instead of being slammed away for thirty years, Jenoff fully expected to get the minimum twenty- to twenty-two-month sentence for having helped convict the rabbi. Once out of Camden County Correctional, Rooney said that Jenoff planned to rake in the money from TV, book, and movie deals based on the fascinating mess he was embroiled in.

Rooney read from a letter that Jenoff had written him from jail in June expressing enthusiasm that the Supreme Court had issued a ruling saying that so-called "Son of Sam laws," which prevent criminals from profiting from the rights to stories about their crimes, had been ruled unconstitutional. "I can profit from all of this after the trial and after the verdict," Jenoff wrote.

"Did Mr. Jenoff indicate to you that the only way he could profit would be if Rabbi Neulander was found guilty?" Jeffrey Zucker asked.

"Yes, sir," Rooney replied.

Rooney said Jenoff reported being in touch with TV producers about his story, and even Barbara Walters, but he felt that for anything to happen, Rabbi Neulander would have to be convicted of murder conspiracy.

A small group, including Rooney, Jenoff's wife June, and Jenoff's barber, Jack Reed, had already held meetings about a possible book or movie deal, Rooney said.

During his cross-examination of Rooney, prosecutor Lynch asked whether, despite the apparent profiteering attempts, Jenoff had ever told him that he was indeed hired by the rabbi to kill Carol Neulander. Rooney replied that the first he heard of the story was when Jenoff had confessed to authorities and been jailed. "Has he ever varied from that statement?" Lynch asked. "Not since he's been incarcerated," Rooney replied.

Afterwards, Rooney told the local *Courier-Post* newspaper, "To put someone to death on the testimony of Len Jenoff would be a sin. He lives in a fantasy. One minute Lenny is very lovable, giving you his shirt, but the next, he's in the CIA mode," Rooney said, adding succinctly, "He's a screwball."

CHAPTER TWENTY-FOUR

IT was seven years to the very day since Carol Neulander had been murdered, and now it was time for the attorneys on both sides of the case against Rabbi Fred Neulander to make their closing arguments.

As they had for the preceding eleven days, both sides stuck to their main themes as they wound up their presentations.

For the defense, it was the argument that absolutely no one had presented any physical evidence to suggest that Fred had killed Carol, and that the witnesses for the prosecution were all either known liars and criminals, or people who had reasons to wish Fred Neulander ill.

For the prosecution, it was a process of piling small brick loosely upon small brick until the overall structure of their argument took shape. They admitted their evidence was circumstantial, but they argued that their explanation of a murder-for-hire scheme made more sense than all the defendant's counter-arguments.

Defense attorney Dennis Wixted got out ahead of any condemnations of Fred Neulander's character and conceded that his client was not going to be playing the moral decency card when it came to his defense. "Mr. Neulander's behavior in this case has been despicable, it's been disgusting. It's a betrayal to his family, a betrayal to his synagogue," Wixted said. "Not that Fred Neulander isn't an S.O.B. as a person, not that he isn't a little, miserable piece of dung as a human being, not that he isn't an amoral man . . . What he did is dead wrong, but it's a long way from there to the conspiracy to commit murder," Wixted said.

Drifting apart from one's spouse, and even cheating on her, "doesn't make anybody a murderer," he said. "No matter what you think of his conduct, no matter what you think of the powerful emotions drawn into this case," Wixted emphasized, "it cannot be used as a substitute for proof."

Saying that if the state was seeking punishment for moral lapses by a rabbi, then Fred Neulander was already a "beaten man," Wixted pressed his point forward on the murder charges. "Fred Neulander is finished. He is a pathetic creature. He has one thing left as he sits here: the presumption of innocence. He is an innocent man," Wixted said, adding that, by the same token, the state's case was made up of shortcomings, "emotional smoke screens," and reasonable doubt.

"It's just too important for them to say to you, 'The man's guilty,' but deny you the building block to prove the case. This is murder. This is first-degree murder. This is capital murder;" Wixted said.

From the first day, the prosecutor's office had considered Fred Neulander a suspect, and everything they had done subsequently had been viewed through that prism, insuring that, with every new revelation about the rabbi's faults, the prosecution saw it all in only the worst possible light, Wixted argued. "What's the proof for a conspiracy?" Wixted asked. "Where is it?"

Implying that the whole case had been railroaded to fit the prosecutor's working theory, Wixted pointed out that the only real piece of physical evidence police had found on the scene of the murder was a human hair in Carol's outstretched hand that did not appear to be hers. No attempt was ever even made to match it to either Jenoff or Daniels. Was it a significant oversight? Wixted said he would leave it for the jury to decide.

But it was really only Jenoff that tied Neulander in

any specific way to a murder conspiracy, and Jenoff had every opportunity, every inclination, and a range of possible motivations to have made up the stories implicating the rabbi, Wixted argued.

Maybe Jenoff was bitter about being dismissed as an investigator by Neulander's new legal team; maybe he wanted to be the lead character in a made-for-television true-life drama that would give him both the money and the tough-guy notoriety he had always craved; maybe it was some crazy combination of all that and more; but Wixted argued that, whatever one thought of Len Jenoff's motives, there was no way to know what was fantasy and what was reality when it came to his testimony. "This man's a pro. . . . He's been lying and confounding people for a long, long time. . . . Nobody knows when he tells the truth and when he lies. . . . His imagination is twisted, demented and sick," Wixted hammered.

"He wants to con a verdict from this jury," Wixted said, adding with a flourish, "Ladies and gentlemen, Mr. Jenoff murdered Mrs. Neulander and seeks to profit from her murder—and he needs your verdict."

Referring to the combination of Daniels and Jenoff together, Wixted said the state had merely re-proven what the defense had already asserted: they killed Carol Neulander. "One knew nothing about Mr. Neulander and the other couldn't tell the truth if it fell on him."

As Wixted sat back down at the defense side of the table, Lynch rose and faced the jury for his rebuttal, the last remarks of the long trial that would soon be in their hands.

Lynch argued that, as despicable as some of his witnesses had been, they had little real reason to admit to something that they hadn't actually done. And in order to believe that Neulander didn't do it, the jury would have to believe that everything Neulander had said, done, and left undone in the two or three years preceding

November 1, 1994, and in the months afterwards, had been taken out of context.

Neulander, Lynch suggested, was someone with the "solemn bearing of a religious leader." But, he added sarcastically, to believe he wasn't responsible for Carol's murder would mean that her death could only be explained by a string of coincidences and "some conspiracy of liars to bring down this good and distinguished man.

"Isn't that what this is? Just a horrible, horrible list of coincidences?" Lynch said sarcastically. "This is a man who has the bad luck to lose his precious wife, has the bad luck to have the people who committed the murder come to his house on the one night his son wouldn't be there to protect his mom, and who has the bad luck to hire as an investigator one of the three people in the world that does not want to see that crime solved.

"Every piece of bad luck, every coincidence, makes him look guilty," he continued. "Coincidence upon coincidence upon coincidence upon coincidence, and this poor, innocent man can't catch a break, can he?" Lynch sneered.

Singling out Jenoff, Lynch agreed that Jenoff was "a little wacky" and that he had a "strange résumé," but Lynch argued that the choice to include him in Carol Neulander's murder was the work of Fred Neulander, not the Camden Country Prosecutor's Office.

The point, Lynch said, as he paced and quoted everyone from Abraham Lincoln to Martin Luther King, was that somebody killed Carol and the jury needed to ask themselves who had a reason to want her dead. "Who had the motive to kill Carol Neulander?" Lynch asked rhetorically. "Was there a lengthy list?"

There was only one person who had expressed an interest in seeing Carol disappear, he thundered, "and that one person is Fred Neulander.

"This was not something which was an unfortunate

circumstance arising out of a failed robbery," Lynch said. "This is a planned murder of a human being.

"Who in the world could have possibly wanted Carol Neulander dead?" Lynch wondered aloud before continuing. "All of the motive falls at the feet of one person. All of the motive surrounds and buries one person . . . Fred Neulander.

"This is a case about lust. It's a case about greed. It's a case about arrogance and betrayal. All of those characteristics you have had the opportunity to see first-hand in this defendant," Lynch roared out at the jury as he paced between them and Neulander. "This was a man who had it all . . . but everything was not enough for this defendant. In this man's mind, the sun and the moon and the stars have to revolve around him," Lynch said. "There's nobody else who's important in this world.

"This is a man who looks shiny and bright and wonderful from the outside . . . but when you open him up and you look inside, there is nothing of substance there—no honor, no decency," Lynch said, rolling into his building conclusion. "This is a man, the defendant, bereft of character. This is a hollow man. This is a man capable of hiring someone to kill his wife."

Lynch held up an enlarged photo of Carol Neulander for the jurors to see. "This is Carol Neulander," he said simply. "She had a life taken from her seven years ago for no good reason. It was taken from her as the result of the actions of the person that she confided in and relied upon and trusted and loved, a person she decided to spend the rest of her life with and raise her children with and had every reason to believe cared about her."

With that, it was the jury's case to consider.

CHAPTER TWENTY-FIVE

IT was still the anniversary of Carol Neulander's murder when the six men and six women who had made the final cut out of the original 1,200 juror candidates retired back to the jury room and commenced their deliberations.

That first session lasted just over an hour before the court called it quits and recessed for the day, but already jury watchers and pundits were settling in for what they were predicting would be a long wait.

Like the art of tea-leaf reading, jury watching has its own aficionados, born mostly of boredom. Participants and lawyers dare not stray far from the courtroom, lest there be a message from the jury, or the verdict itself. Reporters drive themselves mad trying to make each uneventful deliberation day into a story worth reading for those who had heretofore been able to track developments by the hour.

Usually signs of what a jury might be thinking are incredibly subtle, like the request for a readback of a particular piece of testimony from the trial. More instructive yet are questions about a particular point of law from the judge's instructions, which can often indicate how far a jury has progressed in their thinking process. But the Neulander jury went one better in the early hours of Friday morning and sent one of the clearest signals possible that things were on their way to a deadlock.

In a note sent to Judge Baxter and read to the hastily re-assembled courtroom, the jurors wanted to know what would happen if they could not reach a unanimous verdict. It didn't take a paid legal analyst to figure out that this almost certainly meant that right off the bat there were at least two people who were willing to go to the mat with absolutely firm, and diametrically opposed, views of Fred Neulander's guilt or innocence.

Baxter's reply to the jury was that it was premature to answer such a question with less than a day of deliberations behind them, and she asked them to resume their discussions in hopes of reaching a unanimous verdict. After spending six hours on it that Friday, the case recessed for the weekend.

Monday brought a new wrinkle that came as a godsend for reporters, who had spent the weekend recapping the trial highlights and were now utterly bereft of a fresh story. Fred Neulander was spotted carrying a white book in with his pack of yellow legal pads, and reporters craned to see what his choice of reading material was at such a heady moment in his life.

It turned out to be a book entitled *Keep Your Mouth Shut and Your Arms Open: Observations from the Rabbinic Trenches*, and its purported author was listed as Rabbi Adam Plony. To those familiar with Jewish culture, the name Adam Plony is the equivalent of "John Doe"—it's more of an expression than an actual name; it means "everyman." Reporters started making phone calls to learn more about the piece of literary theater they were watching, and quickly confirmed their suspicion that Rabbi Adam Plony was a pseudonym for Neulander himself. This was the book that he had spent the past six years writing, first in his office at the synagogue, then, after his resignation, in the home where Carol had been murdered, and then, after his bail was revoked, from his plain eight-by-ten-foot beige jail cell in Camden County Correctional.

The book purported to be an interesting compilation of anecdotes about life as a rabbi, and an "inside" account of the situations such members of the clergy reg-

ularly confront. Reporters on the jury watch beat spent
hours of free time scouring it for any reference, however
veiled, to the murder, but there was nothing even re-
motely connected to the issue now at hand in the courthouse. There were, however, plenty of double entendres
and unfortunate comparisons that could be gleaned from
the text, depending on just how cynical the reader
wanted to be. A couple of examples were the quotes
listed as "musings" throughout the book, including one
by Benjamin Disraeli reading, "All power is a trust," and
one from Zohar that stated, "A little hurt from a kin is
worse than a big hurt from a stranger."

Little of import happened during the first of the
week as the jurors debated Monday before getting a day
off on Tuesday, Election Day, November 6, and then
resumed with an uneventful session on Wednesday.

On Thursday, the jurors began their day by asking
for extensive readback of testimony. They wanted to
hear the complete testimony of five of the witnesses and
part of Len Jenoff's testimony again. In an eyebrow-
raising move, especially for a jury that had been contin-
ually admonished not to pay any attention to media
reports about the case, the jurors also asked in their note
that the reporters covering the trial be excluded from the
readback, because they didn't want the press to be able
to speculate about where the jury was in the deliberative
process. Baxter denied that portion of the note, saying,
"Under the laws of the State of New Jersey, a court
cannot really grant that type of request," but she set up
the readbacks as requested.

After re-hearing the testimony, the jury retired back
to the jury room and at 4:20 P.M. sent out their third note
to Judge Baxter. In it, the forewoman wrote that, after
four full days of discussion, "We the jury have come to
the point of our deliberations where we have come to a
complete standstill. Our discussions have been complete—if not exhaustive—of every bit of evidence and

testimony . . . We don't anticipate any changes. We understand the significance of a unanimous decision and unfortunately are not in agreement with regard to all three counts." Baxter told the jurors that she and the lawyers would meet Friday morning to discuss the situation.

Friday began with a change of heart by the jury and, in another note sent out to Baxter, they said they wanted to continue. Baxter replied that that was what she was going to urge them to do anyway, given the length and complexity of the trial that had taken place.

The jury would break for the weekend and earnestly give it another shot on Monday, but on Tuesday, November 13, 2001, what the retired school principal, two nurses, two engineers, two teachers, and five other suburban Camden County jurors had initially suspected within the first few hours of deliberation came to pass. They had deliberated, argued, and cajoled one another hoping to convince their doubters of the righteousness of their viewpoints, but there was no budging towards a unanimous verdict. It had taken forty-three man-hours over the course of seven days scattered across three separate weeks, but the jury of twelve peers had hung up on the fate of Rabbi Fred J. Neulander. Within moments of receiving the note from the forewoman, Judge Baxter went ahead and declared the Neulander case a mistrial.

The move sent a wave of relief through the defense camp; any day your client isn't sentenced to death is a good one, even though it still left another trial looming, and questions of Neulander's future hopelessly unresolvable in the meantime. "He's certainly relieved," Zucker said to reporters after the mistrial was announced, although he added, "We look forward to trying to resolve this in a situation where our client is fully exonerated."

Prosecutor Lee Solomon vowed to try Neulander again, to once more seek the death penalty, and to continue to oppose releasing him on bail pending that new trial. Judge Baxter soon agreed that Neulander still had nothing to lose and everything to gain by fleeing the jurisdiction, so she continued to deny him bail, and Neulander continued to sit just a short distance away from Courtroom 33 in the Camden County House of Corrections awaiting his return appearance.

Just how long that wait would be was a question that consumed much of the first half of 2002. There were lingering technical issues from another death penalty case that had ended with a hung jury which might have prevented a second trial of Neulander on the capital murder charge, but the New Jersey Supreme Court ruled in April that such cases could in fact go forward to new trials. Within hours, First Assistant Prosecutor Lynch told reporters that it was certainly the intent of the authorities to try Fred Neulander again on terms that could get him lethal injection if a jury decided in their favor.

In the days and weeks after the trial, Judge Baxter would fight a running battle with the Philadelphia-area media over an unusual ruling that she issued barring reporters from interviewing and reporting on the jurors and their deliberations. Citing the possibility that further media coverage of the details of the reported 9-to-3 split in favor of convicting Neulander could taint a future jury pool, Baxter used every power at her disposal, including issuing contempt of court citations to several reporters, to try to keep the press in line. A judicial appellate panel also agreed with her a few months later, and let her ban specific juror reporting pending the second trial.

Citing the fact that the Neulander case had been "front-page news" every day of the trial, Baxter decided to have the second trial exported from Camden County to Monmouth County, New Jersey, which sits next to New York City. With the new trial tentatively scheduled for the fall of 2002, Baxter seemed to be gambling that after the attacks on September 11, 2001, perhaps potential jurors in Monmouth County had their attention riv-

eted primarily on local news while the first Neulander
trial was underway.

While the rabbi awaits his second trial in his cell in
the Camden House of Corrections, he passes the time
receiving lawyers, as well as some family members and
friends who still stay in touch with him. He also tutors
other prisoners on basic reading skills, and continues to
offer spiritual advice to those inside the prison who will
hear it. Elsewhere in the same dim building, Jenoff and
Daniels live in a similar limbo. Both of them have already confessed and pled guilty to aggravated manslaughter, but their plea deals and any leniency they
might get in a final sentencing can only take effect after
they have testified fully and completely in any and all
trial actions the state brings against Fred Neulander.
Their fate is inextricably tied to his. As he waits, they
wait.

THE DARTMOUTH MURDERS

Two kindly professors...
Two teenage suspects...
One brutal crime...

Eric Francis

On January 27, 2001, popular Dartmouth College professors Half and Susanne Zantop were found slain in their home in the wooded outskirts of Hanover, New Hampshire. Both had been stabbed repeatedly in the head and torso with twelve-inch combat knives. The crime—unprecedented in the bucolic college town—sparked a nationwide manhunt. Then, weeks later, a CB-radio call aroused the suspicion of an Indiana cop, leading him to a truck stop east of Indianapolis—and the arrest of two suspects. Their identities would be as startling as the crime itself...James Parker and Robert Tulloch were two clean-cut, straight-A, Vermont high school students with impeccable reputations. Investigators couldn't imagine any motive they might have had for the vicious killings. Could these boys have snuffed out the lives of perfect strangers with such intense, cold-blooded fury?

DAR 04/02

ABANDONED PRAYERS

A Shocking True Story of Sex,
Murder, Obsession and a Father's Secret Life

GREGG OLSEN

"A searingly tragic look behind the headlines that broke America's heart. Brilliantly researched, wonderfully written."
—Ann Rule

"A riveting and deeply disturbing chronicle of true crime. Olsen has done a superior job."
—*Cleveland Plain Dealer*

COMING SOON
FROM ST. MARTIN'S PAPERBACKS

A HANDSOME OVERACHIEVER AND A BEAUTIFUL
HONORS STUDENT MADE THE ULTIMATE LOVE PACT...
MURDER.

BLIND
LOVE

THE TRUE STORY OF THE TEXAS CADET MURDERS

PETER MEYER
Author of The Yale Murder

Nothing could come between high school sweethearts
Diane Zamora and David Graham—but something did:
beautiful blonde sophomore Adrianne Jones. After she and
Graham had a sexual encounter, a tearful Graham confessed everything to Zamora. Enraged and out-of-control,
Diane Zamora insisted that there was only one way to
restore the "purity" of their love...so together they murdered Adrianne in an isolated spot outside of their home-
town of Mansfield, Texas. There were no suspects in the
murder until months later, when Diane confessed the crime
to her military school roommates, shocking friends, family, and a picturesque Texas town...

AVAILABLE WHEREVER BOOKS ARE SOLD
FROM ST. MARTIN'S PAPERBACKS

BLIND L 11/97

The Case That Shocked the Nation

THE MOTHER, THE SON, AND THE SOCIALITE

The True Story of a Mother-Son Crime Spree
Adrian Havill

Once mistaken for a young Elizabeth Taylor, the weathered, 64-year-old Sante Kimes may have lost her movie-star good looks, but she never lost her pathological ambition to con, steal, and murder, and to use her emotionally explosive son as a pawn in her twisted schemes. Eighty-two-year-old Irene Silverman was suspicious of the surly young man she had just rented a $6000-per-month apartment to in her Manhattan mansion and was planning to throw Kenneth Kimes out. Then she suddenly disappeared without a trace—except for the bloodstains outside of her luxury townhouse. Linked to an unbelievable cross-country crime spree that may have included as many as four brutal murders, police finally caught the Kimeses. In the sensational trial, damaging evidence was presented that left no doubt in the jurors' minds as to the Kimes' guilt in the murder of Irene Silverman. Now, *The Mother, The Son, and the Socialite* takes you behind-the-scenes to reveal a story of two master criminals who thought they would get away with anything—including murder...

"Crime journalism at its best! Well-written, carefully researched, and as timely as the headlines that captured attention from coast to coast."
—Jack Olsen, bestselling author of *Hastened to the Grave* and *Salt of the Earth*

Visit our website at: www.stmartins.com

**AVAILABLE WHEREVER BOOKS ARE SOLD
FROM ST. MARTIN'S PAPERBACKS**

MSS 04/02

Gilad Atzmon grew up in Israel. National Service in the army made him a convinced anti-Zionist. He now lives in London where he is a prominent jazz saxophonist, playing with the Orient House Ensemble. Since 1998 Atzmon has toured with the late Ian Dury's legendary backing band, The Blockheads.

www.gilad.co.uk

A Guide to the Perplexed

Gilad Atzmon

English translation by
Philip Simpson

Funded by the Arts Council of England

Library of Congress Catalog Card Number: 2002110980

A complete catalogue record for this book can
be obtained from the British Library on request

First published by Keter Publishing House Ltd, Jerusalem, in 2001

First published in this English language edition in 2002
by Serpent's Tail, 4 Blackstock Mews, London N4 2BT
website: www.serpentstail.com

Printed by Mackays of Chatham, plc

10 9 8 7 6 5 4 3 2 1

Preface

This book which is here presented to you constitutes another chapter in the process of research into Israeli Hebrew culture, as conducted by the German Institute for the Documentation of Zion. This ongoing project is designed to bridge the chasm of spiritual silence that has been opened with the fading of the Zionist dream. It is no longer a secret that the cultural contribution of the State of Israel to the intellectual life of the globe, in the sixty years of its existence, was modest indeed. While the shelves of book-stores are laden to overflowing with sage words from the workshop of Jewish intellectuals of the Diaspora, from the temples of reason of the Jewish State, not one item of wisdom has emerged, nothing worthy of respectful consideration at the global level, consideration that finds its expression in foreign translation. The German Institute for the Documentation of Zion, under my personal supervision, has set itself the objective of deciphering this paradoxical phenomenon. What is it in Jews that paralyses their brains and turns them into imbeciles when they are gathered together? Professor Gunther Wünker, whose journal is presented here, expressed himself on numerous occasions on this issue. In various seminars he used to say, ironically, that in Jews there is something resembling chemical fertiliser. Chemical fertiliser, if distributed evenly over a broad swath of land, has the effect of promoting growth, but if it is concentrated at a single point, it acts as a deadly toxin. Through this analogy Professor Wünker used to hint at the life-enhancing element inherent in Jews dispersed by the Diaspora, and the life-threatening element inherent in their gathering together.

A century or so after the foundation of the State of Israel, and some forty years since its downfall, we members of the Institute find considerable relevance in the study of those sixty years of doomed existence. Why did the Jewish State suffer from the collective intellectual retrogression that led to destruction? Why do Jews *en masse* revert to a fanatical and pernicious religious enslavement? Why was the story of Massada chosen as a central myth of the regeneration process? What is the secret of collective schizophrenia? Why do the Jews never see disaster looming? Why have Israelis and Jews forgotten to respect their language, to treasure it? The Hebrew language, in which the words for "sword", "wilderness" and "destruction" are closely related, deriving from a single verbal root, could have taught them something before it was too late.

Questions relating to that destruction are beyond counting, and accordingly there is no shortage of answers to them. Therefore, we members of the Institute, instead of consuming our time with endless questions, have opted for an analytical approach, attempting to examine the structure and logic of destruction as exposed in the journals of intellectuals born in that country. For the past thirty years we have been trying to locate intellectuals who identified the cultural sickness of their homeland, intellectuals who constituted a kind of "awkward minority" and who described calamity according to their understanding and their view of the world. The German Institute is looking for academics who had the foresight to warn and even to mourn their homeland while there was yet time. We sincerely believe that a nation dreaming of its renewed existence, a people that links its right hand with its forgotten capital, needs a process of perpetuation if only for the sake of the improvement of the renewed existence when it comes.

Professor Gunther Wünker, born in Ramat Gan in the 1960s, a modest man who gained worldwide renown at the end of the last century, was invited by the Institute shortly before his death to put into writing the story of his life. Gunther did not have time to finish the work and for this reason his journal has about it something of the nature of an unfinished symphony. We members of the Institute see in the document presented here a personal testament of rare quality.

Friedrich Sharavi

German Institute for the Documentation of Zion
Autumn, 2052

13 September 2031

My name is Gunther, a name given to me by my parents or, more precisely, by my grandfather, my father's father, whose appreciation and admiration of German culture were boundless. For him, German culture was the foundation stone of aesthetic-philosophical and spiritual poetry on the one hand, and on the other, the powerhouse of industrial enterprise in the tradition of Mercedes, Telefunken, Bosch and others. In fact, my grandfather's urge to celebrate German culture was exceeded by his desire to play down his Lithuanian origin and if possible to ignore it altogether.

Grandpa, who emigrated to Germany in the early thirties, on completing his medical studies in Warsaw, was well aware of the depth of the gulf between the small-town provincialism of the *shtetl* where he grew up and the secular reality flourishing in the ivory towers of Berlin and Frankfurt. The Germany of those years was rich in culture and art on the one hand, but on the other was also bruised and wounded, like a boil liable to burst at any moment. Such eruptions led, finally, to the outbreak of the Second World War. Even then Grandpa understood well enough that this enlightened culture, at its best, with all its vitality and qualities, was capable of turning its sword against the web of ideas, ideas of freedom and of liberty, that used to stand by its bedside. Things did indeed turn out this way.

Grandpa, who saw a lofty objective in integration and

assimilation among the German people and especially among the shining exponents of German culture, encountered intense and lasting humiliation in Prussia. Educated and astute as he was, he never succeeded in rising in the eyes of his Aryan neighbours above the despised image of the *Ost Juden*. So it was that in fact he remained a lonely alien throughout his time in Germany.

Grandpa wasn't devoid of understanding of reality, or of dread of the impending Holocaust, not at all. On the contrary, Grandpa was equipped with enviably acute antennae for sensing persecution and chaos. For this reason he left Germany as early as the mid-thirties. In the late summer of thirty-six Grandpa went to live in Palestine. By one of those ironies of fate, what he failed to do in Germany, you could say, he achieved somewhere on the shores of the Mediterranean, on the fringes of the East. In Palestine he was seen by his Polish neighbours as a "*yekke-putz*", a combination of words which fitted him perfectly. As for his reception, soon after his arrival Grandpa found himself connected in some way or another with a closed and exclusive social club of high-class émigrés, intellectual refugees from the elite German universities of those years.

Since he attached no particular value to his Jewishness, seeing it as nothing more than a sleeve for the reality into which he had been propelled by an accident of birth, Grandpa spared no effort in the quest to mingle his blood with the blood of a German girl. Grandpa wanted to sink into the arms of a pure Aryan maiden, in so far as it was possible, and the sooner the better. He used to say, "What the hand can't reach by means of brain or cash, can be got between the sheets". In accordance with this principle, Grandpa invested a great deal of physical and intellectual energy in the business of assimilation. Untroubled by inhibitions, he roamed among the isolated German settlements that were scattered around Palestine in those days, expending much sweat in pursuit of white-skinned Aryan girls, from the surviving remnant of the German

Diaspora living in the Holy Land on the eve of the outbreak of world war.

Thinking back, from the vantage point of today, I myself can testify and confirm with confidence that Bavarian and Prussian girls have something special, something for which there's no substitute. It could be there's nothing more wonderful than a love-dance between the legs of a healthy and fragrant Aryan chick. There between the sheets the truth becomes blindingly clear. There between the white thighs, rubbing your lust on blonde downy hair, you grab a share of the kingdom of the good. Screwing white-skinned women is like capturing the enemy's command-bunker. As for the Bavarian woman, even when she's taken she's still not available, she's an iron fortress planted in the heart of a spiritual moat and she's pouring down boiling oil from the ramparts. She's impregnable, even when experiencing conquest.

For example, it's said that short men love tall women and yet there aren't many men who have grown taller as a result of seducing giantesses. So, for all Grandpa's efforts in chasing and even screwing German women, when confronted by his loneliness, before his reflected image in the bathroom mirror, the shame of his circumcision continued to haunt him. For all his clinging to those German blondes, he could never free himself from his degrading Jewish origins. So Grandpa used to slake his lust in the seduction of Aryan women and pour his anger into them too. Those Germans, Kristina, Helga, Frederika, were all apparently available for a brief moment, but the next, they were lost forever. The fact is, Grandpa didn't turn into an Aryan as a result of screwing all those white-thighed "Helgas". He didn't turn into an Aryan, any more than short men grow taller as a result of grazing in the pastures of out-sized women. Although Grandpa was well aware of this, till his dying day he never ceased longing to be on that wavelength of horny transcendentalism.

When Grandpa had exhausted all his strength in searching, he settled for a compromise, finally marrying a nearly pure

Aryan wife. Grandma Gertrud was in fact a German of suspected Jewish extraction, something which Grandpa succeeded
in suppressing almost entirely. Despite her total lack of inspiration or sense of humour, Grandma acquired for Grandpa, from
his point of view at least, a respectable place in westernised
society.

Not content with being a systematic lover of Germans,
Grandpa went further and became, in his own way, a hater of
Israel, exploiting every opportunity to needle his Jewish neighbours. He particularly enjoyed trampling on Holocaust sensibil-
ities. It was clear to him beyond any doubt that: "There's no
business like Shoa business."

Although Grandpa took the view that the Holocaust, in
essence, had been a terrible event (after all, of his own family he
was himself the only male survivor) he was at pains to point out,
incessantly, that the slaughter had to be seen in depth and from
a totally different perspective. He believed that the destruction
had to be studied from another angle, the German for example.
With a kind of morbid energy, he would insist on reminding
me, over and over again, of the tired old cliché that most of the
peoples of Europe had been implicated, through some strange
compulsion, in the German slaughter effort. Thus my entire
childhood was spent in an exercise in suppressing the memory
of the Holocaust. To begin with Grandpa would diminish
German responsibility by dividing the blame equally among all
the peoples of Europe. When he realised that he'd finally worn
me down and I was prepared to accept any conclusion expected
of me, if only to get a bit of peace, he took to raising, on a regular basis, that shitty key-question. The question that I was
already capable of quoting as the occasion demanded. The
hackneyed question that had the sole purpose of convincing me
that the Jew, whoever he may be, is nothing but "a creature
automatically provoking aggression".

"What is it about the Jew that makes everyone want to see
him dead?" he used to ask me almost every day. Being an unruly

child, I didn't rate my Grandpa highly as a teacher; on the contrary, I saw him as a generous contributor to the decay of my teeth. In practice he used to buy my loyal support in his campaign of Holocaust-suppression with free samples drawn from his illegal trading in golden honey-sweets (a brand no longer in existence).

Although in my infantile company Grandpa's ideas went down well enough, among his neighbours he came a real cropper. When he raised his hackneyed question in his circle of acquaintances, he left behind him a cloud of head shaking, bemusement and scorn. Grandpa used to carry on and on as if driven by obsession until, at a certain stage, his constantly repeated question turned the man himself into a pathetic figure, like the commercialised image of the Holocaust against which he had fought with such determination. In his old age Grandpa became such a pathetic figure that he was left utterly alone. Pathetic figures don't oblige those around them to respond in any way or even take them seriously. So Grandpa gradually turned into a demented herald crying alone into the wilderness.

In Palestine of those years in general, and in Ramat Gan where I was born in particular, much use was made of the pathetic principle as an easy method of evading awkward issues. Whenever a troublesome subject was raised, people would excuse themselves on the grounds that the subject was pathetic, a matter of clichés. The idea that sometimes, something as big as the dignity of humanity, or a nation, is nothing more than a pathetic issue absolves those present from any obligation whatsoever. The more that I've examined this question myself, the clearer it's become. Paradoxically, it turns out that the most substantial questions, the issues most urgent in daily life, they of all things sound to our ears like meaningless babble, as irritating as tinnitus.

For example, my darling Lola, God bless her, the woman who has lived with me and comforted me in my old age for a number of years, asks me about six times a day, at fairly regular intervals, if I still love her as much as I used to. I guess there could hardly be a more substantial question in relation to my life and hers, and to this of all questions I'm incapable of putting together a meaningful and interesting answer. I prefer to treat my loved one as a pathetic figure, and this most of all as a means of excusing myself from any in-depth analysis of her question and of her presence, which has become tiresome over the years. Sometimes, when my self-confidence fails me for a while, I feel a sudden stab of fear. Could it be that she's smarter and more subtle in intellectual terms than I ever suspected? Is she asking me if I love her just as a way of giving me a tranquillising drug? Is this her way of turning herself into a dull monotone, freeing herself from my sterile posing? So in fact I carry on living and growing old beside her in a kind of perpetual mutual impenetrability. It turns out that the pathetic principle is a mechanism liable to conceal more than it exposes. That's the way it was with Grandpa: even the big questions that he asked, including the tiresome and repetitive ones, including those going to the very root of life and experience, were left unanswered. So Grandpa became in old age a man despised by his peers, and I was left as his living memorial tablet, walking among people adorned forever with the name of a German aeronautical engineer.

2

I, for my part, got nothing out of my bogus Aryan origin, or so at least it seemed in my early years. As a child I was mocked and derided by all those around me. No five-year-old can be expected to walk the streets of Israel bearing the name of a German rocket scientist, and no court of law in the land would say otherwise. Sending a defenceless puppy out into the damp and anxious world of the coastal plain of the sixties could be classed as a serious crime, only a short step away from gross parental irresponsibility, and it almost led to my death, as you will see.

So far as my memory doesn't mislead me, I realised at a fairly early stage that I wasn't like other people, certainly nothing like the hordes of home-grown *sabras* around me. I was so different from them that I set myself the objective of turning into an undiluted, thoroughbred native. I actually imagined myself mutating into the root of the cactus-plant that gives the *sabras* their name and with this in mind, at a certain stage I even tried growing thorns. It wasn't just that I wanted to turn into a decorated and irritating Israeli pioneer, I'd also developed a powerful urge to die in Israel's wars. I was forever dreaming of those tuneful dirges, of mourners having orgasms over my open grave. I dreamed of them, in torment and in floods of tears, wailing up above, while I, the shattered corpse, sink luxuriously into the clods of earth down below. When I saw my funeral in my dreams, for some reason I visualised my grave from above, from a bird's-eye view. Repeatedly, I saw my body wrapped in a shroud, slumped in the open pit, as if the spirit was already detached, quitting my body to wander innocently among the tearful onlookers. It's very important to me to get this in the right context, seeing as that time, when I began to feel a burning desire to die a patriotic death filmed from above, was long before cemeteries and state funerals became high-ratings TV entertainment in my homeland. In fact my funeral, which I dreamed of every night, was one of the first entertainment programmes that I produced for myself and me alone.

A few years later, when some forgotten Egyptian president began humming tunes of peace, I suffered my first panic-attack. Fool that I was, I feared that this meant no more battles, no more opportunities to die a national hero.

So I developed a fascination with the heroic exploits of others. I hankered after the antiquated dreams of limbless East European heroes, coming to the shores of the Middle East to be roasted into oblivion. I became a fan of the *Palmach*, wearing a woolly cap in summer and even standing in line at the "Comrades" salon to have my hair styled. And beyond all this, I was well aware that in those songs, songs of mess-tins and the Negev, there was a clearly perceptible message. I had not the slightest doubt that in the heart-touching lines:

> *He didn't know her name*
> *But that lock of hair*
> *Went with him all the way*

– there was a kind of patriotic premonition of mortality. Anyway, the *Palmach* seemed to me in the years of my maturing youth a poetic mechanism for the advancement of destruction at a time when I was hooked, in the folly of youth, on the idea of rebellion against the legacy of Grandpa who had died in the meantime, and doing everything I was capable of to embrace death to my bosom. Gradually I became an enthusiastic devotee of the concept of self-destruction. I searched for original ways to die in battle and the sooner the better, and the military cemetery seemed to me then an elite and exclusive club that should be joined without delay. The silence of death that hangs over the little marble slabs ranged in endless lines, together with all the cherishing and the landscape, turned military cemeteries into the most appealing of locations. Beyond this, needless to say there has never been any record of the war-dead wanting to leave, a fact testifying to the overall satisfaction of the residents of this marble city, in the eternal dwellings allotted them by the authorities.

In fact, in the death-in-battle that I envisaged, there was a kind of necessary patriotic escape. Death was like a liberation from the thick swamp of personal obligation and the web of history being woven around me. Since my earliest childhood all those around me, teachers and parents alike, had been at pains to convince members of my generation how lucky we were to be living this historic moment, the moment that the dream of two thousand years in exile is coming true. But if I'm really living in a historic moment, I thought then in my innocence, it means that the history that's happening around me is an inseparable part of me, the way that I'm an inseparable part of it. And I made up my mind almost immediately, that to perpetuate forever this precious connection between me and history, I need to be implanted in the annals in a colossal sort of way. And you won't find anything more colossal than dying on the altar of history. Death seemed to me then an everlasting covenant between myself and the chronicles of the people, and awareness of my curtailed life expectancy flooded every cell in my body with rapture.

As for rapture of another kind, from my earliest youth I was full of raging hormones, painful and unremitting. Every morning, at the time of the dawn prayer, I would be devoting my entire concentration to the love-stick dangling between my legs. The blanket I would raise heavenwards, like a pyramid of angry masculinity. Aroused, it was as if I was taking refuge in the shade of the exultant pride of my youthful yearning. The blanket dripped with the sweat of serious lust. Buxom women, full-bellied and bare-arsed, used to visit me in my sleep just moments before I woke up. They would ascend heavenwards on a ladder, buttocks shifting this way and that, revealing the melons of desire behind them. In my dreams, I would look up, with yearning gaze, caressing with my eyes the folds of cellulite, raising my lips to the tender skin, and anointing my immediate surroundings with the sticky secretions of my burgeoning youth.

In those days I was ready to sacrifice myself on the erotic altar of any female who came my way, to taste the celebrated fragrance of the womb, the esteemed moisture that perfumes the sheets with the scent of sea-fish. I wanted to bite the pleasure zones of any female that I could hook on my line. Hunger for a woman took me over and left me not even a trace of bargaining power. I wanted to meet my obligation to the Creator in full. I wanted to love every woman on the face of the earth, be she young, adult, old and decrepit, stupid or even totally idiotic.

I was so desperate that I was forced to run home in school-breaks, just to ease the pressure. I was secretly pumping into my hand enough to do real damage to my eyesight, and all this with the aid of a couple of German magazines that I found hidden in my father's private library. The father that begat me, middle-ranking engineer – all that he absorbed from German culture was condensed into a few porno mags, nothing more. He had no interest at all in German music, German philosophy or even German food. Maybe in his obsession with porn there was an element of protest, even contempt directed against my Grandpa, who by all accounts had been a pretty strict father. Out of all the German culture on offer, Dad chose to focus exclusively on the clitoral. Feverish interaction with Dad's meagre library had the effect of teaching me, even then, that however much German men love the pink skin trade, the daughters of Germany themselves love it more. They have turned the flower of their lust into a flag of real and uncompromising freedom on the way to total liberation. There between the yellowing pages they would part their legs and expose the rosy pearl while I held secret and passionate conversations with them, soaked in the sweat of illicit lust. German women, I learned much later, don't compromise. They never give up on their libido, even if this amounts to crass indifference to world wars and to bombs dropping on their heads from the bellies of Allied aircraft. For this reason, I know today, the Germans have no emotional blitz to boast about, not because Dresden didn't turn into an island of destruction but because on the German home-front they never stopped fucking.

Anyway, Dad was essentially a sad man, one who never really fulfilled himself. He married a typical Polish woman whose level of tolerance and sex-drive stood in inverse proportion to a strident and tasteless life. While my mother, Lily, became more and more vocal over the years, Dad went and shut himself away in his private world of German porn. And when I wonder today about Dad's contribution to my education, I reckon that his way of secluding himself in the juicy Bavarian world led me to my first exposure to the new Germany, post-war Germany.

3

At the end of the fifth grade, two weeks before the long vacation, my parents were summoned to an urgent meeting with the headmistress of the school. At first I was asked to wait in the corridor and my parents went into the headmistress's room alone. My mother, like other members of the Polish community, always believed first impressions more important than any content or substance, and so she assumed that even when responding to such an urgent pedagogic summons as this, cheap French perfume and synthetic fox-fur would help to buy her a respectable position in the family of mankind. I personally, trying very hard at that time to adopt a proper human appearance in the hope of growing up one day, could tell even then that the noisy symptoms of Polish social activity were nothing more than transmissions of vocal inferiority. It wasn't easy for me to admit that this strident inferiority was emerging from my mother's throat.

"The child is showing very unhealthy symptoms and the educational committee has decided to recommend immediate referral for treatment," I heard through the door, the headmistress raising her voice, as if repeating this key statement for the second or third time. My mother, who didn't have the brightest of heads on her shoulders, instead of defending me or at least doing justice to the perfumed image that she'd tried to project from the beginning, began whimpering like a slaughtered sheep. I knew straightaway that the summons to enter the headmistress's office was only a few seconds away and I would be required to confront the grief I had caused my parents. I wasn't particularly bothered. Although some people now tend to see me as an unruly person, unstable and even dangerous to those around me, I have never been directly accused by the authorities of any action suggestive of mental instability. Never in my judgment has my picture of reality become blurred to the point of total breakdown. The opposite is the truth. In my estimation, I am the one who sees reality more clearly than almost anyone else. So it was that like my Grandpa, who was smart enough to up sticks and save himself from danger just in time, I too found myself armed with an ability to feel threatened by a dripping tap long before it turns into a blood-bath.

"Gunther, come in please," the carefully composed, conciliatory voice of the headmistress was heard through the door. My father who was a relatively reserved man at least in appearance, and this to prevent any intrusion upon him on the part of the world, gave me a sidelong glance and transmitted a quick message: from his point of view at least everything was okay and the headmistress could go stick her finger up her arsehole.

"Gunther, are you aware of the fact that your marks are deteriorating badly, and the education committee may recommend that you don't move up a class?" the headmistress began.

"Lieutenant-Colonel G. Wünker to you, ma'am," I said.

The headmistress lost her cool immediately and turned a despairing glance towards my mother. Even at that time I knew that people who lose their cool at intervals just aren't cool people to start with. The headmistress turned to my mother, not to my father who was rather amused by his son's psychosis and the artificial intellectual display being put on by the distinguished pedagogue.

"What does this child want from us?" she asked in a pleading tone of voice and added:

"Gunther, we're here to help you. Your father has taken time off work and your mother is very worried."

"Ma'am," I said. "No disrespect, but it's Lieutenant-Colonel G. Wünker to you, ma'am."

"Lieutenant-Colonel G. Wünker," the headmistress corrected herself and continued immediately:

"Have you any explanation for the deterioration in your schoolwork, which wasn't at all bad until recently?"

"No, ma'am."

"Do you know that your progress to the next class is in grave doubt, at least as far as this school is concerned?"

"Doubt is the key to all thorough research," I replied, with a host of sincere intentions. First of all I wanted to suggest to the pompous cow that there were things going on, and maybe also suggest that the things going on were likely to be beyond the range of her intelligence, but most of all I wanted to prove conclusively to her and my parents and anyone else who was interested, that any objection or question she might be disposed to raise, I'd be capable of answering aggressively, and finally.

At this stage I was naturally asked to leave the room and there was no choice but to leave me in the mind-numbing class of the brain-dead woman with French pretensions, for another year, conditionally. Of course, everyone knew the kid wasn't completely stupid, might even be more cunning than the headmistress. At the same time there was no doubt that the kid was breaking off his contacts with schoolwork and immersing himself in some obscure militaristic fantasy.

In fact, in the context of my desperate longing to turn into the perfect symbol of the foreskinless, I operated in a somewhat bizarre fashion, though I was aware at the time that it was exceptional. The first manifestation of abnormality revolved around my apparently genuine belief that I really was a lieutenant-colonel in the victorious Zionist army. At that time, incidentally, members of my race believed their army was indeed a victorious army. Admittedly, this was after the October War which in retrospect was the first in a long series of lost battles in which my homeland suffered disaster after disaster until the final disaster from which it was never to recover. But at that time, the people of Israel, and I among them, were adept at ignoring painful reality in a systematic way. There were few who appreciated the scale of the impending catastrophe and I personally identified with the majority of my people, seeing our army, in the air, on the sea and on land, as a lethal and invincible force.

So when I was fifteen years old I was already known, at least among my close acquaintances, by my new name of Lieutenant-Colonel G. Wünker. Dad took a rational view of the issue. To him, compared with the other eccentricities coming to light in my unnatural development, not least my uninvited sharing in his photo-orgiastic world, hiding behind a prestigious title associated with our glorious army seemed a positive sign. On the other hand Dad saw in his son's Zionist-militaristic-foreskinless complex an act of revenge against his own father, who had tried in every way open to him to implant in him and in me the aspirations of a novice Protestant pastor – not the most trendy of perspectives in that part of the world.

And so throughout my pleasant and tranquil adolescence I saw myself as dedicated to one purpose alone: heroic death on the battlefield. I couldn't actually decide if I was the sacrifice or maybe the altar itself, but I wasn't that interested in profound philosophical speculation, unless it made some clear and substantial contribution to my people as such. Anyway, if you think it through, at least from the point of view of the war victim being eaten in his grave, it's irrelevant to ask whether he's the sacrifice or the altar.

But my most pressing concern in those days revolved around the choice of a girl, someone to fall in love with and a young womb in which to sow the youthful turmoil that I was so amply endowed with in those days.

When it's your destiny to die in battle, you have to establish your romantic and socio-erotic relations with a girl who has positive propensities towards widowhood. As a future patriotic casualty, you can't afford to get involved with a hippy type who smokes, or some unhygienic bimbo, because the one you fall in

love with now, in high school, she's the one who after your
death is going to spend the rest of her life perpetuating your
memory. The last thing that a corpse-in-waiting can bear while
still alive is the humiliating thought that his memory is going to
fall into the hands of a dipso freak or what we used to call in
those days "a chick with skid marks in her knickers".

A few years later, when my own little war broke out, I
realised how important it was to establish a link, before it's too
late, with a potential mourner. As you've probably gathered by
now, in spite of all my fervent declarations on the subject of
heroic death, and unlike some of my best friends, I personally
did not succeed in falling in battle. In that war I was already
almost an adult. In general terms, there's not much difference
between the Gunther of those days and yours truly, leaving aside
the paunch that's developed since then, and what used to be a
glut of predatory hormones that hasn't been a part of my life for
some time.

Scientists from all corners of the world came to the unanimous conclusion long ago that war is a horny phenomenon. I
can vouch for this from personal experience, although in that
war I suffered from severe constriction of the bollocks which
never got to be discharged because the girls I knew, most if not
all of them, were caught up in a desperate bereavement race that
I was afraid would never end. Grabbing a bit of female arse in
those jolly days of death was just an impossible objective. There
was a whole clique of women of the fallen prancing ceremoni-
ously from funeral to *shiv'ah* to tours of gravesites. "Be sure to
get yourself a stiff for the weekend," they used to wish one
another, on weekdays. They weren't all so lucky. I knew some
lonely spinsters who hadn't managed to grab a potential fatality
before the lads marched away to war and were forced to make
do with miserable no-hopers, head-injury patients and occu-
pants of intensive care units, those who could confidently be
expected to die soon. Women, I realised then, have a clear phys-
iological tendency towards bearing memory and they scramble

over it, whether it's possible, whether it's appropriate, or otherwise.

Since understanding of this simple fact was part of my armoury from the age of fifteen and a half onwards, all that remained from my point of view was setting up the apparatus of socio-erotic relations with my future widow. Unfortunately, romantic skills weren't my strong point then, any more than they are now. I haven't got and never had the guts to stand in front of a girl, look straight into her moist eyes, bore myself a hole in the seal of her heart and thread myself through it. No one has ever discovered the slightest spark of romance in my baggage. Women who see me as a romantic figure, and there have been a dozen or so like that, are just exercising their creative imagination. In fact I understood even then, that for someone really to love me, a lot of imagination would be needed. Aware as I was of my awkwardness and romantic deficiency, all that was left to me was the development of a style of courtship bordering on tactical suicide. The persona I had adopted was that of a military man, cool-headed and cunning, spitting nationalistic fire at every mammary gland that crosses his path. Being so afraid of face-to-face combat, I trained my tongue in irrevocable fashion to scour every crevice on the face of the earth. Even in my tender childhood I understood that a woman, by the very fact of being a woman, has the ability to leave me exposed, hurt and defenceless. When I see the face of a beautiful woman, when I see her moist eyes, I have to save myself from the oppressive weight which descends on me, out of fearful pain and awareness of a gap that perhaps will never be filled. When I confront the embodiment of tenderness, I'm gripped by utter gloom and a shaming tear appears at the corner of my left eye. It's as clear to me as daylight that if I divest myself of my arsenal of verbal weaponry, then this fair sex, with its outward inwardness, is capable of turning me into a pitiable spent force.

Even then, at the end of the fifth grade, I realised that time wasn't going to stand still just for my sake. There was much work to be done and catastrophe close at hand. I needed to be trapped in the net of a girl meeting all the complex criteria of bereavement. And sure enough salvation was not slow in coming. Avishag caught me on her hook.

4

Avishag, my Avishag.

In the first woman you find the essence of the greatest secret of all. What you don't grasp there, you'll never grasp. Apparently life is sketched out like a stately progression of constant wisdom, but the truth scorches like white-hot steel on a bare arse. What I didn't know when I came to Avishag, not one of my other women has succeeded in teaching me. I don't know what women really know about the rearing neurotic, but from my point of view, in these final moments of completing my life's work, I admit and confess that in spite of a wealth of experience, with regard to the cunt I remain as ignorant as I was that Friday with Avishag.

The cunt. It's like life and like war. You can study it, learn about it, develop theories and even lay down doctrines. But the first encounter exposes the oh-so-terrible truth: the world is chaotic and within this totality, the cunt is chaos in miniature. At that time I didn't even pretend to be an expert in matters of love and sexuality. I came to Avishag a certified virgin. All that I wanted was concentrated on the project of laying the founda-tions of a quorum of females who would cherish my memory. Ecstatically, I imagined the congregation of mourners jostling roughly around my open grave, a phalanx of the bereaved and the broken-hearted coming to say farewell to Eric (a pet name that I gave to the love-bone that used to rear up from my body at intervals) for the last time before the stone is rolled into place. I saw them huddled together, scratching, weeping, screeching

and staring, bemoaning the bitterness of their fate and the loneliness that they would suffer in my absence. In one of my dreams
of this DIY funeral, enriched by the pain of my loss to these
women, I clearly remember how suddenly, through the hubbub
of weeping, a Moroccan rutting-call was heard splitting the air,
that North African reverberation produced by rolling the
tongue – *lululululululululululululu . . . leyeyeyeyeyeye . . .* Years later
I tried in the course of a prolonged session of self-analysis to
understand how and from what source Moroccans had invaded
my dream and my funeral as well.

"What was that Moroccan woman doing at your funeral?" I
would ask myself, sucking on a pipe and winking at myself with
pride and self-importance.

"Were there refreshments? Were there Moroccan cigars?"

As in those days I wasn't yet acquainted with the erotic
charms of North Africa, I reckoned maybe this had been an
echo from the future, trying to drag me out of my grave and
back among the living.

My Avishag wasn't the fairest of women, but I'd realised at an
early age that with an appearance like mine, I'd better be content with whatever I could get. Nor was she the smartest human
being alive, but then Eric wouldn't have sailed through any
intelligence tests either. The reader won't be far wrong if he
assumes that Avishag and I could have been described as the
ultimate in mediocrity. Although we were spectacularly ordinary, we were very much in love. We were so much in love that
sometimes I forgot I had to die, and I so much forgot I had to
die that thoughts of crowds of mourners over my open grave
began to give way to dreams the colour of lettuce with lots of
sky around. When people are really in love, they want to live in
the country, as if to keep up the link with nature, to give meaning to the expression "Mother Earth". Earth and fertility turn
into a direct extension of the womb.

So at the age of sixteen at Avishag's side I understood
some things in a deeper way than I was capable of understand-

ing at any stage in my later life. At Avishag's side I understood the most primal connection between man and woman, earth and green growth, blue of the sky and the smile of a kid. Life in general then took on a mythic quality that included impressions of life itself and life as a concept. My Avishag, I, and the earth seemed to turn into a kind of oneness, so big and so huge that it was also tiny and personal and as intimate as it could possibly be.

That weekend up Avishag's rear end I learned a first and last lesson that I'll never forget. So wrapped up in my pointless fantasy role of a cool military guy that the furthest I dared go was a peck on the cheek, I suddenly felt fingers groping around in my underpants. I did a quick count of my fingers and discovered to my amazement that the ones in my pants weren't mine. I was flustered enough to go apeshit, and the same could be said for Eric, who had no idea how to cope with the intruder. My throat dried up straightaway. With what was left of my strength I tried to raise some saliva, in an effort to block this terrible sensation of death through loss of fluids. My heart was already on the point of bursting and then she really touched me, a proper grope this time, and it was like nothing I'd experienced in my life. It was good like only the absolute embodiment of goodness could be. Even at this moment, decades later, I feel a cold spasm passing through me. Confusion and delirium led me to my first post-childhood initiative and I gave my fingers free rein. Despite the fact that I was something of an expert in the science of the clitoris, as a result of my secret indulgence in Dad's photoheritage, even so the blind virginal probing of my fingers there between Avishag's young thighs brought me to the highest pitch of excitement I had ever known. I'm still roaming like a poisoned mouse in those bushy thickets, eagerly searching for something – I'm not quite sure what – and suddenly my fingers are filled with that hot jelly, like molten lava welling up from the depths. Suddenly and without warning I start spluttering, panting, snorting, gagging and I know at once something isn't right, something isn't the way it was the day before yesterday, and I'm heading straight for an electrical short in the consciousness or maybe even an explosion of electro-static cells in the region of the upper brain. Fear of death creeps up on you suddenly from an obscure direction, palpitations and cold sweats and God knows what else and then miraculously at the very last moment without any warning, a dam breaks in me in the region of the loins causing immediate dissolution of the nervous system. After a minute or two, while I'm still gasping on my lover's neck and wallowing deliciously in my gunge, the order is given to return to normality and prepare for renewed movement. With Avishag, my Avishag, I discovered the real meaning of bonding between man and woman, and the power that lies in the difference between them, and I loved her. I loved Avishag so much.

I loved Avishag so much that certain parts of my body, especially the bits that tend to stick out, began to show a clear and emphatic aversion to the ridiculous idea of patriotic suicide. In a general way, and this I realised only when I was much older, I was suffering in those times from an alarming personality-split. While I knew for a fact that Avishag had chosen me, Lieutenant-Colonel G. Wünker, because of her inclination towards widowhood, I, for my part, confronted by her charms, began to show renewed interest in living. Since I understood even then that the world didn't revolve according to the template implanted in my head but in ways of its own, I turned into a kind of double agent on my own behalf. From the point of view of those around me I continued to be second-in-command of an armoured brigade, if not more. My best friends also adopted this militaristic/militerotic approach and became staff officers, captains and platoon commanders in my outfit. On the other hand, I myself, in my heart of hearts, began to develop a full-blown aversion to this ridiculous dance among the bullets of the enemy. If my memory doesn't mislead me, in fact I didn't dare face up to this fear, not even for a moment and I sure as hell didn't share it with anyone. I was so afraid of fear I didn't even dare let myself in on my thoughts. On the contrary, the more afraid I was, the more macho and surly I appeared, even though I myself couldn't see the point of this display of aggression. A favourite author of mine, one whose name always puts me in mind of the scent of roses, once wrote that the problem of double agents is that testimony to their success is bound up with their ability to become so well integrated among the enemy that no one can tell the difference. The agent is liable to invest so much energy in copying the appearance and thought-patterns of the enemy that only a matter of time separates his status as an implanted alien from his decisive transfer to the ranks of the enemy. And I, between the sheets, writhing in the arms of my little girl, lost my alien status. I became a member of society, an implant. While I was still a toy town general when it began, through the constant back and forth, in and out of Avishag's foaming pussy, new songs began to reverberate in me, songs of eternity and fertility. I deserted to the ranks of those eager to live. I no longer wanted to die for the Zionist dream; I wanted to live for it and serve it on the procreation front. Somewhere along the way I lost faith in oblivion as an objective. I lost the sense of strangeness. I joined a Kibbutz.

In spite of the lust for life which was raging in my flesh and playing havoc with my mind I was still lumbered, till death apparently, with a bunch of numbskull "officers" eager for combat. A herd of goats celebrating their approaching death, the legacy of their master and mentor, yours truly. Much to my surprise, I came to the conclusion that I was endowed with an excessive degree of charisma which had the potential to bring disaster down on me. What was I supposed to do with my gang of pseudo-officers, all of them intent on battle, while I myself, for myself, wanted nothing more than the precious pearl I had discovered. As if all this wasn't enough, as the holder of the most senior rank in this absurd organisation I was also required to behave appropriately, act stern and decisive, when in fact I'd lost interest in the whole bloody game. In those days of emotional turmoil, it became absolutely clear to me that while stupidity is nothing more than a passing evil, charismatic stupidity is liable to be a permanent disgrace and disaster.

With Avishag I spent the most intense phase of my youth in the solid inner belief that maybe this would be the only relationship of my life. In retrospect, it's not that I don't regret things didn't turn out that way, but it's clear to me now that in our youthful innocence then there was something that could have cast a shadow over the rest of our lives. Other women didn't concern me at all, they just didn't come into my field of vision. I never betrayed Avishag's trust, something I can't say about any of my other women. We were so innocent in those days, when we thought of ourselves as transparent within a world of glass. We spent our finest years as if life was a leisurely stroll through the glass maze in Shlotzkilski's Lunar Park. We would spot one another, run towards one another, collide with the glass walls and burst out laughing. In this glass mirror there's a different view of the world, a view that I don't underestimate today, far from it. As I've grown older, I've become further and further removed from myself and from the great family of mankind. I no longer have unmediated access to those pure thoughts and desires. The world has turned darker from day to day and I've become adept in navigating a path among its shadows and blind alleys.

I didn't know then, and it never occurred to Avishag that I, her personal general, the first man to get close to her, was turning gradually into a tormented and haunted coward. So ignorant were we of ourselves, that Avishag herself began to play an active part in my dumb fantasy world. The climax came when she proposed a surprise party for one of my classmates who had just received a pretend promotion. We were all of us then, the command-group, sitting in orderly fashion on a cloud, suspended and drifting in the heart of blue skies. To the majority of us even death still seemed an alluring prospect, although I

venture to confess that I was beginning to have occasional
flashes of intelligence. I sensed even then that sooner or later I
would fly on a blacker cloud to a distant land with especially
grey skies.

Throughout the tangled web of my life, I have never taken a holiday, except for those two weeks of enforced liberty between final graduation from school and the call to the colours. At every stage of my secondary education, my teachers took pleasure in marking me down just before the long vacation, a kind of child- ish revenge on the part of the crippled by accident of birth.

"He hasn't studied all year, so he must study over the summer."

It was a conspiracy. On a regular basis they vented their frus- trations on me, delaying my progress to the next class, giving me extra work and making me sit transitional exams. Most if not all of my teachers, who seemed to me even then a bunch of unut- terably boring shits, had no idea that they were doing me a huge favour. There was nothing that repelled me more than holidays and nothing that excited me more than studying by myself, alone in my room, if only for the simple reason that I could spray adolescence juice around any time I felt like it. In my free time I would read or retire to my bed according to the demands of my biological metabolism.

I don't have and I've never had any inclination to break off from the work that I've done. *Arbeit macht frei*, how true that is! To my mind, liberty and idleness create stultifying routines of their own, denying free rein to ideas and aspirations which are constantly mutating. Those two weeks of unchallenging idleness taught me that if no challenge is put in front of you then you have to invent one for yourself.

Alberto and I decided to subject ourselves to the toughest tests of physical endurance. Alberto, incidentally, was the person closest to me in those years and perhaps ever. From the start of elementary school we were never apart for more than a few hours, and that's why Alberto's disappearance from my life and the fact that he left me alone in the world amounted to such a big deal for me. If Alberto had stayed alive, everything could have looked different. Alberto was the most extraordinary figure I've ever known. He outshone the rest of us in every possible way: he was without any doubt the fastest, the strongest and even the tallest. In every sphere you could think of – schoolwork, sports, girls even and God knows what else – Alberto scored the highest points. In spite of this, he used to smile a moronic sort of smile at us and talk a load of gibberish sometimes, just so he'd be accepted in our gang, in that absurd command-group. We always knew we didn't have a lot in common with Alberto, we knew he was destined for great things, whereas we were going to rejoice forever in our mediocrity.

And yet, over the years bonds of friendship were formed between me and Alberto, friendship of a kind I haven't experienced with anyone since, to this day. We used to sit around day and night indulging in senseless fantasies. We used to see ourselves as astronauts, champion fornicators, Wehrmacht officers and even tycoons in the student travel business. You could say there wasn't a single illusion, daydream or macho fantasy that we didn't exploit to the full. We made plans for our future commercial partnership, so we'd have something to fall back on in the event of our not succeeding in dying in battle, our first choice. We reckoned that as our relative strength lay in initiating way-out fantasies, we could maybe turn this into a marketing opportunity, offering the masses the chance to travel to their heart's desire, their own personal Shangri-la. We were going to set up an agency selling flight-tickets to the very limits of the imagination and we even had a name for the agency: "Imagination Tours".

In those days of enforced pre-army freedom I was secretly hoping that in some miraculous way my military prowess of the past would return to me. In fact, as the day of my enlistment came closer, I could feel my valour steadily draining away. Still, the army was just around the corner and a final toughening-up exercise wouldn't do us any harm. So for the two weeks pre-ceding enlistment Alberto and I walked the streets festooned with weights, spent three days in the desert without food or water, indulged in naïve survival games. To prepare ourselves for the rigours of the P.O.W. camp we whacked our own toes with belts, set fire to our pubic hair. We even conquered the highest peak in the coastal plain, so we'd be ready to scale Hermon, if necessary. So as the fateful day approached I thought maybe something of my lost heroism had been restored after all.

Alberto and I enlisted on the same bitter and frenetic day. Within an hour Alberto disappeared from the selection centre. He was secretly assigned to a hush-hush elite reconnaissance squad, so hush-hush even the Chief of Staff hadn't been let in on the secret. Classification of members of the squad was so rig-orous that besides awareness of your own existence you weren't supposed to know anything, even about your comrades-in-arms, so rigorous that sometimes a group of soldiers within the squad lost contact with themselves.

Soldiers in the squad were strictly forbidden to possess any knowledge, relevant or irrelevant, so Alberto and his mates had to practise forgetting. Amnesia exercises were among the most arduous military training routines in those days, and the training schedule of this unit, which admitted into its ranks only *la crème de la crème*, was beyond any level of endurance that the human mind could imagine. Because the unit took in real tough guys like Alberto who were experts in the techniques of warfare and physically strong enough for any operational duty even before enlisting, the unit adopted a spartan system of training which was in fact the absolute opposite of the tradition of the army and its ethos of warfare. And so, even in the earliest days of their service, members of the unit engaged in combined operations demanding competence in flying and diving, and prodigious physical strength for the purpose of trekking hundreds of kilometres behind the enemy lines.

Very gradually and in a calculated manner, throughout the remainder of the course, an unprecedented effort was made by the best army psychologists and *cordon bleu* chefs on reservist service to downgrade the physical and intellectual capabilities of the soldiers of the unit to the extent of turning them into lumbering, retarded fatties, spoilt brats prone to sudden and prolonged outbursts of infantile grief. The initial training of the unit, which had focused on developing the soldier's talent for forgetting culminated in a gruelling march of oblivion in the course of which the squaddies got themselves lost in the vicinity of their homes, walking around in circles and leaving no traces behind. Furthermore, in an emotional ceremony attended by nobody, the few who had reached the finishing line, Alberto among them, received their amnesiac's wings and a beret of indeterminate colour (for reasons of field security). The beret was incidentally fitted with a bleeper, an electro-optical sensor triggered by absence of contact with a head and designed to prevent loss of the beret. Naturally enough, members of the forgetting squad had a propensity towards losing berets at a quite unacceptable rate, although on the other hand by losing berets they proved their talent and their commitment to their illustrious role as elite amnesiacs.

It goes without saying that behind the military mode of thought that led to the formation of the forgetting squad, there lurked a high degree of understanding and a deep insight into military philosophy. Members of army counter-intelligence, who are the smartest guys to ever put on a uniform, were smart enough to realise back then after the war of October '73 something that the majority of generals never realised. The army, to their mind, was perceived as such an absurd organisation that as a means of forging within it an imaginative, critical and creative

element, men had to be trained in anti-military thinking to the
point of revolutionary stupidity.[1] It's worth pointing out that
although there's no shortage of literary material dealing with
ordinary military stupidity, it's hard to find any mention anywhere of revolutionary anti-military stupidity. This was a new
theory of warfare, which had to be worked out from scratch.
Since counter-intelligence was itself a part of the army and a
symbol of excellence, those chosen for the role of stupid negative amnesiacs needed to be the best, the most analytical and
intellectually gifted of the nation's soldiers. Soldiers who in
other circumstances would have turned out to be the most
"decorated", platoon commanders, chiefs of staff and prime
ministers. Those with the physical and mental stamina to repel
whole columns of enemy armour single-handed.

My friend Alberto was assigned the almost impossible
mission of criticising the military set-up from inside, without
inhibitions.

Throughout our period of service, every Friday, on the rail-
ings opposite the Baraka café, the command group used to
assemble, or at least those of its members who'd got weekend
leave. We used to sit for hours, eyes smarting, with our perky-
titted girlfriends, trying to amuse ourselves by exchanging
impressions and exposing military secrets. The more you're able
to break the silence and scatter the greatest number of military
secrets to the wind, the closer you reckon you're getting to the
nub of things. In the first months of training, while most of us

[1] Editor's note: There can be no doubt that in this instance Wünker is expressing himself in terms of the meta-indoctrinational principle with which he
became obsessed in his later years. We do not have much information at our
disposal regarding the "forgetting squad", but it may be assumed that the idea
behind the setting up of this elite formation derives from the failure of the
"conception", the failure which led to humiliating defeat in the October War
and in countless confrontations thereafter. The military establishment found
itself unprepared and for this reason sought to reach a creative "in-house"
solution.

were boasting about our impressive aptitude for dismantling some rifle or another, or even for washing in cold water, Alberto was already piloting helicopters, planting mines under water and wandering casually behind enemy lines. We knew well enough that Alberto had surpassed us all, he was the stuff of which generals are made. Cold, calculating and analytical – that's what he was. By the time we ourselves had begun flying in choppers and strolling behind enemy lines, Alberto was becoming more and more reticent. Gradually he stopped filling us in on all the things he'd been up to, and we believed in him and acknowledged that we weren't entitled to share his secrets. As time went by he stopped calling us by our names, or got them mixed up. In our ignorance we took this for an example of typical top-brass humour. The look in his eyes turned glassy, dreamy and full of mystery, and he began putting on weight. It took us some time to realise he'd stopped coming to our meetings altogether, but we'd known all along, even without him confiding in us, that he was involved in some pretty heavy stuff and the fate of the nation rested on his shoulders. Two months before he was due for demob, Alberto was killed in mysterious circumstances.

Years later I discovered that he'd just had enough of forgetful stupidity. In a document leaked to me from the secret files of counter-intelligence I found a few lines from a funeral oration delivered by his commander, the amnesiac-in-chief:

Lieutenant-Forgetter Alberto Algernetti
Killed in the line of duty, in his revolutionary anti-army stupidity
Alberto showed great commitment to his assignment
And something else that I can't remember just now, but I'm sure
there was something else he showed ... Now what the fuck was it?

6

As I grew up it seemed to me in retrospect, that in the strange world I'd been raised in, the distinctions had been blurred between self and history, between identity and identification, between sacrifice, the victim and the spilling of guts. If I hadn't been given the opportunity to discover before it was too late that I'm a professional coward, I would definitely have been crushed to death beneath the wheels of history. As a coward I soon realised that if history had wheels it would have fled for its life, which is what happened at the end of the day.

From the moment I discovered I was a coward, my life alongside creatures imagining themselves historical became a much more interesting adventure. There are few things more wonderful than living in a paradise of fools, few experiences more pleasurable than wandering among people full of intentions and aspirations. Historical creatures seemed to me funnier and funnier. They saw every truth in a spirit of determinist vision and self-abasement.

Although I was aware even then, in my late teens, of a rapid diminution in my desire for death or, to put it another way, a perceptible increase in my will to live, I was still unable to take the necessary steps. I couldn't take off my uniform. In fact, I never did take off my general's uniform; it was simply taken from me by force and in the most humiliating manner. That sweltering August, two weeks after final graduation, I turned up at the recruitment and selection centre armed with two vests, a change of underwear and a toothbrush. There, without ceremony, without a sympathetic glance or as much as a word of commendation for my past activities, I was busted down from my senior rank to the status of a raw recruit, as if I'd been accused of crimes against humanity, the state, or God knows what else. There, in the recruitment and selection centre, I knew just how Dreyfus must have felt.

In my very first hours in the reception centre I realised that unlike the playground–militarism in which I'd scored such impressive achievements during high school years, in the real army my prospects of fitting in amounted to zilch. It was just that everything made me laugh so much, so much it hurt. Until you've been a real soldier, you'll have no idea what institutional stupidity means. My dad and other adults had taken the trouble to point out to me now and again that the army was a passing evil – just get through it and forget about it, but in my silly youthful rebelliousness I ignored them, with contempt. After two hours in the army I realised what I should have known all along: I'm a guy who's incapable of accepting authority. Not in childhood, in adolescence or adulthood, and definitely not in old age – I've never accepted authority. In the past, whenever a woman turned me down, I refused to accept the authority of her refusal. I kept at it, digging away and licking with my sharp tongue until I found a way through to her heart.

The prospect of two or three years in the army was enough to convince me that what I wanted most of all in the world was to sink between Avishag's thighs, close my eyes and never wake up. The nightmare was unbearable. I didn't have the faintest notion where I was going to find the strength of mind even to begin the tortuous and terrible process of surviving in the absurd, strident, dictatorial morass of the army.

Of course, the simplest option available to me was an immediate interview with the mental health officer. I'd heard at that time of soldiers getting themselves discharged with no trouble at all, by using the "elephant routine". The elephant routine is performed in the mental health officer's room and in his

presence. It's a simple exercise and it requires no special expert-
ise. You turn your front trouser pockets inside out, to make a pair
of big ears, unzip your flies, pull out your dick and announce:
"I'm an elephant!"

I personally know three soldiers who got out of the army by
claiming to be elephants, and I heard of a female mental health
officer who experienced a traumatic encounter with a jumbo in
the reception centre in Haifa and suffered a severe breakdown
as a result. It's said that throughout the remainder of her service,
before she'd go into her office, her superior had to go there first,
open the door and shout: "Elephants, sod off! Elephants, sod
off!" Only then was she prepared to go into her office – to sift
through mental health cases.

The elephant routine wasn't an option for me, for the simple and embarrassing reason that the best I could expect would
be getting discharged as a *baby* elephant. Make of that what you
will.

Anyway, it was clear enough to me that I wasn't going to be
discharged for psychological reasons. At that time, despite a
vague and troublesome inkling, I hadn't yet grasped the full
extent of my cowardice, or to put it crudely, I didn't know for
certain that I was the most scared-shitless coward on earth.
Today I realise that the moment you become aware you're the
most scared-shitless coward on earth you can solve all kinds of
problems with the simple statement: "I'm a coward." Later I discovered that people in general don't resent or despise cowards;
on the contrary, the respect they give them is out of all proportion. The reason for this is wrapped up in circus logic. On the
one hand, the guy who admits he's afraid doesn't despise the
coward because he identifies with him. On the other hand the
gallant hero trapped in the lions' den facing a dozen savage
beasts is bound to, and dependent on the coward, because it
takes a coward to recognise his heroism. He recognises it by the
shrinking and freezing of his bollocks. The coward thus turns
out to be a vital component in the social order.

But I belong to the worst strain of all, the strain that has no place in circus logic. I, Gunther, belong to the family of mega-cowards who set themselves up as national heroes. People like me make a show of despising the coward while not saluting the hero. As if this isn't enough, I'm a member of the exclusive clique of those who always find a way and a ploy to absent themselves from the battlefield. People like me send others to die their deaths for them. From the moment it began to dawn on me that I was nothing more than a playground-hero, I knew for a fact that when the chips were down, a rallying cry such as "Follow me!" would never pass my lips. I knew I wasn't one of those lions of battle who roar impressively and go storming forward. I believed in the more courteous approach: "After *you*, my heroic brothers!" – or an enticing cry such as "Volunteer to attack now and win a weekend pass to visit your Maker!"

So, while I in my innocence was trying to figure out a way of retreating with dignity from the dream of patriotic death, time was passing and I was still in uniform and a corporal, no less. A corporal, in an allegedly crack regiment, when war goes and breaks out. My war, in which I was supposed to be putting my head on the block. Incidentally, we'd been predicting this war since the end of our last term in high school, two years before it broke out. We knew we were in a war-cycle, and some of our names would be inscribed on the brass plaque at the school gates. Like menstruating women, leaders of nations have periods too, in weird cycles of their own, and we knew the nation's menstrual blood was going to be *our* blood. We used to joke that if "our war" didn't break out at the appointed time, it could mean the State was pregnant. And we knew the timing of the war in advance. Leaders the world over schedule wars for the first week in June, perhaps because they can't stand the heat of summer wearing ties and encased in dark suits. I reckon leaders prefer to spend the summer months in air-conditioned command-bunkers rather than holding populist rallies in parched, sleepy, dead-end southern townships.

When you're an infantry soldier, the most oppressive thing on earth is the journey towards your advancing death in a battered, swaying army truck. You're anxious, paralysed by fear, and nerves have made your bladder swell to the point of bursting. The journey goes on hour after hour amid endless columns of pissy-pants, trapped like you in steel boxes and puking over their boots. The combination of the searing sun overhead and the roar of the lurching steel monsters, plus the clatter of caterpillar-tracks on asphalt, turns time into a whirlpool. It's as if you're daydreaming of your anticipated end. In the din and the chaos around you, you find nothing personal in the death that awaits you at the end of the road. You feel like living and tormented flesh, in the lobby of the kosher sausage factory.

As you get closer to the front you hear the thunder of artillery and the sirens of ambulances screeching as they sweep past you from the front to the rear, ferrying bits of broken people. Time passes slowly, every second an eternity to you. Very gradually, to the rhythm of melancholic pounding, the head of the column disintegrates and you're shoved forward to fill up the gap, the mummified apex of your approaching death. And you don't care, as there's no point bursting into tears over the grave that you've dug for yourself, and the night comes down, darkness like the plague of Egypt and already I'm stuck in an exchange of fire with something that's shooting at me in a desperate effort to put an end to me. I hide behind a spur of rock and every now and then toss a grenade or fire at random, if only to signal to the enemy that he might as well carry on shooting seeing that I, as far as I can tell, am still alive and breathing. For two long hours I play with the gang of murderers, until at a certain point I've had enough of this ridiculous game in which the whole world is united against me in a desperate attempt to turn me into a sieve. So, in a sudden surge of energy that even today I can't explain, I load a magazine full of goodies, switch to automatic, aim directly at my ankle and squeeze the trigger, with a yelp of pain that comes out as an authentic and blood-curdling battle cry. I've put a whole fusillade of bullets into my foot. From this point on I feel as relaxed as I would be between Avishag's thighs, nuzzling her neck in those languorous post-coital moments. I fall into a contented sleep.

The next day I wake up in a hospital in the middle of the country to the bright lights of popping flash bulbs. To my surprise it turns out that I'm the hero of yesterday. I'm told that my brothers-in-arms, hearing my orgiastic battle cry which they knew so well from the early stages of our training, immediately interpreted it as an order to attack. They stormed forward, thinking they were following me. Once they had conquered and destroyed and were checking the dead, they realised I wasn't there. They rummaged among the bodies of the enemy, thinking maybe I'd gone in there just using a bayonet. They hunted for hours around the objective until suddenly, just as dawn was breaking, they found me lying unconscious at the foot of that spur of rock, a broad smile on my face. As if I'd seen, before passing out, that they'd finished the job that I had initiated with my cry in the night.

So for a whole week I was treated to visits by all the top people in the land, coming to be photographed beside the national hero in his hospital bed.[2] I was doped up to the eyeballs with all kinds of painkillers and I couldn't even lift up my head to see what was left of my foot. Every day my bed was surrounded by swarms of professional coffin-chasers, whom Avishag took great pleasure in getting rid of. I knew even then that every single one of these bereavement-freaks would have let me in on her most intimate secrets as a member of the mammary brigade, if only given the chance. I've noticed that women reveal their oral talents in the shadow of the fear of desertion, or alternatively by the light of simulated closeness, when confronted by a bulging hard-on.

With the first intermission my former subordinates from high school came on pilgrimage too. Even Alberto turned up for a short visit, his eyes blank and the smile that I remembered so well now strained and heavy. I was bathing during those days of grace in a thick and sticky broth of adulation blended with chocolate. Only after two weeks of condensed compassion did the coffin-chasers begin to scale down their visits, leaving just Avishag and me, and my parents who came occasionally to

[2] Editor's note: The Hebrew political elite had a well-known weakness for hospital wards and sickbeds. Government leaders conducted desperate media battles among themselves for the right to be immortalised at the bedsides of war-cripples and alongside grieving families. They came to give succour, and left succoured.

bombard me with questions about my future. It was clear to me that I had to sever all links with the old world, and as soon as possible. If they were to find out that the sieve-style perforation of my ankle had been self-inflicted, in a moment of uncontrolled panic, if they were to find this out and especially after the media orgy that had surrounded me – they would throw me out of the window of the hospital ward and call the municipal disposal services to come and pick up what was left of me. According to my own judgment, I couldn't be accused of anything. All I did was shoot myself in the foot with a heartrending cry and fall asleep. I didn't claim to be a hero, although when I admitted this to reporters the morning after, this too was taken as reflecting credit on me, evidence of my modesty and humility.

I'd been given a great opportunity to extricate myself from my image as fixed in my eyes and the eyes of those around me. I'd been given the right to escape by a new and unknown path. I discovered that when somebody is seen as a hero, eccentric behaviour patterns are accepted with excessive tolerance. What was painful was the knowledge that my Avishag, who had been hovering around my heroism like someone who's won the lottery, would soon be disappearing from my life. She loved someone else in me. A man who never was and never had been. So I deliberately cultivated the image of the self-indulgent battletrauma victim.

After some two months in the hospital and a few days before I was discharged, I told Avishag that I needed a little time to myself. The fact that I was speaking fluent male-ese was a clear and accepted sign that the loving and lovely bond between us was no more. The love of my youth had run its course.

I felt an overpowering need to tour other worlds, chase distant women, one-night stands – or five-minute stands come to that. I wanted to collapse, my heart broken by a girl passing me by in the street. As she disappears from sight my longing for her soars beyond endurance, as if the love of my life is

slipping through my fingers. I wanted to kiss women I didn't
know, give love-bites to foreign chicks on the bus. I wanted
to sniff the seats of anonymous bicycles, whisper lewdly into
ear lobes, close my eyes and wallow in my lust forever. Then,
in my youth, I didn't yet understand that at the crossing-
point between the lobby of love and the escalator of time there's
a heavy burden of futile fantasies. You work your way up
through time to your abstract love. Sometimes you even see her
coming closer, you're filled with longing, breathing heavily and
clasping her naked body ever closer and then, at the finishing
line of this imaginary marathon, you yourself are exposed
as the destitute beggar that you are, and all that there was
between her and you is nothing but the futile fantasy of the
crossroads.

   Leaning on a stick I went out into the new world as a limp-
ing fornicator-major. It didn't take me long to realise – and this
contradicted what I used to think in my youth – that nubile
peace-campaigners represented my best prospect of getting laid.
In those post-war days the country was already under the control of a tightly knit and extremist clique of nationalist Jewish
fundamentalists, and the flag of enlightenment was carried by
ephemeral peace movements. The enlightened peace-seekers
saw bright light at the end of the tunnel, and I screwed up my
eyes along with them, as if I too could make out some abstract
rosy radiance filtering through to us from the future. In this situation of guaranteed rosy radiance up ahead and the darkness of
the tunnel in the present, they all wanted to share a little
warmth, and that's how I got close to the nubile and enlightened. When we were naked they would scrutinise my body,
focusing on my damaged foot and intoning fervently: "No more
war" – before straddling me and swallowing me whole. Women
of the Left have a sort of poetic compassion for war casualties,
it makes them horny as hell. There was even one crazy lefty who
loved rubbing her erogenous zones on my perforated ankle until
she got where she wanted to be, with some heart-rending battle

cries on the way. I stood and stared at the weirdness of the world. I finally stopped taking the family of womankind at all seriously.

As time passed the Left and the enlightened in general began to seem to me a foolish waste of time. I detected in those enlightened lovelies a violence that reminded me of the opposing camp. In the carnivals of peace in which I took part sometimes, I noticed a brutality that really disgusted me. On the other hand, I learned to use these protest marches as a way of pumping up my libido to unprecedented levels. In these parades, the men used to march at the front like a kind of human shield, standing shoulder to shoulder in a grotesque parody of brotherhood and leaving me to limp to my heart's content among their womenfolk. The women would stride eagerly in the centre, trumpeting empty slogans of peace with truly impressive pathos. Sweat trickled from their armpits, spines, cleavages, sometimes a cheeky droplet glistened in the region of their gaily-belted waists – direct product of the prodigious, cock-crowing effort that they were involved in. They all moved together, girls, adults, fat, thin, faded, sick, beautiful and even very beautiful, filling their lungs to a regular rhythm and spewing out into the world tarnished and inharmonious pearls of peace. And I would be stumbling among them, walking amid the streams of sweat mingled with the scents of flesh and hair. Desire made me shudder. Sometimes I used to block my ears with both hands and imagine them panting and yelling above me. Then I would swing round on my axis and tremble with fear, fear of this stupid beauty, the smells of sweaty armpits, the perfume and the tampons. They used to screech in unison, growing louder and louder until they reached a mass orgasm, then collapsing, spent and in desperate need of a break. They were so beautiful in their debilitation I wanted to stay alive to sleep with all of them. I knew they were in the mood and I couldn't let them spend the night alone. In those days of priapic campaigning for peace, excess of libido even led me to identify with the plight of the Palestinian people.

As a crippled reservist, recognising the justice of the enemy's cause, my prestige rose in the eyes of members of the fair sex to the point where I was admitted to the ranks of the enlightened. Through fleshly contact, my women would share with me my opinions of equality. Even then, I was clearly endowed with a prodigious ability to implant myself in the brains of women with the power of words. I screw intellects in all senses of the word. Conventional chatting-up techniques not being my forte, as I've mentioned before, my way to carnality winds between liquid sparks of original ideas which I reveal with perfect timing. Women, although they aren't usually subtle, have a high regard for reason and for the other. Since deprivation is at the root of their existence, the desire to receive and to curl up in the shade gives them motive force. It's only natural that they present themselves with legs wide open to the thing that they lack and they covet so much. Since in the world of erections my name wasn't one to conjure with, I used words as a means of correcting this inadequacy. My women learned to lust after my word power and I learned to come up with the goods. They soon learned to fuck my wordiness in every conceivable position. Because women don't know what *petite mort* is but know all about constant and insatiable desire, I, with my verbal skills, used to sweep my women to the horizon of fulfilment, somewhere in the abstract zone where sexual delight unites with total desire.

The body of a man may fall, worn out by ejaculation to the point where he needs a proper rest, and yet reason never goes down the tubes. On the contrary, it is fertile and it creates the instinct to procreate. It seemed only natural that I learned to present to my loved ones the fruits of reason that were withheld from them. I brought women to illumination.

Illumination essentially shows the surfaces of things from an unfamiliar angle. At the same time, when the surfaces of things are illuminated, they become more familiar, and richer, in their new form. So I used to sneak into the souls of my women like a little god, plundering their minds and turning them into my property.

But always, despite my talent for unflagging verbosity, there were women I never got anywhere with. Those who were way ahead of me intellectually. They instilled in me a kind of terror, a cold shudder. They were castration personified, and yet in spite of this my lust for them knew no bounds. The more I failed to make headway with them, the more they cleft my virility into innumerable pieces; the more I wanted them, the less they wanted me, the more I wanted them and so on and so on ... I mustered all my intellectual powers, all my logical apparatus, and they spurned all that I had to offer. They made cold and calculating use of me and turned me into a template of inadequacy; alongside them, in the shadow of their all-embracing masculinity, I became the woman. I longed for them. Such a one was Lola, who accompanied me at intervals through the third decade of my life. At intervals she came and went and everything that I had, I gave to her.

8

Lola invaded my life for the first time in a corner of the famous cafeteria of the Faculty of Humanities. In Humanitarian circles, intellectual activity is concentrated amid coffee cups and cigarette smoke. There, in the cafeteria, the intuitive prodigies of mankind discuss, with pathos and hyper-energy, subjects of which they have only the vaguest understanding. They do this, not as a means of honing their powers of reasoning, but essentially as a means of impressing one another with empty eloquence. The more abstruse the topic that you raise, the better your chances of leaving your competitor standing in desolation, unable to reply. Since creating desolation of the mind is reckoned a worthwhile achievement, over the years the Faculty of Humanities and its cafeteria have turned into an intellectual wilderness – in other words, an ideal stamping-ground for me, seeing that when it comes to empty verbiage, I'm the undisputed champion. For hours we used to pursue penetrating debates, awash with sentiment and enthusiasm, on the least significant subjects imaginable.

In this barbarian landscape a lot of attractive girls used to nest, and there was one strange bird, Lola by name, who looked like an inverted straw-broom with a pair of slack tits. You could tell that Lola was a puzzled sort of bird, incapable of digesting the world around her. Her speech was a kind of slow, phlegmatic drawl, and the few occasions she opened her mouth, I noticed she could string out one syllable to the length of a whole sentence. While we were surfing on the waves of empty rhetoric, and especially in the dreary interludes between proposition and rebuttal, Lola would be watching us from the sidelines with those calf's eyes of hers, wrinkling her brow with an intensely earnest expression. As she was never drawn into the babbling circle, you could never tell what she was made of, for better or worse.

I used to notice her sometimes, sitting alone in the corner of the cafeteria. I imagined she was watching the world go by, and once I noticed the way she was staring, bemused, at a passing student with a look of agitation and hunger for love. In this prolonged and fragile look of hers there was something that made me shudder. Her feeble vulnerability contained a beauty that I wanted to embrace. After all, way back in my childhood, when my father used to take me to watch migrating birds, I used to feel the greatest empathy for the storks that brought up the rear, that lagged behind the rest. In Lola there was a kind of slow, veiled melancholia, as if she was looking out at the world through the glass of a Coca-Cola bottle. Lola had something that ignited my imagination – and maybe just a vague hint of desire as well.

One of those evenings between autumn and winter, when the sky is so grey you're sure world war must be imminent, when nobody wants to sleep alone – one of those evenings I found myself sitting next to Lola on the back seat of a number 25 bus. I wanted to bring up some topic, or even just hold a commonplace conversation, but what I could do in public, in front of a crowd, I was too shy to do on a one-to-one basis. The bus rolled on from stop to stop and already I was running out of time; on my own initiative I had taken the seat beside her and here I was, silent and wrapped up in myself. And now my stop was approaching and I was fated to get off without us exchanging a single word.

"How come you're so quiet for once?" – I suddenly heard her slow, phlegmatic, indifferent drawl.

"I was thinking about Descartes," I replied with a silly air of superiority, as I saw the stop where I was supposed to be getting off receding.

"What's so great about Descartes that makes you think about him and not me?" she persisted in the same slow and indifferent tone, turning her vulnerable, bovine eyes to stare at me, while I cleared my throat, trying to dredge up something plausible that would account for the way I'd ignored her presence up to now.

"I was thinking about the strange progression from 'I think therefore I am' to proof of the existence of God," I said with ultra-earnestness. To which she rejoined in the same phlegmatic style:

"If you had even a fraction of the reasoning-power you think you have, you'd have realised long ago that existence precedes thought. 'You are and therefore you think.' As for God, that's another story altogether."

Her voice was so low I had to make a real effort to hear. I swallowed spittle and came close to bursting into tears. This phlegmatic shithead had shattered me in three moves. Checkmate – and I might just as well be dead. In fact if I only could, I'd willingly have thrown myself in front of the wheels of that sodding bus, waiting calmly for my death and the end of everything. She, on the other hand, wasn't letting up for a moment:

"Tell me," she said, drawing it out into a kind of absurd glissando. "Instead of fucking my mind, why not have a go at fucking the rest of me?"

That was it, I knew I was drowning, my end had come. I tried to speak, I even managed a few rhythmic lip-movements, but no words came. I was choking. The phlegmatic madam had plucked all my feathers to the very last one. While I was still flailing like a fish just pulled from the water she continued, there on the back seat, to pulverise what was left of my pride. So with an air of calm and lazy assurance she asked:

"I live here near the bus-stop, are you coming up?"

Without waiting for any response on my part she grabbed me like a harassed mother dragging a morose infant. Lola took me off the bus and towed me, hobbling unsteadily, to the door of her apartment.

Nervously I entered her apartment and even before slamming the door she turned to face me, pinning me against the wall, clinging to my body under the cover of darkness. Clueless in the shadow of the mane of hair, pressed between soft and pendulous breasts, I grabbed hold of the two rounded segments of her arse and bit her neck. My lips nuzzling her throat, I pull her crotch towards mine, on the point of submission to her, as a man to a woman, and then it's as if Lola is gently pushing herself away from me and asking me:

"Tell me Gunther, do you think a man could love me?" To which I reply, instinctively and sincerely:

"Lola, I myself am already terminally in love with you."

In a ruthless tone of voice, she ripped into my flesh again:

"No Gunther, I mean a real man."

Still fastened to her neck, pressed against her crotch, I began shedding quiet tears of real despair. Lola didn't want me, she just fancied a little warmth, to avert the threat of the black sky. As for me, I was already incapable of living without her. I wanted her as a woman for all climatic conditions. She on the other hand despised me, as she despised the whole world, and with reason.

For a whole night she lay without moving a muscle while I exerted all my resources in the attempt to rattle her foundations. I felt like a tin soldier engaged in a futile and impotent assault on an impregnable fortress.

Maybe I really can't get it on with her, the alarming thought occurred to me at the very moment of plunging into the interior of her motionless body. I have to admit that, speaking for myself, the whole business of penetration has always seemed bizarre to me. There's something very indecisive about penetration. You attack and withdraw, enter and leave, leave and enter, into a highly lauded temporary permanence. I have no doubt at all that where penetration is concerned the man shows a very indecisive face, the pleasure of prevarication. Sometimes, just when I was trying to have fun inside a woman, I used to hear my mother's imperious tones resounding in my head:

"Gunther, either come in or go out but close the door!"

This never failed to blow away what was left of my concentration. I would try to dispel her and to regain the concentration she had stolen from me in her venomous Polish:

"Mum, leave me alone, let me be, let me screw in peace, I'm a big boy now."

As a rule, during the third decade of my life I was prone to severe concentration problems. In retrospect, I sometimes thought it would have been a good move by my parents to send me, in my early childhood, during one of the summer vacations, to a concentration camp, something which did indeed become popular among sensation-seeking Israeli youths. When it came to fucking, concentration problems were a particular worry, seeing that the act itself, all that storming in and pulling back, was a bit unfocused anyway. A friend who acted as my confidential mentor in my adolescence told me he had once spent the night with a girl who was so boring, that to hold on to his concentration and be sure of getting his rocks off, he had to imagine he was masturbating. This really was helpful advice.

All that night, while I'm going in and out of Lola's sleepy gates, trying to erase the fact that she's succeeded in plucking all my feathers one by one, instead of experiencing the gloomy reality of the pair of us, I invent an experience in myself. I'm wanking Lola in her innermost parts; I attack and retreat, biting her neck, one hand caressing her little round buttocks and the other clutching at her skinny waist. I imagine her groaning, gasping, fondling and as I'm still in the process of inventing her I spurt into her a rainstorm of sticky reality, the early rain in fact, presaging the winter of us both.

Only then, after spraying my juice inside her, do I realise how much more bitter the reality is than anything imagined. She's sleeping the sleep of the just, as if unaware that something has just invaded her entrails. I ask myself: is there any bottom to the pit that I've been shoved into these last few hours, or will I go on falling for ever? Just as I'm getting used to the idea of tumbling down the endless slope into Hell, I suddenly hear her phlegmatic tones:

"That was so good," she whispers. I catch a handhold on the cliff-face and I could weep for joy, as I clutch with the last remnants of my strength at the caper-bush jutting out from the rock and she continues in a self-indulgent murmur:

"Stay with me tonight and stroke me until I go to sleep, please."

I'd already twigged that where Lola was concerned it was best to economise on words and obey. So I obeyed. I leaned over her, threading my right hand under her head and on to the bony furrow of her shoulders, and the other hand I moved, barely touching, in tender arabesques between the jaw-line and the upper cheek. Then I changed direction, taking the back of my hand from the base of the throat to the ear and back again. Her eyes closed, she was serene as an angel. So beautiful and fragile in her sleep, and with winter just around the corner I wanted to be sure she was properly covered. I felt myself falling helplessly in love.

So I went on caressing her hour after hour until the dawn rose, the sun beginning to roll back the last vestiges of the night, and as the first rays of light percolated through the shutters I became aware of the sea of paintings and fragmentary sketches surrounding me on all sides. Only then did I perceive for the first time the background scenery of the room in which I'd had my way with her. I reckoned in my innocence that even if she threw me out as soon as she woke up, I personally wouldn't have come out of it too badly: a shag and a bit of culture too. But I soon realised that Lola's paintings were something that was happening in the future and had filtered through into the present of her room.

Lola painted like no one had ever painted before. Gradually, as the light breaking through the shutters grew brighter, her designs were revealed to me. First I saw isolated shadows, then what seemed to be a broad expanse of shadows gradually changing colours and becoming non-dimensional forms. Suddenly I saw designs in their entirety: a veritable symphony of such emptiness, it would be pointless even attempting to describe it in words. In any case, the works of Lola Bentini are today very much in the public domain and may be observed in any of the mobile exhibitions roaming among the various galleries of western capitals.

Quietly I got up from her bed and wandered among the empty shapes and the painful voids. I stepped forward and stepped back and refused to believe. Until that day I'd had no real contact with art and in spite of that I could feel Lola's handiwork sending me into a cold sweat. The sun was already making determined progress towards the centre of things, and with a glance through the crack of the shutter I could tell that the intimidating grey skies of yesterday had melted away. After more naked wandering among the exhibits on show I returned to the bed, took Lola's face in both my hands, kissed her warmly on the forehead and whispered, partly to myself, partly to her and maybe to both of us:

"Lola, you're a genius."

She opened her calf's eyes. I repeated what I'd said, but this time with added detail:

"Lola, you're a genius, I'm in love with you, I'll make sure you're always happy, I'll give you children, I'll water the plants, cook, wash the dishes, earn lots of money, brush my teeth, go to sleep after you, I'll learn how to give you pleasure, I won't mind your cold feet, I'll come after you, come before you, soap your back for you, we'll go for walks at weekends, I'll never grow a paunch . . ."

Lola interrupted me, her diction as lazy as ever but her tone resolute:

"Gunther, calm down. I don't know how to love. I've never loved and I don't think I ever shall."

I wasn't deterred. I assured her I'd be content if she'd just let me take refuge in her shadow and enjoy the fruits of my love for her on a one-sided basis.

Lola didn't reply to this. She sat up in the bed and stretched her arms above her head. She looked like a boyish kind of broom now, with soft little breasts tilting gently with her body, even when her body wasn't tilting at all. Lola got up and walked naked to the window as I watched every movement and twitch of her bony body; there's nothing that turns me on more than a hairy love-slot, glimpsed from the rear, hiding bashfully behind the cleavage of the arse.

I was obsessed by the thought that she really might never love me. Suddenly I found myself overawed by her beauty and

I knew there weren't many who could appreciate that kind of beauty. Maybe, I thought, her beauty would be my private property and I wouldn't have to share it with anyone.

"Lola," I said, as she opened the shutters, exposing the room to the blue sky of the morning, "do you want me to leave?"

"Gunther, it's been many years since I knew what I wanted."

She spoke without looking at me. I saw her face in profile, and the slow-moving, interlocking legs emerging from her tiny backside and I detected in her an excessive burden of grief. I came to her from behind and hugged her as if trying to wrap the whole of her in my arms while she went on looking out into the street and didn't move a muscle.

10

Many months passed and I was wrapping myself around Lola in a cosy kind of embrace. I learned to sense her intentions and her desires before she was aware of them herself. I was good at disappearing and leaving her in her artistic solitude, and I was good at enfolding her too, and even coaxing her into indulging with me in some natural and not so natural humping. At intervals I also let her trample on my dignity, and I moved into her room in the heart of the metropolis long before she herself knew that was what she wanted. Lola's life was hollow, but I knew she was destined for great things. I wanted to be there in her shadow when she hit the big time; more than that, I wanted to be a layer of bricks in the tower of her achievement. Lola herself didn't attach any great importance either to herself or to her art. She painted as if she had no choice in the matter. Being a creature of a different strain, a creature of futuristic qualities, there was no way she could forge a substantial bond with the family of mankind. She created her own world with her paintings, and at the same time she practised her art as a way of creating the world around her, our world that she didn't understand at all.

From her earliest childhood Lola had adopted that phlegmatic style of speech, just so she'd be accepted as a fully accredited member of the human race. Maybe she affected stupidity so she wouldn't be thrown out on account of her eccentricity, maybe so someone would make space for her. There's something rather amusing about these geniuses, trying so hard to be assimilated among us. Lola with her phlegmatic speech, Alberto with his silly smile, both of them key-figures in my life and both apparently from a different strain, a strain of silent greatness implanting itself in the folly of the noisy majority. Not being like other people, Lola and Alberto tried, each in his own way, to disguise their alien side by adopting decidedly degenerate human practices. In their behaviour there was a kind of innocent reflection of the dark layers that are a part of us. As if to be reckoned a solid pillar of the community, you have to pick your nose and talk a load of crap. As a member of the family of mankind, I reckoned it was a privilege hanging out with those types; it was like picking up telepathic transmissions from the future.

I enjoyed getting close to my girl-of-the-future, but I knew that to her mind, though she never said it, her relationship with me was a total waste of time, like a relationship with an endearing pet. A woman of her standing, a stately mare, can amuse herself from time to time with a shaggy poodle, but tying her destiny to his just isn't an option. I knew Lola was only keeping me by her side until she met the hero of her life. In fact, these people of the future can sometimes waste a whole lifetime waiting for that bloody saucer to take them back to their lost world. Not being a believer in time-tunnels or flying saucers I realised even then, though still in a vague sort of way, that Lola and I were deeply intertwined, and the guys Lola was going to meet, the ones who'd be hanging around her the moment she made it into the limelight – most if not all of those heroes would soon turn out to be empty illusions and she'd come back to me, broken-hearted. I knew I could never refuse her.

And sure enough, she used to return to me with wings clipped and feathers drooping. The desperate quest for unfading love, for perpetuity, for celestial curiosity, intellectual delight and sexual fulfilment, was simply hopeless. For some reason people tend to expect life to offer them something total, complete and absolute – all this while ignoring the fact that life is a finite and shitty experience which lies in wait for man in his isolation. You have to learn to be content with little. It's best to see consolation in shadows and bless the light even if it's out of reach.

Surprisingly, the higher the tally of Lola's disappointments mounted, the greater was her desire to exploit what she believed to be her right, her elementary prerogative. She used to come back to me broken-hearted, her body exuding strange scents and her womb awash with hostile juices. With an ease that amazes me now I learned to take pleasure in the favour of her return, to wallow in the shade of the oppressive tenderness of degradation. I was her right-hand man. She would lay her head on me and fall asleep within moments while I caressed her forehead late into the night. She used to stay with me for short intervals until the hunger arose in her again, and then she went back to looking for something that the world has never had to offer, to her or to any other person. She went from me to her lost loves, and I knew for certain that I'd be incapable of refusing her on her return.

At times such as these, left alone in her apartment which had in the meantime become our apartment, I would find solace in bought love. I realised that in my complicated situation there was a lot to be said for sex as a liquid asset. With sellers of love you're not expected to get into a lasting relationship. When you're buying love you're paying a wad of money for a wad of time, and infinite time is outside the exchange rate of commercial eroticism.

In bought love, by the nature of things, money flows like water, until that split-second of climactic upheaval. Until the very moment of sublime satisfaction you're prepared to give away everything you possess, but when it happens you turn into a shagged-out tramp, motivated by the most basic acquisitive urges. At the peak of pleasure you turn from a big spender to a tight-fisted creep. Somewhere, at that moment of descent from the seventh heaven to your *petite mort*, you experience a sensation of self-defilement mingled with guilt, and in tandem with this, the lust for money comes storming back. Sellers of love for their part are alert to the fluctuating rhythms of their regulars, in terms of the pre-ejaculation hard-on, which is why they try to squeeze out the contents of your wallet before you get to shoot your load. It's only on the way up to the peak of bliss that you're prepared to give it all away.

Being aware both of my profligate horniness and my liquidity problems, I developed systems of my own. Coming cheap was my speciality. In peep shows I used to try everything in my power to encourage and accelerate my bodily rhythms while stemming the flow of cash from my pockets. I'd even dash into peep shows with half a hard-on already in my hand, and all this for reasons of economy alone, or maybe calculated stinginess. I learned to exercise strict control of my libido, and over the years I became renowned as a world authority of the subject of peep shows. In the dossier of my life, thousands of hours of peeping are recorded.

In the end, the enforced economy of my love-practices proved their worth, when I was approached by a well-known publisher, one of those specialising in guides for dumb tourists – lighting up the darkness for creeps who'd get lost on their own doorsteps – and asked to produce a guide for peepers the world over. So my first significant foray into the world of literature consisted of my best-selling book "Gunther's Guide to the Voyeur", a book translated into twenty-five languages including Assyrian and Amorite. Incidentally, I should point out at this juncture that not only am I not at all ashamed of my first book, sometimes I even find myself flicking through it again and nostalgically reliving those merry youthful days.

The collection of impressions and insights that I gathered during my stifling seclusion in peep shows was one of the most complex I have ever experienced and anyway, in my complex personal relationship with Lola, there wasn't much left to me besides voyeurism of one kind or another. Voyeurism is nothing but commitment to ritualised curiosity. There are so many women in the world and they are so different from one another:

Jacqueline has a slack arse and Bridget has pointy tits; Clare looks intelligent and Josephine has hairy legs. Only there in the theatre of lust, when you take your destiny in your hand in the unseen presence of women stripping off for you, only there do you understand the scale of the difference. In those years I realised that the fabric of our lives has turned into a wank, a market-culture of self-release. More and more we are turning into consumers of simulations rather than dealing with life itself, actors who have left the stage and moved into the stalls. We need magazines, films, inflatable dolls and even puncture repair-kits, because the experiences we admire and boast of, experiences that were once within our grasp, have long since stopped exciting us at all. Apparently we celebrate the issue of sexuality in our progressive culture, while sex as such slipped through our fingers long ago.

In those crevices of lust, fornicating in my imagination before naked reality, I came to understand the secret of hidden personality as it is revealed in the awesome combination between Gunther the obscure and Gunther the onanist. In my practical life it was easy to distinguish between "Gunther the onanist", the one who clutches the soap, the grinder, the conscious, the alert – and "Gunther the obscure", the intangible and the unconscious, the one who hides behind the back wall of the projection-booth, and transmits shafts of light that draw shadows on the screen of consciousness. But I've never succeeded in getting hold of this metaphysical Gunther who stands at the base of the combination of the two. The Gunther who understands the secret of the linkage of obscurity with onanism, the Gunther who produces his phenomena while remaining hidden and never exposed.

When they join together in the context of post-climactic slump, the onanist and the obscure leave the secret of hidden personality impenetrable forever and ever. In their mutual destructiveness they reveal the most personal "I", to the point where I too am motivated to get to the bottom of it, a kind of inaccessible, secret Gunther, a Gunther who participates in all the strategies of existence and is never exposed; so close, full, whole and comprehensive that he is absolutely intangible.

In those days of sweaty release, slumped in an armchair in the peep-show booth, watching scores of nubile chicks stripping off behind a window, I realised that the hand-job is nothing other than a mechanism of private amnesia in which the misty and obscure self is silenced for the benefit of its perverse manifestations. Lusting so much in my imagination during the process of auto-debilitation, I was forgetting what it is that enfolds me totally. Myself.

Just as I realised I was wanking a dream of private amnesia, I also came to recognise masturbatory culture as a mechanism for collective amnesia. The culture of endless orgasmic release seemed to me the ideal instrument of shared forgetting. The two pillars of culture: on the one side, lustful and hidden obscurity and on the other, the connected consumer-onanist suddenly disintegrate in a mutual fashion at the moment of fleeting satisfaction. They are soothing the unbearable pain of existence, consigning to oblivion the catastrophe that lies ahead. In the shadow of onanism, culture seals intangible experience in a steel safe, for fear of getting to the bottom of it.

When Lola used to leave me, I would wander among the capitals of Europe, visiting knocking-shops, porno theatres, peep shows and back-street dives. I used to spend my money on nameless German women, forgetting so I could remember. I was screwing women without faces, without awareness of space and time, using myself up so much it hurt, loving them all from the depths of my sincere soul, not loving them at all in my bisected mind.

Often, when Lola was away on one of her jaunts, I used to wander among the pleasure-centres of European capitals, and as I
roamed between lust and desire, trying to assuage the pain of
loneliness, I learned to appreciate the qualities of European culture at its best. And while I studied the magnificence of Europe
in the kitchen, in contemplation, in dark corners and in bed, I
became gradually aware that in my homeland all the
magnificence was ebbing away. I knew Lola and I would have
to go into exile, and the sooner the better. In those years, with
the outbreak of the first uprising of the hungry Palestinian
people against the increasing nihilism of my overfed people on
the other side, I had no doubt that my beloved nation was lurching on a zigzag course towards certain annihilation. Since I
didn't see myself as a part of any national ensemble, just someone yearning to stay close to Lola, nothing more than that – I
made every effort to persuade her we had to pack our bags and
head for the vibrant world.

Lola for her part was comfortable at home, where she
was beginning to make a name for herself among "the gay
artistic mafia", sometimes even earning genuinely encouraging
criticism. Occasionally she was crowned with powerful and
prestigious epithets such as "the Rothko of the Coastal Plain"
or "Jackson Pollock of Givataim" and countless other unclear
descriptions all of them working in the key word "post" with a
kind of abstruse logic. In general, the whole "post" movement,
which soon after its invention had turned into intellectual

testimony to the barrenness of reason, was in my country a yardstick for westernisation and progress. Circumcised post-ism was the flag-bearer of a kind of neo-enlightenment. Anorexic intellectuals began inserting the word "post" as a prefix to almost any word, even concrete nouns. Under the influence of the expiring post-modernist trend, the shagged-out of Zion started broadening their terminological world by using all kinds of empty verbiage. Thus the post-historical perception came into being, not to mention the post-Zionist, the post-theatrical, the post-sexual. There were even post-modern dictators. Design students at a prestigious art school in the capital began developing the post-door, post-baby buggy, post-coffee cup and so on.

The plethora of "post" definitions littering the columns of criticism relating to Lola's work seemed ludicrous to me. It was clear as daylight that success in our parts, with all the bombastic descriptions, was nothing but empty delusion and useless frivolity. The fact that a local self-appointed pundit could describe Lola as a "post-aesthetic artist", for example, was to me conclusive evidence of intellectual blindness, because by its very nature the aesthetic can't become post.

In the course of my wanderings in the world I gained a clear awareness that the West, by its very nature, is located in the West and the East, for the same reason, is located in the East. For this reason I didn't see the point of the tantalising dream of the New East, as spoken of by daydreamers. The dream of subjugating the magic of the Orient for the benefit of some vague western futurism looked to me like a hallucination. What's the point of planting the West in the East? What reason could there be for re-inventing America in a place where "Niagara" means a flushing toilet? The obsessive dream of reviving the West in some desert outpost, alongside an oriental theme park, seemed to me not only morbid but tragically humorous as well. Why install the poetic dream of a "new Middle East" and invest in it wealth and prodigious effort, when for the price of an air-ticket you can travel straight to the heart of the dream? Meanwhile, the good old West is ready and waiting.

So most if not all of the members of my race began behaving as if they'd undergone unsuccessful treatment for the transplant of feathers. Feathers of progress. The radio was overloaded with the grunts and squeals of pseudo-London piglets, local cinema limped along with an air of confused pretentiousness, and the theatre was crying out to a beloved country. Likewise there was a sudden proliferation of pubs and clubs which were in reality just humus-counters for the night hours. My city was collapsing beneath the weight of empty representations of a mouldering culture. And in the midst of this huge, self-deluding void Lola carried on working in her innocence, Lola who was immeasurable, who was above and beyond; even those who sensed her greatness were incapable of grasping just how great she really was.

I myself, as one suffused with Holocaustic terrors, knowing how to read the map long before the eruption of the impending catastrophe, made every effort to persuade Lola to join me in exchanging our joke-domicile here for a domicile with a future. "The hour-glass is running out," I used to tell her. I don't remember when exactly I knew for certain that my nation was indeed dashing towards certain ruin, since like most of my mates at that time I was essentially an opportunist. After all, in us human beings, there's a sheep-like variety of behavioural opportunism. Even now I dimly remember some lines from one of those sheep-like leftist anthems of the time:

"It's going to be fine, going to be fine,
Sometimes I'm broken,
But tonight, yes tonight,
I'm staying with you . . ."

The idea being that even amid the greatest of disasters you can find the positive. The world may be collapsing around us, and yet love and the night can still console us with their intoxicating charm.

But I, even at my most sheep-like, couldn't soothe the terror in my mind. The fearful thrill of impending disaster kept me awake at night. And so, out of fear and sleep-deprivation, I came to sobriety, the sobriety that leads to action.

Back then, towards the end of the eighties, I had already convinced myself that my country was transmitting its final geriatric palpitations, the kind of death-throes where the intellect expires long before the body finally wears out. As if the body is left to twitch in shameful disarray, putting on show the disgrace that is life in the absence of intellect. I remember noticing how the people around me were becoming more stupid, more blind, more credulous, more pious, and less and less in touch with reality. As if huddling together in a kind of collective culture, just as a means of sailing with confidence on the calm seas of forgetfulness. "Tonight, yes tonight, I'm staying with you", in order not to see, not to remember and not to prophesy.

"Come on, let's run away together," I used to urge her.

"Come on, let's walk arm-in-arm through the streets of Marseilles."

"Come on, let's travel by train from city to city, sit in the restaurant car, get drunk and watch the world racing towards us."

But Lola was content with modest success in a nation of dwarfs. Or maybe she was afraid to admit she could never be contented. I was just incapable of understanding how a girl stuffed with genius such as hers could think it worthwhile, sitting in the shade of a palm-tree in the middle of an intellectual desert. I knew so well that the roots of that palm had dried up long ago. It was obvious to me that not only was the fruit doomed to disappear from the top, but shade too would soon be denied to those sheltering beneath it, as the foliage slowly withered.

"The dream of emigration is a wet dream."

I used to batter away at her sealed ears, in an effort to infuse a little juice into the desiccated and indifferent and phlegmatic zones of her existence. I tried in every way I could think of to breathe into Lola a little zest for a different life, an aspiration to climb above the familiar. I knew that emigration, the strangeness and the alien identity, would be good for Lola. Even then, I truly and innocently believed that the new world belonged to migrants. Migration is the identity of the unidentified, and where lack of identity is concerned – Lola had it in spades. She lived in our world as if she'd just stepped off an inter-galactic cruiser.

Migrants have a wonderful ability to see things in their nakedness, as if out of childlike innocence. Unlike the natives who surround them, migrants judge every issue without prejudice and they're not bound by any local mind-set; they're simply original whether they like it or not. Thus they create new worlds, apparently without investing any effort. Migrants never become members of the family, being an alien people among their neighbours. They are created – something out of nothing – and that's the way Lola was too. She was created second by second in her unfamiliar image, born with her paintings into her unidentified identity. She painted her world according to the template of her innocence, but in our eyes her painted world was our other world. Her world was in our view unattainable; intimidating, sensitive, disturbing, delightful and yet in spite of all this – still out of reach.

I insisted that her natural alienation required the strangeness of a great city, an endless city, a city without corners, a city unconnected and out of touch, a city that she could get lost in. Despite constant efforts to convince her of this, all my speeches and arguments fell on deaf ears. I discovered to my sorrow that the more effusive my praise of the wonderful world beyond the sea, the more determined my efforts to magnify and extol, to instil a little enthusiasm in her, the less my words seemed to count. In fact, she had lost all interest in anything I had to say.

Aware that Lola was refusing to join me in my flight, and still knowing for a fact that disaster was just around the corner, I was left with no choice but to go by myself. I hoped Lola wouldn't be slow to follow, as I saw myself as the mean-time man of her life, the one shagging her in the mean time, between one knight in shining armour and the next. So, as I was kissing the dawn of the fourth decade of my life, I had the sense to get out while there was still time, never to return. This deed, which in the eyes of those around me was an act of craven desertion, seems to me in retrospect the most rational thing I ever did.

Like my grandfather, I have an innate propensity towards survival. I have a phenomenal ability to sense danger, to feel threatened even by a box of matches. Grandpa made a substantial contribution to this ability. When I was still at a tender age he used to drum his survival precepts into me. His words are deeply engraved in my memory and have accompanied me all my life.

"The wise left Germany in thirty-three," he would begin in a resolute tone, before continuing with an air of malicious scorn:

"The foolish left in thirty-six, the idiots in thirty-eight, and those who were so feeble-minded they never left at all, paid the price for their stupidity in their incinerated flesh. As for those who survived that lapse of reason, the remnant – they were poured like human cement into the foundations of the State-in-the-making, on the road to Latrun. They were rewarded with the personal and recurrent spectacle of the most sophisticated slaughtering machine in human history."

And he would go on to regale my infantile ears with portentous and highly intellectual ditties from the Palmach songbook:

"History repeats itself, nothing is lost, nor forgotten . . ."

Songs like this were his way of teaching me to be alert, and to save myself before it was too late. And just as Grandpa saw fit to escape when the opportunity arose, so I too had a clear presentiment of dying at a ripe old age, and in my own time.

Without Lola, I packed my belongings and made my way to the airport and, by the first available flight, to the land of the

Germans. Why the land of the Germans? Because their land was the answer to all my needs. Germany was contemplation at its best, music in its most sublime moments; a symbol of total diligence and order personified. I travelled to Germany because I wanted to go home. Germany because of German women, Germany because of Helga, Margarita, Frederika, Ingrid and Elza. Germany, because it was everything my homeland aspired to be, and never was.

Germany bubbled in me like an intoxicating drug. I was captivated by the appeal of a people that not only sees itself as chosen, but also makes an effort to rationalise and justify this. Even when I was a student in that intellectual shit-hole back home, I was feeling a growing sense of admiration for German thought, and although my teachers didn't have a lot to say about the wisdom of Germany or the wisdom of Germans, I was lucky enough to lay my hands on a few key-books. I became ever more conscious that German thought, even the nationalistic variety, had a lot to teach us. You could find all kinds of good things there: on slaves and masters, on forgetting, on existence and on the forgetting of existence.

I used to think then in my innocence that if for example my teachers had devoted a little of their attention to the subject of relations between the "slaves" and the "masters" of the land in which they lived, they might perhaps have rescued all of us from disaster while there was still time. If they'd only listened to their language, their ancient tongue, perhaps they'd have remembered an existence which they had succeeded in allaying in a systematic way. Even the greatness of my darling Lola I learned to express in a new and a fresh style, with a gusting German wind blowing in my face. German thought does a fine job of embarking on the stormy seas of aesthetic reasoning.

But more than all this, I loved to love German women. There's nothing to compare with a love-dance between Aryan German thighs, nothing more wonderful than the gorgeous, full-bodied, ash-blonde Aryan chick, gagging for it, opening green eyes and moaning in the guttural cadences of that rich language. Nothing cheered me up more than having a sleek Aryan stretched out underneath me.

"I am Gunther," I used to mutter to myself as my senses swam, at the moment of penetration. "I am Gunther, of that race that was destroyed, I am the brand plucked from the burning and I'm fucking you from behind, from the front and from the side, for the sake of my six million brothers."

Thus, to avenge the blood of my brothers, I poured out my wrath among the Gentiles.

12

It didn't take me long to realise that in Germany most doors were wide open to me, maybe because as a survivor of the ovens, I aroused feelings of spontaneous remorse. In fact, I never fully understood the source of the friendliness I encountered. Was this really a sanctimonious response to my apostate origin, or did they perhaps see me as a comical figure? From an economic point of view, things were definitely improving, and I was actually quite rich. Royalties from my first book supplied all my needs, so I wasn't obliged to work at all. At the same time, just for fun, I agreed on several occasions to appear as a guest speaker at various social or academic gatherings. At such events, I addressed myself to my first book and the tantalising subject, "the psychology of voyeurism". These lectures, which began as an intellectual curiosity, soon became an unprecedented hit, turning me into a popular lecturer and even an accredited teacher in some prestigious universities.

I was roaming the length and breadth of the continent, holding forth on the theory of voyeurism and the eroticism of the glass partition. Gradually my subject evolved into a genuine science, to the point where students began submitting postgraduate theses in voyeurology (peepology) and its practical implications. Today, courses such as "Introduction to Voyeurology" or even "Postgraduate Seminar in Applied Peepology" are accepted as an integral part of the curriculum, but in the not so distant past, in the last decade of the previous century, the peepological insights that I presented were a refreshing novelty in the unutterably boring academic land-scape.

The surfeit of insights that I acquired in the field of voyeurism, I attribute to the fact that I was an alien among Europe's windows of desire. In the glare of red neon lights assail-ing me from all sides, I was like a Gentile embarking on a sea of sanctity. I used to wander around there feeling embarrassed, among scores of ripe women, sucking cigarettes in long and sensuous holders, while leaning sensually in the doorways of dark buildings and projecting their colossal tits so far across the pavement, they seriously impeded the progress of three-legged pedestrians. Strolling there for hours on end, I was staring fixedly, painfully even, at their crowning glory, the coy crevice between bosom and bosom. They for their part would reward me with a plastic kiss or an empty whisper, as if we had been long acquainted.

And in fact, from their point of view they had known me a long time since they, the street-tarts, were women absolute in their generality and their wealth of experience, while I was the gawky one, the isolated man, the lonesome flea. I was struck dumb by the spectacle of their overwhelming, overflowing fem-ininity. To prevent myself bursting into tears of tormented long-ing, I would summon up my last reserves of strength and pretend to be on my determined way to a business appoint-ment. So I wandered around there as a stranger. It's possible, I thought then, they all feel like strangers in these streets, but then the opposite could well be true – meaning the only solitary alien there was me. Maybe, I reckon today, maybe there are some who feel at home there, in that environment of manufactured sex. I'll never know this for certain.

Because my childhood, boyhood and youth I had spent as a conservative in a conserved society, the way things turned out – in my adult journeys through this sensual world – I went through such an intellectual battering that I was driven towards profound contemplation and analysis. As I've mentioned before, the migrant perceives the world with a vibrant and unflinching gaze. As a stranger among the fleshpots, I arrived at a variety of contemplative activity based on the casting of doubt, the drawing of conclusions and the pursuit of deductions. After all, doubts and conclusions are the very cornerstone of voyeurological research. You stand in the doorway of the nooky-shop, not sure of the quality of the merchandise, you go inside, choose from a plethora of porno slots, insert a coin and from that moment on, in your isolation and your allotted time, you draw all kinds of weird and wonderful conclusions, as you confront the unvarnished truth that is stripping off before you.

In the study of voyeurology in general, it's all a matter of casting doubt and drawing conclusions. The guiding concept in voyeurological research – of which I myself, so it seems, am the father and the pioneer – seeks to examine our experience in the new world, as if, in a spirit of alienation, watching from the sidelines the game of life as it is played. While the arena of voyeurological research begins with peepholes, the theory itself constitutes a very useful critical tool, with conclusions relevant to society and all its component elements. The central problem at the root of peepological research touches on the onanistic structure of liberal democratic society. A society which indulges itself in deceitful fantasies of freedom, integration, ideological metabolism and the like. Peepological research seeks to trace the roots of the self-lie with the aid of models of pornographic consumerism. According to the working hypothesis of peepology, the range of activity of the fly-man masturbating before a woman stripping off in virtual space can teach us something about our innate ability to ignore ourselves. The man who comes in secret teaches us about the human tendency to sketch a delightful reality in the eyes of the mind, in blatant disregard of oppressive circumstances and of the ambient world.

My most talented pupil, Wolfgang Von Hausmann, who has made a name for himself over the years, performed a number of behavioural-voyeuristic experiments. These were long-term experiments involving groups of human guinea pigs who were put into a sexual maze, constructed under laboratory conditions. The mass of conclusions he drew from his experiments, which were often quite cruel and even life threatening, he connected in an academic-analytical manner with the mass of occurrences that led to the rise of the National-Socialist regime in Germany in the thirties. Wolfgang, in my estimation, is the most interesting historical-behaviourist peepologist working today in the theoretical field and, for my part, I'm glad that until quite recently he has kept in touch with me, sharing with me his thoughts about current peepological trends.

Anyway, the voyeurological theme I chose to pursue touched on the sudden eruption of emporia for the sale of artificial sex, which spread through the streets of the West a few years after World War Two, emporia dealing in the marketing of imagination, as if to bridge the illusory chasm that had opened in that war. These sex emporia, which were a world in themselves, on the one hand turned the female body into a liquid economic asset, and on the other made it inaccessible. Woman became a simulated reality which we celebrated with great gusto. The lust industries flourished, arriving at the bizarre, almost absurd state of affairs where both women and men began consuming virtual sex almost exclusively.

Sexuality, which essentially is the least virtual of experiences, became in these establishments an intangible virtual event. Grown men started playing with dolls, and women finally learned to change batteries by themselves, without the assistance of an adult male. And all of them together, women and men started using up their leisure time, every individual closeted alone in blue-tinged lechery, in the darkness behind sealed curtains. Unlike the good old brothel, where the customer used to do his thing in an introspective sort of way, in commercial porno slots the new sexual customer has climbed to new heights. He's created himself in his imagination. When you're a slave to virtual reality, reality as such holds no further interest for you.

Margarita, my first steady girlfriend in Germany, was of the inflatable variety. Inflatable loves have advantages that are not to be dismissed out of hand. As I did a lot of travelling in those days, from capital to capital, from hotel to guesthouse, from train to plane, it was very convenient, carrying my loved one around with me, deflated and neatly folded in a suitcase. Besides which, my doll Margarita was exceptionally amenable. I never found myself trailing along behind her, weighed down by heavy bags in the course of an interminable shopping expedition. It shouldn't be deduced from this that I didn't shower her with presents. I used to buy her the best French perfumes then available and sprinkle them on her delightful elastic neck. I put rings in her ears, gold rings studded with precious stones, using holes specially designed for this purpose. I particularly enjoyed kissing her behind the ears and on her permanently rosy cheeks. After my lectures, she'd be waiting for me between the sheets, her blue eyes open to just the right extent, as if in a perpetually orgasmic state, and I would leap into my loneliness with her. I used to flip her over in the air, kissing her shoulder and taking her from the front and from behind. There are innumerable advantages to inflatable love. She never asked to sit beside me at dinner-parties of the academic fraternity and, needless to say, was never given the opportunity to talk rubbish and embarrass me in public. Women just have a natural propensity for talking rubbish at social events, something that arouses an excess of compassion on my part. She never complained about my circumcision either, although it meant that I differed from her compatriots in having a piece of me missing. So, while she made no contribution towards running the house, didn't clean, or wash, or cook, she never bothered me either. In fact, Margarita succeeded in blending into the fabric of my life, my aspirations and desires, more than any other woman I've known.

Were it not for what happened I think that the pair of us,

Margarita and I, could have grown old together quite happily, I into my biological dotage and she until the onset of fabric-fatigue. Having grown so accustomed to Margarita, my suitcase girl, at a certain point I even stopped expecting Lola to appear and fuck up my life for the umpteenth time. At Margarita's side, for the first time in my life I came to know true peace. The world around me was honouring me as an original thinker and a witty raconteur and at the same time my sex life was stable and entirely satisfactory.

So when the summer came, feeling relaxed and happy I decided, after consulting Margarita, to take a short break in the countryside. We thought it would be so nice to pack a few things, two or three books I'd never got round to reading, and relax for a few days in the countryside, near the foaming Rhine, if only as a break from the routine of the city. However, although I'd planned our leisure time down to the last detail, determined not to fall into the trap of inactivity – that well-deserved rest was destined to turn into unspeakable tragedy.

For me, this fresh air holiday with Margarita was supposed to be a decisive step towards coming out of the closet. None of my friends had the slightest inkling about her. They all knew I was involved in a close romantic relationship with a woman, but no one imagined my love was such a doll – and an inflated one at that. Besides, as I had long ago acquired a reputation as an authority on the subject of femininity, it was inconceivable that I would choose a woman who was so ideal, she wasn't even flesh and blood. Until now, since the moment I became a celebrity, I had refrained from confiding in anyone over my bed-time preferences, with the result that my private life became a public issue, and all kinds of bizarre rumours were flying around. In spite of this, or because of it, I decided that my holiday with Margarita would be a joint cry for freedom. It was time to come clean.

Two days before our scheduled departure, I went by myself

to the new shopping mall on the outskirts of town to buy my Margarita the best that German fashion had to offer. I wanted her to feel like a queen beside me. And when we set out that morning, Margarita could have passed for a supermodel on the cover of an expensive fashion monthly. She wore a broad-brimmed straw hat, tied with a pink ribbon under her pointy chin and her wrap-around Gucci shades accentuated her retroussé nose and the finely crafted lines of her face. As for underwear, here too I'd spared no expense. I chose a padded bra and split-crotch panties, both of black lace and perfectly match-ing the garters that I bought on the personal recommendation of Wolfgang's girlfriend; that's Wolfgang my star pupil. So, with her in a black summer skirt and high heels, sitting beside me under the open sunroof of my cheeky car, we set off for the countryside. Incidentally, Margarita being as light as she was, I had the sense to tie her down to the chassis, so she wouldn't fly up and away through the sunroof. We started out on the city ring road and from there took the autobahn, heading west towards the Rhineland.

As we drove I noticed the attention we were getting from other drivers. They were pulling all kinds of suicidal manoeuvres just to get a glimpse of Margarita from the side, or admire her beauty in a rear-view mirror. Truckers were the most persistent; they simply wouldn't leave us alone. We gobbled up the kilo-metres, while alongside us the truckers gazed down at Margarita with lingering, lustful eyes from their high vantage points, hoping for a glimpse of thigh under the billowing skirt. Margarita for her part showed no particular interest in the bevy of admirers around her. She was waiting patiently, quietly, for the coming night's orgy in our hotel-room in the country.

It didn't come as a total surprise to me when I became aware that, the more interest the other drivers were showing in my partner, the more I was desiring her myself. In my abdominal region things were beginning to stir and stiffen like beasts scent-ing prey. I left the autobahn and took a side-road, and then a side-road off the side-road and so on until we reached the side-road centre of the universe. I stopped with a squeal of brakes.

In the grass, with birds looking on and earthy smells all around, I threw Margarita to the ground and leapt on her, gagging with lust – and then what happened, happened. I dispensed with foreplay and was in the process of penetrating her, kissing her neck, when a sodding thorn pricked her delectable arse. So just as I'm congratulating myself on another successful seduction, there's a loud bang, followed by a hissing outrush of air from her nether regions. My lover has turned into an empty scrap of synthetic skin. My bodily fluids still intact, I find myself encased in a flaccid plastic bag. At first, what distressed me most was the sight of her underclothes, hanging limply on her ruined, deflated body. But after a few moments I pulled myself together and finding I had some initiative left after all I stripped off her clothes and set out in search of a garage specialising in tyre repairs. At the end of the day, it was only a bloody puncture.

Sweating and still in shock I drove a few kilometres through a typical rustic region until I came across a typical rustic service station, servicing agricultural machinery but with a puncture repair facility on the premises. The mechanic, Walter, was a hearty, smiling, middle-aged guy who greeted me cheerfully, walked round the car, kicked the right-hand rear wheel and asked how he could help me. For a moment I worried that, as a rustic, he might not feel much sympathy for my friend's predicament. But there was no going back now. Having come this far, I decided I should at least try to breathe new life into Margarita. The Germans are without any doubt a nation of smilers, and Walter was a champion smiler. He even admitted he too had an inflatable friend; it was a relationship encouraged by his invalid wife, who didn't want him pestering her. Affable and eager to help as he was, Walter was no genius and by the time I realised this it was already too late. To locate the puncture in Margarita's body, he immersed her in a tub of filthy water, with a sediment of oily sludge and tyre debris. Her hair was transformed instantly into a tangled mess resembling wire wool, her blue-tinted contact lenses fell out and even the warm hue of her skin had faded. She looked like a victim of radiation sickness.

When he'd patched the hole in her arse and pumped a healthy dose of air into her, Walter took the trouble to jump on her himself, to prove she could stand any treatment, then handed her over with a smile full of self-importance and professional pride. I paid him what he asked for and then, shot through with grief and pain, returned to that place in the back of beyond, that delightful spot where Margarita breathed her last, through her backside. With my bare hands I dug her grave. Her dress I put down as a soft lining, and the girl herself I folded with trembling hands and laid to rest. Mournfully I placed the garters and the panties and the bra on her inert body, took off her earrings and slipped them in my shirt-pocket. I wiped away a tear, wished I'd never be hurt this badly again, said goodbye to her and covered her with the clods of earth that were scattered about. When she was completely covered, I planted her high-heeled shoes in the soft ground and put the broad-brimmed straw hat on top. I bade her a final farewell and returned to the city and my cold apartment.

On returning to the city I made every effort to preserve my privacy, as far as it was possible. I decided not to share with anyone the remotest hint of Margarita's demise, and I certainly wasn't going to say anything about the events of that disastrous day on the way to the Rhine. I realised I wouldn't get a lot of credit if the truth came about, and besides this, I knew that Margarita's memory wouldn't be treated with the reverence she deserved. While it was relatively easy to deflect the interest of my friends, using the excuse that the pain was too much and I just didn't want to discuss it, the upsurge of curiosity on the part of the women around me couldn't be restrained. Women get so horrendously bored, they can't resist sticking their noses into the business of others. I noticed then that the fatter the woman, the stronger her impulse to poke a proboscis into things that don't concern her. I was so convinced of the truth of this, I became suspicious and anxious in the company of plump women, preferring to graze in the embrace of leaner specimens – bonier ones even.

I never confided in anyone the secret of Margarita's plastic nature. No one ever imagined that my woman, Margarita, was nothing more than an inflated being from scalp to arse. That is why she turned into an admired and ideal figure. In the eyes of my womenfolk, she was the **absolute woman**, intimidating and impossible to equal; on the other hand, among my disciples, she was a key concept in the field of peepological analysis. Since, in a number of auto-peepological articles I had discussed, in very general terms, the course of my relationship with her, Margarita became public property.[3]

As far as my readers were concerned she was the archetypal feminine icon, a figure so fascinating that a whole batch of monographs were published on the subject. Professor Theodor Sliverstein, a Jew by origin, went so far as to collate, meticulously, all the various articles dealing with Margarita and published a compendium which became an obligatory text in the field of peepological research. His book, *From the Culture of Icons to Margarita and Back Again — Collected Peepological Studies*, was required reading in modern approaches to the world of virtual sexuality and its socio-political implications.

In a certain sense, Margarita was to me a private saint, my sex-goddess, created in the recesses of my mind and yet, though she came into being within me, I worshipped her as if there was something in her beyond my understanding. For eight months from the day she breathed her last, I abstained from female company. In fact, I imposed on myself a period of mourning, so as to relive in my memory those fine moments we spent together. Wistfully I remembered the hotel rooms, the spacious beds and the scent of crisp, freshly laundered sheets. I remembered how, in a kind of ritual that was repeated time and time again, I used to stand in the middle of the room and inspect the arena of desire, how I used to draw the curtains, adjust the lighting and position the mirror at just the right angle. So, when the room was awash with repressed desire, I would throw the suitcase on the bed, gleefully pull Margarita out, fill my lungs, and in the space of seven and a half minutes, put more and more life into her. Having breathed spirit into her, I would cover her, kiss her forehead and go out to attend to my academic duties, in the sure

---

[3] Editor's note: It appears that here Prof. G. Wünker is for the first time admitting the truth about the plastic identity of Margarita, a fact which demands analysis and re-reading of all those scientific texts relating to Margarita and to the peepological implications of her colourful figure.

knowledge that she would be awaiting my return, alert and available. For eight months I imposed upon myself a grieving way of life, saturated with memory and self-pity.

During those sorrowful months, I kept well away from the fleshpots and from women in general; and yet, in spite of the emotional silence I had decreed upon myself, there were still some women prancing around me — fat ones and bony ones, the neurotic and the bashful.

Among the bony women of that time was Eva, my student. Eva, who was excessively bespectacled and exceptionally bony, set herself the goal of prodding me towards resurrection. Out of pity for my loneliness, and the mistake of seeing me as an admirable person, she wanted to draw me closer to her; with girlish self-confidence she reckoned she could bring me back to life and with charming feminine presumption assumed she was the one to represent life itself — and offer it to me. Maybe, seeing me as an accredited scientist, she made up her mind to sacrifice her body to science. I was then in my thirties and beginning to notice a certain cooling of the abdominal fires, and for this reason I found myself intrigued by the notion of a love-nest in the lap of a student some years younger than me.

This is perhaps the place to point out, to celebrate the fact, that Eva was endowed with extraordinary physical qualities, such that no one would imagine possible. She was the wettest woman on the face of the earth. Despite her bony frame, and although she abstained from fatty foods and alimentary excesses, her production of love-juices was phenomenal. At times of ascent to sensual heights, her vaginal vestibule would be awash with a foaming torrent of sweet secretions, tidal waves of happy-tears streaming down from between her legs, threatening to drown us both. I sometimes reckoned that making love to her without a lifeguard standing by was distinctly hazardous, but I kept this to myself and told no one. Like a holiday-maker I would swim towards her naked, battling desperately against the current, burying my head beneath the waves, closing my eyes as the cataracts cascaded on my face, marvelling afresh each time at the natural wonders presented to me and diving into her.

Impressive though it was, this behaviour of her body inevitably entailed some lapses in discretion. To put it plainly, it was simply impossible for us to perform in enclosed spaces. When Eva felt the first stirrings of libido she would flee for her life to open country. I chased her through the green fields, throwing her down amid the vegetation, setting sail on the lakes of her desire and finally, with resolute masculinity, plugging her leak. Coming, in her, was simply adding a drop to the ocean. Like one person we navigated the river of her love, she gripping my arse with her legs and I taking the whole of her in my hands, she enfolding my neck and I sliding the full length of my thumb into her bum-crack, delving deep into her anal passage while she moans joyfully. So we sailed to a safe shore. Eva was like a blast of fresh air, restoring my youth, like a bubbling, invigorating spring in the desert. I felt no reservations about a relationship with her, on the pedagogic or any other level.

The process of getting to know one another was conducted at a somewhat leisurely pace — and that was the way we liked it. We used to prattle for hours on end, and we even learned to love hearing ourselves prattling together. Eva showed a lot of interest in the convoluted story of my life, and I sensed she was falling helplessly in love with me. Although I had loitered in the company of numerous women up to that time, only a few of them saw me as a lovable figure. In fact I realised then that, being the way I am, hesitant and nervous, I hadn't been the object of any woman's love before Eva. Maybe that's why Eva was the first woman to try to cajole me into marriage and also, to the best of my knowledge, the only one who ever egged my seed. Women, I knew even then, have a definite propensity towards procreation. What we men understand only at a fairly advanced age, women naturally grasp at the beginning of the second decade of their lives, sometimes even earlier.

I sensed that Eva wanted children from me. I realised she saw me as the man of her life, and this did have a certain appeal, the only snag being that I didn't see myself as completely free yet from my one-sided obligation to Lola. Even though Lola herself was making no effort to find out how I was faring, I still felt obligated to her; I needed her consent before taking up my new status as proprietor and custodian of Eva's womb.

It was while trying to locate Lola in my damaged homeland that I became aware of the unhappy state of my former compatriots. The more eager my friends were to pass on exciting news, the more surely I knew they were edging ever closer to the fatal blade. When they told me proudly about peace rallies and pilgrimages by the Polish ruling junta to various Arab capitals, I perceived at once, as an international peepologist, that peace had become an object of collective onanism and would therefore never find release. Peace was like the fantasy of the naked woman revealed through the glass of the peephole. As is known today to every peepologist worthy of the name, the worst fear of every peeper is realisation of the fantasy. The peeper doesn't want materialisation of the woman in flesh and blood; the peeper wants her as an illusion, a desirable concept trapped behind glass, no more than that. To be without being, is the peeper's definitive reply to Shakespeare and his vacillating hero.

In the days when I was looking for Lola, to demand my freedom, there was a legend going around in my native land: the legend told of a certain king, a commander of armies who though he had waged wars all his life, was suddenly exposed, on the very day of his death, as a secret lover of peace. That day, the day of his return to his Maker, there came to that king a messianic ass, who shot him from behind and turned him into a sieve.

The story goes on to say that all his people put on sackcloth and grieved for their king and lamented the lost prospect of peace. As they mourned his death by candlelight in the square, I was sitting in foreign parts. I was melted by the poetic and touching beauty of the tale; the cloudburst of tears drowning the last remnants of rationality among my people really touched my heart. As an expert I knew that bitter grief for their king, who became a legend on his death, and only on his death – was nothing more than paying lip-service. Mourners by candlelight are just jerking off into the void, coming with a hand outstretched to peace. The rallies of grief were in fact a voyeuristic and onanistic display of *joie de vivre* and smiling acquiescence. There was in them a kind of captivating poetic foolishness. I knew that peace was a lost cause.

In reality things never turn out the way you expect. For all the effort I put into searching for Lola, I couldn't find a trace of her. She was gone. I found out later that during the time I was searching for her she was in India. Like many other Jews from my former homeland she experienced a spiritual revelation. What drew them to the East? What was there in India for Lola, I wondered.

I have a lot of respect for spiritual experiences, and even more respect for those prepared to endure exile for their sake. And yet, to me this hankering after India remains an unsolved problem. Judaism, the religious cornerstone of my race, is the universal source of inspiration to the revealed religions. Every believing Christian and every devout Muslim understands this. And yet my people, in crass disregard of this, make arduous pilgrimages to the monks of Buddha. I don't doubt the beauties of Buddhism. On the contrary, to my mind all the great faiths and religions are directed, like philosophy and art, towards the most sublime essence and highest meaning. This being the case, what is the magical attraction that sends lost souls out wandering?

Firstly, I found that in the Zion of that time, the business of disseminating the Scriptures had been hijacked by a coterie of born-again magi whose wisdom was concentrated in the structure of their names. They adorned themselves with two forenames: Rabbi Moshe David, Torah supremo Yitzhak Yosef, genius Amnon Yakov. In the new culture of sages with two forenames there was a kind of denial of generality, challenged by the absolute concretisation of the individual. As opposed to the abstraction of surnames which transmit distant anonymity, the new culture was based on drawing hearts together in intimate and uncompromising proximity. Unfortunately, the new rabbis failed to find a way to the hearts of distinctive individuals such as Lola, demanding special and personal revelation, here and now.

So the lost ones began searching for foreign spirituality, a laudable step in itself. Except that spiritual Jews are, by the nature of their being, hampered by considerations of greed and materialism, as was explained to me by a dear friend, a compatriot of mine who over the years was to become the most prestigious jazz drummer of his generation. When the aspirants arrived in a Europe offering a plethora of creative spiritualities in the spirit of the West, the lost of Zion were forced to confront their cultural and emotional ignorance. While in Zion they proudly carried the flag of western culture, and some of them made a point of listening to Wagner on the Day of Atonement, in the West, their shaved fannies were exposed. By the western yardstick they were primitive, uninspired outsiders. My visionary brothers did not absorb the teaching of a single one of the fathers of European spirituality, a spirituality based on the striving for freedom, the emancipation of the spirit against a backdrop of self-effacement in relation to divine ecstasy.

Having failed and been rejected by western culture, the lost sought a transient spiritual alternative. It wasn't slow in coming. They suddenly discovered the wonders of the East, the truth in the mysteries of Ganja. As if that wasn't enough, by Indian standards they were suddenly super-rich. Discharge-gratuity from the army was enough to finance three years of luxurious accommodation in ashrams; they could even be mistaken for westerners.

Lola too, that wisest of mortals, was drawn to the East. She spent years hanging around shrines, smoked dope, dressed in rags, fucked yogis, babbled in Hindi, and all this time evaded my searches, which didn't extend as far as India.

So, unable to inform Lola of what was happening, I decided in the end that the best thing I could do, for myself and for Eva, was devote myself to her love and fill her up with embryos. And that's how it was. One fine summer evening, at the end of August, coming home from the Academy, I was barely through the door when I saw that Eva had prepared for the two of us a celebratory meal on the balcony. As we clinked our wineglasses together Eva had a formal announcement to make: we were already at an advanced stage of the procreation process. A new generation of voyeurs was putting on skin and sinew in her womb. Eva began to swell, a ball-shaped mass sprouting in her bony frame and growing bigger from day to day.

14

On the advice of the ante-natal nurse, I did my best to suppress any trace of libido on Eva's part. Her unstoppable hydraulic apparatus could endanger the foetus, and I made strenuous efforts to tone down the sensual side of our relationship, encouraging her to keep her love-lake inside for the sake of our potential offspring. It's a well-known fact that pregnant women need an inordinate degree of cosseting, and their demands for clitoral stimulation are all the more irresistible for being unattainable. So I set about enriching the intellectual side of our lives, from discussing existential issues and logical paradoxes to dumb crosswords gathered from specialist time-wasting magazines and vapid computer games.

Every evening we would stroll for an hour and a half in the lush greenery of the Schillergarten, its western side bordering on the street where we lived. For kilometre after kilometre we talked about the baby on the way, and how the baby's room was going to be furnished, but equally we spent hours discussing the future of peepological research, the ruination of the psychological sciences, the collapse of the western democratic ideal, and so on. Eva was a typical daughter of Germany. She was immersed in continental culture, a quality that I couldn't really claim for myself. For all the time I spent plugging the cultural gaps, and however many books I read, I was still backward in comparison with the people around me. In my youthful years in Ramat Gan, not one of my teachers had ever taken the trouble to instil in me an awareness of classical studies – and as a result both western languages and western philosophy remained beyond my reach. Despite the effort I expended trudging through the byways of European thought, this was still essentially a closed book to me, and Eva, not content with being my loved one and the mother of my child-to-be, also made a crucial contribution to my education. It was she who pointed out to me that even my wackiest ideas had been rising to the surface in one form or another since the dawn of the western intellectual experience.

As a result of this, while still in the early stages of my voyeuristic career, I decided it would be instructive as well as amusing to approach peepological analysis as if it were a kind of *Guide to the Perplexed*, showing the way of mankind towards the new world – since by the light of the torch ignited by Eva in the void of my consciousness, I became aware that peepology is nothing but a re-running of ways of thought that have been present in the spiritual void since the dawn of human experience.

So I began searching out voyeuristic notions in ancient texts. I realised, for example, that the concept of the peep-hole is essentially no different from the categorical theory which forms the basis of the *Critique of Pure Reason*; similarly I concluded that the peepological experience is virtually identical to the experience of catharsis, and this led me to probe more deeply into the wisdom of the Greeks. So there I was, digging away among great piles of crumbling tomes, a slave to ancient wisdom, while Eva went on growing, to truly impressive proportions.

In those jolly days when the fruit of my loins was putting on skin and sinew in Eva's womb, different insights began to crystallise in me, insights going beyond the realm of idle chatter. I began to give more and more attention to the concept of existence. I began to experience different insights into almost everything. Even before the birth, I felt I was in the throes of a process of metamorphosis. I was surprised to find myself longing for my kid-in-the-making. Even in women I suddenly saw something different and infinitely more complex. Until that time I had thought of women as organic beds for the implantation of sticky juices, but as a father-to-be I was aware of obscure conceptions coming to the fore, conceptions I couldn't fathom at all; it was as if sensations of kinship were rising from the depths. I reckoned that in matters of love and parenthood there was no room for peepological insights.

I soon realised how mistaken I was. The closer the big day approached, the more anxious Eva became, even going so far as to read a load of crap literature on parenting – the kind of books written by publicity-hungry paediatricians and redundant midwives. Eva wanted me to be there for the birth, and also to take part in an ante-natal course; although I refused to commit myself on the birth itself, I had no choice but to agree to attend the ante-natal classes, an experience that turned out to be the ultimate voyeuristic event. I found myself sitting, embarrassed, in a yellow-painted classroom, surrounded by a dozen gigantic women, crouched in parturient poses before a nurse-instructor.

Although the course was intended for couples, besides me there were only two males there, sensitive green types who had also decided to share the experience of birth with their womenfolk. What could compare with the voyeuristic fellowship between the three of us? Three bleeding-heart-liberal males, suddenly, in mid-life, imagining themselves as women.

The nurse spoke for about an hour and a half on the thighbone, and I sensed I was in real danger of dying of boredom. As a rule, when I'm bored I need to piss. I left the room to go to the toilets at least four times in the space of two hours, going out and coming in, back and forth, something which drew the attention of the big-bellied women around me and rather embarrassed Eva too. All the same, I have to admit that I kept up the solidarity exercise with a commitment that surprised even me. I dispensed forced smiles in all directions, rolled my eyes when alarm was required, and there was no shortage of alarming details in this gala opening session. I even asked one question which went down remarkably well. The nurse-instructor declared this was an intelligent and perceptive question, worthy of a commendation.

As a peepologist, master of assimilation, it was only natural for me to identify with the woman in her finest moments. So I and my classmates absorbed the wondrous subtleties of the vagina and the pelvis, over two hours, until in fact there was nothing more to be said about the womb, forceps, fingers, underwater birthing, placenta, epidurals and laughing-gas. When the nurse was satisfied beyond any doubt that all theoretical issues relating to the genital region had been addressed, we moved on to practical exercises. The classroom turned into a mini-state of squeezing, pushing and relaxing. As a reward for my enthusiastic contribution to the theoretical session, the nurse chose Eva and me to act as a model couple. We were chosen to present, for the benefit of our classmates, the pushing and yelling exercise. I was asked to stand beside Eva and squeeze as hard as I could, while emitting a heart-rending cry. Although I'd had experience in the past of cries incorrectly interpreted, I couldn't resist this foolishness. So as I'm squeezing, gulping in air and yelling at the top of my voice, reaching the very peak of simu-lated effort – and bearing in mind that I didn't have a womb of my own in those days – what happened happened. The fruits of simulated solidarity ripened in my bowels in the form of some-thing spectacularly airy, which burst into the room like a fra-grant hurricane.

Engrossed as I was in the solidarity exercise, I wasn't aware that an apology was required. On the contrary, I was expecting another commendation from the nurse, for showing such dedi-cation to the role. In my innocence I believed that if in child-birth there is indeed some similarity with distension of the bowels to the dimensions of a watermelon, then my monumen-tal fart counted as direct posterior solidarity. To my sorrow my display of solidarity, genuine and sincere as it was, didn't encounter appreciative nostrils. It was a humiliating experience, finding myself at a loss, surrounded by bulbous women exchanging knowing smiles, smiles that proved beyond any doubt that for the umpteenth time, I had become a laughing-stock.

Offended to the depths of my soul by the unsympathetic response, to my mind a glaring display of anti-Semitism, I informed Eva I had no intention of attending any more womb-workshops. Besides, what was done couldn't be undone, and there was no way I could shove my disgrace back where it had come from. I insisted the birth must take place in a different hospital, on the other side of town.

15

On the other side of town, amid much emotion, my son, Gustav, came into the world. Being born in Germany to a German mother, his birth was a kind of closure of a circle. A circle that began with Grandpa's tenuous germanity. Gustav, on the other hand, was of German identity by right of birth. Although I was assimilated in my own fashion, a proportion of Gustav's blood was vintage Prussian.

Despite the fact that in my youthful years I'd found no personal interest in the issue of procreation and reproduction, one thing was absolutely clear to me: I realised that if I ever raised a new generation, it would have to be abroad. I knew, and I'd always known, this was something I would never do in my homeland. I knew that in my childhood haunts kids grow up into a smoky and absurd experience of crude and violent emptiness. That's how my Dad grew up, how I grew up, and that's the way the kids of my former friends were being raised. My son Gustav, on the other hand, grew up in a pastoral European atmosphere. Gustav was raised in a fertile cultural setting, a place seeing a purpose in healing the wounds of the unforgettable war.

The more I associated with the European peoples, the more I realised how eager they are to discuss the wounds of that terrible war: the horror, the destruction, the loss, the obliteration and the miraculous escapes. People talked about flight, about hiding and comradeship, people wept over ruined cities. Eva used to spend hours drawing out her parents' memories of

Armageddon; with all the energy of her bony frame and her thick bifocals, at intervals she used to relive their disaster as if to preserve the longing for ease and reconciliation; as if she was keeping the nightmare of the war and the horrors of that time alive for the sake of our Gustav, so he would turn out to be a green-tinted peace campaigner. I didn't mind the thought of my kid growing up to be a Green, expending his anger on the conservation of peace and the quality of the environment. Ecological blunders seemed to me a suitably absurd focus for the discharge of juvenile wrath.

As for that war itself, it seemed to me it almost qualified as an inherited trauma. Just as my native land was overloaded with organisations, institutions, private bodies, professional victims and an excess of artists too – all of them, though of the second and third generation, experts at making a living out of nightmare visions of the Third Reich – so too in Europe I discovered people could sometimes live their parents' memories as if this was their own experience. They did this as a way of underlining principles, improving behaviour. There was no doubt in my mind that because the nightmare of that war was too much to bear, the memory of the horror turned into a value preserved from generation to generation. Maybe this is the secret of continental reconciliation.

At first I thought there was something plainly absurd in the re-running of that war, since I and the friends I grew up with had counted five wars before we even reached our thirties. But the longer I lived among the pink-skinned races, the better I came to understand that their western wars and our eastern wars are totally different. I realised that however many wars my fellow-countrymen have experienced, these were nothing more than marginal skirmishes, battles that on the scale of the European mincing-machine were mere pinpricks. I came to the conclusion that if histories and the annals of the times are like nutshells tossed on a foaming river of blood, then at least from the perspective of my people in the East, there was no room to speak of any kind of history. However much it was discussed among my compatriots, and in spite of the orgy of grief in which they were accustomed to indulging night and day, in rallies and in torch-lit processions, refined rivulets of blood were all that their flesh ever exuded. Not only did the sons of my nation not flood riverbeds with their blood, their delicate drops fuelled nothing more than a winding stream of tears, evaporating in the sunlight as it trickles down the face of a chalk cliff. In the regions I knew as a child, my compatriots never awoke to the reality of ruin, never woke in the morning to find that the city where they'd gone to sleep no longer existed. Among my people, the tormented howl remained an unclaimed orphan, and in the stock exchange of nightmare, no one was bidding for it. They didn't absorb the taste of true horror and because they didn't absorb it, they never really uttered an authentic howl. So their howl became a simulated reality, their cry a theatre of florid grief. When people gathered together in rallies they learned to experience grief as a systematic orgasm and to discharge their anger collectively.

In those years the world was turning into a kind of small village, a focus of electronic revelation. Nothing could be hidden any more from the eye of the camera. Visions of horror, sport and leisure were flashed around the globe with the speed of lightning, sometimes as simultaneous transmission. In the evening, when Eva and I were curled up together on the sofa, waiting for tomorrow's weather forecast, we used to see the media-filtered shadows of national sob-fests, megalomaniac displays of bereavement patented by members of my race, somewhere in my anguished homeland in the East. I remember it was Eva who drew my attention to the fact that bereavement and pain in my homeland are phenomena essentially different from what is experienced among other peoples.

At first I thought this was an anti-Semitic dig at me, but to my surprise I found that she was right. I realised that in the grief and mourning stakes, there's a distinct difference between the practices of my people and those of other races. Funerals of American G.I.s, for example, are noted for their restraint. A tight knot of relatives gathers around the grave, as a squad of riflemen stands by. Pop maintains a resolute exterior; the loving wife and mother shed a single tear apiece, wiped away with a clean handkerchief prepared in advance for just this purpose. To the sound of gunfire, the body is lowered into the grave, in a smart coffin draped with the national flag. As the echo of the shots dies away the ritual comes to its dignified conclusion, men and women alike taking refuge in the private grief that will remain with them for the rest of their lives.

In my country, on the other hand, although a handful of families might use their bodies as a physical barrier against the intrusion of crowds or the media into the territory of their grief – the death business had become a public issue, turned into a national sport with many participants and no shortage of supporters. Patriotic funerals began to resemble tribal gatherings of football supporters. These bereavement-buffs were divided into several categories: middle-aged women who yelled their heads off, girls whimpering decorously, macho soldiers who suddenly broke down at the graveside, even blubbering paratroopers and sympathisers sent by political parties. In a complicated logical process, the latter used to link pain and lamentation with acts of vengeance on an almost cosmic level. Furthermore, as in any football game, as well as supporters there were also team players on the field. These were simply family members of the first rank, some of whom went so far as to leap into the pit as the crowd voiced its approval, covering their heads with dust to the sound of thunderous applause, scratching themselves, talking bullshit, etc., etc.

Local TV stations in my homeland had the sense to recognise that images of real grieving were infinitely more popular than any artificial Hollywood substitute. Death-based programmes such as 'The All Weeping Show' on the national channel, or 'Grief of the Day' on the commercial channel, pulled in the ratings like nothing else. The TV screen was a peephole into the suffering of others. Members of my race treated sorrow as the most pleasurable spur of the imagination. On hot summer days, when the air stood still for hours on end, hairy-chested men used to sprawl on their balconies, hopping from channel to channel and from funeral to mortuary, from autopsy-room to heartbreak. They watched the players of the sport of death, one hand gripping the melon-slice dipped in Feta cheese and the other indulging in long-range grief.

As one who is drawn to investigate the secret of things and their hidden reality, I tried to understand the difference between the restraint of American obsequies and the orgiastic approach of the circumcision-brigade. I asked myself how it is that America the great, the ultimate kinship-society, appears to us more estranged from the stiff being lowered into the pit than the most distant circle of bereavement-buffs in the land of my birth. Why is it that abroad people maintain their self-respect while in my country the cycle of heartbreak and funereal self-abasement has become a national sport? If grieving was ever accepted as an Olympic sport, my country would be right at the top of the medals-table.

Although at the time the Olympic Committee rejected Israel's proposal to stage inter-continental grieving contests, my compatriots did at least succeed in converting pain into an economic asset. At a certain stage, when destruction had already reached the point of no return, pictures of the crisis became Israel's primary export. Postcards of girls bending over tombstones, and tearful paratroopers, were sold to Christian pilgrims coming to bath in the floodwaters of the Jordan (which had dried up long ago), and wood and glass dolls of 'women in black' became popular items in tourist souvenir shops. The women in black were in such demand that they even pushed off the shelves the ever-popular Bedouin dolls and caravans of camels. Despite the fact that my country never was a river foaming with blood, lamentation became the athlete's diet. Images of bereavement were marketed overseas, to buy the indulgence of recognition and justification.

In our quest for the weather forecasts, Eva and I sometimes came across images of the strident fantasies of my compatriots. Eva used to smile at me with a kind of complicity in my ancestral pain while I, not wanting to look at myself, would look instead at my son, little Gustav. When he was asleep in his cradle, I used to think in my innocence of my darling boy growing up in the green-tinted tranquillity of a world at peace with itself, a world capable of looking into itself with ease. I was so glad I had severed the umbilical cord between my origin and the fruit of my loins, relieved to have taken my seed far away from the riots.

I discovered then that in the infant there is a kind of fresh outlook on the world. In his own babyish fashion, Gustav changed the order of my life to an extreme degree. He was the first to impose his company on me, and demand my solidarity. Before my child came into the world, I used to choose my circle of acquaintances with care, while in relation to my Gustav, I found myself drawn to my seed as if by an irresistible force. This social conditioning, which caused me some apprehension at first, developed rapidly. Gustav became the love of my life. His smiles from ear to ear, which came ever more frequently, earned him the place of greatest honour in my heart. I loved him as I've loved nothing else in my life, and the more I loved him, the more marginal became the sea of nonsense around me. My arid and anxious homeland was far away, and even Eva I sometimes saw as nothing more than a milk-stop in the process of development of my little peeper.

Observing Gustav with great admiration, I came to a firm peepological conclusion: the development of little Gustavs was nothing other than constant widening of the peephole. The human infant, the gosling-Gustav, begins his journey in an initial state of blindness and develops slowly towards the status of a systematic peeper. As if there's opening before him a growing gap in the mechanism of intellectual restriction.

While still in his first year, Gustav gave up sleeping altogether. He would yell for hours, calling for the help of neighbours, authorities and the international community. His screeches would rise and fall in pitch in a random fashion, seldom repeating themselves, as if to show his distaste for monotony. At first we thought that as the scion of a radical family, Gustav was declaring war. But why fight against sleep, we used to ask, our eyes strained and nerves frayed.

It wasn't long before we figured out the cause of the weeping. Gustav wanted milk. Lots of milk. Lots more milk. He wanted all the milk in the world, and not because he was hungry but because milk had turned into a peephole into Eva's heart. Milk means I'm loved, he must have been thinking.

As night fell we prepared ourselves for the battle of the milk, a battle becoming ever more complex and rapacious. Milk, it occurred to me then, is the baby's high-precision scientific instrument for measuring the mother's capacity for sacrifice. Lactation-relations become a complex set of emotional ties.

I realised then that like Gustav, man begins his life as a biological mechanism whose metabolic purpose is concentrated in the destruction of nappies, changing his skin in the agreeable shadow of boobs and becoming a peeper. Few human beings are capable of attaining in the course of their development a profound meta-voyeuristic understanding. The meta-voyeur understands that the world revealed to him is just a peep show and no more.

The sober awareness that sees the world as a peep show and no more reflects a great deal of scepticism and cynicism in relation to almost every possible form of conception. The understanding that the world is nothing other than a peephole, is the mother of all conceptions that form the basis of self-mockery. The deep awareness that as a human being I am nothing but a peeper places all my conceptions relating to the world in limited liability. The sensible peeper resolutely refuses to take himself, his race or his homeland too seriously. The wise peeper is revealed to be full of scorn for all; he is a malicious sceptic, monstrous and poetic.

When I walked in the world, among collapsing empires, I became aware that when self-mockery is absent, you may be sure that ruination is already upon you. Peoples bereft of humour, those lamenting the bitterness of their fate, those convinced they are the chosen ones, those indulging in mass-lamentation – their end is at hand.

Just as I was able to perceive collapsing people and peoples, so I was capable of admiring and revering elite conceptions. Most of all I appreciated the supreme quality inherent in a person's perception of himself as a stray leaf, bruised and enclosed in his own temporality. The moment the individual properly understands that the reality with which he is confronted is nothing but invention, or alternatively isn't such a great find after all, this constitutes a profound conception in relation to his experience as a human being.

When I noticed Gustav's curiosity, Gustav's first encounters with the reality around him, his persistent attempt to talk with cups, converse with the pictures on the wall, rage at the plastic birds above his bed, when I realised that Gustav was offended to the very roots of his being by the vase beside his bed, I knew that Gustav, like other infants, came into the world with a wondrous capacity for invention which I wanted to preserve in him forever. I wanted to preserve his creative voyeurism. I wanted him to grow up pinko-green and poetic. I wanted to give him all that I could, to enable him to invent his world in its entirety. I hoped that in the process of invention he would dominate, craft and create his world, discover within himself the root of poetic scorn which is the foundation and the façade of all things.

16

Towards the end of my thirties, I experienced a series of steep declines. Without any advance warning, Eva sank into a severe depression from which she never really emerged until the day of her death. Within a few days, or maybe it was just a few hours, she lost her vitality and withdrew into a chilly and suffocating shell. There was no way of figuring out what was going on in her head. As one with a keen interest in the secret workings of the mind, I believed then that this was a cry for help, but that wasn't the way things were. Eva went on dissolving from day to day. Gustav, I and the rest of the world became utterly irrelevant as far as she was concerned.

Wrapped up as she was in despondency and trapped in permanent and impenetrable inertia, she found consolation in the deadly tipple. Not that I've anything against booze; on the contrary, I'm an enthusiastic fan of substances with intoxicating properties. I believe that someone stoned out of his head on alcohol sees a different reality, a reality sometimes a whole lot more interesting than the one he's used to. When you're inebriated, you're no longer subject to the demands of discipline, morality and justice. Freed from all limits and restraints, Eva sometimes took to showing me, and the world, just what was burning inside her, and most of it was anger. Speaking in broken syllables and fragmentary words, she rounded on her parents, who had been rotting away nicely for years now underground, ripening into prime manure; she was angry about Dresden and the destruction of her childhood somewhere in the East and, it turned out suddenly, she hated me. She even began seeing Gustav as a threatening force, a tyrant depriving her of freedom. Needless to say, she didn't have the highest opinion of herself, either.

As I've already pointed out, I didn't marry Eva because I was madly in love with her. To me she was like a stepmother in my acquired homeland. She was my warm home and the mother of my child and from my perspective these two factors were enough to make me see myself as bound and committed to her to my dying day. I won't deny that I was fond of her bony appearance and her fragile flanks, that I admired the cataracts of love bursting out from her nether regions. If it was up to me, I would have thirstily imbibed the happiness of her youth and luxuriated between her legs for as long as I lived. But I wasn't tied to her by bonds of infinite love. Our life together, which began as a wet event, suddenly turned into an extended nightmare. Eva no longer strolled with me in the magical paths of the Schillergarten. Instead she spent whole days slumped in the leather armchair beside the big window, the window overlooking tranquil Heinrich Heine Boulevard and beyond it Berthold Platz, the central square. Friends explained to me that in Eva's depression there were elements of typical northern mania. Hysterical outbursts are a widespread phenomenon in northern Europe, almost as common as flu used to be in my childhood haunts. The many hours of darkness in the winter and the endless hours of sunlight in the summer constitute a greenhouse for the nurture of a certain kind of neurosis. Eva would sit there motionless, staring out the window, embracing the silence and the dusky gloom of the perpetual twilight. Usually there would be at least three empty bottles on the floor beside her. Gustav and I no longer interested her and gradually she stopped relating to us altogether.

I spent hours trying to talk to her. Sometimes, motivated only by the sense of obligation which is the basis of partnership, I tried to rekindle her passions, but with the exception of one solitary occasion, when a jet of concentrated lust sprang suddenly from between her legs, I failed abysmally. Eva remained in her frozen world, as if trapped behind a wall of silence. I reckoned it wasn't doing Gustav any good growing up in this atmosphere of bitter dejection and I tried to keep him close to me, even at the cost of isolating him from his mother and his pals. I used to take him with me almost everywhere: Gustav used to sit beside me at my lectures in the academy, share my immersion in the silence of the library and accompany me on my overseas trips. We spent hours on end strolling, hand in hand, I an ageing buffer and he a plump infant, bespectacled and jaunty.

I believe it was on account of my tutelage that Gustav tended to grow outwards rather than upwards. As a child he swelled and ballooned above and beyond any of the conventional scales of paediatric medicine, and this because he drew his nourishment from two sources; one being the sugared candyfloss that I used to buy on almost every street-corner, and the other, the vanilla ice-cream garnished with chocolate sauce and nuts that was on sale in all the public parks. Knowing how much my son, my dearest one of all, was missing his mother, I saw fit to sweeten his life in every way possible. Because Gustav was beside me throughout his childhood, I used to discuss almost any subject with him, even introducing him to the principles of peepology. Sometimes, before taking part in erudite seminars, I used to try out my lectures on him, and he, peering beyond the pink candyfloss, or the ice-cream cone, would enlighten me, correcting mistakes in the language of Holy Writ, the German tongue. He even had his say in regard to structure and content and I was immensely proud of him.

It seems that the prodigious efforts I was making to distance Gustav from his increasingly deranged mother meant that I had to neglect Eva herself. Her mind deteriorated to the point where in fact she lost her reason altogether. She was visibly declining from day to day, approaching a state of utter abstraction from any conventional perception of reality. The grey skies visible through the window, together with the cold and the inactivity, sublimated her isolation and it was as if she was turned to stone, sitting – uncherished and undignified – in an armchair covered with a woollen tartan rug, a souvenir from one of my lecture tours and a visit to the Scottish Peepological Society.

Eva stopped eating meals and when the pangs of hunger attacked her she would binge with unrestrained animal instinct, not only dispensing with knife and fork but somehow contriving to smear food all over her fingers, her hair and her clothes – you name it. My friends urged me to put her in an institution and even sever all ties with her, but for some reason I couldn't do this yet. Maybe it was inherited stubbornness, or maybe I too was in love with melancholy in one way or another. Sometimes I used to observe her as if she were a wounded animal, studying her behaviour patterns.

While initially Gustav used to try to get his mother to talk, being tied to her in umbilical fashion, gradually he found himself rejected by her, but he stayed by her side and spent days and nights as I did, watching her slow decline.

Although I saw danger in this way of life, I had no clear knowledge of how I was supposed to act: whether I should isolate my son from his mother by depriving her of freedom, or perhaps give Gustav a completely free hand to rebuild his relationship with his mother. As a result of this, inadvertently, Gustav began to develop leadership skills. My plump kid breathed a spirit of life into the gaping void left by his mother. I observed all this happening and despite my experience I didn't realise that my son's sacrificial project would one day be turned against me, in the form of implacable anger.

17

My home being a wreck, I found myself focusing more and more on the course of my own life, from myself and for myself. I was living in a household that was the very embodiment of dysfunctionalism. Eva had turned into a slut and there was even the stubble of a beard starting to sprout on her cheeks, in the manner typical of bag ladies. Gustav supported her willingly and with love. It was obvious to me that we couldn't carry on like this forever. At the same time, my circle of peepological admirers was still growing, a tidal wave of sympathisers, believers and adepts soaring higher from day to day. Much to my amazement, despite the upsurge in peepological studies and the plethora of quotations from things I was supposed to have said, I found myself a stranger to myself in my own specialist field. I was incapable of constructive thought, while my awareness had flown out of my skull and was roaming the world without me. My individuality was lost forever.

The whole business of peepological research was beginning to seem empty of any content, a passing intellectual trend and nothing more; peepology, like other new sciences, was making use of intellect and understanding as an expression of style and not of substance. Though wisdom, by the nature of things, is supposed to underpin the universe, those held to be wise had become an exclusive club speaking a single language. More and more poofs and eco-egoists were debating, ostensibly on my behalf, and this out of artificial reverence for my utterances. It wasn't long before the post-peepological concept came into being, spreading like wild fire among fantasists whose brains were like chaff. Post-peepologists attacked me, accusing me of sexist and male chauvinist attitudes, and blatant disregard of the glass/glee duality. In the view of these well-connected gays, the glee principle provided a solution of sorts to the peepological problem. They saw glee as a form of ascent, going beyond the peephole and even shattering the mirror and converting it into plain glass. The ideological posers, in their grubby and self-consuming experience, tended to believe, mistakenly, that in identical otherness there's a kind of invalidation of the peephole. I myself, seeing voyeurism neither as a burden nor a boon but as an essential condition of existence, was quite unaffected by the glee-criticism.

The more attention was paid to my theses, the more I felt repelled by my own utterances and by the eggheads who were my self-appointed champions. It became ever clearer to me that if there is any person who is incapable of discerning the substance of voyeurism, or the empty delusion of gleeful transparency – then he and I do not belong to the same human strain and there is no dialogue between us, only an ocean of silence. To me, the peephole was the metaphysical condition of human existence. The axiom "I peep therefore I am" is one that I used to drum into my students, but I also remember the existential proposition "I am therefore I peep".

If our picture of the world is not an imagined collection of shapes filtered through peepholes into the void of the consciousness, then all that remains is to seal the shutters. To my mind, existence that is not voyeuristic existence doesn't count as human existence and therefore I have no truck with it.

As if it wasn't enough that stray fragments of my utterances found themselves an independent route to empty praise, I myself, delving further into German wisdom, realised that the objective of voyeuristic understanding had been there all along. The Germans understood long ago that reality, insofar as it's revealed, is nothing other than a peephole evolved out of a world whose secrets "as they are in themselves" we shall never understand. And as if this wasn't enough, the Greeks knew it all too, and even earlier.

If they had all known all this way back in the past, I thought naively, then in my arrogant ignorance I had dug myself a grave, I had stormed a continent that was already colonised. And what of my disciples rooting around in the recesses of my arrogant ignorance? They were digging graves for one another. So every night I went to sleep scared, my mind in a ferment, wondering how it had come about that the fanciful nonsense emerging from my fevered brain had suddenly become a cult phenomenon.

It wasn't only that I found voyeuristic research implanted in the foundations of European thought, I also discovered much to my surprise that in the wisdom of my own people, the voyeuristic notion was a powerful element. It seemed to be rooted in the very basis of things, in the Hebrew language, in the duality of the covenant of the word and the rite of circumcision, the covenant between mankind and language, the covenant that paves the way giving mankind access to his world. The Hebrew word, *mila*/circumcision is an ideological root, striving towards the apex of wisdom, way beyond our material world. The circumcised are therefore close to primeval awareness of expulsion from the Paradise of "things as they are in themselves".

In my forties, my household collapsed and my vocation lay on me like a curse. My vocation, which for the past fifteen years had led me to believe that I did indeed belong to the small and select band of philosophical pioneers, turned in my eyes into a strident concoction of externalised ignorance. For a moment I was assailed by the crippling fear that this was the reason behind Eva's descent into the recesses of her mind, the perception of me as a charmless nonentity. But even in this whim I was guilty of arrogance and self-importance; Eva sank simply because she was heavy.

As might be expected, the veil of silence that I imposed on myself, in regard to questions and problems of voyeurism, didn't do me any favours; in fact it induced my fan-club to latch on to the implausible and grotesque idea that I had up my sleeve a tin of intellectual cemtex liable to explode at any moment. The more resolute my silence, the brighter my halo shone, and the higher rose the anticipation of my utterances, my future revelations. Were it possible, I would have peeled myself from myself and run away to the desert, hiding from the shame and the disgrace that I had brought on myself.

Just as I was sinking into comprehensive ruin, between my disintegrating family and the snowball of peepology, liable to melt at any moment, as I was losing interest in any kind of interaction with the world around me, I found one especially wintry morning an urgent letter on my desk in the Peepological Institute of the German Academy, a letter that had just arrived by registered post:

Dear Gunther,
It's years since we've spoken to each other or even been in touch. I've been following your activities over the years, and I am greatly impressed by your success, less so by the materials on which it is based. The day after tomorrow I will be arriving at the Academy for a two-day visit. I'd be glad of the chance to meet over coffee. I'd be glad of the chance to meet as lovers. I'd be glad to find there is still goodwill between us after all that has happened, and we can be joined together forever. I'm desperately in need of love.
  Yours hopefully,
  Lola

Needless to say, I was stunned. There was an uninhibited kind of arrogance in Lola which could be the very thing that would save me at this precise moment. A moment of self-contempt. A mid-life moment. The self-disgust that my vocation aroused in me, combined with the all too familiar mania of my wife, cleft open in me, so it seemed, a bay into which Lola could sail serenely. Lola, the lumbering battleship of my life's love, on the move again but this time heading for an anchorage. I had no doubt that from the rain of contempt descending on me, only good could emerge. As if contempt from an external source could save me from the contempt I felt for myself. Lola could grind me into thin powder and then proceed to reconstitute me. I was all a-quiver with intellectual and carnal curiosity. The hours passed lazily. In my eyes, life suddenly took on the appearance of dawn – life in the shadow of anticipation.

Despite the joyful excitement, I was prey to a few obvious worries such as: the nature of the relationship between Lola and Gustav, who unfortunately didn't share so much as a syllable of a common language. Besides this, I wasn't sure enough of how Lola felt about kids in general, and adolescent kids in particular. Gustav's reaction was a worry too: how would he react to a new figure emerging from his Dad's bedroom? With regard to Eva, I felt virtually no qualms of conscience. I'd already made up my mind to institutionalise her as soon as possible, and on any terms. Besides these predictable fears, I couldn't help wondering if Lola would find anything interesting in me at all, seeing that fifteen years without contact can't just be passed over. A formidable paunch masked my nether regions to the point where I'd lost all visual contact with my third leg, my libido had declined somewhat, my hair was thinning and what remained of it was turning grey.

So I embarked on a lethal two-day diet. Contrary to the widespread opinion which holds that problems of overweight are caused by excessive eating, I saw obesity as decisive proof of slimming-gene deficiency. I was full of optimism. I registered at a health club, made an appointment with a trichologist and even bought myself a check suit several sizes too small, for the lean and happy days that lay ahead.

Some three months ago I was approached by Professor Friedrich Sharavi of the "German Institute for the Documentation of Zion" and invited to put my memories into writing. Having never attached any special value to my life and its vicissitudes, I recoiled from the idea quite vehemently. I wanted to spare myself and the world the story of my life's mazes and dark passageways. I don't see myself as an endearing personality and as has already been explained, even the flashes of wisdom attributed to me were in most cases the product of chance if not of stupidity. It's no secret that Professor Wünker became a name to be conjured with in the peepological sciences, but as I've mentioned before, by my estimation, all the axioms associated with me have turned out over the years to be empty husks. This isn't false modesty. In all sincerity I didn't reckon then, three months ago, that in the course of my life there was anything special or worth sharing with a broader public. I didn't believe my life could serve as any kind of history lesson. I admit, I did a good job of predicting some of the decisive events relating to the morbidity of Zionism, but I never put this down to excessive wisdom, rather to the instinctive directness that underpins my experience. To my mind, then as now, those events weren't a matter of chance; they were inevitable and it was lethal blindness that prevented my compatriots perceiving their impending disaster. I suppose it was existential joy, unbiased and unlimited, that taught me about the future, my crude desires that brought me closer to things as they are to me, to myself in the most personal way possible.

Professor Sharavi wasn't deterred and for three hours he worked at persuading me to put my memories into writing. Finally I gave in, and from the bottom of my heart I thank him for his persistence. I find that the process of reliving has turned out to be a blessing to me, as my life returns with added vitality, strength and energy such as I haven't known in a long time.

For close on three months now I've been absorbed in writing my memoirs. I'm not getting any younger and it could well be that my end is near. I should add that recently I've become aware of a misty haze bearing down on me from the future, and over the horizon I already clearly see heavy clouds advancing, ready to discharge the terminal deluge that will wash away the last vestiges of life from my aged body. My senses aren't as acute as they were, but often I'm aware of a strange smell invading my nose and throat, reminiscent of the smell of preserving fluid that pervades school laboratories, where all those embryos are pickled in sealed jars. There's no room for doubt here: the reek of the grave is taking up residence in the extremities of my body.

Although throughout the course of my life I never paused even for an instant to listen to the quiet ferment of life, to touch the breath of the moment, to taste the flash of joy – now, as I'm living my life afresh on paper, I find myself feeling the pain and the laughter of those wonderful moments that slipped through my fingers, that I couldn't hold. Today, from the vantage point of my years and in spite of terminal exhaustion, I'm living my youth as I never lived it the first time round. I bite my lips and touch, unflinching, the sticky secretions at the base of Avishag's abdomen. I close my teeth on Eva's nipples, and thrust my tongue into every available cavity, even body parts devoid of any explicitly sexual charge, such as nostrils and navel. Again I fondle the erogenous zones of all my womenfolk. I'm tired and confused but I don't let up, sending out my fingers, stroking and caressing, and afterwards rubbing my fingers together for hours on end. Sometimes, swamped by memories of love, I put my fingers to my nose and try to follow the joyful scent. I remember the cramped, airless room, interminable shagging late into the night, into the morning and back again. I remember the bed-space wrapped in fragrant vapours of desire, recalling the aroma of rubber tyres scorched by emergency stops. I let my former loves pour intoxicating scents into the domain of my melancholia, effacing myself in awareness of my shortening days. I'm not in a hurry to go anywhere. I let time get on with the job.

As memory comes, as my life turns over and turns into a chisel constantly at work in me, I realise that nostalgia is the longing for missed experience. Experience that remained hidden at the time, unexploited. I'm coming to understand the cruelty that lurks at the foundations of existence; just at this moment, as the exultant fragrance of spring is rising in my imagination, my flesh is filled with the musty smell of autumn. And perhaps this is the reward of existence: it gives to every axiom an untimely spell of validity, rejuvenation following decrepitude.

Confronting the sharp teeth of the hidden hourglass of my life, I know I will not have time to complete the story of my life. My personal temporality is breathing down my neck. At the moment I have reached what is approximately the mid-point of my life-story, the days of Lola's return, but my strength is ebbing and the rhythm of my writing is slowed as my intellect withers. I spend whole days indulging in drunken forays into the voids of desire. I don't know if my manuscript has any historical worth, and anyway all these questions no longer stir the tip of the prick that went back long ago to being just a willy. But I'm happy and at ease, and I've shaken myself free from the doom that used to lie in wait for me behind every corner. I thank you, Mr Sharavi. May you be singled out for long life and when you reach a ripe old age, don't *you* forget to record your memoirs too.

This morning I received an official invitation from the Palestinian Government to attend a peepology seminar at the University of El-Kuds. On any other occasion I would have ignored such an offer and yet — although for many years I have found little to interest me in peepology and even less in Palestine — just now, in the middle of writing my memoirs, I suddenly feel a strong urge to travel. I'm ashamed to admit it, but I'm beginning to experience pangs of separation, and longing. It's forty-five years since I visited my childhood haunts. The idea never occurred to me for a moment. In the light of the temporality of the shortening wick of my life, it's as clear as day that another opportunity won't arise. I have an uneasy feeling that I'm going to accept.

In expectation there is an element of the personality looking into itself. As people grow older, the sense of expectation, with its burden of hopes and delusions, gradually melts away. The unknown fades, to be replaced by the known and the acknowledged, which in turn are themselves washed into the chasm of oblivion. The known dispels every hint of surprise. In your childhood, the unknown outweighs the known, while in your dotage a sea of details sweeps away almost every trace of the wilderness of primeval blindness.

Knowledge introduces itself, dishonestly, as mankind's best friend. It purifies life with a kind of heavenly light, light that kills the age-old darkness on the face of the abyss. In practice, this is a serious deception, since knowledge spells death to the sense of insufficiency, those little voids and duplicate identities behind which you thought you could hide forever. My personal view is that lack of knowledge and darkness in general induce a kind of fluttering of the guts, which is a more sober brand of knowledge. In darkness, in the gloom of the abyss, I find great happiness, yearning heartbeats and intoxicating fear. Expectation invalidates the present, the actual. Life in the shadow of expectation becomes a collection of incidents craving for the mists of the road ahead, the blind future to come. This is the ultimate pleasure to be found in lack of readiness for any possible eventuality.

While enjoying the sense of expectation for Lola, I contemplated the purpose of longing and the excessive self-denial inherent in the awareness of the here and now. For two whole days I had been imagining our meeting, carefully rehearsing my words, trying to lose weight, and reshaping the story of my life up until this moment. Even as I sat waiting for her in the cafeteria, in the corner we'd agreed on in a brisk phone conversation that morning, I found myself still preparing myself, dreaming, rehearsing, smiling to myself in cosy foolishness. I was still engrossed in visionary mode when suddenly, she was standing there in front of me, tall and bony, with the addition of a smattering of wrinkles at the corners of her eyes. It was obvious she was at least as excited as I was. Maybe, the hope occurred to me, she won't notice how obese I've become.

"Hello Gunther," she began in that poetic-phlegmatic tone of hers that my ears had forgotten for so many years.

"Hello," I replied.

She planted herself on a seat facing me and with a fairly serious expression took the trouble to inform me that I hadn't changed at all. For the sake of politeness I assured her that she too remained as she was, but knowing it wasn't healthy to rebuild our relationship on the basis of such blatant lies, I amended this, telling her there were a few changes perceptible in her, but they didn't bother me a bit. "On the contrary," I said, "it's only by the faint light of your mild decrepitude that I can tell how much I'm tied to you by a bond that will never be broken."

Lola for her part wasn't one to leave this unchallenged, and she retorted at once in that slow and raptorial tone of hers: "I wanted to believe you had acquired a modicum of manners during your time in the West, but since you have yet to learn how to behave when meeting an old friend I may as well tell you straight, where decrepitude is concerned, you should do something about that hideous pot-belly of yours that's sticking out in all directions. Be careful, that clumsy shambling around of yours could knock Planet Earth out of its orbit."

I was left stunned by the effrontery of my former lover and

by the stinging insult delivered to my bulging waistline. I sat twitching over the cup of superior Italian coffee, lacking the strength to lift the spoon and take a second mouthful of strudel, or think even a mild thought in criticism of the iced *sahne* trickling gracefully from the baked apple at the apex. As in the good old days, the days of my repressed youth, I was paralysed, gripped by the chill that had the power to inflame my erotic urges beyond measure.

"While on the subject of slimming and waist-trimming, you'd do well to steer clear of all these frothy, creamy things, and besides that, you should devote a little of your time to some physical activity," she saw fit to inform me in her imbecilic voice that had turned arrogant over the years. And she added in the best of her traditional style: "If we're talking about physical activity, you have my permission to join me in my hotel room, where you can exercise your body in any way that appeals to you. Personally, I'm gagging for it."

I tried to recall the contents of the letter that had landed on my desk just two days before. There was mention there of meeting for coffee, but not of drinking coffee. Within the first minutes of meeting Lola I was deprived of my freedom. Sodding freedom, who needs it anyway? Of my own free will I handed over my freedom to the thought-police, the Clitoral dictatorship, responsible for activating the love of my life. As in the good old days Lola took my hand and led me through the alleyways of my city to her rented bed in a tiny *Zimmer* at the corner of Kaiser Strasse.

Without any romantic gesture on her part, she sat me down on her bed, took a step backwards and turned her back on me. I realised she was waiting for me to unzip the back of her dress, and this I did. Still with her back to me, she peeled off her flimsy underskirt and stood there before me bare and bony-arsed, wearing only a pair of garters hitched to black fishnet stockings. She bent over, sticking out her bum and giving me the opportunity to glimpse the moist delights of her fragile pussy. Without a word, lean and naked, she turned to me and pressed her pubic mound against my flaring nostrils. She persisted with this somewhat violent movement and her centre of gravity, concentrated in the joints, pushed me backwards. As I was falling and the room heaved around me, I noticed that my forehead was serving as the saddle for a pair of thighs that had become a blend of delightful scents and other encouraging secretions. I began nibbling and caressing while she spurred me on tirelessly, uttering plaintive chants in a phlegmatic tone.

I have no doubt that in terms of tongue-movements, lips, gums and palate, I grew very thin those afternoons. Lola the dominatrix established the order of things and I, with my abiding interest in human beings and their sexuality, saw an ideal opportunity to act as investigator, peeper and protagonist of the first rank.

After a few hours of energetic equestrianism on my brainbox, my face bore the imprint of her blissful contours. I love looking at women from below, from the unique point of view defined in engineering language as "rear-end projection". I love pleasuring women as they ride on my forehead. I stick out a tongue full of life and let them slide along it, back and forth; I woo their orifices and they fuck my brain until all my senses are numbed.

Suddenly Lola reared into an upright position and before I had time to unfasten a single one of my shirt-buttons, her knees were kissing my ears and her pleasure-machine trickling tears of joy on my bruised nose. She stretched out her arms, backwards, emitted a sigh of relief and fell fast asleep beside me. The room was filled with phlegmatic snores, rising and falling like those of a Tolstoyan Siberian Cossack.

I was left alone. In fact I was always alone, but loneliness at Lola's side used to leave me as an empty vessel. What greater pleasure is there than to be a willing empty vessel, a vessel surrendering its freedom to a master and thereby purchasing its freedom forever, since the root of coercion lies in free will. In devotion to Lola I surrendered to the dark forces of the occult. Beside Lola I was the proverbial Negro slave. I did as she told me and I could go. I liked being a Negro and I liked to go. This time I had somewhere to return to.

20

Drenched in Lola's scents, clearing my throat, trying to expel the pubic curls that lodged there as a ticklish souvenir, I walked smiling down the street till I reached the door of my house. I went home to my Gustav in the certain knowledge that we must prepare for drastic changes in the structure of our family unit. Eva was already trussed up in a straitjacket somewhere, so it remained for me to rescue my son and myself. The more I pondered Lola's motives, her sudden re-appearance from nowhere, the clearer it became: it wasn't passion for me that brought her to the homeland of the Germans, but the need to escape from her own, ravaged homeland.

The western world in those years was thronged with Israeli refugees in positively implausible numbers. First there were the refugees fleeing for their lives from the worst excesses of Jewish fundamentalism; then came those fleeing for their lives, empty-handed, from the cataclysmic war erupting around them. The decisive majority of Israelis I found as repellent as ever. Even in myself I discovered a sizable store of nauseating Hebraic vestiges, enough to fill me with self-disgust and keep me awake at night.

My compatriots seemed to me creatures greedy for power and money, whether they were hired assassins, haters of Arabs, or inept fantasy-philanthropists. Of all of them, the most obnoxious in my eyes were the bleeding-heart-dreaming-of-the-West liberals. I recoiled from provincial pacifist campaigners, green-tinged visionaries, devotees of a just peace fresh off the Peace

Now production-line, those who kept the faith in hollow, leftist Zionism, which in practice was nothing other than National-Socialist stupidity. Perhaps what I was most afraid of was the notion that I'd been created in their image, a bleeding-heart crawling on his apparently rational belly. The peace-mongering Polish junta, kicked out of office at the end of the last century, aroused real nausea in me, even more than the millions of rightwing hoodlums whom I really considered subhuman. In an amusing and pitiable fashion the majority of my friends, including Lola, put their trust in the clique of sandal-wearing analytical Poles, academics dreaming of the New Middle East, a dream which to my mind was merely the by-product of over-exposure to the glaring light of the Mediterranean sun. The wise ones among the circumcised cured themselves of this vision by drinking a lot of water and sitting in the shade. I was cured by taking regular gulps from the Holy River, the Rhine.

I used to think that in Europe I'd succeeded in escaping from the burdensome presence of Israeli Jews. Not so. With the dawn of the new millennium these proud beasts became an integral part of the human landscape of western capitals and their financial sectors, not to mention crime and prostitution. Scores of pistachio, hummus and falafel counters sprang up overnight in shopping malls, festooned with "Kosher" signs to greet the Hebrew glutton. I found myself for the second time engulfed by swarms of strident barbarians. The old derogatory tag of "*Ost Juden*" acquired a new lease of life, being applied to many thousands of refugees, uninvited arrivals from the East as they were. To the people of Europe, accustomed as they were to migrants, these many thousands were an unwelcome novelty. This was a new brand of asylum seeking, characterised by haughty indigence and insolent stupidity. In many respects this ungracious idiocy was nothing other than a direct extension of the Hebrew-Jewish conception of the world in general. The Jews consider themselves a chosen people. A chosen people that lives by gathering alms and oppressing others.

The Hebrew, even before his homeland collapsed, was revealed as a type full of bombast and lacking in dignity, exposing his soft belly for money or a powerful gesture. My homeland, which prided itself on shattering the stereotype – bearded, stooped, exploitative and corrupt – was revealed in the evening of its days to be the natural nursery of all this morbidity.

The Jew slipped back into the distorted image, hiding behind beard and side-curls, shyster and crook, or alternatively, the slum-landlord driving a smart car – gleaming magnesium wheels on a background of metallic red. Neo-Nazis assembled once more in Bierkellers, muttering abusive slogans, their ideology revived. It wasn't easy, seeing my compatriots demeaning themselves, but there was nothing I could do about it. From the perspective of Israel-haters I too had turned into an enemy.

For years I have been dogged by the question: did I do all that I could to save my friends and family from this disaster? I knew where things were leading. At the beginning of my third decade, the hiss of the guillotine blade was already keeping sleep away from my wandering mind. Whenever the subject came up for discussion, my sensitive liberal friends raised various arguments opposing the notion of emigration, arguments which I believe are worth the effort of recalling. According to the system favoured by Professor Friedrich Sharavi, if we understand the Jewish propensity for clinging to clods of earth belonging to someone else, we shall also understand the Jewish tendency to be slaughtered like sheep. How did it happen that my friends preferred to build a ramshackle wall to keep at bay the dark reality materialising before their eyes?

The arguments put to me by my friends were regularly invalidated by basic logical flaws. The silliest argument of them all was the one constantly being raised by Dalia, ex-girlfriend of the late Alberto: "If you and I and everyone else go, then who will be left?"

This argument, which astonished me with its simplicity, suffers from an essential logical flaw. If you and I and everyone else leave, then no one will be left. If no one is left, obviously there will be no one in a position to report on the scale of the residue. Taking the thought further, you could say that it's enough if only I am not left, for me not to know who is left. If you're not part of the residue, you're not qualified to comment on its composition.

Bill asks Ben: "Tell me Ben, have you been to Yad Vashem yet?"[4]

And naturally, Ben replies: "No, I haven't been to Yad Vashem yet."

To which Bill retorts: "If you haven't been to Yad Vashem, what gives you the right to say that you haven't been there?"

To be in a position to declare with certainty that he hasn't been to Yad Vashem, Ben should have been there to see with his own eyes that he wasn't there. If I don't stay with the residue that is doomed to slaughter, how shall I know who's staying?

It emerges that with the existential logic of the Chosen People, they're all staying and being rounded up for slaughter so that they can verify with their own eyes who is staying. The logic of assimilation away from the slaughterhouse is much more appealing: when Pinch-me and I go down to the sea, Pinch-me always drowns and I'm always spared.

With the exception of my Lola, my friends and family remained trapped in their deaths, caught up in a logical mechanism of lethal opportunistic curiosity. I, having chosen assimilation as a convenient ideology, sat facing the screens and watched them die, dying without honour, dying without dignity. On one level I was amused, on another I was deeply grieved: these friends of mine from long ago were perhaps the only true friends I ever had.

---

[4] Editor's note: Yad Vashem – formerly a memorial hall commemorating the victims of the Jewish holocaust. The hall was built in the outskirts of Jerusalem on the site of the abandoned Arab village of Ein Kerem. Today the place serves as a universal memorial hall, in honour of all victims, of all races and persuasions.

Predictably, I accepted the invitation and travelled to the conference in Palestine. To mark the quarter-centenary of the foundation of the State of Palestine, the Arab Academy of Behavioural Sciences was holding a conference to debate the issue of "Applied Peepology in the modern Middle East". The Dean of the Academy, my former pupil Professor Antoine El Said who over the years had become a key figure in peepological research, insisted on my attendance at the opening ceremony.

Professor El Said is one of the most fascinating figures in the field. He first acquired a reputation through his researches into the subject of identity and exile, and in the closing years of the last century he developed some interesting theories relating to displaced populations. He himself belonged to a refugee family originally from Lod, was born in the Sabra Camp in Lebanon and emigrated to Germany with his parents at an early age. Having distinguished himself in postgraduate study of psychology at the University of Nuremberg, he was exposed to concepts of peepology, a discipline then in its infancy. He obtained his doctorate from the University of Beirut, which had become an influential peepological centre, for his analysis of the Palestinian dream of return, at that time one of the wettest dreams of all.

Delegates to the conference were to include prestigious peepologists active in the world's leading research centres. I myself, as one who had by now washed his hands of peepological analysis, was intrigued by the idea of accepting this unique invitation. Despite my age and infirmity, the prospect of visiting my homeland after an absence of four decades excited me: I'm going home, to the landscape of my childhood, to the smell of aromatic herbs, to the olive trees, to the invigorating aridity. I'm returning to my native land, to eternal spring, brotherhood of man and place, to the pain soaring faraway until the end of time, like first love.

The first step was to buy tickets. The thought of flying with the Palestinian national airline (Yas-Air) made me feel highly honoured, but then the whole notion of Palestinian sovereignty was still a novelty to me. When I severed my links with my homeland, my compatriots still saw the Palestinians as "stoned roaches in a bottle". And here I am, on the way back to my native soil, borne aloft not by inebriated beetles but on the wings of eagles, eagles returning to their nests.

At the airport I was surprised by the number of flights to Palestine. Besides mine, there was a charter flight operated by the subsidiary (Air-Afat), as well as a late, supplementary flight courtesy of "Ra'is" Airlines. Naturally enough, the Palestinian people felt tremendous respect for their national leader who had led them in their struggle for freedom and statehood. Here too there was a novelty for me. When I left home, this great leader was just "a man with hair on his face". Which goes to show, even men with hair on their faces deserve respect. After all, the visionary founding father of Zionism wasn't short of facial hair, either.

Before boarding the plane I was politely asked by the ground-stewardess, dressed in traditional national costume, whether the distinguished gentleman would prefer hummus with pine nuts, or perhaps hummus with hot chick peas ... with or without egg ...

It was an exhilarating experience, sitting amid two hundred hummus-guzzlers at an altitude of thirty thousand feet. A sky-scraping experience. Towards the rear of the plane, Boeing

Airbus Inc. had installed a specially designed brick-built oven for the continuous supply of hot pittas. As we touched down, the pilot switched on the public address system and welcomed us, to the tuneful strumming of the *oud*, the rhythmic beating of the *darbuka* and heart-wrenching patriotic songs.

Before I had even reached the exit-ramp, I was hit by a blast of Mediterranean breeze, a breeze bearing the torpor of spring combined with the smell of growth, a smell which only a son of the Mediterranean would recognise, identifying all its permutations; a sweet smell that scorches the inner nostrils with a gentle caress, a caress reminiscent of picking your nose with a match – a lighted one.

The meeting with Antoine was encouraging. We hadn't met in years and in the meantime he had done very well for himself. He waited for me at the gate of the terminal, before passport control. Since my visa identified me as an "Ibn Isaac" (as members of my race were evidently dubbed by the new bosses) I was liable to undergo stringent interrogation and demeaning body searches. The Palestinian border police weren't in the business of encouraging refugees from the "Ibn Isaac" community to return to their homeland. I was spared all these indignities, and whisked away to the official air-conditioned limousine, a Peugeot 404 Reissue, the car which had once served as the symbol of the Palestinian struggle for liberation. We set out for the hospitality wing of the University of El-Kuds, situated on the slopes of Mount Scopus.

On our way we passed through the western city, now a crowded urban ghetto, a congested vista of closed balconies. Many members of my race had stayed on to live in their homeland under Palestinian sovereignty – those of limited means who were unable to flee for their lives in time, and idiots who were so committed to their real estate that they turned into real estate themselves. Real estate people intrigued me especially. A few of my friends and relatives were numbered among them. In the

Jewish nature there is a pathological devotion to property, and some members of my race even value property above life itself. In the run-up to the collapse of Zion most assets lost their value. In fact, there's no more reliable indicator of impending disaster. In spite of this, until the last, cataclysmic moment, the Ibn Isaacs were still wheeling and dealing, buying and selling houses and apartments. They moved from a one-room apartment in a condo to a two-room apartment in the same condo and from there to a three-room apartment with triple air-conditioning. They move again, and this time they find themselves in a triple air-conditioning apartment with two bomb shelters. Then it's a freestanding house with land attached, an investment opportunity. When they finally arrived at their dream-residences, the men of property discovered that their assets had disappeared along with their State. So obsessed were they with moving from condo to complex, from one abode to another, they failed to notice the dissolution of the State. Clutching their title deeds they turned overnight from a race of complacent landlords into a race of penniless serfs. What is it with Jews, that induces in them such primeval blindness?

Having introduced me to the glories of the Palestinian capital, El Said suggested we should meet for supper in the restaurant of the American Hotel near Sheikh Jarrah. I went up to my room, sat facing the window and looked out at the desert, stretching away from the soles of my feet to the horizon. Hey, I'm home, confronting the landscape of my boyhood, hills where I used to cavort alongside my youthful loves, hills that I charged across in basic training. Here I am, facing the interminable hills of chalk and dolomite which lead to the end of the world. I fell asleep full of mountain air pure as wine, to the sound of bells.

I dreamed, I remember it clearly, that Avishag and Alberto were beside me. Alberto and I running, racing across the chalk hills and far away into the horizon. Suddenly Alberto stops and I stop too. Alberto turns to me and looks into my eyes and bursts into laughter, laughing the way he used to, a rolling laugh that knows no limits and suddenly I am laughing too. We laugh for hours and then our eyes meet again and suddenly we are both weeping, weeping as we never wept before. Within my dream, amid the bitter tears, it suddenly occurs to me that I never actually wept for Alberto. In fact I never wept at all. I weep a whole lifetime's worth of tears, and we fall into one another's arms. And then, in an instant our eyes meet again, and Alberto is laughing again and I am laughing too. We laugh and weep and weep and laugh. Our weeping amuses us and our laughter grieves us — and suddenly Avishag is laughing too.

The sound of knocking at the door roused me. I woke exhausted, sitting in the armchair facing the window, drenched in tears and sweat. I stood up and opened the door. Antoine seemed alarmed by my puffy and dishevelled appearance, but he understood at once the emotional strain I was experiencing. I washed my face and changed my shirt, and we walked to the hotel lobby. In the restaurant, Antoine ordered *tamarhindi* flavoured with rose water for both of us and at once, without preamble, began explaining to me the importance of the conference and the reasons behind my invitation. I was told that the Palestinian Government was determined not to repeat the farrago of fatal mistakes that led to the collapse of Zion. Palestinian politicians were intent on bringing about a civic revolution, forging an egalitarian society in which all the different races could live together in mutual respect. Antoine saw fit to inform me that the rump of the Ibn Isaacs remaining in Palestine preferred to shut itself away in ghettoes and avoid any interaction with the ethnic blending going on around them, aside from minor criminal excursions. Jewish ghettoes such as "Mount Francewi" and "Mount Eskolawi" had become lawless wastelands strewn with stolen cars. Antoine was adamant that by means of a process of applied peepology it would be possible to heal the flaws of Palestinian society and to accept the Ibn Isaac on equal terms. I felt the need to return to my room. I promised I would give the matter some thought, took my leave of Antoine and hurried to my room.

In the room in the night, facing the open window and a blast of desert breeze, I sit in the armchair, as moonbeams shimmer on towers and turrets. To the warbling of the muezzin I sink back into my lost world. I'm lying naked in the desert. Avishag underneath me. I'm biting her neck and fucking her ferociously. My bollocks scrape the chalky rock and my fingers, cupped round her tight little arse to protect her skin from stones and thorny cactus, are cut to ribbons, wounds in the living flesh. I go on fucking relentlessly like a real macho man and she squeals. I try to hush her; after all we're screwing in the middle of a hostile Arab neighbourhood. Blood streams from my fingers, the nails are torn and broken. In the morning I wake up unscathed.

I shower and go down to the opening session. I see all those who revere my memory, even though I'm still alive. I meet Wolfgang Von Hausmann and other former pupils of mine. They too are no longer young. I sit at the head of the presidential table, while all around me complex peepological propositions are raised, their meaning lost on me. They drift above my consciousness like airy wisps of cloud, finding no inclination to linger in my decaying brain. Professor El Said introduces the central problem facing delegates to the conference – how to establish a civil society based on equality by means of the mirror of peepology. I want to go back to the armchair of my life, weep with Alberto and fuck Avishag. I'm old and my reputation is secure, I have the right to leave and go to my room.

I stand facing the window of my life. Late morning. Prenoon. A herd of goats trails down the slope. I listen with keen concentration and succeed in picking out the bleat of a frisky nanny goat and the breezy tinkling of a bell. I settle in the armchair, waiting for Avishag and Alberto. Breathing the air of Jerusalem, which penetrates through the nose into the lobe of the brain and grabs the roots of the hair from within. I'm already dreaming. A light blur and then again I'm naked, skipping over the hills, gazing up into the sky and running like a maniac. What am I doing here? Even I, the dreamer, can't quite understand it. A few seconds later it all becomes clear: this time it's Margarita, my inflated doll, soaring aloft like a balloon released from its mooring. My Margarita, flying in tight loops and spirals, sometimes diving to attack the ground before climbing back to the heights. I prance naked in her wake and she, the perpetual tease, doesn't let up for a moment – swooping, ascending, never landing. I feel spurned in my nakedness, an island in a river of goats that lick my exposed skin. My eyes raised, I continue to monitor her untiring flight, while a Bedouin shepherd looks on with amusement, grinning innocently. I stare at him with alarm, covering my embarrassment. "Margarita! Get the fuck out of my dream!" I yell from the armchair. "I want Alberto, I want Avishag." And she, offended to the depths of her soul, goes into ground-attack mode and buzzes my scalp, before climbing and banking for a fresh assault. I hide and she waits for her chance. How has Margarita changed from an inflated German into a Syrian dive-bomber? – I ask myself.

The phone rings. Much to my surprise, I'm naked and my forgotten pride is rearing in an unexpected fashion. It's a long time since I've experienced such an erection. I don't remember undressing and I'm beginning to feel that my mind is out of synch, but I'm enjoying every moment. The phone is still ringing and I have to get up and answer it, just to get rid of the troublesome interruption. Antoine, at the other end of the line, implores me to honour the conference with my presence and give my opinion of methodological proposals for the solution of Palestinian social problems. I promise to attend the evening session, which is also the closing one. In the meantime I return to the window, and its tapestry of the shadows of my life. A desert afternoon, the languor of the day, neither man nor beast. I sink back in the armchair, close my eyes and sleep. I don't dream this time, or perhaps I don't remember.

In the evening I went down to the conference-room, curious to hear about proposed solutions based on applied peepology. My former star-pupil Wolfgang Von Hausmann put forward a fascinating analysis of the Jewish-Arab disintegrative issue. Wolfgang drew the attention of the delegates to the banal fact that on the sub-textual level conquest is violent sexual interaction between conqueror and conquered, between victor and rape victim. In crude terms, conquest is a carnal battlefield on which women of the defeated side sacrifice themselves to the unbridled lust of the victor. The conqueror turns into an instinctive cluster-bomb, raping everything that stands in his way.[5] The laurels of victory the conqueror plucks from the conquered one as she weeps silently, spread-eagled, helpless, beneath him.

There was nothing offensive or alarming in this peepological perception. It was simply an encapsulation of objective fact, a state of affairs not to be ignored. In the course of the German *Blitzkrieg*, soldiers of the *Wehrmacht* exacted the spoils of their victory on Russian soil. They fucked all the way to Moscow, leaving burnt and broken women at the roadside. When the tables were turned, the Red Army took its revenge, planting the seeds of Stalin's wrath in every young German womb encountered on the way to Berlin.

That is the way things are in the West. In the Middle East, on the other hand, there is no precedent for violent sexual activity in a military context. The Arab Legion resisted any temptation to rape the daughters of Ramat Rachel while the Zionist army, throughout its history, avoided carnal contact, consensual or otherwise, with the daughters of Palestine. Apparently this would tend to testify to the high moral calibre of the hawks, but the peepological interpretation casts doubt on this. In Wolfgang's opinion, sexual restraint is a symptom of lack of mutual respect. Just as you don't expect a dog to fuck a camel,

[5] Editor's note: Sometimes even innocent sheep and other agricultural animals.

so the Arab man refuses to fuck a Jewess, and vice versa. In the Middle East there is a clear disinclination on the part of hawks to see themselves as equally entitled members of the great family of mankind. To solve this bizarre problem, to begin the process of mutual recognition of the humanity of the other, Wolfgang proposed a programme of integrative coercive sexual activity, adding the judicious recommendation that statutory rape-days needed to be organised and supervised by the authorities: on Sundays and Wednesdays, there would be the systematic rape of the daughters of Isaac by their cousins, while Tuesdays and Thursdays would be set aside for the systematic rape of the daughters of Ishmael by the sons of Isaac. Members of the Druze community, in the centre of the scales and cast in the role of unwilling collaborators, would be granted dispensation to rape and be raped on any day of their choosing.

I thought this an interesting practical solution. I expressed my support, went up to my room in the hotel, packed my possessions, glanced for the last time at my personal window of opportunity and took my leave of Avishag and Alberto. They smiled at me with rueful understanding, knowing deep down that I couldn't stay with them forever. Margarita was still engaged in her land-forces support exercise, soaring skywards, banking sharply and diving. I jerked a thumb in her direction, ground-crew style, and waved goodbye to her. A last fond look at Avishag and Alberto. I saw them walking towards the horizon, hand in hand. I made my way to the airport and my return-flight to Germany.

E-Mail to Professor Friedrich Sharavi
12.1.2032

Dear Professor Sharavi,

I don't suppose you will ever know how grateful I am to you for your persistence in persuading me to put my memories into writing. For the past three and a half months I have been waking in the morning and rushing straight to my desk, fired with enthusiasm.

At first I felt considerable resistance to your project, but then I came to perceive with greater clarity the hidden wisdom on which your method is based. I have to admit that at this moment, in the lengthening shadow of my life's work, even I find in my experience an instructive lesson which, had it been given to me in time, could have changed the course of my life entirely.

Three and a half months ago, when I took on myself the challenge of writing, I did so with the clear intention of giving a thorough and exhaustive account of my life, at least on the chronological level. Unfortunately I am not in the best of health these days and I need medical supervision. It is also emerging, so I am told by those around me, that my mind is fading and in decline. I'm becoming a nuisance to my surroundings and also a target for derision and mirth. Yesterday, for example, I went into a local McDonald's, near Weimar Platzen, and insisted that I wanted "Cow's foot jelly with red horseradish, no chips, and a large Coca-Cola". In retrospect I suppose this was a somewhat eccentric order. Big fucking deal. Lola, the old witch, stands there looking embarrassed and pretending she's nothing to do with me. All this last week, since I got back from Palestine, I've been having nostalgic gastronomic urges that are hard to control. I long for a portion of Sabiah.[6] I want to drown myself in a barrel of chutney, eat my way through a pile of mango slices. I wish I could put on gumboots and trudge through endless fields of chickpeas. What I really want is to embark on a sea of gluttonous memories, reclining on a mattress of soft carrots as I grapple with the rudder of my gefiltefish-gunboat, ploughing through the raging surf of spiced nuts and almonds.

To get to the point, tomorrow I shall be putting my fate in the hands of doctors, who will try to identify the source of the ailment that is

[6] Editor's note: Sabiah — a traditional Ramat Gan delicacy, a miraculous gastronomic concoction with no medical properties whatsoever. Sabiah in its traditional form comprises five ingredients each of which has its origin in an entirely different culture: first, aubergine, originating from Turkey; second, hummus, originating from the Sahara Desert; third, mango chutney, which is a delicacy originating from South-East India; fourth, egg, originating from a chicken — and it is particularly important to note that the fifth ingredient, nothing other than the **pitta** into which the four above-mentioned ingredients are stuffed, originates from outer space. Neo-post-Jungian gastro-scholars are of the opinion that the pitta constitutes compelling evidence of a rich process of correspondence between people of the Ancient East and extra-terrestrials. The pitta in its Jewish form does indeed resemble a flying saucer, and in those years it was customary to stuff the pitta with a far greater quantity of food than could possibly be permitted by its modest dimensions. Thus the pitta defies the laws of physics and is a mystery that has yet to be solved, a cosmic secret from outer space. As if this were not enough to inflame our curiosity, it emerges that after the pitta had been crammed with enough food to feed a small army, the solitary gourmand would lean forward with legs parted, engage his teeth and dispatch it within a few seconds, leaving no evidence that it had entered his stomach at all. The pitta is thus revealed to be the black hole of oriental culture. A unit of infinite energy. The gourmand used to consume it in such a minimal space of time that sauces and fragments of pickle would cascade between his legs, staining public property and also his own shoes and trousers.
If indeed we accept the premise whereby Sabiah represents a cosmic encounter between cultures, then we have to re-examine the hidden meaning behind the apparently innocent name of the great Sabiah-emporium of Ramat Gan. "Zion-Central Sabiah Joint" seems to imply that it is the name of a place rather than a simple eatery. It could be that this was an inter-galactic meeting-place, perhaps even the very centre of the Milky Way.

corroding my mind and sapping my vital energy. I may as well tell you that both Lola and Gustav are doing everything they can to rid themselves of me, once and for all. Lola hates me and is ashamed of me, while Gustav, all fired up with careerist zeal, wants me out of his sight, and preferably out of his life too. Incidentally, in about a year from now he'll be the commander-in-chief of the Luftwaffe.

However funny or distasteful it may sound, all my former admirers are turning away from me, and making no secret of it. In fact, Friedrich, you may be the only person alive who takes any interest in me at all. I'm not asking for pity. But I do want to apologise for not finishing the composition of my memoirs.

I shall now set about making final adjustments to my text. From tomorrow onward, you are welcome to visit my home and collect all the material. I hope you will find what you want there. I myself shall be elsewhere.

Yours,

Gunther

P.S. If you see fit to publish my memoirs, I should be grateful if you entitle them A Guide to the Perplexed. If there is any lesson to be learned from my life, it consists of the illumination cast upon the perplexity inherent in the frenetic, unthinking existence of the "chosen". While researching the sources of the intolerance of my compatriots, I have concluded that the roots may be traced back to Rabbi Moses Ben Maimon, the celebrated doctor who demanded that love of God be preferred above human values, and the sanctity of the Sabbath above the life of a Gentile.

Afterword by Professor
Friedrich Sharavi

The following day, as requested, I paid a visit to Professor Wünker's house to collect his memoirs – the volume that is presented here in its entirety. Later it transpired that Professor Wünker, having left his home that morning to keep an appointment at the medical centre, never arrived at his destination. Since that day all trace of him has been lost. There are some who allege that in the months preceding the date of his disappearance, and especially during the last week, following his return from Palestine, his mind was becoming unbalanced and he was suffering from a form of dementia which is not uncommon among his age-group. From this it might be inferred that his disappearance occurred under tragic circumstances. But the contrary is also possible, and it should be noted that as against the tragic inference, a more optimistic scenario has been mooted. A number of investigators have concluded that Professor Wünker deliberately cultivated a senile image, as a means of compartmentalising his links with the outside world more meticulously. If this theory is examined, the possibility emerges that Professor Wünker left his home that morning intent on embarking on a new course. This interpretation may account for the fact that on returning from Palestine, Wünker closed the majority of his bank accounts and transferred the funds to an obscure and untraceable location.

Although there is no positive confirmation, over the years there has been an accumulation of reports from all kinds of sources, persistent reports according to which Professor Wünker has been sighted on a number of sun-drenched holiday beaches. Palestine, the Caribbean Islands, Miami Beach, Thailand and the South of France are among the places mentioned. It should further be noted that all these reports are identical in nature: they describe the elderly Wünker reclining on a beach, wearing only a sombrero, surrounded by a bevy of young girls whom he entertains with his theories. The girls have been observed leaning over his body, straddling his spread-eagled limbs and anointing him with aromatic oils. He rewards them by pinching and biting their bottoms, as they giggle and mew like kittens. Such reports are still arriving in peepological centres to this day, some twenty years after the morning that he left his house, never to return.

If there is no truth in these reports, then it may be confidently asserted that a new cultic myth is taking shape before our very eyes.

An Appeal for Public Assistance

Professor Gunther Wünker was last seen on 13.1.32 near Weimar Platzen. Professor Wünker is believed to be 72 years old, and is of average height and average build. Colour of eyes – brown. He has no distinguishing features whatsoever, and for this reason it is believed that he can be easily and positively identified. Members of the public are asked to be vigilant and to report any information regarding his whereabouts immediately to the nearest police station.

Missing Persons Department
Weimar Police

In view of the success of the first two editions of *A Guide to the Perplexed*, and a growing interest in the life and activities of Professor Gunther Wünker, it has been decided to include in the current edition a number of personal letters and other writings, some of them very personal, which are now being made public for the first time.

Professor Friedrich Sharavi

(From Professor Wünker's agony column, "Ask the Peepologist", in the distinguished periodical *Peepology Today*)

Reply to a wife whose husband has left her for another woman with an exceptionally large posterior.

Dear Frederika,

Before proceeding to advise you, I should remind you that I have no miraculous solutions at my disposal, and the only advice I am capable of formulating is confined to the peepological context. The first point to be made is: Philip has made a mistake, and a serious one at that. It seems that this bimbo with the massive haunches represents nothing other than a conceptual posterior devoid of content. This is my first impression from reading your letter, and it is not likely to be changed.

Regarding the substantive issue, i.e. that for Philip the arse-woman is a catalyst, my opinion is that drastic and renewed efforts should be made towards the immediate dissolution of the partnership-package. If indeed Philip is disillusioned with the current mechanics of his life and is genuinely and sincerely seeking a change, pleas will be of no avail; they will not bring him home. If this is indeed the situation, and there seems to be a reasonable prospect that it is so, then the gangrened flesh needs to be cut and the sooner the better. But another possibility exists, one which in my estimation is very realistic. It is highly likely that Philip is no expert when it comes to analysing his own thought processes. This being the case, he is becoming aware of his true intentions by means of a process known in professional parlance as "negative dialectic". According to this concept, Philip is becoming acquainted with his perceptions not through positive consciousness, i.e. what he feels at this moment, but rather through sorrow and regret mechanisms which will be evoked in his mind in the future. In a case such as this, Philip is immersing himself (consciously) in quicksand as a means of becoming aware of himself (the unknown) through a painful series of (necessary) existential contortions.

In my professional judgment, this insoluble equation should be ditched without delay. If Philip wants to leave, he must go at once. If this is what he genuinely wants, there is no other solution. If on the other hand Philip is motivated by a superficial desire to torment himself (by a process of negative dialectic), then the business of torment should begin. I envisage that the torment and the regret will start within the early hours of the painful destruction of his current life, within the gloomy isolation at the side of his fat-arsed mistress. I urge you, anyway, to cut all ties without delay. If Philip wants a holiday, take a holiday yourself. Have affairs with everyone who comes to town, and please don't forget your paragon of an adviser from Berlin.

Furthermore, I empathise with your grief and sincerely hope that sorrow will be an uplifting experience. In sorrowful happiness it is possible to find great happiness in the long term.

To conclude on a flippantly cynical level, I just wanted to tell you my dear Frederika that from all the letters you have sent me, I have the impression that you have always seen yourself as Sisyphus. And now for the first time you're being invited to carry that rock all the way to the top of the hill. At long last there is a point to accumulated nagging.

Professor G. Wünker

Dear Bill, ✶

    I was and am still astonished by the degree of spite directed towards you recently. But what shocked me most was seeing the dumb face of the fat floozy with the stained skirt. This is a spectacle which appears utterly absurd: someone in your position, a world leader and a handsome man by any reckoning, indulging in erotic frolics with a woman so lacking in either charm or discretion.

    I can understand the anal fixation which impels you to shove a cigar up an arsehole, since the cigar is the predominant phallic symbol of capitalist affluence, while the fat arse is outside the spectrum of symbolism. The fat arse represents itself and nothing else. Therefore, by a simple process of analytical reduction it emerges that your sexual proclivities testify eloquently to the fact that for you, the arsehole is where capitalism belongs. I agree with you wholeheartedly. As I'm sure you remember, my opinion is that the whole world is one big gross arsehole.

    As to the specific issue – your question regarding the attraction of men like us towards the ugly and the monstrous – as I see it the issue is quite simple. Masculinity by its very nature comprises an element of conflict and challenge. We trek across deserts, wrestle with sharks, dive out of airplanes, drive too fast, jump traffic lights and fuck incessantly. And why do we fuck incessantly? Not because we want it or need it but because in the cunt there is something that calls out a challenge to us, in the swivelling buttocks there is something confrontational, injurious and painful. Something demanding to be subdued and skewered. Fortunately for us, and perhaps here there is further proof of the existence of God, the female organ melts when we enter it and greets us with a libation of rapturous tears. So it is too with the arse, stuck out behind in anticipation of the rampant erection that threatens to split it like a sword.

    The attractive ones among them, sharp-nosed and mischievous of spirit, have no difficulty turning us on. But this is also their weakness.

✶ In his time Wünker served as confidential adviser to several world leaders. This letter, as is clearly evident, is part of a correspondence over a number of years between Wünker and a former president of the United States of America, a man of striking good looks who attracted widespread publicity on account of his intimate relations with a girl of Jewish origin. (F. Sharavi)

They don't threaten us. Firm bottoms and perky tits are a passing fancy. We're prepared to get inside them every day, at any time, whatever the weather, just because we're enthralled by their captivating beauty. The true and thorough test of male valour consists of venturing into the monster's lair: the fat, the ugly, the smelly, the stupid, the decrepit — and if possible a combination of all these. Only there, in the shadow of fear, do we become real and dauntless men. When we are challenged, fear of the shame of detumescence is something to be worn like a medal.

At the same time there is a further detail to be taken into account. When we set about screwing attractive women — rock starlets, high-class strippers, cover girls — we are engaging in a public act. We enjoy reading about our exploits in tacky gossip-mags and issuing vehement denials. Fucking the uglies, on the other hand, is an ascetic process best passed over in silence. We do this as a demonstration of valour and determination behind the enemy lines, overcoming the impulse to flee for our lives. Most of all, in such cases, we are challenging ourselves. The irony is that the majority of ugly women tend to appreciate the favour that nature has done them, in terms of the masculine propensity towards asceticism. Unfortunately for you, that fat little slag of yours saw you as a social event, suitable for sharing with her chattering friend. Incidentally, we can agree that her friend is no oil painting either.

Bill my old friend, take it easy. Go on sticking cigars up arseholes. Without knowing it you have acquired a permanent place in the mythology of sexual relations. We understand where you're at and we identify with your needs.

Keep in touch,

Yours,

Gunther

To: Yocheved117@hotmail.com

My Yochi,*

Evidently those around me see me as a nuisance. For some reason my ideas are not being accepted and properly understood. As for

* One of many others, apparently. (F. Sharavi)

your question, why people are incapable of accepting my revolutionary ideas without losing their senses or resorting to violence, the
answer is simple. My ideas cannot be refuted. They are too abstract
on the one hand, while on the other they lick the arsehole of human
existence. I strip people of their content, nations of purpose and the
whole world of hope. I stroll smiling down forbidden paths and fuck
sacred cows behind the hedgerows. Whatever does not submit to me
I rape and whatever submits to me I leave behind, bleeding and hungry for love. My opponents are spiritless invertebrates, desiccated
shadows of annoying emptiness. They are lack of identity striking
meaningful poses.

And you my love, my sexual identity,

Thirsty flower, insatiable always.

Do you really understand what I'm about,

Or are you too just wrinkling your brow as a mark of esteem?

When your brow is wrinkled and you are nodding your
head on hearing my words, my body is filled with power. I long to get
inside you and break you down into factors. I want to bite your buttocks and make a sandwich out of your flesh, grip your pussy-hair
between my teeth and shake my head like a puppy. Are you my partner or, like the daughters of Eve who were here before you or maybe
those who will fill the void you leave behind when you depart, are you
just pretending to be my partner?

Please dear lady, protect me from your ignorance, conceal your
stupidity, save me from ever knowing just how dumb you really are.

Yours,

Gunther

Letters to Elza
From the personal archive of Elza Hoffmann★

Dear Elza,

I hope that you are well and that your research is proceeding at a satisfactory pace. It was tough for me, having to return to my home and my own bed, but it seems that I'm feeling more relaxed and emotional tensions are not disrupting my unconventional daily routine. Today is the 22nd of the month, meaning that it's been more than two weeks since I parted from you, a fact which is not easily concealed from the watchful and beady eye of the environment (environment in the feminine gender).

It seems to me that I am religiously devoted to the process of redis-covering the significance of a question that does not really exist. Inspired by you, I suppose, I am finding myself ever more interested in the Hebrew language, which is most assuredly "a Holy Tongue" (though not yet "the Holy Tongue"). If you have succeeded in scaling the heights of my latest research, at least as far as the introduction to Heidegger's ety-mology is concerned, you will definitely find quotations regarding the primal language and its origins. In my research I discuss the issue of "covenant of the word". Covenant of the word which is, quite simply, covenant with the word. While mankind is embroiled in covenant with the word, God the absolute ascends and hovers above the discourse, which is nothing other than declaration of open warfare between the signifier and the signified. Man is bound by covenants and God is free. According to Hebrew insight, the word itself has its origin in God. I came to this conclusion some time ago, and it isn't original at all. This week, however, two new insights occurred to me, which are no less

★ It is now public knowledge that the late Professor Wünker led a double life, sharing his bed between Lola Bentini and Elza Hoffmann. According to infor-mation which has not been positively confirmed, the ageing Wünker spent most of his nights with Elza Hoffmann, thirty years his junior. Hoffmann, a renowned beauty and a former model, became acquainted with Wünker while composing her doctoral thesis on the subject of "The Peepological Connection in Study of the Scriptures". On at least two social occasions, Bentini and Hoffmann are known to have exchanged exceedingly crude verbal invective.

alarming: the first concerns the notion of language. Language (safa) refers to tongue (lashon), meaning the system of relationships between signifier and signified but at the same time "language (safa)" in itself constitutes a signifier which belongs to the system and signifies border or limit, such as the safa of the sea, of the street etc.

This being the case, the holy language is not necessarily the language that speaks of holiness but rather the border beyond which the greatest holiness begins. And because a thing is defined by what it is and as well as by what it is not, it follows that the holy language defines holiness by way of a negative dialectic. If the Jews are a chosen people, their path is via negativity, and their yearning for the absolute is fundamentally dialectic. Therefore, the meaning of their being chosen is that holiness begins where they end. The Jews were chosen to anticipate holiness. They are "the difference between sacred and profane".

The other issue that I've been engrossed in this week is the notion of obligation (ne–chuyavut). Man tends to feel obligated to God, to him-self, to spouse/partner etc. In this too we are trapped in a minefield of double meanings, created in the deepest recesses of Jewish consciousness and the Hebrew language. There is a subtle connection between obliga-tion (ne–chuyavut) and love (chiba), words sharing a common Hebrew root. The Jew is obligated by his faith, but he is also commanded to love God with all his soul. Obligation to God is abstract commitment to the unknowable, but at the same time it is supposed to be the unquestioned bond of love. Unknowable because we don't know how to break it down into factors. There is no way of justifying love, desire, yearning. Obligation and love are bound together in a mutual and bi-directional manner; there is no place for love without obligation and no place for obligation with-out love. This is the basis of the partnership nucleus, the family nucleus and so on up to the national nucleus. The connection between man and his mate, man and his place, and man and himself is revealed as a fusion of love and obligation ultimately defying dissolution and separation.

With love and pain,
Affection and longing,
Yours,
Gunther

Dear Elza,

I sat up all last night reading your article. I am studying your work with great interest and it appears that you are on your way towards a discovery of prodigious dimensions, a discovery that will boost your academic standing and confirm your status as a Biblical scholar of the highest importance. The proposition that the Scriptures, in their entirety, are nothing other than a peephole, is both entertaining and thought-provoking. If I understand you correctly, your assertion is that the Bible is an accumulation of episodes lacking any historical continuity whose entire purpose is to expose the word as meaning in flux within the anecdotal context. This idea, which is essentially Hegelian, points to the end of the dance of Jewish history, at least on the scriptural level. It is amusing to find that all that Jewish blather which is still heard from time to time, about "historical right", turns out to be empty rhetoric, and this from a Jewish scriptural viewpoint.

The breathtaking notion that the Bible is an apparatus of dynamic context presenting the liquidity of meanings of the language which it itself speaks, is the most fascinating of interpretations for the understanding of holiness in general and the holy language in particular. If I have indeed understood your reasoning: unlike a dictionary, which gives explanations which themselves require explanations and so on, the Bible in its entirety is the explanatory context of itself. The dictionary establishes meanings and the Scriptures flow. The dictionary requires periodic updating while the Bible needs no renewal. It restores itself by itself and from itself. I fear this is an idea enchanting in its beauty. I love you . . .

If I've got it right, the Bible is no longer a historical context on the one hand, and on the other it raises a series of metaphysical questions, obscure questions enmeshing the reader in a web of notions we will never fully understand.

Elza, this is the most marvellous insight of all. You are giving back a little credit to my genocide-obsessed roots and I'm just longing to play with your tits and pussy.

Yours,
Guntosh

P.S. I haven't forgotten, dear. Here, after extensive research, is my recipe for geckte Leber (chopped liver).

<u>Ingredients</u>: *2 onions (chervil), a whole garlic (canobel), three spoonfuls finest Schmaltz, ten fresh chicken livers, three slices dry bread, three hard-boiled eggs, parsley, salt and pepper.*

<u>Preparation</u>:
Fry the chervil and canobel in the Schmaltz, until it turns as brown as a Nubian's cheek.
Add the chicken livers and fry well.
Allow to cool.
Depending on your stinginess, add bread and eggs in inverse proportion to the quantity of liver.
Grate up small in an old-fashioned mincer.

<u>Presentation</u>:
Place spoonful of concoction on largest dish you can find, and squash with fork until it covers entire expanse of dish, creating optical illusion of abundance.
For garnish, add parsley to taste. As an optional extra, dice the hard-boiled egg with a cheese-grater (Reibeisen) and write a blessing with the breadcrumbs.
Guten Appetit

My Elza,

Sometimes I find myself wondering about the roots of happiness. What is the source of radiant enthusiasm? In my childhood, I remember, my uncle Yankele was the absolute ultimate in cheeriness. He rejoiced in his lot in an uncompromising manner. He was so happy he wanted all of mankind to share the secret of his good cheer. He was always ready with a joke or a humorous poem to fit every possible occasion, and his booming laughter was a byword within the family and outside it too. I also clearly remember how surprised I was, still a youngster and barely into adolescence, when Uncle Yankele jumped to his death from the eighth floor of an office block. I remember the funeral, scores of

mourners, women in fashionable Polish headscarves, and men wearing
Ray-Ban pilot-style shades. They told one another they hoped they
would know no more such grief, while knowing full well that grief was
an integral part of their lot in this world. It was only when the mourners dispersed and it was just the family left, the innermost circle of relatives, that the gloomy atmosphere shifted to one of levity. Presiding over
a table laden with goodies, my father expressed the scientific axiom that
although Yankele jumped to his death from the eighth floor – it wasn't
the fall that killed him, it was hitting the ground. All members of the
family dissolved into a seven-day-long paroxysm of mirth.

I realised even then, on the verge of adolescence, that peals of laughter and unbearable pain are close neighbours. Behind the jokes, fearful
distress sometimes lurks. Sometimes jokes are just the straws that we
clutch at, sinking into a gloomy morass.

Other members of the family insisted, naturally, that my uncle's
jovial behaviour masked a desperate cry for help. So every time I felt a
laugh coming on, I wondered if I too was crying out for help. The
impulse to grin brought with it the fear that this was the beginning of
the slippery slope leading down to my ultimate destruction. When I
laughed, I wondered if it was time to jump.

The conventional belief is that moments of happiness are capable of
killing existential fear, that gaiety has the power to blur the oppressive
weight of pointlessness. It may be that happiness comprises a form of
delight, but in my experience the opposite is the case. Whenever I
grinned, to myself or in public, I heard the echo of my mother's whisper:
"Gunther, you're getting more and more like Uncle Yankele".

When I made myself laugh, when I rolled down the endless slopes of
the absurd, I caught a whiff of the wondrous scent of the unrelenting pain
of existence.

Towards the end of their relationship

Dear Elza,

For years I have been aware of the substantial degree of indignation
aroused in people in response to the coldness emanating from my emo-

tional responses. Usually from the direction of women like you, desperately insistent on delving into my arsenal of deep feelings. Suddenly you're demanding my heart. When you were between my sheets, you accepted and understood with perfect clarity that your role was that of a loin-cooler and now, suddenly, you want to pluck my emotional strings. You were so determined to stick around, to belong, that you used to declare proudly you were just a carefree urchin hanging around the empty doorways of momentary gratification. You and girls like you, when you're awash with primal lust, melting in the heat of your insides, gratefully receive any token of affection, even if it's only the paltry tribute of a flabby hard-on. But once you've had your fun, riding on the waves of orgasm and high-octane gasping, you start singing new tunes, a soft wheedling sound that rises to a pitch of strident demand. Without any advance warning, you and your ilk are asking for permanence — children, weekends, Sabbaths, holidays, even a house in the country. Suddenly you're extolling the merits of everlasting love. I wonder how we have come to this. How is it that the innocence of mutual libido has turned into a one-sided apparatus of emotional whims and demands of a decidedly material nature?

I have never understood the female obsession with hyper-emotionalism and permanence. I myself am a two-dimensional person, an individual devoid of feelings. Even when I sense searing resentment and consider putting an end to my life, I see this as nothing more than the product of a mechanism of metabolic relations. We exchange materials, opinions and sensations. We trade in bodily juices, converting proteins into impulse, impulse into erection, erection into resurrection. I'm not one to fall into the trap of unbridled, overwhelming emotion. I treat it with metaphysical scepticism.

For all my researches into the nature of love, I haven't really succeeded in getting to the bottom of it. Thinking on a deeper level, it isn't possible to point to inner feelings in an explicit manner. This applies to love as much as to the aesthetic appreciation of beauty. What I have learned is that I loved you because I hated you, because I missed you, because I longed for you, because you turned up naked in my dreams and sucked me, because you sat on my face, because I never wanted to see you ever again and I knew I couldn't live a moment longer without you. Love is just an amalgam of confused sensations relating to you, an empty verbal signifier, a signifier with nothing to signify, carrying with it a sack-full of illogical behaviour-patterns. The word "love" is like a magic wand, imposing order on the chaos and proposing a solution to the riddle, apparently shedding light, the hazy light of "love". I find that I hate because I love, love because I hurt, I'm sad because I'm happy, I desire because I'm in torment and so on.

Love depends for its sustenance on the totality of confused sensations. It flourishes by the light of contradictions; it is the impossible conjunction of two poles — the general and the particular. In the shadow of your love I want to be the hero of your dreams. The absolute, complete man, the summit of your feminine aspiration. I want to symbolise before your spread-eagled body the masculine ideal, in a permanent state of erection. In your shadow I want to scale the Olympian heights of the universal, to be the most general man on the face of the earth but at the same time the most individual. I want you to love the personal Gunther, the man with the bulging waistline, the indefatigable fucker of minds, the one with piles, runny nose and sweaty armpits. In the light of love I want to be the absolute ideal of individuality, anonymous and particular. This is the nature of love between the sexes.* This is its strength

---

* It appears that Wünker is here expressing his radical and provocative perspective on the marginal ideology, a perspective that earned him many opponents in liberal circles. From Wünker's point of view, love between man and woman comprises the possibility of contact with the root of dialectical experience. Insofar as Wünker's perception can be understood, love between the sexes resolves the ultimate dichotomy between the general and the particular. In the act of love, lovers are capable of visiting the Garden of Eden of the absolute. Love between man and woman, in his view, is a temporary sharing of sublime experience and the basis of an aesthetic.

While in contact between the sexes, each partner represents to the other the ideal of his or her sex, in gay relationships there is no place to speak of idealistic representation. When Joe and Jim fall in love, they cannot represent mutually and also temporally the absolute ideal of their sex, since in doing this each is mutually denying the other. Hence, according to Wünker, gays have no access to the territory of dialectical inspiration. They are prevented in a *and also its weakness. The desperate attempt to become absolutely general and at the same time individual and personal, is by its very nature of temporary duration. It is impossible to be general and particular forever. In the end we submit to the law of compromise and abandon our aspirations towards eternity. We learn to be content with little, with steady affection that nourishes itself with transitory, opportunistic and purchased affairs. In pain and in brooding grief we abandon the desperate attempt to find in love what we don't find in life. Sadly we discover that love, the ultimate dialectic, invites us to the threshold of the spirit and at the same time expels us from the gates of the Garden of Eden for all eternity.*

Love me in the way of the flesh, as I love you.
Yours,
Gunty

My Gunty,
Your last letter left me in a state of emotional turmoil. I feel deceived and betrayed.
As I'm sure you realise, I understand perfectly well what you're getting at. You're not the first man in my life and judging by the way things are going, it seems you won't be the last either. I'm convinced that you know how much I love you, and you're an expert at exploiting this. In fact, I've never loved anyone the way I love you, and sometimes I reckon that before I met you, I never experienced true love at all. But I also know only too well what a dreadful old man you are – devious, fat and malicious. You're a man without feelings and without any respect for

conditional fashion from visiting the realm of the sublime. Wünker claims furthermore that since gays are deficient in dialectical aspirations, their vital faith is focused on style and not on substance.

It has to be remembered that in his time, in the dark days of the era of Political Correctness, Wünker attracted vociferous criticism on account of his ideas, which were interpreted as homophobic and even morbid. Wünker for his part never took the trouble to respond to his critics, and in fact there is no evidence that he engaged in any debate on the subject, which in any case is no longer a hot political issue. (F. Sharavi) *others. And although I'm well aware of all this, I love you and I miss you. I don't have, and I never had, any desire to change you. I accepted you as you are: a bundle of narcissistic instincts, driven by unbridled verbal impulses. I love to sit on you and I'm addicted to your sharp tongue even when it's burrowing tirelessly between my legs.*

In addition to all the negative attributes that I've already thrown at you, it seems to me you're also a rotten and incorrigible coward. Why can't you stand up like a man and tell me you don't love me any more? Why do you have to insulate yourself with philosophical shit to get away from me? I feel so humiliated after all these years, years of waiting for you to get shot of that bloated crap-artist of yours, your wrinkled old whore who fucks everything that moves in the name of art.

Seeing that you've stolen the best years of my life, I'm entitled to demand something in return. As you know, if there's one thing I can't give up on, it's having a child. You promised and I'm insisting that you keep your word. If you don't, I swear I'll make your life Hell till your dying day.

I want a child from you, whether you come here and plant it yourself or wank into a test-tube and send it to me by special messenger. For my part, I've already made an appointment at the clinic and tomorrow afternoon I'll be getting rid of the I.U.D. that you shoved into me more than ten years ago. I don't intend to give up on this and I hope that's as clear to you as it is to me.

Now, turning to the philosophical content of your letter: in your habitual fashion you have touched on the root of things, the nature of the purpose of existence. The glorious idea that in love mankind is exposed to the dialectic is indeed the very essence of pain. The apparently simple idea that in the shadow of love man finds within himself the root of the sublime puts all contemporary Biblical research on a very flimsy footing.

The three religions of revelation are unanimous in the absolute prohibition of excessive and indiscriminate copulation. "Thou shalt not covet thy neighbour's wife", the three of them agree, submissively and self-righteously. Is it reasonable to suppose that the good Lord, who endowed us with the faculty to copulate without purpose and in thousands of ways, should suddenly demand of us that we abstain from the one bodily pleasure that He planted in our bodies? For what purpose did God put lips between my legs if they are unable to speak? Why did God give you a sceptre and no kingdom, just so you could fill my body with good things, so I could pleasure myself with your body? I don't suppose there exists any theosophical tract which will justify clitoral gluttony, which is essentially endless and inexhaustible pleasure. I want a man, and if it's still possible I want you and I want more from you, without respite, forever and ever.

It seems that the theory you raise in relation to the temporal nature of love is definite and irrefutable. It is true that it's impossible to maintain over a period of time a state of union between the universal self and the particular self. At its climaxes love is momentary and the dialectical pleasure is short-lived. If this is indeed the case, in order to maximise our visits to the fields of bliss, we should try to fall in love afresh day by day and copulate endlessly, indiscriminately and without compromise.

Evidently the three monotheistic religions recognised before it was too late the revelatory nature of love and its ability to exalt the human heart. They understood that through anguish of the heart it's possible to catch a whiff of the fragrance of God's backside. Except that this God isn't in heaven, nor on the earth, nor accompanied by legions of angels. This Holy One is I. Through my hunger for your body I am discovering in myself the spirit of God. As if I am breathing on the face of the abyss.

This, it seems to me, is the reason why sexual liberation has led to a mass migration from Judaeo-Christian western ideals in favour of a spiritual frenzy over eastern perceptions. Perceptions that seek out the quality inherent in mankind, what is sublime in humanity and what is holy in the self.

Gunty, you bastard son-of-a-bitch, you're opening my eyes. I hate you. I want you to make a baby with me, and I'm pleading with you not to leave me. Love me. I need you. Contact me, now.

Elza
De Profundis

Glossary

Arbeit macht frei Work brings liberation. A German slogan welcoming prisoners to Auschwitz death camp.

Darbuka A traditional Arabic drum

Druze A tribe of brave warriors and combat lovers. The Druze can be found in northern Palestine and southern Syria. In general the Druze will join forces with any given regime just for the pleasure of holding a gun and the chance of using it against living organisms.

El-Kuds Jerusalem (in Arabic)

Givataim A suburb near Tel Aviv, even smaller than Ramat Gan

Hermon The highest mountain in the Golan Heights. Regarded by the Israelis as a prime strategic point because it is the only place in the region where Jews can ski. It was conquered twice by the Israel Defence Forces, first in 1967 and then in 1973.

Ibn Isaac Son of Isaac

Kibbutz A Zionist communal socialistic set-up based upon total sharing. According to the Kibbutz philosophy, every Kibbutz member contributes as much as he can and gets very little back.

Kosher food A collection of Jewish religious restrictions concerned with food ingredients and general diet. The kosher laws protect: pigs, prawns, frogs, horses, camels and oysters from the Jewish cuisine. Since Kosher food is available in Jewish food shops only, it guarantees zero assimilation of Jews with the surrounding environment.

Massada A symbol of the Jewish 'heroic' communal suicidal act. Can be seen as the foundation of Jewish radical, national and religious fundamentalism.

"Mount Francewi" and "Mount Eskolawi" Two Jewish settlements in east northern Jerusalem. Both were built on Palestinian land after 1967.

Ost Juden An eastern Jew. Refers mainly to Chasidic Jews who migrated to central and Western Europe from Poland and Russia in the late 19th century. The *Ost Juden* can be easily distinguished by his heavy black medieval dressing code. In most cases he will hide his face behind a large beard and dated dark glasses.

Oud A traditional Arabic string instrument

Palmach Jewish paramilitary commando force. It was dissolved with the declaration of the state of Israel. At the time, it achieved a very limited reputation for its military success. On the other hand, it also became the pillar of the early Israeli leftist culture. The *palmach* became known for its liberal sexual attitude and was established as the best institutional barbecue party around.

Petite mort Little death, a French poetic way to describe male orgasm. Refers to the post-coital terminal feelings and bodily fatigue that come with ejaculation.

Ramat Gan Small suburb near Tel Aviv

Sabras Common Israeli expression referring to the Israeli young native male Jew as if he is a strong, rude, clever, combat pilot, marine commando hero, Rambo. In short — better than anybody else. Somehow, the expression predicts that the Sabra will have hairy legs and wear biblical-type sandals. In general, Sabra people always wear their Ray-Ban sunglasses on the top of their heads rather than over their eyes.

Sabra Camp Palestinian refugee camp on Lebanese soil. Became famous after the "Sabra and Shatila massacre" (1982), a genocide that was committed by Lebanese Christian paramilitary forces while under Israeli occupation. In the international community Israel was regarded as responsible for this atrocity. Following internal and international pressure the minister of defence (Ariel Sharon) had to resign. Mr Sharon was banned from any ministerial job for life.

Shiv'ah A Jewish ritual gathering lasting for seven days of grieving after a Jewish death

Shoa A Hebrew word invented to describe the Jewish holocaust. It would appear that 'Shoa' refers to Jews only, depriving any other innocent people from being Nazi victims, i.e. Gypsies, Poles, Russians, homosexuals, disabled people, German political opponents etc.

Shtetl A Yiddish expression referring to a form of Jewish urban settlement that guarantees zero assimilation with the surrounding environment

Tamarhindi A drink made from dates

"Yekke-putz" German dick head

Yiddish Jewish form of linguistic communication that guarantees zero assimilation with the surrounding environment